D0876285

EVERYDAY MIRACLES

The Healing Wisdom of Hasidic Stories

EVERYDAY MIRACLES

The Healing Wisdom of Hasidic Stories

HOWARD W. POLSKY
YAELLA WOZNER

JASON ARONSON INC.
Northvale, New Jersey
London

10 9 8 7 6 5 4 3 2 1

Jason Aronson Inc. gratefully acknowledges permission to quote from TALES OF THE HASIDIM:THE EARLY MASTERS by Martin Buber and TALES OF THE HASIDIM: THE LATER MASTERS by Martin Buber. Copyright 1947, 1948 and renewed 1975 by Schocken Books, Inc. Reprinted by permission of Schocken Books, Inc., published by Pantheon Books, a Division of Random House, Inc.

Permission to use line drawing "Dancing Hasidim" has been given by the artist, Tully Filmus.

Library of Congress Cataloging-in-Publication Data

Polsky, Howard W.
Everyday Miracles: the healing wisdom of Hasidic stories / Howard W. Polsky and Yaella Wozner.
p. cm.
Bibliography: p.
Includes index.
ISBN 0-87668-880-6
1. Parables, Hasidic—Psychological aspects. 2. Hasidim—Legends—Psychological aspects. 3. Pastoral counseling (Judaism)
4. Hasidim—Psychology. I. Wozner, Yaella. II. Title.
BM532,P56 1989 88-21999
296.8'33—dc 19 88-2CIP

Manufactured in the United States of America.
Jason Aronson Inc. offers books and cassettes.
For information and catalog write to
Jason Aronson Inc., 230 Livingston Street,
Northvale, NJ 07647.

Dedicated to
Our Parents
Jacob and Sarah Polsky
and
Elyakim and Ayala Ben-Menahem

Their knowledge, love, and practice of Jewish tradition inspired this book.

In Memory of
Martin Buber and Louis I. Newman

Their imaginative renditions of Hasidic stories have shown us their profound psychological wisdom.

Contents

Part III. *Hasidic Teaching*

Part IV. *Storytelling*

Part V. *Epilogue*

Preface

The Teaching of the Soul

> Rabbi Pinhas often cited the words: "A man's soul will teach him," and emphasized them by adding: "There is no man who is not incessantly taught by his soul."
>
> One of his disciples asked: "If this is so, why don't men obey their souls?
>
> "The soul teaches incessantly," Rabbi Pinhas explained, "but it never repeats."
>
> (*Buber, Early Masters, p. 121*)

A story is like a soul: It "teaches incessantly," because one story leads to another story.

* * *

There is always the danger when emphasizing one particular religious and cultural movement in Judaism that it will appear to take on more significance than other equally important philosophies. Obviously, the sources of the value systems that constitute contemporary Judaism are in no way exclusively Hasidic. Because of its popular mass base in Eastern Europe and Russia for two hundred years, Hasidism contributed importantly to the present Jewish character, but many other sources and forces before and after early Hasidism were of equal importance.

The Hasidic movement, in a very short period (1760–1810), gave birth to a dazzling galaxy of creative saint-mystics in the wake of the towering Baal Shem Tov (1700–1760).

In his great seminal work, *Major Trends in Jewish Mysticism* published in 1942, Gershom G. Scholem theorizes that Hasidism was essentially an attempt to reveal the world of Kabbala to the masses of Jewish people. Hasidism introduced a new emotional enthusiasm and a joyous positivistic outlook in raising the fallen divine sparks of the Almighty.

According to Scholem, Kabbalism became an instrument of psychological analysis and self-knowledge. The rabbis turned their mystic-talmudic minds toward an intense preoccupation with the human mind and imagination and toward both ordinary and grand human impulses. What emerged in Scholem's felicitous phrase is "the mysticism of the personal life."

In this new transformation of Jewish life, the personality of the rabbinic leader became as important or even more important than his scholarship. The rabbis became advocates of the simplicity, strength, and grace of the common man. Life and God and the community were with the people and not exclusively in the yeshiva. Direct, spontaneous religious experience took the place of mediated, abstruse *pilpul* and commentaries. God truly was everywhere, not only in the synagogue or house of study.

To this new marriage of esoteric spirituality and the uncommon common sense of the shrewd, wily, and independent Jewish villager, a new humanistic psychology was born, which was every bit as modern and sophisticated as any of our current schools of psychology and social work.

On the Way to Karlin

A Hasid was on his way to visit the Karliner Rebbe. A rav met him and said: "Can you not find a rabbi nearer than Karlin?"

"No, I cannot," answered the Hasid. "I read the thoughts of all the rabbis, and I find them to be spurious."

"If you read thoughts," said the rav, "then tell me what I am thinking now."

"You are thinking of God," answered the Hasid.

"No, your guess is incorrect; I am not thinking of God."

"There you have it," remarked the Hasid. "You yourself have stated the reason why I must go to Karlin."

(Newman, *The Hasidic Anthology, p. 155*)

The Hasidic movement represents an important leap in the development of the Jewish heritage of world culture as well. Its main strength lies in its harnessing of a profound faith in humanistic spirituality to help people with practical daily concerns and problems. This is the message of Hasidism, and it is preserved in the thousands of stories that Hasidim told and retold and later wrote down.

Neurolinguistic Programming, originally developed by Richard Bandler and John Grinder, has helped us understand how the Hasidic healer effectively used the language of the story, gained the support and cooperation of his "client," and influenced the subconscious to effect conscious changes in behavior.

The stories fulfill two main functions: They afford sound, practical psychological guidelines for people with problems that stand in the way of their reaching desired goals, and they serve as an effective educational method for disseminating Hasidic values.

We have used three main sources for the stories we selected to analyze: Our primary source, Martin Buber's *Tales of the Hasidim*, is a very careful selection of stories that enlarges the reader's understanding of Hasidic life. Louis I. Newman's *The Hasidic Anthology* and its companion volume, *Maggidim and Hasidim: Their Wisdom*, contain over 4,000 tales, teachings, anecdotes, and sayings culled from 121 Yiddish and Hebrew books.

Our main purpose in writing this book is to show how the Hasidic rabbis served their followers as counselors and teachers by telling stories. We use stories to illustrate psychological principles and techniques that have impressed us with their sophistication and modernity. The wisdom and practical utility of the Hasidic stories continue to surprise us:

The True Wonder

They asked Rebbe Elimelekh: "In the Scriptures we read that Pharaoh said to Moses and Aaron: 'Show a wonder for you.' How are we to understand this? It would have been more logical for him to say: 'Show a wonder to me.' Rebbe Elimelekh explained: "Magicians know what they want to accomplish and

> how to accomplish it. It is not a wonder for them, but only for the beholders. But those who work it know of no whence and no how, and the wonder which rises out of their doing overwhelms them. And this is what Pharaoh meant: 'Do not pretend to me! Get you a wonder from the true world, so that it may thus testify for you.'"
>
> (*Buber, Early Masters, p. 262*)

Finally, we returned to personal family experiences, where there were strong Hasidic ties, and have summoned our professional expertise in psychology and education to tease out in some systematic fashion the most significant connections. By analyzing the stories' structure and cultural background, we have been able to determine how it is that the stories have a lasting power for us today.

What has actually happened is that the stories have helped us understand better our own past as well as contemporary psychological theory and practice. The universal wisdom of Hasidism will do the same for you!

ACKNOWLEDGMENTS

We thank our friend, Prof. Mordechai Rotenberg, author of *Dialogue With Deviants: the Hasidic Ethic and Theory of Social Contraction*, for stimulating us to wed Jewish traditional wisdom to a scientific theory of the mind. Milton Erickson taught us how our stories and metaphors could be used in therapy.

We also wish to thank our spouses, Dr. Zita Norwalk Polsky and Dr. Yochanan Wozner, whose encouragement helped us over many difficult hurdles.

Dr. Milton E. Polsky helped us understand Hasidic stories as drama which engaged the listeners' heart, mind, and soul.

Dr. Howard W. Polsky
Columbia University
School of Social Work
New York

Yaella Wozner
Jerusalem

Part I

CULTURAL AND THEORETICAL BACKGROUND

INTRODUCTION

The Lost Girl Finds Her Father

Once upon a time, a carefree young girl who lived at the edge of a forest and who loved to wander in the forest became lost. As it grew dark and the little girl did not return home, her parents became very worried. They began calling for the little girl and searching in the forest, and it grew darker. The parents returned home and called neighbors and people from the town to help them search for their little girl.

Meanwhile, the little girl wandered about in the forest and became very worried and anxious as it grew dark, because she could not find her way home. She tried one path and another and became more and more tired. Coming to a clearing in the forest, she lay down by a big rock and fell asleep.

Her frantic parents and neighbors scoured the forest. They called and called the little girl's name but to no avail. Many of the searchers became exhausted and left, but the little girl's father continued searching throughout the night.

Early in the morning, the father came to the clearing where the girl had laid down to sleep. He suddenly saw his little girl and ran toward her, yelling and making a great noise on the dry branches which awoke the girl.

The little girl saw her father, and with a great shout of joy she exclaimed, "Daddy, I found you."

This is a striking metaphor of our relationship to Hasidic stories. There are, of course, thousands of Hasidic stories with great practical meaning for us, and in this "forest" of stories every reader will find those that have the most meaning for him just as the lost girl found her discovery of her father as the most important event in her life.

In other words, what we are saying is *trust yourself*. What works for you will probably work for others. This has been our experience. It was also important to us to explain why the stories are enjoyable and instructive, which may help you to find parallel or new discoveries in the stories.

Through some mysterious, magical process, a story will often pop into your head suddenly, help you to define your problem more clearly, develop a strategy for working at it, and then anchor itself in your mind, to be used again when it is helpful.

Each Hasidic tale has a "striking image," some symbol which encapsulates or succinctly summarizes the essence of the tale and its significance for you.

One such story is the oft-told tale of Rabbi Akiva and the drops of water on the rock. Rabbi Akiva came to the study of the Torah late in life. He was an ignorant peasant, so the legend goes, but he sought the hand of a well-to-do young woman who had fallen in love with him. Her father, however, was extremely unhappy about Akiva's status. Akiva wandered about very depressed, until he chanced upon a rock in a meadow and noticed that single drops of water falling on this mammoth rock had bored a huge hole that was about to cleave it in two.

It suddenly struck Akiva that, whatever he was now, persistent activity based on faith could be powerful in redirecting his life. He recognized immediately that a persistent and consistent routine could, little by little, achieve untold wonders.

From that moment Akiva assiduously applied himself to the study of the Torah and became a renowned scholar. Needless to say, he also won the heart of the young woman and the respect of her father.

This story is a variation on the tale of the tortoise and the hare. When Kohelet says in Ecclesiastes that "the race is not to the swift," the implication is that less is achieved by flashes of performance than by steady, consistent daily effort.

This is a powerful tale about the importance of working persistently at what one most values in life. In moments of disappointment or frustration, this striking image of the steady drop of water serves both as an inspiration and as a methodology, if you will, for pursuing your most cherished goals.

This may not work for you, but even if it doesn't, it may still work for others with whom you are associated. So it becomes tricky. Sometimes, a story's practical use can only be discovered by telling it to different people and in subsequent discussions. And this is a second revelation. Telling a story to someone else engraves it more deeply in your memory so that it becomes part of you and your way of life. Telling a story anchors it in your psyche so that it has the double payoff of reinforcing and guiding someone else as well as yourself. In this sense, every storytelling combines helping someone else with helping yourself. The most important criterion we used for selection of a Hasidic story was if it worked for us as practical, helpful, enlightening, and/or entertaining.

But the more we read and discussed the stories, another criterion "jumped" at us. We became intrigued with stories that initially stumped us and made us wonder about their meanings. We discovered that the richest stories initially puzzled us, and continued to work in our subconscious until the "aha" popped up.

To get into this Hasidic mood, consider the following dilemma confronting a rich merchant—one that you may also have felt at times in your life:

How to Become Spiritual

In the days of Rabbi Dov Baer of Mezeritch, known as the Great *Maggid*, a well-to-do merchant, who refused to have anything to do with Hasidic teachings, lived in Mezeritch. His wife took care of the shop. He himself spent only two hours a day in it. The rest of the time he sat over his books in the House of Study. On Friday morning, he saw two young men there whom he did not know. He asked them where they were from and why they had come, and was told they had journeyed a great distance to see and hear the Great *Maggid*. (A *maggid* is a preacher who uses mainly stories and parables to make his points.) Then he decided that, for once, he too would go to the *maggid's* house. He did not want to sacrifice any of his study time for this, so he did not go to his shop on that day.

The *maggid's* radiant face affected him so strongly that from then on he went to his home more and more frequently and ended up attaching himself to him altogether. From then on, he had one business failure after another until he was quite poor. He complained to the *maggid* that this had happened to him since he had become his disciple. The *maggid* answered: "You know what our sages say: 'He who wants to grow wise, let him go south; he who wants to grow rich, let him go north.' Now what shall one do who wants to grow both rich and wise?" The man did not know what to reply. The *maggid* continued: "He who thinks nothing at all of himself, and makes himself nothing, grows spiritual, and spirit does not occupy space. He can be north and south at the same time." Those words moved the merchant's heart and he cried out: "Then my fate is sealed!" "No, no," said the *maggid*. "You have already begun."

(*Buber, Early Masters, p. 108*)

1

Hasidism

It is told . . .

Near the magical wooded Carpathian Mountains, a new spirit was scheduled to enter humanity in the early 1700s and spread in all directions to every part of the globe.

A man of the common people with very little formal learning, Israel ben Eliezer received the call. As a child, Israel often played hooky from *heder* and was caught wandering deep in the forest near the town of Okup, in the Ukrainian province of Podolia. Even as a boy, Israel followed his very own star and was regarded as "strange"—the child most likely to get into trouble.

While still a young man, Israel traveled around the country as an ordinary holy itinerant. Israel told marvelous stories that entranced his growing number of followers. Soon he was invited to bigger towns and cities. He performed miraculous cures, foretold the future from dreams and assumed self-hypnotic states that he had practiced in the mysterious forest near Okup. In his presence, his followers were able to attain ecstatic communion with God.

Israel gradually came to be known as the Baal Shem Tov (The Master of the Good Name). This sounds like a title, but originally it was an affectionate nickname. You remember from your childhood the importance of nicknames? How did Israel get this nickname?

It is told . . .

A group of Israel's followers who were now called *Hasidim*, the "pious ones," were extolling his uncanny powers and extraordinary virtues. Each Hasid tried to outdo the previous speaker.

Finally an elderly man arose and said quietly: "Israel ben Eliezer is a good man." Everyone fell silent (a sign of a divine spark from Heaven).

Many, many minutes later another Hasid dared to enter the silent meditation with an additional comment: "And everywhere Israel travels he has a good name!" For a second time all the Hasidim fell silent.

This is true.

To be the Master of the Good Name, the *Baal Shem Tov* or Besht (an acronym of the Hebrew words), was to be thoroughly and consistently honest. Among Jews to say that so-and-so has a good name is like receiving a Nobel prize for exceptional integrity. The Besht's honesty was terrifying and inspired awe and trust among his followers. The Master of the Good Name was incapable of uttering a self-serving false word. Indeed he often spoke openly and frankly about his shortcomings, including his lack of Talmudic scholarship. For some people, "Cleanliness is next to godliness"; for the Jews, "A good name is next to godliness."[1]

The Besht was always close to the common people and identified with them and their lot. The poor were powerless and degraded. They were ciphers in the synagogue dominated by rich merchants and "legalistic" rabbis who kowtowed to the wealthy and split esoteric hairs over Biblical commentaries.

The Besht and his followers burst into this oligarchic cabal and tore asunder its ideological and political hegemony. Hasidism's alternative path was the creation of a mystical and ecstatic bond with God. Hasid and God evolved a personal intimate relationship.

---

[1]The term "Baal Shem" (Master of the Good Name) predates the Baal Shem Tov and was used by itinerant preachers and rabbis to ward off evil spirits and promote their followers' well being.

This passionate relationship released tidal waves of joy at being alive and experiencing daily God's magnificent creations. The Hasidim are the modern originators of the power of positive thinking and positive feeling and positive behaving. They joyously affirm success and failure, fortune and misfortune, death and life; they emphasize compassion for the less fortunate, promote individuality and proclaim the dignity of all—rich or poor.

A populist spirituality caught fire. How were the Besht and his successors able to transform his life and beliefs into a movement that spread to millions of Jews throughout Eastern Europe and retains until today enormous vitality among a variety of small contemporary Hasidic sects?

The Besht launched two new powerful social forces: The first was the revival and development of the concept of the *tzaddik*, a superior human being and role model because of his special spiritual capacity to adhere to God. His second social innovation was the role of *kavvana*—motivation and intention—in *all* human affairs.

The *tzaddik* was somewhere between a messiah and an ordinary human being. Since the *tzaddik* was always struggling, like the rest of us, to become as holy as he was capable of becoming, he could never claim a messianic role and so every generation could produce an abundant yield of *tzaddikim*.

The *tzaddik* was a unique concept. The criteria for becoming a *tzaddik* were not codified. There were no exams and no certifying board. A *tzaddik* did not have to be especially learned. Once a *tzaddik*, always a *tzaddik*—he could not be disbarred and become a former *tzaddik*. He was appointed (or anointed) for life. Of course "appointed" means that people gradually began to recognize him as special—a kind of "holy person."

Above all, a *tzaddik* was imperfect—he had to struggle every day, as we all do, against "unholy thoughts":

The Limits of Advice

The disciples of the Baal Shem heard that a certain man had a great reputation for learning. Some of them wanted to go to him and find out what he had to teach. The master gave them permission to go, but first they asked him: "And how shall we be able to tell whether he is a true *tzaddik*?"

The Baal Shem replied: "Ask him to advise you what to do to keep unholy thoughts from disturbing you in your prayers and studies. If he gives you advice, then you will know that he belongs to those who are of no account. For this is the service of men in the world to the very hour of their deaths: to struggle time after time with the extraneous, and time after time to uplift and fit into the nature of the Divine Name."

(*Buber, Early Masters, p.* 66)

The idea of an imperfect holy man was profoundly democratic. Every Hasid was on the same level with every other Hasid in his potential for becoming a *tzaddik*. This actually resulted in a variety of *tzaddikim* and the eventual rise of invidious comparisons among them. There could not possibly be a broader basis for a religious democracy than Hasidism, which conferred upon everyone the right to become holy individuals. It is certainly more democratic than becoming a "holy person" via formal academic degrees and certification or by traveling to some Tibetan monastery for six months. (Of course, there were no women *tzaddikim*.)

The Hasidim had a check on the non-*tzaddik* rabbis with the *tzaddikim*. This curb on the rabbis was significant. Every Hasid, including rabbis, had the right to maximize his sacred capacities to become a *tzaddik*. Needless to say, in a society where everybody was everybody's equal in his ability to become a special holy man, there was growing disbelief in an elite group. In the ordinary sense any Jew could be a *tzaddik*, even a mitnagid.

Hasidic belief during the eighteenth century was full of variety and disorder and justified pride in the principle of equality, especially before God:

The Name of God

Rabbi David of Lelov once heard a simple man who was praying say the name of God after every verse. The reason he did this was that there are two dots, one above the other, at the close of each verse. The man took each to be the tiny letter Yud (pronounced Yid by many Yiddish speakers, exactly like the word meaning "Jew"), and since the name of God is sometimes abbreviated in the form of two Yuds, he thought that what he saw at the end of every verse was the name of God.

The *tzaddik* instructed him: "Wherever you find two Yids (Jews) side by side and on a par, there is the name of God. But whenever it looks to you as if one Yid (Jew) is standing above the other, then they are not Yids (Jews) and it is not the name of God."

(*Buber, Late Masters, p. 185*)

Hasidic rabbis followed in the Besht's footsteps in adopting nicknames (or titles): "The Angel," "The Great *Maggid*," "The Seer of Lublin," "Zevi, The Scribe," "The Yehudi," "The Rav" (master), "The Spola" (grandfather) and others.

The Hasidic rabbis began to vie with one another for status and prestige in the absence of the living, unifying force of the Besht:

The Two Lights

Rabbi Mendel of Rymanov was asked: "Why cannot two *tzaddikim* have their seats in the same city?"

He replied: "*Tzaddikim* are like the lights up in Heaven. When God created the two great lights of Heaven he placed both in the firmament, each to do its own special service. Ever since, they have been friends. The great light does not boast of being great, and the small light is content with being small. And so it was in the days of our sages: There was a whole skyful of stars, large stars and small stars, and they lived together in all brotherliness. Not so the *tzaddikim* of our day! Now no one wants to be a small light and bow to a greater. So it is better for each to have his own firmament all for himself."

(*Buber, Late Masters, pp. 129–130*)

Although the Hasidic rabbis nostalgically bemoaned the "old" solidarity, their rivalries were much healthier than the emergence of one dominating charismatic figure. Gradually, the mantle of leadership in various Hasidic groups began to pass from father to son. Eventually, the Hasidic movement splintered into sects with several, such as the Lubavitcher group, dominating the field.

Thus the first institutional revolution centered on the roles of the Hasid, the rabbi, and especially the *tzaddik*, with the central idea that every man has direct access to God and that all are equal in finding bliss in Him and receiving His blessings.

The second major institutional revolution was cultural and developed around the concept of *kavvana*, which can be roughly translated as intention, commitment, will and, in the broadest sense, motivation—the person's conscious and subconscious reasons for his behavior.

The Besht and his followers originally were greatly influenced by the Kabbala, the tradition of Jewish esoteric-mystical lore. The *Zohar* (The Book of Splendor, the basic work of Kabbala, composed in the thirteenth century), the writings of the Ari, Rabbi Isaac Luria of Safed, and books by other kabbalists profoundly influenced Hasidism at its inception, and the Hasidic movement in turn altered profoundly the kabbalistic influence in its applications of *kavvana* to the practical realities of the poor and non-scholarly masses of the Jewish people.

Kavvana was a revolutionary form of popular prayer and dedication to God in daily general behavior. Prayer and behavior in general were profoundly spiritualized, so that, through focusing on God as a kind of "partner," the Hasid broke down the barrier of his earthly existence by connecting continuously to the Divine Presence. He "wills" his soul to God's spirit through his heart and his faith and creates an internal vacuum which is filled by God's spirit, which connects to man's soul and acts and "speaks" for him:

What the Mouth Will

> The Baal Shem said: "When I weld my spirit to God, I let my mouth say what it will, for then all my words are bound to their roots in Heaven."
>
> (*Buber, Early Masters, p. 51*)

The Besht is saying that in this ecstatic state the mouth continues to speak but the spirit, God's spirit, supplies the thoughts. The generalization is that whenever a person prays or acts with *kavvana*—full intentionality of connecting to God—a transformation occurs wherein that person ceases merely human activity and is moved by God's spirit acting through him.

The practical result of this *kavvana*-oriented religious emphasis was to open up dramatically the internal, subjective side of man, his innermost thoughts, feelings and fantasies. A new and powerful psychological dynamism was released which exploded the all too human propensities for pretense and self-deception through "correct" behavior:

Speaking the Truth

Rebbe Elimelekh Lizensker once said: "I am sure of my share in the world-to-come. When I stand to plead before the bar of the Heavenly Tribunal, I will be asked: 'Did you learn, as in duty bound?' To this I will answer: 'No.' Again I will be asked: 'Did you pray as in duty bound?' Again my answer will be: 'No.' The third question will be: 'Did you do good, as in duty bound?' And for the third time I will answer: 'No.' Then judgment will be awarded in my favor, for I have spoken the truth."

(*Newman, The Hasidic Anthology, p. 167*)

Since the concept of *kavvana* is so central to understanding Hasidism, we want to illustrate through the stories the extreme (ridiculous?) extent to which the rabbis were swept away with the idea of being fully motivated in what you do:

With the Proper Intention

Said the Besht: "When we petition God, let us ask for understanding and firmness to do His will. Then we shall also obtain other favors in a form as unlimited as is God Himself.

"We should be cautious, however, lest we be deceitful in our intention: We must not affirm that we offer prayer and acts of piety for love of God, and not for anticipated rewards, whereas in our heart we remember that we will profit thereby. There is a story to the effect that a poor man asked his rich brother: 'Why are you wealthy, and I am not?' The other answered: 'Because I have no scruples against doing wrong.' The poor brother began to misconduct himself but he remained poor. He complained of this to his elder brother, who answered: 'The reason your transgressions have not made you wealthy is that you did them not from conviction that it matters not whether we do good or evil, but solely because you desired riches.'

"How much more applicable is this to doing good with the proper intention!"

(*Newman, The Hasidic Anthology, p. 438*)

This is quite a prescription for successful connivance: "Do it with a pure heart."

Or consider the following strange instruction to a boy of four:

Pray Like a Child

When the Bratzlaver fell ill, his daughter's child, a boy of four, entered the room. The Bratzlaver asked the lad to pray for his recovery. The boy replied: "Give me your watch and I will pray for you." The rabbi smiled and said: "See, he is already a 'good Jew.' He wishes to be paid for his prayer." The Bratzlaver handed his watch to the boy, and the child exclaimed: "Dear God, dear God, let grandpapa become well!" The Bratzlaver commented: "This is the real way to offer prayer. Any other way is futile."

(*Newman, Maggidim and Hasidim, p. 66*)

"Be paid for prayer?" Does the means of pay or "bribery" to get full motivation really nullify the child's whole-heartedness?

Or consider the case of the rabbi who was severely beaten because of mistaken identity:

According to Intention

Rabbi Abish once spent a night at a tavern where he was unknown. The wife of the tavern-keeper was distressed to discover that eighty thalers were missing, and she accused the guest of taking them. The rabbi was searched, and, by a coincidence, exactly eighty thalers were found on him. The tavern-keeper beat him severely and took the money away from him. A few months later the tavern-keeper's wife found the money she had mislaid. Her husband searched out his guest, was told his identity, returned the money and tearfully implored the rabbi's forgiveness. Rabbi Abish replied: "There is really nothing which I need forgive. It was your intention to punish a thief, not an honest man."

(*Newman, Maggidim and Hasidim, p. 133*)

We doubt that such a defense would hold up in a modern court of law.

Now, of course, in all three of the above examples, the rabbis are speaking tongue-in-cheek. Nevertheless, the issue must be addressed in its most stark form. Were the Nazis perpetrating all their unspeakable horrors from the most ardent and fullest conviction of *their* "hearts"?

Kavvana does not exist in a social and cultural vacuum. The Jews had their law and code of humane conduct which is embodied in the Torah. *Kavvana* is complemented by the *tzaddik*—the Hasidic ideal, the role model who "lives Torah."

The Tzaddik *and His Conduct*

Said Rabbi Leib Saras: "A *tzaddik* is not a person who preaches Torah, but rather lives Torah. Not his words but his actions should teach Torah to the people. I visit *tzaddikim* not to listen to their interpretations of Torah, but to observe how they conduct themselves from the time of their arising in the early morning until the time of their lying down to rest at night."

(*Newman, Maggidim and Hasidim, p. 29*)

In fact, many rabbis decried Hasidim who sought help through prayer, rather than changing their behavior.

The Many and the Few

The Ropshitzer was accustomed to say: "Many come to my house, but few come to me." Rabbi Solomon Sopher explained this as follows: "Many come to the tzaddik to seek his prayer in their behalf. But few come to seek to know his holy conduct, and to learn from spiritual perfection."

(*Newman, Maggidim and Hasidim, p. 29*)

A true *tzaddik* is one who fearlessly examines and probes his own motives, and is thus enabled to empathize in a most profound way with his Hasidic followers:

Two Kinds of Tzaddikim

Said the Lizensker: "There are two kinds of *tzaddikim.* One is a true saint, but he knows it and believes he need not repent since he does not sin. Such a *tzaddik* cannot influence others to repent, because he does not himself adhere to repentance.

"The other *tzaddik* is likewise a true saint, but of a higher type. He constantly passes judgment upon his own actions, to discover whether they were performed from holy motives only and for the sake of pleasing the Lord, rather than for the sake of his own soul's benefit. If he discovers an impure motive in his conduct, he repents of it with fervor. Such a *tzaddik* is able to influence others to repent, for he himself cleaves to repentance. This is the meaning of the Talmudic saying: 'Greater are the penitents than the perfect *tzaddikim.*'"

(*Newman, The Hasidic Anthology, p. 531*)

We believe this severe uncompromising self-examination is the single most endearing quality of the Hasidic heritage and is the key to each *tzaddik*'s finding his unique path:

The Greatest Tzaddik

Said Rabbi Hirsch Rymanover: "Some *tzaddikim* serve the Lord in the old way: They walk on the state road. Others at times adopt a new way: They walk on the side road. Still others pursue a way of their own choosing: They walk on the path. The last reach their destination first."

(*Newman, The Hasidic Anthology, p. 529*)

As the Hasidic movement spread, its ceremonies and rituals reflected more and more their followers' joyous identification with God. In their own *shtiblakh*, or prayer houses, they prayed at the tops of their voices, swayed and clapped their hands and spontaneously chanted in an exuberant cacophony of voices. They created their own tunes, called *niggunim*, and swayed and danced to them—often in trances. Their practices spread all over Poland and into Lithuania.

The traditional Jewish establishment—which stressed Halakhic scholarship—regarded Hasidism as an outrage. The early Hasidim found a dedicated enemy in Elijah ben Solomon Zalman (1720-97), the *Gaon* of Vilna, a man whose secular and religious knowledge was awesome. He regarded Hasidic claims to ecstasy, miracles, and visions as lies and delusions. The idea of a "*tzaddik*" was idolatry; obsessive concentration on prayer and devotion to God was an affront to scholarship—the *raison d'être* of Judaism. The Gaon believed that the Hasidim should be repudiated, suppressed, and relentlessly pursued with all manner of punishments. The anti-Hasidim became known as *mitnagdim* (opponents).

The Hasidim replied in kind with their own "excommunications" and they were locked into religious strife for generations. What the Hasidim lacked in scholarly learning, they easily made up with their caustic wit:

Concerning the Messiah

> In jest, a man once asked Rabbi Shneur Zalman of Liadi, known as The Rav: "Will the Messiah be a Hasid or a *mitnaged*?" He answered: "I think a *mitnaged*, for if he were a Hasid, the *mitnagdim* would not believe in him; but the Hasidim will believe in him, no matter what he is.
>
> (*Buber, Early Masters, pp. 270–271*)

The *mitnagdic* attempt to destroy Hasidism failed. Hasidism exerted a permanent and significant influence on Judaism. It spread west into Germany and the United States and throughout the entire world. The internal war abated as all religious Jews began to face a new common enemy—the Haskala, the Jewish movement for secular enlightenment.

From a larger societal perspective, the Hasidic rabbis were not naive about what was happening in the world. They saw the rapid secularization of society and the movement from a closed communal order to a more open commercial society. The world was becoming competitive, individualistic, greedy, impersonal, and less God-loving.

The Marketplace and the House of Prayer

> The Berditchever opened his discourse: "A world turned topsy-turvy I see before my eyes. In years gone by, the Jews spoke the truth in the streets and the marketplaces, but in the House of Prayer they told a lie. It is the other way around now. On the streets and in the marketplaces they all speak falsehood, but in the House of Prayer they tell the truth.
>
> "A riddle? The explanation: honesty and good faith were the torches lighting their paths in the olden days. And so they made good the Scriptural word of a righteous aye and nay, and all their trading was done in good faith. But when they came into the House of Prayer, they would beat their breasts and say: 'We have defrauded, we have robbed.' That was then a lie, for they had been true to God and their fellow man. Today it is the reverse: in the trading place, they lie and defraud, and in their confessional prayer, they speak the truth."
>
> (*Newman, The Hasidic Anthology, p. 519*)

The early Hasidic rabbis tried to stem the tide toward commercialism, chicanery, and connivance:

Protecting the Weak

> The Sadigurer Rabbi rebuked a wholesale merchant for being too harsh in his dealing with the retailers. The merchant remarked: "Rabbi, why do you live in a city and interfere with the merchants? Why do you not live in a village, and commune in solitude with God as the Besht did?"

> The rabbi retorted: "In the time of the Besht, the robbers lived in the forests, and hence the *tzaddik* lived there in order by his prayers to protect the passers-by. Today, however, the robbers live in the city, and the *tzaddik* is compelled to live there as well, in order to protect, if he can, the weak."
>
> (*Newman, The Hasidic Anthology, p. 195*)

It became clear to the Hasidic rabbis that the two worlds were becoming increasingly split, and this is what the Berditchever is really talking about. The ironic outcome is that lying in the marketplace enables the Hasidim to be truthful in the synagogue, a huge ironic joke that clothes a great truth.

In this new titanic confrontation between the sacred and the secular worlds, the Hasidic rabbis found themselves in retreat. The world was indeed changing and it was almost as if people lived to work rather than to serve and to live according to God's law:

Out of Travail

> Once, at the close of the Day of Atonement, when Rabbi Shlomo was in a gay mood, he said he would tell each Hasid what he (i.e., the Hasid) had asked of Heaven on these holy days and what answer was intended for his request.
>
> To the first of his disciples who wanted to be told, he said: "What you asked of God was that He should give you your livelihood at the proper time and without travail, so that you might not be hindered in serving Him. And the answer was that what God really wants of you is not study or prayer, but the sighs of your heart, which is breaking because the travail of gaining a livelihood hinders you in the service of God."
>
> (*Buber, Early Masters, p. 280*)

Don't ask God to help you with your work, but ask God to help you "sigh" so that your work does not prevent you from serving others and believing and conducting your life according to God's will.

The Berditchever Rabbi took this "sigh" one step further and infused it with another challenging *kavvana* for Hasidim:

The Uses of Life

> A Hasid once asked the Berditchever Rabbi to explain why the Lord did not provide him once a year with sufficient funds for his annual needs, and thus free his mind for spiritual activities.
>
> The rabbi replied: "We cannot comprehend God's reasons. Perhaps he desires to see what use you will make of the life He has granted you, while you are burdened with the task of carving out a living."
>
> (*Newman, The Hasidic Anthology, p. 152*)

In the above story we return to the key force in Hasidic life—*kavvana*—the commitment to God must be heartfelt and wholehearted. This is the Hasidic response to modernization.

THE HASIDIC STORY

The Hasidic rabbis put new life into a form that was to become their "Talmud"—the Hasidic story. In a dazzling display of stories that flowed from and to the people, that spoke to the people in clear unadorned language and familiar images, the rabbis were able to demonstrate to the people of the *shtetl* how faith in God could be used in a practical way in their everyday life.

The Hasidic story was successful then and is also highly successful in influencing people today, because the rabbis and others who told and retold these stories in a naturalistic style were very close to the people and responsive to their feedback. They knew what "worked" because they were constantly experimenting with these stories in telling them over and over again from one generation to another.

Hasidic stories had four main functions:

- To serve as a continuous bridge from the past to the present and sustain the Hasidic tradition.
- To continuously connect the rabbis and *tzaddikim* to their Hasidic followers through psychological counseling and support.

- To reinforce the core values of Hasidism that comprise the foundation of its philosophy.
- To serve as a main source of entertainment—the radio, movies, television, theater, and nightclub of Hasidic life. All work and prayer and no play certainly could not be joyous for very long!

Since this book deals with these four themes in depth, we will begin with an introductory overview.

THE STORY AS A TRADITION-CONSERVATOR

Tradition is a guide to the present and the future, not a dictator. Continuity with the past does not mean that the vital present and exciting future must be subsidiary to tradition. People are what their predecessors were *and* much more!

The Hasidim, thanks to the iconoclasm of the Besht and its early irreverent tradition (the subject of many stories), strove to revere tradition *and* not be trapped or encased by it. Thus, there are many stories that emphasize tradition *and* the importance of striking out in new, fresh and original paths different from the past. The following stories illustrate these blending trends in the Hasidic tradition:

In Every Generation

> One evening, several of Rabbi Hayyim of Kosov's Hasidim sat together in his House of Study and told one another stories about *tzaddikim*, above all about the Baal Shem Tov. And because both the telling and the listening were very sweet to them, they were at it even after midnight. Then one of them told still another story about the Baal Shem Tov. When he had ended, another sighed from the bottom of his heart. "Alas!" said he, half to himself. "Where could we find such a man today?"
>
> At that instant, they heard steps coming down the wooden stair which led from the *tzaddik's* room. The door opened and Rabbi Hayyim appeared on the threshold, in the short jacket he usually wore in the evening. "Fools," he said softly, "he is present in every generation, he, the Baal Shem Tov. Only in those days he was manifest, while now he is hidden."

He closed the door and went back up the stairs. The Hasidim sat together in silence.

(*Buber, Late Masters, p. 99*)

Such heavy homage definitely would not have pleased the Besht. He would have been rather delighted with the following story:

In His Father's Footsteps

When Rabbi Noah, Rabbi Mordecai's son, assumed the succession after his father's death, his disciples noticed that there were a number of ways in which he conducted himself differently from his father and they asked him about this.

"I do just as my father did," he replied. "He did not imitate, and I do not imitate."

(*Buber, Late Masters, p. 157*)

This story represents more truly the Besht's legacy to Hasidim.

THE STORIES AS PRACTICAL AIDS TO EVERYDAY LIFE

One of the most charming aspects of the Hasidic stories is their offering of very practical ideas as well as general philosophical guidelines for living a good life. Who in his right mind could possibly find any fault with the following cardinal principle:

Give and Take

Rabbi Yitzhak Eisik said:

"The motto of life is 'Give and take.' Everyone must be both a giver and a receiver. He who is not both is as a barren tree."

(*Buber, Late Masters, p. 220*)

Beware takers and givers of the world who are only one or the other—your life is utterly fruitless!

A somewhat more practical bit of advice is the homely Hasidic counsel about the wisdom of pacing yourself in the pursuit of your goals, especially when you tire along the way:

Up the Mountain

> Rabbi Yehiel Mikhal said: "It is written: 'Who shall ascend onto the mountain of the Lord? And who shall stand in His holy place?' For the sake of comparison, let us take a man who rides up a mountain in his carriage, and when he is half-way up, the horses are tired and he must stop and give them a rest. Now, whoever has no sense at this point, will roll down. But he who has sense will take a stone and put it under the wheel while the carriage is standing. Then he will be able to reach the top. The man who does not fall, when he is forced to interrupt his service, but knows how to pause, he will get to the top of the mountain of the Lord."
>
> (*Buber, Early Masters, p. 153*)

In general, the Hasidim valued learning directly from experience and especially by talking to and observing their role-models, the *tzaddikim*. The Hasidim not only believed in learning by doing, "life" was the best teacher; they consciously formulated these principles and incorporated what Gregory Bateson calls "meta-learning," into their stories:

The Program and the Play

> In the days when Rabbi Bunam still traded in lumber, a number of merchants in Danzig asked him why he, who was so well-versed in the sacred writings, went to visit *tzaddikim*. What could they tell him that he could not learn from his books? He answered them, but they did not understand him. In the evening, they invited him to go to the play with them, but he refused. When they returned from the theater, they told him they had seen many wonderful things. "I know all about those wonderful things," said he. "I have read the program."

"But from that," they said, "you cannot possibly know what we have seen with our own eyes."

"That's just how it is," he said, "with the books and the *tzaddikim*."

(*Buber, Early Masters, pp. 8–24*)

THE STORY AS A TEACHER OF VALUES

Every Hasidic story, implicitly or explicitly, espouses a Hasidic value; so when you embrace the stories, you adopt also their system of values. We will examine in detail the stories as promoters of the Hasidic belief system in Part III, Hasidic Teaching. Perhaps the following simple tale best illustrates the humanistic foundation of the Hasidic faith:

How to Love God

A learned but ungenerous man said to Rabbi Abraham of Stretyn: "They say that you give people mysterious drugs and that your drugs are effective. Give me one that I may attain to the fear of God."

"I don't know of any drug for the fear of God," said Rabbi Abraham, "but if you like I can give you one for the love of God."

"That's even better!" cried the other, "just give it to me."

"It is the love of one's fellow men," answered the *tzaddik*.

(*Buber, Late Masters, pp. 151–152*)

If the preceding stories seem a bit soupy, one should balance the real concern that Hasidim have for others with their keen appreciation of self-interest as a major motivator of behavior. The Hasidim were realistic and experts at constantly reconciling individual interests with concern for others and the community:

The Best Kind of Prayer

Rabbi Yaakov Yitzhak of Pshiskhe, known as *Der Yid* (The Jew), became dangerously ill, and the inhabitants of his town

> proclaimed a fast and universal prayer for the rabbi's speedy convalescence. A villager chanced to come to town, and went to the tavern for a drink of brandy. Several townsfolk overheard him and informed him that drinking was prohibited for the day.
>
> The villager at once went to the synagogue and prayed: "O Lord, please cure the Holy Rabbi, so that I may have my drink."
>
> Soon after, the rabbi began to recover his strength and said: "The prayer of the villager was more acceptable than any of yours. He expressed the greatest and most earnest supplication for my prompt recovery."
>
> (*Newman, The Hasidic Anthology, p. 64*)

The Hasidim, and the Besht above all, were keenly aware of how stories could teach their followers in ways that would prove to be superior even to prayer. Stories captured the listeners' imagination and riveted their attention:

Profane Phrases of Holiness

> Said the Rizhiner: "Abraham wished to enable men to devote a portion of the day to the Lord, and he, therefore, instituted the Morning Service. The Satan conspired against this, and succeeded in capturing it by filling it with distracting thoughts. Isaac said: 'I will institute a brief service, through which men may perhaps be able to pray with the proper concentration.' This proved of no avail. Jacob then said: 'I will proclaim a voluntary evening service; perhaps the Satan will not trouble to introduce alien thoughts into an optional service, since a man may choose not to read it.' But this, too, proved unsuccessful. The Ari said: 'I will institute the practice of silent meditation'; but this too, proved unsuccessful. Hence, the Besht said: 'Let the good man who cannot pray properly recite aloud profane phrases or tales and endow them with a holy meaning.' This proved a successful remedy against the machinations of the Satan."
>
> (*Newman, The Hasidic Anthology, p. 158*)

THE STORIES AS ENTERTAINMENT

Hasidic stories cover the gamut of emotions from pathos to sentimentalism, from the lofty to the flat and trite; they go from light-heartedness to mystery and ecstasy and awe, and often to the comical and the ironic through the expected as well as the astonishing. All of these are part of the Hasidic heritage.

The high and low drama of the stories is quintessentially captured in one of our favorites:

The Watchman Who Brooded

Rabbi Bunam once said: "It sometimes happens that a man becomes sinful and he himself does not know how it came about, for there was not a single moment when all his thoughts were not on guard." And he told this parable:

A great nobleman once had a race horse in his stable. He valued it more than anything he possessed and had it well guarded. The door of the stable was bolted, and a watchman was always posted in front of it. One night, the owner felt restless. He went to the stable. There sat the watchman, obviously brooding about something with great effort.

"What are you brooding about?" asked the master.

"I am wondering," said the man, "where the clay goes to when you drive a nail into the wall."

"Just you go on thinking about it," said the master. He returned to the house and went to bed. But he was unable to sleep and after a while he could not stand it, and went back to the stable. Again he found the watchman brooding in front of the door.

"What are you thinking about now?" asked his master.

"I am wondering," he said, "where the batter goes when you bake a doughnut."

"Just you go on thinking about that," said his master approvingly. Again he retired and again he could not stay in bed and went to the stable a third time. The watchman was sitting in his place and brooding. "What is going through your head now?" asked the master.

"I am just wondering," said the watchman. "There is the door and it is bolted. Here am I, sitting in front of it and watching: and yet the horse has been stolen. How is that possible?"

(*Buber, Late Masters, pp. 246–247*)

One can picture a deadpan Hasid spinning this story, emphasizing the watchman's curiosity as a positive quality and then showing how his diligence and dedication, normally highly valued character traits, are turned on their head by his crazy obsessiveness. Can you picture the story-teller mimicking the guard at the end, spreading his hands in wonderment and disbelief: "How is that possible?"

We can also imagine a Hasid warning a finicky friend about being over-meticulous by simply reminding him of the "brooding watchman." So traditions are built, counseling is gently suggested, values are promoted, and a really good time is had by all. Each story plays many roles and fulfills many functions in reinforcing Hasidic culture and society.

Humorous tales keep the Hasidim from taking themselves too seriously all the time. A Hasid prefers a clever and honest profane point-of-view to false pieties:

Three Excuses

> Three youths hid themselves on a Sabbath in a barn in order to smoke. Hasidim discovered them and wished to flog the offenders. One youth exclaimed: "I deserve no punishment, for I forgot that today is the Sabbath." The second youth said: "And I forgot that smoking on the Sabbath is forbidden." The third youth raised his voice and cried out: "I, too, forgot." "What did you forget?" he was asked. The lad replied: "I forgot to lock the door of the barn."
>
> (*Newman, Maggidim and Hasidim, p. 191*)

In the chapters that follow, we will be discussing many other important Hasidic values, but we would like to highlight, in concluding this chapter, a Hasidic preference for deviant, zany, impractical or even crazy behavior that comes through in many stories and is hinted at in the last story. This tendency to favor the deviant is related to the Hasidic belief that the intention or motivation underlying behavior is as important as the behavior itself—perhaps even more important. Hasidim were distrustful of pretense and mechanical conformity—the "nature of man"—which could be overcome through God's spirit. They believed in the spunky deviant.

Poor Man, Rich Spirit

> Said the Kossoker: "If you give a donation to a poor man, and the latter returns it, asking for a still larger gift, your acquiescence to his request will bring you a boundless reward, since it is contrary to the nature of man."
>
> (*Newman, The Hasidic Anthology, p. 39*)

This story is a fitting ending to our brief introduction to Hasidism and its spiritual-humanistic core, and an equally appropriate beginning to the Hasidic stories that follow. Someone forced by circumstances to seek donations, says the Kossoker, need not become a beggar in spirit. Every great spiritual movement profoundly respects and nurtures the dignity of *all* persons. Hasidism is exemplary in this respect.

The Kossoker's remarks may remind you, the next time you meet a beggar, that like *tzaddikim*, not all beggars are alike.

2

The Psychology of the Hasidic Story

INTRODUCTION

Neurolinguistic programming (NLP) is a school of psychology that has developed a body of skills for understanding patterns of human behavior and influencing behavioral change in the context of a useful therapeutic model of linguistics. The latter, called "meta-model," is a set of linguistic strategies developed by NLP for responding productively to people's verbalizations.

This chapter introduces three interlinking steps NLP utilizes to effect therapeutic change:

- Assessing the client's evaluation of his situation through careful attention to his language and nonverbal behavior as he describes and evaluates his difficulties, desires and goals. This is the meta-model.
- Gathering information about the client's situation and desired goals and gaining rapport and cooperation. This process is called "pacing."
- Helping the client evolve from present state to desired goals and anchoring this desired state into the client's ongoing behavior. This is referred to as "change-behavior strategies."

Each of these steps will be discussed in detail later in our analysis of Hasidic stories. This chapter will present more generally Hasidim's strategies for assessing the Hasid's understanding and distortions of his situation by analyzing how he verbalizes his problems; gaining the Hasid's rapport and cooperation, and, helping the Hasid utilize his own resources to achieve his desired goal.

THE META-MODEL

We talk to ourselves in pictures, sounds, feelings, and words. When this internal talk is not aligned with actual sensory experience in the real world, distortions emerge. Such incongruities can be useful at certain times and deliberately cultivated, like daydreaming through a boring meeting or generating a pleasant fantasy while in the dentist's chair.

The lyrics of songs, for example, are purposely vague and ambiguous, so that the listener fills in the generalities with associations of his own:

You must remember this
A kiss is still a kiss
A sigh is still a sigh.
The fundamental things apply
As time goes by.

This verse from the song "As Time Goes By" (from the film, *Casablanca*) abounds with what NLP refers to as "meta-model violations:"

You must remember this. Who is the *you*? Everyone? *Must remember* Is it imperative? What if one doesn't? *A kiss is still a kiss.* Not an orange! *A sigh is still a sigh.* Nothing more? For how long? Forever? *The fundamental things apply.* These are fundamental? When? Apply to what? *As time goes by.* When, specifically?

Stories, as we shall soon see, also abound in generalities and vagueness—"once upon a time"— to draw the listener into an appropriate mood and to elicit associations that can blend with the story's line and its message. For example, in the

Hasidic story the client's name (if he is not another rabbi) is never given. The rabbi-counselor's name is invariably given. The anonymity of the client may help many listeners to fill themselves into the situations with their own associations.

In some counseling situations, however, it is detrimental for the counseling to proceed without a clear and specific picture of the client's problem. The client who comes to a therapist with "Boy, have I got problems!" will not get very far without more details.

Many of the Hasidic stories are a strategic blend of meta-model violations and challenges to the meta-model violations:

Alien Thoughts

> A man came to ask the Rabbi of Lublin to help him against alien thoughts which intruded on him while he prayed. The rabbi indicated what he was to do, but the man went on asking questions and would not stop. Finally, the rabbi said: "I don't know why you keep complaining to me of alien thoughts. To him who has holy thoughts, an impure thought comes at times, and such a thought is called 'alien.' But you—you have just your own usual thoughts. To whom do you want to ascribe them?"
>
> (*Buber, Early Masters, p. 316*)

The rabbi is suggesting that his petitioner come to terms with the true origin of his own thoughts as a first step to doing something about them. The rabbis were keen about each person facing up to the reality of his situation, and they helped their followers by cutting through distortions which covered up their real problems.

In the story above, the petitioner is not "owning" his thoughts. He does not see himself as the "cause" of his "alien thoughts." This is a tough confrontation and an important first step for the petitioner who wants to do something about them (see, for example, "The Sin of the Melancholy" on p. 81).

It is important to stress that the client's view of his problem is only a first step in treatment; a counselor would want to know many more specifics: alien thoughts about what, when, where specifically, the petitioner's strategies for dealing with them, etc. The Lubliner Rabbi appropriately made the petitioner take the first step toward coming to terms with his problem by recognizing that he himself is the author of his alien thoughts.

The following story masterfully draws the reader into a specific situation from which he learns a general truth which can be applied to many of his personal situations that can transform his life:

Can and Want To

> Once, when the Yehudi (i.e., the *Yid* of Pshiskhe) was walking cross-country, he happened on a hay wagon which had turned over.
>
> "Help me raise it up!" said the driver. The rabbi tried but he could not budge it.
>
> "I can't," he finally said.
>
> The peasant looked at him sternly. "You can all right," said he, "but you don't want to."
>
> On the evening of that day the Yehudi went to his disciples: "I was told today: We can raise up the Name of God, but we don't want to."
>
> (*Buber, Late Masters, p. 228*)

In this artful story, the rabbi's "can't" is changed to "won't" and gains the profound insight that what we often think we cannot do for objective reasons is very often a misperception based on fears and doubts within ourselves.

Compare this with Shakespeare's *Macbeth*: "Our doubts are traitors and make us lose the good we oft would attain, by fearing to attempt."

The Yid's faith in God is re-energized. And he subtly brings his audience into the revelation with "*We* can raise up. . . ."

Many who heard the tale back then could begin to see that many of their own personal problems stemmed from the difference between "can't" and "won't." Even today, those who frequently catch their own verbal and nonverbal "can'ts" and substitutes "won'ts" for them can see more clearly how many of their problems are fueled by inner doubts and fears.

The Hasidic rabbis were keenly aware of the power of imagination for good and evil, as a tremendous boon to mankind and as a cunning snare and trap:

The Horse's Shadow

A storekeeper complained to the Premishlaner that another man had opened a store near him and was taking away his livelihood. The rabbi answered:

"Did you ever notice that when a horse is led to a pool of water to drink, he stamps with his hoof in the water?"

"Yes," said the man.

"The reason is as follows," continued the rabbi. "When the horse bends his head to drink, he sees his shadow. He imagines that another horse is also drinking and, fearing there will not be sufficient water for him, he attempts to chase away the other horse. In reality, he is afraid of his shadow, and there is plenty of water for many horses. You, likewise, are afraid of an imaginary foe. God's abundance flows like a river. No one can touch the other's livelihood, since Providence grants sustenance to everyone according to His will."

(*Newman, The Hasidic Anthology, p. 150*)

PACING

One of the most powerful tools in the repertoire of the therapist is pacing the client who has problems. Pacing consists of two parts: The first is tuning in to the client in order to feel and understand not only the specific problem from his point of view, but also all of the feelings that surround and often contribute to the problem. Much of this, of course, is nonverbal and depends upon the tone and pace of speaking, the words that are used, the timing and, of course, the intensity of feeling accompanying the words.

The Hasidim were profoundly aware that the implicit message conveyed by gesture and tone is as important as the explicit message of a story in influencing the listener:

The Tone of a Request

Said the Dubner: "A student wrote a letter to his father, asking for extra spending money. The father's secretary read the lad's letter to his employer in a loud, harsh voice: 'Father, send money immediately; I need shoes and an overcoat.' The father became incensed at the seemingly impolite tone of his son's letter and refused to answer him. Later he gave the same letter to his wife to read. She read it to him in a low tone of modest entreaty. The father, thereupon, wrote out a check and instructed his wife to mail it to his son.

"From this we learn that he who prays quietly makes a better impression than a noisy worshiper."

(*Newman, Maggidim and Hasidim, p. 143*)

But hearing where the client is existentially, so to speak, is only half of pacing. The other part is letting him know that his counselor knows where he is coming from not only in relation to the problem he has, but also as regards the client's feelings. It is important not to parrot back to the client, because that is phony and can be regarded by the client as mimicking him/her. Thus, pacing is getting on with the client in such a way so that you get into his rhythm and also acknowledging overtly and covertly, that you know where that person is at this moment. The Hasidic rabbis were very close to the people and knew them intimately. They were the settlement and street social workers of their time. The modern idea of networking includes a "central figure" who serves as a focal point of support and service to others in the network. Such was the role of the Hasidic rabbi.

Hasidim believe (Newman 1944) that a person's intention, motivation, or reason for doing or not doing something can be as powerful as the act itself. This, as we have said before, is embodied in the concept of *kavvana*, and its essence is captured by something the Lubliner Rabbi once said: "I love more the wicked man who is aware of his wickedness than the good man who is aware of his goodness."

We have also pointed out earlier that the rabbi-counselor's task is to match with his heart the Hasid's trouble, which means being at peace with his own heart. For Hasidim the heart was the seat of understanding, empathy, and compassion. It far exceeded the senses in penetrating the real intention of an individual. Thus, the Koretezer Rabbi (Newman 1944) once said: "The true *tzaddik* is always able to see without his eyes and to hear without his ears. A man comes to ask my counsel, and I hear that he himself is telling me, unknowingly, what I should advise him." "Unknowingly," the Hasid's heart reveals the truth, and the rabbi helps the Hasid tune into it. Thus, before it is possible to lead a troubled person out of his troubles, it is necessary to start where he is now:

Climbing Down

> Rabbi Shlomo said: "If you want to raise a man from mud and filth, do not think it is enough to keep standing on top and reaching down to him a helping hand. You must go down all the way yourself, down into mud and filth. Then take hold of him with strong hands and pull him and yourself out into the light."
>
> (*Buber, Early Masters, p. 277*)

As this story shows, the rabbi-counselor was aware of the importance of matching his follower's troubled situation. Every modern school of psychology stresses the need for the client to know that the counselor realizes how troubled he is.

Paradoxically, the rabbi in one story tells a Hasid that he cannot help him now because he "knows" how deeply troubled he is!

The Other's Tribulations

> A poor man came to the Berditchever and petitioned him to offer prayers for his deliverance from poverty. The rabbi asked the man to remind him of his request the next day.
>
> "But, rabbi," protested the suppliant, "today I have a chance for a free trip home."
>
> "What can I do?" replied the rabbi. "At this moment, my heart is full of another man's troubles. When the Lord will aid him, my heart will be free to take up yours. I can assist you only when my heart feels your trouble as much as you do yourself."
>
> (*Newman, The Hasidic Anthology, p. 119*)

The rabbi is the master of troubles of the heart. In this instance, the rabbi was burdened with another person's troubles, but he was also aware of the depth and intensity of the petitioner's situation. In effect, the rabbi was saying that he truly felt the depth of the petitioner's problem by telling him that he could not, in fact, feel it yet as strongly as the poor man did!

The rabbi showed profound sympathy for the petitioner, and he let the latter know that he realized how deep and difficult his situation was indeed! The petitioner could not help but take some consolation from that.

What is paradoxical about the rabbi's prescription is that he helps the petitioner by not helping him. But on a much more profound level he does, indeed, help him by pacing his problem by letting him know that he understands how difficult it is. The petitioner himself may not have realized the depths of his troubles, and the feeling that the rabbi indeed was aware of how troubled he was would calm him. Knowing this, the becalmed petitioner can then begin to think about what he might be able to do. He will be able to work on his problem himself, or he will return to the rabbi less agitated and ready to begin to work in a more intensive, practical way on his problem. It is in this sense that the rabbis in being so close to their people, were able to quickly tune into the depth of the emotional field in which their followers' problems were embedded. They had a healthy respect for those feelings and how they were related to problem-solving.

The superb and stunning modernity of the rabbis as sophisticated psychologists is best revealed in their ability to tune into and monitor their own feelings in counseling others. They were fully aware of what is broadly called today "countertransference," the evocation of feelings in the counselor by his own unresolved problems, which mirror the client's difficulties and interfere with the counselor's helping the client. Note the exquisite sensitivity of the rabbis' monitoring their own feelings in helping their clients.

A True Healing

> Rabbi Isaac of Ziditchov learned much of the art of healing during the many years of his 'wandering' in the earlier period of his life. When his grandson fell sick, the lad's father

implored Rabbi Isaac to do something to aid him. Rabbi Isaac was buried in thought and did not utter a single word in response. The sick boy became steadily worse. A second grandson, Judah Zevi was sent upstairs to the room of Rabbi Isaac. At the door he coughed and, when he was allowed to enter, he said: "Grandfather, Joshua Heshel has improved a little. Can't you hasten his recovery?" Rabbi Isaac went over to a cupboard, took out a container of herbs and said: "Have these brewed at once, and let the sick boy drink the brew." This remedy brought about the patient's complete recovery. The rabbi thereupon made this explanation to the boy's father: "You, my son, disturbed my thoughts with your dire report about your sick boy. In my anxiety, I found it impossible to collect my thoughts and forgot the remedy at hand. But when Judah Zevi came to me with encouraging news, my fears were allayed, and I was able to think aright."

(*Newman, Maggidim and Hasidim, p. 63*)

Deliberation in Advice

A rich Hasid visited the Kotzker Rabbi and asked for immediate advice concerning a settlement on his daughter who was about to be married. The rabbi replied: "I cannot give you advice instantly. It is not granted to me to ascend to Heaven and see the future decreed for a man and his family. When I am asked for advice, I feel a sense of pride. I find myself unable to reason correctly until my sense of pride has abated. When this has happened, I weigh the matter in the scales of ethics and law, and then I offer my advice."

(*Newman, Maggidim and Hasidim, p. 165*)

The Berditchever Rabbi was one of the most sophisticated psychologists of his, or any other, time. We have learned a great deal from the powerful way in which he paced his "clients." His ability to understand exactly where they were at the moment was so uncanny that his brief surgical interventions were transformative.

By matching external appearances precisely with what is going on inside a client, one can influence the client to make important changes:

Perhaps

A very learned man who had heard of the Rabbi of Berditchev—one of those who boasted of being enlightened—looked him up in order to debate with him, as he was in the habit of doing with others, and refuting the rabbi's old-fashioned proofs of the truth of his faith.

When the learned man entered the *tzaddik's* room, he saw him walking up and down, a book in his hand, immersed in ecstatic thought. The rabbi took no notice of his visitor. After a time, however, he stopped, gave him a brief glance and said: ". . . but perhaps it is true after all!"

In vain, the learned man tried to rally his self-confidence. His knees shook, for the *tzaddik* was terrible to behold, and his simple words were terrible to hear. But now Rabbi Levi Yitzhak turned to him and calmly addressed him: "My son, the great Torah scholars with whom you debated wasted their words on you. When you left them, you only laughed at what they had said. They could not set God and His Kingdom on the table before you and I cannot do this either. But, my son, only think! Perhaps it is true. Perhaps it is true after all!"

The enlightened man made the utmost effort to reply, but the terrible *perhaps* beat on his ears again and again and broke down his resistance.

(*Buber, Early Masters, p. 228*)

This is a superb example of how the Hasidic rabbi was able to peer into an individual's soul—what we would call today his psyche—and go beyond the surface appearance to the heart of the matter. One general rule of psychology is that the more resistive an individual is to hearing any opposition to his own ideas, the more inner conflicted and ambivalent that individual is about his own "truth." The Berditchever Rabbi had gathered sufficient information about his visitor, namely his boasting about his enlightenment, etc., that he knew what was going on inside this learned man's head.

How ingeniously the rabbi paces his visitor. He invites the learned man into his room and shows him an alternative way of learning—not only through the mind, but through the heart—the way of "ecstatic thought." This is somewhat disturbing and heightens the inner conflict within the learned person.

Now the rabbi deals with him head on by doing something that no one else has done. Everyone else has tried to debate the learned person on his terms, on his "turf," and they have "lost." The Berditchever is not disposed to take this track at all. He has three choices before him: to tell the "enlightened" skeptic that he is right and let it go at that (who needs more problems?); to tell him he's wrong and offer proof, thereby increasing his resistance; to tell him that maybe he is right, and maybe he is wrong. This requires no proof. It is a psychological truth which the learned man is resisting, and it eventually demolishes his resistance.

Imagine the psychological skill of this surgical operation! One word, "perhaps," can dissolve such powerful resistance!

The Berditchever's reply is an example of perfect pacing, followed by the leading of the listener to the point where his internal conflict is intensified and he becomes vulnerable to another point of view. The rabbi's position, of course, is one of complete faith in God, but this would have been ridiculous to set before his visitor. As he says: "I cannot set God and His Kingdom on the table." He must be satisfied with the step before that, and that is the *possibility* that God *could be "set on the table."* And that answer is enough to persuade somebody who has come armed and ready to argue "to the death" against anything the other person says.

The broader implication here is that logicians often like to see issues neatly categorized, so that they can be dealt with one at a time—rationally and objectively. The Hasidim were much more aware, because of their "understanding hearts," that most events in life were contradictory, ambivalent and ambiguous at best. This is another reason why "perhaps" so shook the learned scholar. The visitor was not prepared to get to the heart of the matter with his heart, and there, after all, lay the "heart" of the matter.

One of the greatest contributions that the Hasidim have made to society and culture is the realization that although learning is of vital importance, it has its limitations. They brought the "heart" back into learning and considerably enhanced scholarly work, because the scholars were enabled to realize their own limitations. This is beautifully expressed in the following story:

The First Page

They asked Rabbi Levi Yitzhak: "Why is the first page number missing in all the tractates of the Babylonian Talmud? Why does each begin with the second?"

He replied: "However much a man may learn, he should always remember that he has not even gotten to the first page."

(*Buber, Early Masters, p. 232*)

What the Hasidim resented among their scholarly opponents, the *mitnagdim*, was not their vast storehouse of learning; in fact, they envied that. They were disturbed that learning became an end in itself and led to egotistical displays of their superiority and caused them to separate themselves from ordinary people and from God's compassionate spirit. The above story emphasizes that one can be a learned person and humane as well, with a heart and soul that are connected to God. Hence the critical importance among the Hasidim of modesty and humility.

Since the Hasidic rabbi and his followers shared a common religious cultural heritage, it was not difficult for a sensitive counselor to quickly gather the essential information about his client:

The Doubter

A disciple of Rabbi Pinhas was tormented by doubt, for he could not see how it was possible for God to know all his thoughts, even the vaguest and most fleeting. He went to his teacher in great anguish to beg him to dispel the confusion in his heart. Rabbi Pinhas was standing at the window and saw his visitor arrive. He entered, greeted his master, and was about to tell him his troubles, when the *tzaddik* said: "My friend, I know. And why should God not know?"

(*Buber, Early Masters, p. 122*)

Rabbi Pinhas sees that his follower is sad and "knows" that, whatever the problem is, it has to have at its source a crisis in his faith in God. In this story, the disciple's problem is his doubt about God, and Rabbi Pinhas surgically and miraculously dispels his doubts with irrefutable logic: If he, Rabbi Pinhas, a mere agent of God, divines he has doubts, then how much more so would God be aware of it. To the Hasidim, however, this story reflects their belief that faith in God enables the rabbis to partake of God's miraculous powers. Stories like this, depicting rabbis who knew what their followers were thinking before they said anything, contributed to legends about Hasidic rabbis as miracle workers.

In the story below, Rabbi Pinhas instantly situates himself in what we call today the "life-space" of his young disciples:

With the Evil Urge

Once, when Rabbi Pinhas entered the House of Study, he saw that his disciples, who had been talking busily, stopped and were startled by his coming. He asked them: "What were you talking about?"

"Rabbi," they said, "we were saying how afraid we are that the Evil Urge will pursue us."

"Don't worry," he replied. "You have not gotten high enough for it to pursue you. For the time being, you are still pursuing it."

(*Buber, Early Masters, p. 132*)

Rabbi Pinhas is conveying to his young disciples that they have not yet matured to the point where they can adequately contest the Evil Urge. At this point, there is no contest—the id impulses are in command!

An unusual example of pacing is the legendary saying that "Solomon in his wisdom was wiser than fools." Now, on the surface that seems a ridiculous statement. Certainly Solomon was wiser than fools. But that was not the meaning the Hasidic rabbis attached to the saying. They commented that, when Solomon worked with fools, he descended to their level; yet even when he did that, he was not tricked by them and was able to help them while he was assuming the fool's role. A fool is regarded by Jews as someone who thinks he knows all the answers, has no problems, and "closes the loop" by refusing any help with his problem. Solomon was able to influence fools by identifying with them and yet not becoming one.

The Hasidic rabbis attached great importance to identifying strongly with people at their own levels, pacing them and then suggesting new ideas and pathways for them to follow—but only when the petitioners were ready emotionally.

This great ability of the Hasidic rabbi to pace his followers suggests to us his close identification with the common folk as teacher, counselor, and human being—a powerful role-model for all of us.

BEHAVIOR-CHANGE PRINCIPLES

In Part II, on Hasidic Counseling, we will detail the techniques and strategies Hasidic rabbis used in counseling their followers. In this overview of behavior-change principles, we point up how modern the rabbis were in their approach to psychological issues and problems.

One important Hasidic principle is to treat every person's troubles in a way that is unique to that individual's personality and resources:

Each Individual Learns Differently

> Said the Koretezer, "We read, Moses said: 'My doctrines shall drop as the rain' [*Deut.* 32:2]. We see that rain falls upon many kinds of plants, and each grows according to its own nature. In the same fashion, let instruction be accepted by all persons; each one will profit according to his inherent ability."
>
> (*Newman, The Hasidic Anthology, p. 459*)

Another basic psychological principle is that the "same reality" can be interpreted differently by different people. Each of us has a very personal map of the world, and it is dangerous to equate it with reality. The map is not the territory.

Every experience is influenced by one's perception and interpretation. With the ability, perhaps the necessity, to interpret our experiences in different ways, we can exert some control over our environment and change our lives, move in new directions.

We can change our feelings and attitudes and take steps to change our situation and ourselves. It is not the world alone that dictates fulfillment or unhappiness, but reality in interaction with our knowledge, perception and actions. The following story is one of the most poignant expressions of this principle that we have found among Hasidic stories:

I Know No Sorrow

> Rabbi Schmelke and his brother once petitioned their teacher, the Maggid of Mezeritch, to explain to them the words of the Mishna: "A man must bless God for the evil in the same way that he blesses Him for the good which befalls" (*Berakhot 54*).
>
> The Maggid replied: "Go to the House of Study, and you will find there is a man smoking. He is Rabbi Zusya, and he will explain this to you."
>
> When Rabbi Schmelke and his brother put their question to Rabbi Zusya, he laughed and said: "I am surprised that the rabbi sent you to me. You must go elsewhere and make your inquiry from one who has suffered tribulations in his lifetime. As for me, I have never experienced anything but good all my days."
>
> But Rabbi Schmelke and his brother knew full well that from his earliest hour to the present, Zusya had endured the most grievous sorrows. Thereupon they understood the meaning of the words of the Mishna, and the reason their rabbi had sent them to Rabbi Zusya.
>
> (*Newman, The Hasidic Anthology, p. 125*)

Here, suffering and evil are experienced by Rabbi Zusya as something "good." This is an example *par excellence* of the power of the mind over reality. If evil can be experienced as good and right, then anything can be "turned on its head."

Accepting what is ordinarily thought of as "good" can have negative as well as positive consequences. The Hasidic rabbi would be the first to agree: One can always challenge an interpretation with another interpretation.

A third principle of change that psychologists emphasize is the importance of soundly projecting a desirable outcome. A well-formed outcome is a prerequisite for evolving an effective strategy and a solution. The following criteria form the basis of a well-formed outcome:

- It is under the control of the client.
- It is specific.
- It is ecological (does not have serious side-effects).
- It is positive (tells what to do rather than what not to do).
- It is in a specific context (compatible with current values and way of life).
- It can always be changed along the way.

The following story will be analyzed with these criteria in mind:

Doubling A Loss

The Lubliner asked his wife to arrange for the preparation of his evening meal earlier than usual, inasmuch as he wished to have more time for the performance of a certain good deed. It chanced that supper was laid later instead of earlier than usual. The Lubliner said: "It would be natural for me to scold the people of my household for disobeying me. But I wished to gain time to please the Lord. Shall I displease Him by becoming angry and thereby double my loss?"

(*Newman, The Hasidic Anthology, p.* 8)

The desired outcome for the Lubliner is to have more time to perform a good deed. It is under his control to achieve; it is a specific goal—more time to perform a good deed; it is ecologically sound—create more harmony at home and collect a good deed by omission of a bad one; it is positive, avoids doubling his loss by upsetting his wife and puts him in a better mood to use the time he has to do a better job with the good deed he intends to perform; and it is in context, in the sense that it serves better himself, others and God!

There is a vital psychological lesson to be drawn from this story. This has to do with an effective way to deal with frustration, whether triggered directly by oneself or others.

Frustration, of course, like any feeling, in a fundamental sense is *caused* by the person experiencing it. A person "chooses" to be frustrated and angry.

The story beautifully illustrates that one sets himself up for disappointment and frustration and anger, just as one does for peace of mind. Why double the loss? In other words, a disappointed person does have a choice: He can stew, become upset, get angry, hit out at others; or he can say, "O.K., it happened, no big deal, let's get on with it. Why double my loss?" The answer to that could be: "because we are human," and the rabbis would surely say that that is also true!

Nevertheless, the story offers an alternative when we are disappointed and frustrated: We can say to ourselves: "Why double our losses?" We have found this to be very calming, and it enables us to make more constructive use of our energy and time.

We have outlined the bare bones of NLP's model of therapeutic linguistics—achieving rapport with the client, pacing him, and then leading him toward his desired goal in ways which encourage him to use his own resources. In the chapters that follow, we will be more specific about the techniques used by Hasidic rabbis to help people reach the desired solutions to their problems.

3

The Drama of the Story

A story has a beginning, a middle, and an end. The beginning prepares a conflict, the middle part complicates it, and the end resolves it. A story is complete in itself; it contains everything necessary for the reader's understanding of its message and its drama.

The storyteller includes any background information the reader needs to know and ends by solving whatever problem has been introduced. Most often, a story deals with a struggle between two sides or two people or a struggle within a person. It cannot end before one side wins the struggle and we, as an audience, understand what happens because of one's triumph and the other's defeat.

By dramatizing a problem or conflict, a story will draw the reader into the fabric of the tale, catch his attention and hold it. The rabbis were keenly aware of this. Here is how they described the use of the parable, a favorite type of story:

A Parable on the Parable

The Dubner Maggid was once asked: "Why does the parable possess such great influence?"

The Maggid replied: "I will explain this by a parable:

"Truth was accustomed to walk about as naked as he was born. No one allowed him to enter a home, and everyone who encountered him ran away in fright.

"Truth felt greatly embittered and could find no resting place. One day he beheld Parable attired in colorful, expensive garments. Parable inquired: 'Why are you so dejected, my friend?' Truth replied: 'I am in a bad situation. I am old, very old, and no one cares to have anything to do with me.' 'Nay,' retorted Parable, 'it is not because of your age that you are disliked by people. Look, I am as old as you are, and the older I grow, the more do I seem to be beloved. Let me disclose to you the secret of my apparent popularity. People enjoy seeing everything dressed up and somewhat disguised. Let me lend to you my garments, and you will see that people will like you as well.' Truth followed this counsel and dressed himself in the garments of Parable. Ever since then, Truth and Parable walk hand in hand, and men love both of them."

(*Newman, Maggidim and Hasidim, p. 136*)

The rabbis and preachers also appreciated the value of outlining their own stories:

The Tailor and the Garment

Said the Mikolayever: "In the same way that a tailor sketches the design and cuts away the extraneous material before making up a garment, so the preacher must first outline his subject of discussion, and with questions eliminate the nonessentials before he brings his analysis to a point."

(*Newman, The Hasidic Anthology, p. 348*)

The following dramatic components make up a story:

- Central Character: Whose story is it, and what does he or she want? What's the problem, what's the vision or dream that this individual has and cannot attain?
- Obstacles: Who gets in the way and why. Often there is an opposing character and the development of conflict.
- What's at stake? In other words, how important is the thing the

central character and others are struggling over? Do we care about it?

- The Dramatic Question: Will so-and-so be able to solve the mystery, find a workable strategy, what are the costs, and so forth?
- Crisis: The turning point at which the opposing sides clash and the issue has to be settled one way or another.
- Climax: The high point of the story, in which the difficulty is finally resolved.

These dramatic components are nicely illustrated in the following story:

Writing Down

A disciple secretly wrote down all the teachings he had heard from the Baal Shem. One day, the Baal Shem saw a demon going through the house. In his hand was a book. The Baal Shem asked him: "What book is that you have in your hand?"

"That is the book," the demon replied, "of which you are the author."

Then the Baal Shem knew that someone was secretly setting down what he had said. He gathered all his people around him and asked: "Who of you is writing down what I teach you?"

The disciple who was taking notes said it was he, and brought the master what he had written.

The Baal Shem studied it for a long time, page by page. Then he said: "In all this, there is not a single word I said. You were not listening for the sake of Heaven and so the power of evil used you for its sheath, and your ears heard what I did not say."

(*Buber, Early Masters, p. 66*)

Let us analyze the dramatic components of this story:

- Central character: The Baal Shem is the central character, and he is upset by the realization that someone has written down his teachings and is using them for an evil purpose.
- Obstacle: The first obstacle to overcome is the realization that someone has been writing down the Baal Shem's teachings.

Then he must find out who did it and study the notes to see whether they are authentic or can be used for evil ends.

- What's at stake? We care about the story because there is an evil spirit in the house that can cause a great deal of harm, paradoxically by utilizing the writings and sayings of the Baal Shem Tov himself. What must be determined here is how the demon is using the Baal Shem's teachings against him and his followers.

- The dramatic question: Will the Baal Shem be able to figure out who has the book and why the writings in the book can be used by the demon to cause so much harm? This raises another question: Is it at all possible to put down the words of the Baal Shem in such a way that they would not harm other people or cause future generations to suffer?

- Crisis: The turning point is when the Baal Shem is able to identify the disciple who wrote down his teachings and to study the book in detail, "page by page."

- The climax: The resolution of the story occurs when, after studying in detail what the disciple has written, the Baal Shem sees that there is a vast discrepancy between what he said and what was recorded, and not "a single word" was accurate. The demon could utilize these distorted teachings to cause great harm to people.

The climax also includes an explanation as to why there is such a great distortion of Baal Shem's teachings in the disciple's notes.

The point of the story is that the disciple was so intent upon recording what he heard that he was not listening with his heart and soul to what was being said about God. The disciple was not listening to the words with his heart; he had an overriding *external* reason for paying attention to the Baal Shem. The means became the end—a desecration of the words.

Recording what the rabbi was teaching without the emotion and spirituality of what he was saying made a mockery of the rabbi's teachings even if they were recorded word for word. And that is why the Baal Shem completely dissociated himself from what was written in the book and said that mere copying of the words does not mean that the scribe had heard the spiritual message.

In fact, the disciple was so intent on merely recording the words that the demon was able to use the disciple's unauthentic record for evil purposes. Listening to a spiritual message is much more than remembering words—one has to go deeper and feel the words with heart and soul.

This is a theme that is met very frequently in contemporary literature. Can a writer distance himself enough to record what is going on about him and at the same time be able to listen with all his heart and soul to what is happening? Does the mere intention of recording and using what people are saying distort what they are saying? Does concentration on transcription distort the writer's ability to listen with his own feelings and heart so that he does not hear what is actually being said?

Many argue that, in trying to record what other people are saying, the writer fatally changes the experience so that in the end he has to distort. Is this what the Baal Shem was thinking when he read what the disciple had written about his own teachings? He did not recognize what was there, because he, the Baal Shem, was not uttering only words, but the spirituality of the words, with the intention of being with God. He was not able to find the spirit of his words in the disciple's recording of his teachings, and therefore they could be used for harmful purposes.

The story is also fascinating because it combines fantasy or surrealistic elements with a very real encounter between a rabbi and his disciple. This adds further mystery to the story—namely, the Baal Shem encountering a demon going through his house with a book and actually engaging him in a conversation. This corresponds to the outcome later, when the Baal Shem is discoursing at two different levels: the words that the disciple has written and on another level, their evocation, their true, implicit reality. The demon and the spirituality of words (and prayer) in the Hasidic orientation point to *kavvana*, roughly the subjective intention and spirituality of an act as being more important than its manifest content.

The disciple is, in a sense, comparable to the demon in that he is using the rabbi's teachings for some personal gain or gratification by jotting down the words and becoming so involved in the writing of them that he loses the spiritual meaning of what is being said.

Satan, the Evil Urge, is a tricky customer. This is especially so because Satan is a master of artful disguises, his favorite being the appearance of piety, of doing a good deed:

Pious Deeds with a Blemish

> Said the Hafetz Hayyim: "When the Satan perceives the futility of luring a great man into the performance of a sinful deed, he frequently makes an about-face and persuades him to perform a pious deed which contains within itself an unsavory element and therefore brings no honor to God."
>
> (*Newman, Maggidim and Hasidim, p. 153*)

This theme runs through many Hasidic stories. The tales of the Hasidic rabbis are mostly about the vast struggle of the rabbis to preserve a holy way of life. The real meaning of a man's sojourn on earth is to be with God every moment of every day. Individuals are caught up with the externals involving egotism and greed, which must be combated by a return to God and the spiritual way of life:

The Busy Man's Prayer

> The Baal Shem said: "Imagine a man whose business hounds him through many streets and across the marketplace the livelong day. He almost forgets that there is a Maker of the World. Only when the time for the afternoon prayer comes, does he remember: 'I must pray.'
>
> "And then, from the bottom of his heart, he heaves a sigh of regret that he has spent his day on vain and idle matters, and he runs into a by-street and stands there and prays. God holds him dear, very dear and his prayer pierces the firmament."
>
> (*Buber, Early Masters, p. 69*)

What a close shave! This story certainly matches the exciting chase scenes that one can see every day on television and in the movies. It is a chase that takes place within the heart and soul of a busy and successful businessman. The central character is a businessman caught up in his business.

The obstacle is the business itself and its magnetic attraction. What's at stake here is whether this individual will be so caught up in business that he forgets why he's alive in the first place and his purpose on earth. The dramatic question is whether he will be able to overcome an involvement with business so intense that he loses all other meaning and purpose in life. The crisis occurs in the late afternoon when it is time to pray, and the climax occurs when he remembers that he must pray.

The Baal Shem holds this person even more dear than someone who is not caught up in business, because the ability of the businessman caught up in his business, to reorient himself and recognize anew what is really important, namely returning to God, results in his prayers piercing the firmament. It is like the rabbi's preference for a wicked man who is aware of his wickedness over the good man who is aware of his goodness.

Because the Baal Shem was able to see spirituality in everything on earth and God's wondrous activity in every person that he was able to say genuinely to one of his disciples: "The lowest of the low you can think of is dearer to me than your only son is to you."

Now if you stop and think a little about what this really means, you will see that there is a profound lesson to be learned here. This one sentence contains a dramatic story: Again, the central character is the Baal Shem; the obstacle is being able to love every person as one loves the most dear one here in his own family. Is it really possible to do this? The Baal Shem goes on to say that the lowest of the low is *dearer* to him than an only son is to his father. Is this because the lowest of the low is someone who often has no one at all? And may be more despairing of God? And so the climax is to weigh the lowest of low who has no one, against the only son of a disciple—and the resolution follows.

We can experience drama in a story with two sentences. The Hasidic stories are dramatic because they embody a dramatic struggle to remain spiritual—authentic, humane, decent—in the face of all obstacles and difficulties in a competitive society that seduces people into being self-centered, mad with greed, and obsessed with security in an insecure world.

Life is a continuous struggle to be true to oneself and to the highest ideals of one's cultural heritage. The conflicts to conduct oneself according to God's ideals make the stories suspenseful. This universal theme is illustrated in countless daily battles that the spiritual person undergoes in overcoming all of the seductions to be certain about life and about oneself. No one ever can rest secure in his holiness because one's holiness lies precisely in struggling to be that: The story on page 9 ("The Limits of Advice") makes this point clearly.

In that story again, the central character is the Baal Shem, and he is required to talk about how to identify a true *tzaddik*. He has to come up with criteria by which to help his followers recognize how to evaluate a *tzaddik* with a great reputation for learning.

What is at stake here is of great import, because the rabbi is challenged to tell his followers the essence of a man of learning and what a true *tzaddik* is and whether they are the same and, in any case, what is the chief trait of such a man. The dramatic question is whether the Baal Shem will be able to come up with an acceptable answer.

The crisis, or turning point, is the Baal Shem's telling his followers that there is no solution to sin; life is a continuous struggle to combat sin, and this is an answer acceptable to his followers. The true *tzaddik* has the humility to live with this "solution."

And how are this ideal to be spiritual *and* the need to live and work in the mundane world to become integrated? This supreme issue is beautifully illustrated in:

The Hosemaker

Once, in the course of a journey, the Baal Shem stopped in a little town whose name has not come down to us. One morning before prayer, as he smoked his usual pipe and looked out the window, he saw a man go by carrying a prayer shawl and phylacteries and walking as intently and solemnly as though he were going straight to the doors of Heaven.

The Baal Shem asked the disciple in whose house he was staying, who the man was. The man, he was told, was a hosemaker who went to the House of Prayer day after day both summer and winter and said his prayers, even when the prescribed quorum of ten worshipers was not complete.

The Baal Shem wanted to have the man brought to him, but his host said, "That fool would not stop on his way, not if the emperor called him in person."

After prayer, the Baal Shem sent someone to the man with a message that he should bring him four pairs of hose. Soon after, the man stood before him and displayed his wares. They were of good sheep's wool and well made.

"What do you want for a pair?" asked Rabbi Israel.

"One-and-a-half gulden."

"I suppose you will be satisfied with one gulden."

"Then I would have said one gulden."

The Baal Shem instantly paid him what he had asked. Then he went on questioning him. "How do you spend your days?"

"I ply my trade," said the man.

"And how do you ply it?"

"I work until I have forty or fifty pairs of hose. Then I put them into a mold with hot water and press them till they are as they should be."

"And how do you sell them?"

"I don't leave my house. The merchants come to me to buy. They also bring me good wool. They have bought from me, and I pay them for their pains. This time I left my house only to honor the rabbi."

"And when you get up in the morning, what do you do before you go to pray?"

"I make hose then too."

"And what psalms do you recite?"

"I say those psalms which I know by heart while I work," said the man.

When the hosemaker had gone home, the Baal Shem said to the disciples who stood around: "Today you have seen the cornerstone which will uphold the Temple until the Messiah comes."

(*Buber, Early Masters, pp. 68–69*)

Told in a dramatic manner, this story illustrates the highest ideal of the Hasidic way of life. The central figure is the hosemaker, a worker who has integrated his spirituality and his work so that one is in the other and they are inseparable. The obstacle or test is the Baal Shem's attempt to bargain with him for his wares and the hosemaker's refusal to lower his price because he feels that he has asked for the true value of his work and will not compromise. The Baal Shem is duly impressed.

The Baal Shem continues to question the man. What is at stake here is the character of a person who embodies the highest ideals of spirituality in his work so that work and spirituality cannot be isolated from each other. He plies his trade with the understanding that it is being done within the framework of his connection to God every moment of his activity.

The man is so involved in this synthesis of work and spirituality that he has organized his life to maximize his work in a spiritual way. This can be done by working at home and having others come to him. But he is not so inflexible that he would not make an exception by visiting a rabbi who asks for his wares, by taking time off, so to speak, to do a good deed.

So the dramatic question is the ability of this worker to blend his work and spirituality throughout the day. Can he demonstrate that he is able to do this during the working day?

The Baal Shem asks him again how he manages to work and pray and pray and work at the same time. The hosemaker easily meets this "crisis" by telling him about his recitation of psalms while he works.

The climax occurs when the Baal Shem has become so impressed with this spiritually integrated worker that he has to pronounce him a true *tzaddik* who will serve as a cornerstone of society and a model for others until the Messiah comes. This is the highest accolade a Hasid can receive.

The Baal Shem was constantly challenged to demonstrate the presence of the holy spirit in every part of the natural world. And so it was inevitable that he would also be challenged by that newly emerging protagonist, the scientist. The dramatic struggle of the scientist with the holy man is reflected in this story:

The Famous Miracle

A naturalist came from a great distance to see the Baal Shem and said: "My investigation shows that in the course of

> nature the Red Sea had to divide at the very hour the Children of Israel passed through it. Now what about that famous miracle?" The Baal Shem answered: "Don't you know that God created nature? And he created it so, that the hour the Children of Israel passed through the Red Sea, it had to divide. That is the great and famous miracle!"
>
> (*Buber, Early Masters, p. 71*)

The central character is the Baal Shem, who is asked by a scientist to justify the miracle at the Red Sea. The obstacle is the naturalist's contention that there is a scientific explanation for the parting of the Red Sea, namely, geological forces active at the time. The stakes are obviously very high here, because the Baal Shem is confronted with a scientist who has an alternative explanation for the divine miracle of the dividing of the Red Sea.

The dramatic question is whether the Baal Shem will be able to answer him in such a way as to uphold the division of the Red Sea as a miracle from God. The Baal Shem meets the crisis by reframing the naturalistic cause: It in turn was created by God just at that moment when the Children of Israel were passing through the Red Sea. In this climax of the story, there is no way for the naturalist to explain why it occurred at the moment when the Children of Israel were passing through the Red Sea.

THE DRAMA IS SUSPENSEFUL AND UNPREDICTABLE . . . BUT PLAUSIBLE

One of the reasons Hasidic stories are so dramatic is that they surprise the reader by upsetting his conventional ways of thinking and feeling. Since the Hasidim were constantly "exploding" conventional wisdom by stressing what is below the surface, namely that which flows from the heart, all kinds of behavior became susceptible to transformation through the underlying meaning of overt action. For example, who would imagine that sinners are more salvageable than the sinless and have a greater potential for becoming holy spirits?

With the Sinners

The Baal Shem said: "I let sinners come close to me if they are not proud. I keep the scholars and the sinless away from me if they are proud. The sinner who knows that he is a sinner and therefore considers himself base—God is with him. For He dwelleth with him in the midst of his uncleannesses. But concerning him who prides himself on the fact that he is unburdened by sin, God says, as we know from the Gemara: "There is not enough room in the world for myself and him."

(*Buber, Early Masters, pp. 71–72*)

The central character is the sinner. But there is a catch. The test and obstacle are that the sinner is not proud. The stake is salvation. The dramatic question is not sin but pride. The climax is that the sinner who is not proud is more holy than the sinless who "burdens" himself with sinlessness so that he is no longer susceptible to God.

In this powerful story, the Baal Shem stresses the importance of being open and struggling to change. The story is a cogent antidote to those who become too self-righteous and points to the danger of the proud religious person becoming tyrannical with those who are struggling to abandon their sinful ways.

The Hasidic story joins the struggle against both the "sinless" and the sinful by stressing a powerful underlying motif: the constant struggle on both sides of the equation, the sinful and the sinless, to fulfill the ideal image of a holy person.

The battle to overcome sin and evil provides the dramatic conflict of many Hasidic tales. Story and philosophy become intertwined. The *tzaddik*, the ordinary person, and royalty—all strive to become good people, and the essence of a story is conflict and rivalries:

The Prodigal's Return

Said the Mezeritcher: "A king had two sons. One was content to be constantly in attendance on his father; the other

> preferred to enjoy himself away from home. There evil companions led him astray. The king was prompted to send his officers to fetch him for chastisement but, out of paternal love, refrained from doing so. Later the prodigal regretted the anguish his conduct had caused his father and, of his own free will, returned with a plea for pardon. The king was overjoyed and showed him more love and favor than he did to the son who had never absented himself. Likewise, when a grievous sinner returns unto the Lord, he receives greater joy and favor than one who has never sinned."
>
> (*Newman, The Hasidic Anthology, p. 387*)

Ultimately, the forcefulness and high drama give the Hasidic story a powerful momentum, because the rabbis were not only very close to the people, but they acknowledged their own vulnerabilities. This was the heaviest burden of all.

The great power and legitimacy given to them by the people was always in danger of being corrupted by the "glory" bestowed upon the rabbis by their followers. That is why they militated so strongly against pride and heeded the biblical warning that "pride goeth before destruction," particularly of those who become holy in their own eyes and believe they are no longer susceptible to deviation.

The rabbis were extremely sensitive about the possibility that they might lord it over their followers. The rabbi was not only the wise counselor in most of the stories but also *the* storyteller. He could easily be seduced by his own "brilliance" and "perfection:"

The Overeducated

> The Lubliner *Tzaddik* said: "The coming of our redeemer is, in great measure, hindered by those Jews who are overeducated in rabbinic legalism. Redemption demands complete repentance, and a person of lofty attainments finds it difficult to experience lowliness of spirit. Therefore he does not fully repent, and the Messiah is delayed."
>
> (*Newman, Maggidim and Hasidim, p. 41*)

No One Is without Sin

Said the Besht: "No true saint would be able to see wickedness in others. The real *tzaddik* would not know if men and women are guilty of offenses. He could not, therefore, under these circumstances serve as an example to others and could not teach the people. It is for this reason that there is no man on earth who does not sin. The sin makes the *tzaddik* humane and enables him to guide others."

(*Newman, The Hasidic Anthology, p. 443*)

4

The Story as a Normative Metaphor

INTRODUCTION

If we examine the Hasidic story from a new angle, we will see that it is a *normative metaphor* which provides the listener/reader with important practical wisdom on both the unconscious and conscious levels and instigates new productive and satisfying modes of behavior. In this chapter we will concentrate on the subconscious impact of the story on the audience.

Every Hasidic story is fundamentally a metaphor. Every situation depicted in such a story stands for a similar situation in the listener's life and suggests a likeness or analogy between them. Our concept of the normative metaphor builds on NLP's formulation of the "healing metaphor." The healing metaphor has two main characteristics (Bandler 1978):

- It is a cogent description of a problem or situation about which the listener desires new approaches and new choices. The metaphor is effective if the client is paced so that his subconscious accepts it as being isomorphic (having a one-to-one relation in structure) with his problem, although he may not be consciously aware that the metaphor is intended to be isomorphic.

- It contains solutions via techniques, strategies, insights, and reorientations which are applied to the listener's situation often without his conscious awareness that the story is intended to provide new personal solutions.

Although this therapeutic model goes a long way towards describing the metaphorical match between the situation in the story and the listener's life situation, we felt that an essential ingredient was eluding us: Precisely how did the story generate within the listener the feeling that his condition was analogous to the one depicted in the story?

It occurred to us that every Hasidic story, upon close examination, contained essentially a normative message about the good, just, the moral way of life. A norm is an idea, formulated by the members of a group or society, that specifies what people *should* do, ought to do, are expected to do under various circumstances. Norms consist of standards to which people are obligated or expected to conform, frequently because they are believed to be functional to the well-being of the group and its members.

For example, one Hasidic norm is the importance of being independent and autonomous. As we shall soon see, many stories set up a variety of challenging situations whose underlying metaphor teaches and reinforces the value and technique of being independent and learning how to be self-reliant, despite the seductions to act otherwise.

We suggest that, if you scratch the surface of each story, you will see that the rabbis created a powerful instrument in the normative metaphor, a tool that teaches subconsciously and reinforces mental health principles and ethical values that promote a compassionate, joyous, and productive way of life.

Let us see, in greater detail, how the normative metaphor works in Hasidic stories.

THE NORMATIVE METAPHOR IN ACTION

In discussing the normative metaphor in Hasidic stories, we will not go into the details of how the rabbi engages and paces the client or his specific techniques for facilitating changes in behavior, feelings and attitudes. Rather, we will focus on the *overall normative metaphor* of the story and specify the isomorphic relationship between the characters in the story and the reader and the implicit (sometimes explicit) norm that the reader is led to confront.

The following story is unusual in that the rabbi explicitly extracts the metaphorical significance of a personal experience for himself, his disciples and, by extension, the reader.

Can and Want To

> Once, when the Yehudi (i.e., the *Yid* of Pshiskhe) was walking cross-country, he happened on a hay wagon which had turned over.
>
> "Help me raise it up!" said the driver. The rabbi tried but he could not budge it.
>
> "I can't," he finally said.
>
> The peasant looked at him sternly. "You can all right," said he, "but you don't want to."
>
> On the evening of that day the Yehudi went to his disciples: "I was told today: We can raise up the Name of God, but we don't want to."
>
> (*Buber, Late Masters, p. 228*)

First of all, we have a metaphor in the story itself:

Yehudi	⟶	Raising an upset wagon
Yehudi and disciples	⟶	Raising up the name of God

This is the explicit metaphor. Underlying this metaphor is the distinction between not being able to do a difficult task ("CAN'T") and not wanting to do it ("WON'T"). This story then raises the norm of *kavvana,* the intention or motivation of an individual, to accomplish a difficult task, such as, for example, raising a wagon and raising up the Name of God.

Thus, the overall normative metaphor reinforces in the reader the importance of *kavvana* for carrying out "superhuman" tasks.

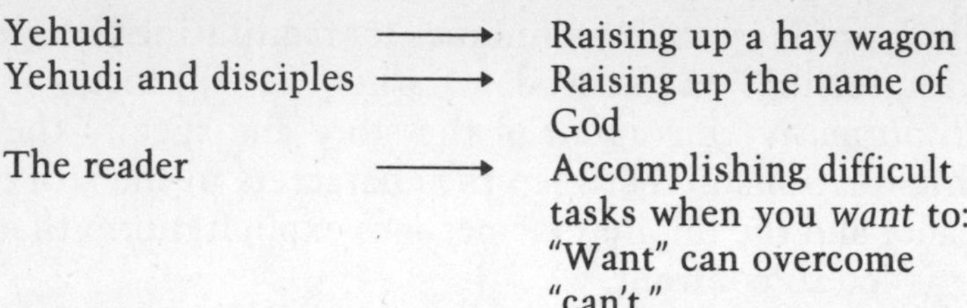

Yehudi	⟶	Raising up a hay wagon
Yehudi and disciples	⟶	Raising up the name of God
The reader	⟶	Accomplishing difficult tasks when you *want* to: "Want" can overcome "can't."

The following two stories could not be further apart in content, and yet the underlying normative metaphors are quite similar. The first deals with cleaning pots and pans thoroughly and the second with horses that are surrealistically transmuted into something other than horses:

Preparation

A disciple of Rabbi Shmelke begged his master to teach him how to prepare his soul for the service of God. The *tzaddik* told him to go to Rabbi Abraham, who—at that time—was still an innkeeper. The disciple did as he was bidden and lived in the inn for several weeks without observing any vestige of holiness in the innkeeper who, from the Morning Prayer till night, devoted himself to his business. Finally, he asked him what he did all day. "My most important occupation," said Rabbi Abraham, "is to clean the dishes properly, so that not the slightest trace of food is left, and to clean and dry the pots and pans, so that they do not rust." When the disciple returned home and reported to Rabbi Shmelke what he had seen and heard, the rabbi said to him: "Now you know the answer to what you asked me."

(*Buber, Early Masters, p. 191*)

Here again, we have a metaphor within the story:

Learn how to prepare the soul for the service of God	Observe the innkeeper thoroughly clean dishes, pots, pans.
To prepare the soul for God	Do everything, including the most mundane activity, with wholehearted, genuine thoroughness.

Reader who wants to prepare his soul for God	The way to reach God is by doing *everything* wholeheartedly and genuinely; every thing (and every act) is full of God's holiness—so treat it accordingly.

The next story takes the same normative message and raises it a notch or two higher:

Concerning Ardent Zeal

After the Great *Maggid* died, Shneur Zalman decided to leave the town of Mezeritch for good. When he parted from the *maggid*'s son, from Rabbi Abraham, the Angel who had instructed him in secret wisdom, his teacher said he would accompany him and got into the carriage. When they were out of the city-gate, Rabbi Abraham called to the coachman: "Urge on your horses, and let them run until they forget they are horses." Zalman took the words to heart. "It will take me a while to learn properly this way of serving," he said, and remained in Mezeritch for another year.

(*Buber, Early Masters, p. 267*)

Reader: How do I know enough to leave my teacher and go on my own?	Shneur Zalman decides to leave his teacher.
(or, alternative): How do I know when I know anything—especially how to serve God?	Rabbi Abraham (his teacher) to coachman: Urge on your horses, and let them run until they forget they are horses.
You will know when you penetrate and have taken to heart the words Rabbi Abraham called to the coachman (which in effect is a metaphor for transcending conscious, explicit knowledge for an ecstatic-emotional communion and understanding of God—a central Hasidic value).	Shneur Zalman changes mind Decides to remain with his mentor.

Clearly, key Hasidic values were being reinforced through the stories in a variety of contexts. These multifaceted attacks are cumulative and extraordinarily powerful in anchoring Hasidic beliefs deep within the followers' subconscious.

In the next section, you will have a taste of how diverse situations and problems all combine to reinforce a single motif embodied in one normative metaphor. The motif we've chosen is independence, autonomy, self-reliance or self-realization. The Hasidim are great believers in individual initiative and the crucial importance of learning how to stand on your own two feet.

Some of the stories are quite explicit in embedding this value in the reader's psyche, and some are very subtle. The methods include irony, direct confrontations and indirect techniques embedded in messages that do not appear at all related to the motif.

THE VICISSITUDES OF LEARNING HOW TO STAND ON YOUR OWN TWO FEET

The normative metaphor of the supreme value of self-reliance is presented in diverse contexts involving an endless variety of situations, people, conflicts and issues. It is our thesis that it is precisely the multiple methods of transmitting the same normative message, often in subtle, indirect ways, that make the normative metaphor such a powerful instrument for influencing the values and behavior of the listener:

The Dream

Rabbi Bunam was told by a Hasid that the latter's father had appeared in a dream and had counseled his son to become a rabbi.

Rabbi Bunam remarked: "The next time your father comes to you, ask him to appear in a dream to the Hasidim, and persuade them to become your adherents."

(*Newman, The Hasidic Anthology, p. 114*)

This ironic story contains the same normative metaphor for fathers and sons (and today, much more than in the past, for mothers and daughters):

Hasid thinking about becoming a rabbi	Hasid's father appears in a dream and counsels him to become a rabbi.
Rabbi counsels Hasid	"Ask your father to appear in a dream to Hasidim and persuade them to become your adherents."
Listener in son's role	Don't be dependent on your father. Do what you want to do.
Listener in father's role	Don't foist your dreams on your children. They have to make it on their own.

The normative metaphor here is "Don't depend on others, rely on yourself to be or become what you desire." There is also an added warning to parents not to make their children dependent on them.

The following paradoxical tale is built on the premise that it is of supreme importance to rely on oneself in order to fulfill one's most important desires:

In Order

It is told:

A villager and his wife came to the *Maggid* of Koznitz and begged him to pray that they might have a son, for they were childless. "Give me fifty-two gulden," said the *maggid*, "for this is the numerical value of the word *ben*, son."

"We should be glad to give you ten gulden," said the man, but the *maggid* refused to accept them. Then the man went to the marketplace and staggered back under a sack of copper coins. He spread them out on the table. There were twenty gulden. "Look, what a lot of money," he cried. But the *maggid* would not come down with his demand. At that, the villager grew angry, gathered up his money and said to his wife: "Come on, let's go. God will help us without the *maggid's* prayer." "You have already been granted his help," said the rabbi. And he was right.

(*Buber, Early Masters, p. 292*)

Listener seeking help:	Couple seek help from rabbi.
. . . you are still responsible for solving your own problem.	Rabbi is too expensive.
No one can get for you what you want except yourself (God helps those who help themselves).	Couple reject rabbi.
	Couple are already helped by relying on themselves.

"The Limits of Advice," which appeared on page 9, is a Hasidic tale emphasizing the supreme importance of self-reliance: It portrays the *tzaddik*, the holiest of Hasidim, as a man vulnerable to "alien thoughts," just like any ordinary Hasid.

The normative metaphor in this story has to do with how an individual can deal with alien (sinful, lustful, greedy) thoughts.

Disciples ask reputed wise man how to deal with alien thoughts.	If reputed wise man tells them how, then you know he is not wise.
How listener deals with alien thoughts.	Nobody else can solve this for you; you have to struggle with them all of your life.

Here is a poignant story stressing the same theme of independence in a very moving, subtle, and dramatic manner.

The Sigh

Silently, his wife held the hungry child. It was too weak to cry. Then—for the first time—the *maggid* sighed. Instantly, the answer came. A voice said to him: "You have lost your share in the World to Come."

"Well, then," he said, "the reward has been done away with. Now I can begin to serve in good earnest."

(*Buber, Early Masters, p. 99*)

Maggid in deep distress sighs.	Sign of doubt, perhaps even distrust of God.
Maggid realizes he is not "entitled" to God's help when he wants it.	*Maggid* punishes himself.
Maggid serves God with no expectation of reward.	*Maggid* serves God "better."
Listener in most desperate situation.	Don't look to God for help. Rely on yourself.

We will delve deeper into this story in Chapter 10 ("Merging with God"), but here it is still another example of rigorous self-reliance.

The rabbis were extraordinary in their ingenuity to take a chance innocent remark and show how it undermines a person's individuality by making him dependent upon another person:

Comparing One to Another

Someone once told Rabbi Mendel that a certain person was greater than another whom he also mentioned by name. Rabbi Mendel replied: "If I am I because I am I, and you are you because you are you, then I am I, and you are you. But if I am I because you are you, and you are you because I am I, then I am not I, and you are not you."

(*Buber, Late Masters*, p. 283)

The normative metaphor here is a bit complicated:

If I am I, separate from you	Then I am I.
If I am I because of you (that is comparing myself with you)	I am not I.
Listener achieves his individuality	By a nonevaluative acceptance of himself.

This story begins to chart some specific ways of thinking about oneself and others in order to realize one's full potential. The following two stories continue this line of thought and describe the positive consequences of self-reliance and the endlessly wondrous adventure of learning more about oneself—*a story without end*:

Resignation

> The Tzanzer Rebbe used to tell this story about himself:
>
> "In my youth, when I was fired with the love of God, I thought I would convert the whole world to God. But soon I discovered that it would be quite enough to convert the people who lived in my town, and I tried for a long time, but I did not succeed. Then I realized that my program was still much too ambitious, and I concentrated on the persons in my own household. But I could not convert them either. Finally, it dawned on me: I must work upon myself, so that I may give true service to God. But I did not accomplish even this."
>
> (*Buber, Late Masters, p. 214*)

The core message here is that once you concentrate on working on yourself, you will have no need to "convert" others, so great is the job of getting to know and improve yourself. Amen.

Finally, in the last story in this series of normative metaphors about self-realization we see the ultimate reward: Understanding the core of oneself leads to cosmic communion with all of God's creatures, with nature itself:

Speech

> The Yehudi and Peretz, his disciple, were crossing a meadow: Cattle put out to pasture there were lowing, and where it was watered by a stream a flock of geese rose from the water with a great cackling and beating of wings.
>
> "If only one could understand what all of them are saying!" cried Peretz.
>
> "When you get to the point of understanding the very core of what you yourself are saying," said the rabbi, "you will understand the language of all creatures."
>
> (*Buber, Late Masters, p. 278*)

We feel strongly that the distinctive contribution of the Hasidim to the story and to literature in general was to embed their practical wisdom in simple everyday situations and events with which their followers could easily identify. In response to their followers' problems and questions, the rabbi-counselors would impart counsel that could be best understood and accepted if given in the context of an everyday situation. And they added puzzlement and surprise, paradox or unexpected endings to entrance the listener into absorbing the message.

One can imagine how a Hasid would delight in a well-turned tale that he could identify with, that would keep him in suspense and then would upset his expectation with a surprise ending. When the same basic theme is worked over and repeated in so many guises, it is obviously a subject that is very important in the Hasidic belief system.

Reach for the normative metaphor in each Hasidic story, be delighted with your discovery, and marvel at the practical wisdom it adds to the conduct of your life.

The Hasidic rabbis were shrewd as well as wise. They not only counseled their followers to be independent, but were always reinforcing their own roles in applying the basic psychological principle (as true today as 200 years ago): "Help the seeker of help to help himself."

The Ear That Is No Ear

> Rabbi Pinhas said: "In the book, *The Duties of the Heart*, we read that he who conducts his life as he ought, should see with eyes that are no eyes, hear with ears that are no ears. And that is just how it is! For often, when someone comes to ask my advice, I hear him giving himself the answer to his question."
>
> (*Buber, Early Masters, p. 126*)

5

The Story's Role in Counseling and Education

This chapter develops an essential thesis of our book: The Hasidic story is a generative invention by which the rabbis counseled their followers about specific, concrete, everyday problems, and *simultaneously* inculcated the core values of Hasidism. This was, indeed, a brilliant idea.

There is not a single Hasidic story which does not have at its core, explicitly or implicitly, a definite set of values which is more or less emphasized in guiding a supplicant to work out his problems. Hasidic values are often interpreted in novel ways which can be used by "clients" to solve practically all their troubles.

It gradually became clear to us which stories had in the foreground the solving of a problem and which emphasized the reinforcement and perpetuation of basic values that made up Hasidic culture. When the emphasis was on counseling, the Hasidic values which served as the context for the problem were in the background; when the stress was upon a Hasidic belief, the helping process was implicit and in the background. The "counseling story" generally is nondefinitive, open-ended, with multiple options from which the client can freely choose and, very often because of its puzzling ending, open to a variety of interpretations.

The "educational story," by contrast, is generally more closed and definitive, with a consensus interpretation.

The next two stories are typical of the two kinds of Hasidic tale. The first one stresses a basic counseling technique often used by rabbis:

The Story of the Cape

A woman came to Rabbi Israel, the *maggid* of Koznitz, and told him, with many tears, that she had been married a dozen years and still had not borne a son. "What are you willing to do about it?" he asked her. She did not know what to say.

"My mother," so the *maggid* told her, "was aging and still had no child. Then she heard that the holy Baal Shem was stopping over in Apt in the course of a journey. She hurried to his inn and begged him to pray she might bear a son. 'What are you willing to do about it?' he asked. 'My husband is a poor bookbinder,' she replied, 'but I do have one fine thing that I shall give to the rabbi.'

"She went home as fast as she could and fetched her good cape, her 'Katinka,' which was carefully stowed away in a chest. But when she returned to the inn with it, she heard that the Baal Shem had already left for Mezbizh. She immediately set out after him and since she had no money to ride, she walked from town to town with her 'Katinka' until she came to Mezbizh.

"The Baal Shem took the cape and hung it on the wall. 'It is well,' he said. My mother walked all the way back, from town to town, until she reached Apt. One year later, I was born."

"I too," cried the woman, "will bring you a good cape of mine so that I may get a son."

"That won't work" said the *maggid*. "You heard the story. My mother had no story to go by."

(*Buber, Early Masters, p. 286*)

Implicit in this story are many important Hasidic values and norms. First of all, the importance of bearing a son is emphasized in relation to both of the aging women. Asking a rabbi to pray for her so that she might bear a son is also stated matter-of-factly as a proper course to take. This suggests the belief that God can bring about this miracle through his intermediary, the rabbi. Another implicit idea is that in order to gain something you have to give up something that is of value to you: the cape for the prayer.

All of the above values are more or less implicit in the telling of the story and in the counseling of the woman who has come for help in her desire to bear a son.

Now, when we turn to the psychological counseling itself, we note how powerfully the *maggid* paces the woman and tells her a story about another woman who was in exactly the same situation. Obviously, this strongly involves the supplicant and enables her to learn vicariously from the other woman's experience. What is stressed in this story is the persistence of the *maggid*'s mother, who "walked from town to town" . . . first chasing the holy Baal Shem and traveling a long distance on foot to return home. This expresses the importance of will and determination.

Now comes an extremely curious twist in the story. The *maggid* tells the woman-supplicant how his mother succeeded in bearing a child by giving a valuable cape of hers, her "Katinka," to the holy Baal Shem who in turn prayed for her. Naturally, the woman's first impulse is to do what the *maggid's* mother did and thereby also bear a son. The *maggid*, however, tells her that it won't work for her to do what his mother did, because his mother did not have a story to go by. The *maggid* tells her: "You heard the story. My mother had no story to go by."

Now the irony of this tale is that the woman did indeed have a story to go by; namely, the story the *maggid* told her about his own mother. But she did not get the point of the story immediately: not to imitate what the *maggid*'s mother did in order to bear a son (namely, give her good cape to the rabbi), because that stemmed from her judgment that it was the most valuable thing she could give up. But that does not mean that another costly cape owned by the supplicant would be the most valuable thing she could give to the rabbi for his prayers, and, hopefully, for the birth of a son.

Subtly, the rabbi is teaching his clients the importance of searching their hearts to determine what they consider most valuable, so they can then give it up. This is the point of the rabbi's counsel: to find and trust one's own way to reach out to God for His help.

On a psychological level, the story emphasizes the importance to every individual of finding his own way and learning how to rely on himself. Over and over again, the rabbis teach and counsel their clients that there are many ways to God, and all of them flow from one source—one's own heart, one's genuine feelings. And so the story also teaches the most fundamental principle of Hasidic life, that *kavvana*—inner feeling and motivation—is the fundamental quality a person should nurture and express.

There are many ways to reach God, but they must all stem from one's heart and soul.

So there is a double message here: the Hasidic principle of *kavvana*, and the idea that every individual is ultimately responsible for himself, that God truly helps those who help themselves.

This latter idea is brought home forcefully in the story when the *maggid* emphasizes that his mother persisted in her efforts to gain help for the most important goal in her life and, having persisted, found her way by herself.

Now we come to the most paradoxical aspect of the story. The rabbi cannot give anyone a ready-made formula for reaching God, overcoming one's troubles, or attaining desired goals. The rabbi is, however, a divine messenger, informing his Hasidim over and over again, in as many different challenging and perplexing ways as possible, that the function of the rabbi is to let them know that they have the resources within themselves to get what they want. The rabbi's *not* telling the woman what to do is his most compelling lesson to rely on herself.

The rabbis were extraordinarily wise clinicians. They understood the old adage that if you give someone a fish he will be dependent on you all his life; but if you teach him how to fish, he can become independent. This is the fundamental principle of all social work and psychology: The counselor helps the clients help themselves. The rabbis reached this conclusion many hundreds of years ago and practiced it diligently in their counseling.

But there is an added element in the Hasidic principle of helping oneself: One also helps oneself by reaching for God, who can help you, and the way to reach God is through the heart and soul, that is, to be honest! The Hasidic morality of authenticity consists in recognizing one's own true motivation. That ferocious honesty gives one the strength, abetted by God, to achieve one's desired goals in life.

As we have said before, counseling and socialization into the Hasidic system of values are inextricably intertwined. We view this process as a two-way bridge, but perhaps that image does not quite capture the essence of the matter. Actually, psychological counseling and education are powerfully interwoven everywhere in the Hasidic story and we separate them solely for analytical purposes.

In analyzing the last story, we emphasized how psychological counseling was embedded in a matrix of Hasidic social values. In the remarkable story that follows, we will see how certain values and qualities highly revered by the Hasidim were converted into extremely potent psychological principles and techniques:

Two Points of View

The Rabbi of Ger once asked one of his disciples who was a guest in his house, what thoughts he had on the way to him. The man replied: "Hasidim come to the rabbi with all manner of requests, some because they have business troubles, others because they are sick or the like. 'What has all this to do with the rabbi?' I asked myself."

"And what did you answer yourself?" asked the *tzaddik*.

"I told myself," said the disciple, "that the rabbi helps those who come to him to make the turning [i.e. to repent] and thus raises them to a higher rung, from which their prayers will more readily be heard."

"I see it differently," said the *tzaddik*. "The rabbi reflects: 'What am I and what is my life that these people should come to me and ask me to pray for them? Why, I am nothing but a drop in the bucket!' And in this way he makes the turning and is uplifted and since he has linked his being to those who sought him out, salvation flows from him into them."

This was the last journey this disciple made to his teacher, for soon after this the rabbi died.

(*Buber, Late Masters, p. 310*)

We begin the interpretation of this story with the observation that the Hasidim revered, to an extraordinary degree, modesty and humility. In part this was a reaction to the snobbishness, arrogance, and haughtiness of their scholarly archrivals, the *mitnagdim*. They often suffered ridicule at the hands of these scholars and therefore were very sensitive about lording it over other people.

Now, this story goes far beyond the views of Rogers and other contemporary psychologists who stressed the importance of empathy and pacing of the client's state of being, particularly his feelings about his problem. The idea behind empathy and active-listening is that if you can help the client come to terms with his own feelings about being able to cope with his problem, he will gradually begin to explore his own resources for solving the problem and thereby maximize his independence.

In "Two Points of View," the rabbi goes far beyond this concept. The lay counseling concept is that the essential problem of a Hasid's coming to a counselor consists in triggering the rabbi's potential for arrogance and being a know-it-all. Presciently, the concept foreshadows a form of transference, since the client is in a very dependent position, somewhat like a child coming to its father for help and guidance.

Thus, according to the Rabbi of Ger, the single most important issue in the rabbi-client relationship is how the rabbi deals with the potential for arrogance when people come to him for answers and how he resists the temptation to "rattle them off," so to speak, to the client.

The rabbi does not even have to let the client know explicitly that he, the rabbi, is vulnerable. But if the rabbi can reflect upon his own vulnerability and his frailties, he will match the client's vulnerable state and thereby give him strength. For he will sense that he is not so terribly badly off if the rabbi himself, the person he is coming to, is also filled with these same feelings of vulnerability. In effect, the Rabbi of Ger is serving as a role-model in stressing to his Hasid the need to recognize his own limitations and "use" them to resolve his troubles, as the rabbi does with all of his vulnerabilities.

This is brought home with special poignancy in the very last sentence of the story. Probably the most difficult experience all of us have to contend with is facing our own mortality. In the face of death, we are all frail, vulnerable, and equally powerless. Before the Rabbi of Ger died, he was able to convey to his disciple the importance of coming to terms with himself by accepting his limitations. And this is especially so in the face of death. The Gerer Rabbi was able to give his disciple his most priceless lesson—a look into the heart of the rabbi himself, with all of his vulnerabilities and frailties; in short, his own humility. And this lesson was so powerful that the disciple also had a "turning" and was uplifted, as are we the readers who participate in this story by linking ourselves to the Rabbi of Ger. Salvation flows from him not only to his disciple in the story, but even to all of us who have become "disciples" of the Gerer.

We believe that the genius of the Hasidim in honing and developing their counseling-didactic stories was one of the most important interventions in all of literature and psychology. It represents a unique synthesis of education in the Hasidic way of life and interpretations of Hasidic philosophy and culture in ways that are of practical-psychological help to Hasidim in coping with everyday troubles and desires. The Hasidic rabbis' practical acumen is so cogent that the stories can still stand on their own and are just as useful to people today who may be less God-centered than their Hasidic forebears. We believe Hasidic counseling was potent because it was so intimately interwoven with Hasidic values; but we share many of those values today, and it is our belief that counseling cannot get away from underlying cultural and moral values. Counseling and education flow from and contribute to a vital cultural heritage. This two-way bridge between counseling and education is formidable in articulating not only powerful psychological techniques which work, but also enduring social values that are relevant to people today.

The Hasidic rabbis' psychological sophistication greatly influenced their attitudes towards traditional values. Nowhere is this more clear than in their evolving attitudes towards sin. We have already indicated that the rabbis were superb at tuning into their clients' feelings and their general state of being in order to match them so that they could begin where the clients were and then bring them along to the point where they could trust themselves more and be able to depend on themselves for *their* solutions to *their* problems.

But it would be a gross error to emphasize only the individual subjective side for the masses of ordinary people, however revolutionary that was in the early eighteenth century. Through the concept of *kavvana* the rabbis were able to study and work with their clients at two different levels—the level of explicit awareness and the level of subconscious motivation; and they could go either way (or, most often, both ways) in their work with clients. That is to say, they could emphasize the behavioral component, or they could choose as their target the subjective or emotional side.

Perhaps the best way to describe the rabbi as a counselor and educator is to picture him as a *wholehearted activist*. He was interested in immediate concrete results. Those results could be either in the form of direct behavioral change or change of the context in which the problem existed or shifts in the client's subjective view of the problem. Of course, these changes are most often interconnected, but the major focus of change emphasizes either a transformation of behavior or a change of perceptions and attitudes.

This is beautifully illustrated in the following two stories about "sin," which elaborate our thesis that the increasing psychological sophistication of the Hasidic rabbis influenced their attitude toward traditional values:

The Sign of Pardon

"In this day and age, when there are no prophets," Rabbi Bunam once said to his disciples, "how can we tell when a sin we have committed has been pardoned?"

> His disciples gave various answers, but none of them pleased the rabbi. "We can tell," he said, "by the fact that we no longer commit that sin."
>
> (*Buber, Late Masters, p. 253*)

The story has a no-nonsense ring to it. As the rabbis would say, "There are no *hokhmes* attached to it." In other words, don't be cute about sin, don't spend hours wringing your hands and heart over being repentant, just stop it. In this sense, action speaks not only louder than words, but much louder than prayers as well. Stopping the sin is not the preferred way to repentance. It is the only way.

Nevertheless, when sin, or thinking about sin, or even the prospect of thinking about sin begins to affect the Hasid so deeply that he becomes depressed, the rabbis are able to shift gears and emphasize the need to cope with those negative (what we call today "neurotic") feelings:

The Sin of the Melancholy

> A Hasid bemoaned to the Lubliner that evil lusts plagued him and made him melancholy. The Master said to him: "Above all else, rid yourself of melancholy, for it is more pernicious than sin. When the Evil One rouses men to lust, it is not his aim to make them sin, but to draw them through sin into the pit of melancholy."
>
> (*Newman, The Hasidic Anthology, pp. 242–243*)

Here again, we must step back and marvel at the incredible psychological sophistication of the rabbis. What they attacked here was not the sin directly but the subjective reactions of the sinner to the sin. Once the sinner is obsessed with his sin, he's caught in a loop which he cannot get out of, because being obsessed with sinning can lead to an obsession with obsessing about sinning and so on and on and on.

The rabbis were able to cut through all this by redefining the "sin" of sinning. When sinning begins to infect the whole personality and you begin to be obsessed with your sin and your sinful thoughts, *that* is the ultimate payoff for Satan, the

Evil One. The rabbi is saying, in effect: "O.K., you sinned, no big deal. You can get over it by stopping it, but don't let Satan drag you into thinking about your sinning and then thinking about thinking about your sinning. Once you get into that loop you will fall into a melancholy or a depression from which it will be difficult, if not impossible, to extricate yourself."

So here the focus shifts from the sinning to the subjective reaction to sinning, and the rabbis reframe the whole problem of sinning in order to be of practical assistance to their Hasidim: Sinning is "successful" only when you are obsessed with it. What a liberating interpretation!

In general, the rabbis were exceedingly wary of excessive thinking, talking, and intellectualizing divorced from constructive actions. Good deeds were favored over prayer, study and verbal repentance. This emphasis on action pervades the Hasidic orientation:

The Borrowed Light

> A rabbi poured out his heart to the Rizhiner, saying: "When I study a subject of the Torah, I feel myself to be encompassed by holy light. But when I halt my studies, I feel myself chilled and surrounded by darkness." The Rizhiner commented: "Whenever you are not occupied with study of the Torah, occupy yourself with the practice of a mitzva, and then the light will not fail you." He continued: "The light which you feel round about you during your studies is a light borrowed from the souls of the Sages. A light, however, derived from your performance of *mitzvot* is your own light."
>
> (*Newman, Maggidim and Hasidim, p. 102*)

In emphasizing the rabbis' remarkable ability to empathize with their Hasidim, we do not mean that that was their only way of helping their followers. Compassion was a necessary precondition for assisting their followers, but we would be remiss not to note that the rabbis were often very daring and innovative and sometimes took enormous risks to puzzle, confuse and shock their clients so that they could be of the greatest assistance to them (Chapter 6 explores this theme in detail).

Nowhere is this more clear than in the following story:

Strange Assistance

Rabbi Moshe of Lelov's daughter, a granddaughter of Rabbi David of Lelov who had been the Yehudi's friend and protector, was childless. Time after time, she beset her father with requests to pray for her. Finally, he told her that only the Rabbi of Radoshitz could assist her in this matter. She immediately made preparation for the journey and traveled to Radoshitz in the company of her mother-in-law, who was also the daughter of a distinguished *tzaddik*. When she had told Rabbi Yisakhar Baer her trouble, he turned on her and berated her as one scolds a spoiled child: "What's all this about wanting children, you impudent baggage? Out with you!"

The young woman, who had been delicately reared and never heard a rough word, fled, dissolved in tears. "Now I shall cry and cry till I die," she said to herself. But her mother-in-law went to the rabbi and asked him why he had shamed the poor woman as he did, whether she had by any chance committed some sin.

"Wish her good luck," answered the rabbi. "Everything is right with her now. There was no other way than to stir her to the very depths." The woman returned to him and he gave her his blessing. Soon after she came home she conceived a son.

(*Buber, Late Masters, pp. 204–205*)

We don't have too many clues about the rabbi's daughter, but we are told that "she had been delicately reared, . . . never heard a rough word" and "time after time beset her father with requests to pray for her." The Radoshitzer Rabbi berated her as "one scolds a child," since he believed that "there was no other way than to stir her to the very depths."

What we are dealing with here is a spoiled young lady. The rabbi's overwhelming opening maneuver is actually very compassionate, because it shakes up the "spoiled rottenness" of the pampered child. His abrasive remarks were completely consistent with what many people thought of her but were afraid to tell her, and the rabbi realized that he could help her only by being "cruel," "insensitive," and highly "confrontative." In this way he forged an immediate link with her and the strange world in which she had been brought up, where all the adults around her had fed her spoiled character and reinforced it.

It is interesting that, when the young woman is confronted, she immediately shifts gears and dissolves into self-pity by saying, "Now I shall cry and cry until I die"—a typical ploy by someone who has been confronted with her own "aggression." The young woman now makes everyone feel very sorry for her so she can get all the phony support she wants and can continue to be a spoiled child.

But the rabbi's "attack" revealed that this young woman was in fact "spoiled rotten." His cutting remarks accurately described what she really was, and he was thus able to forge an immediate link with her. Having established this quick, albeit painful, contact, the rabbi enabled the young lady, for the first time, to seek help without haughtiness, arrogance, and "cuteness."

What we are emphasizing here is the powerful interchange between the use of stories in psychological counseling and their importance in educating Hasidic followers in the true tradition. This is a dynamic cross-fertilizing process.

The Hasidic rabbis began to plumb more and more the depths of their clients' "inner worlds" and they viewed the counseling relationship as an intense, introspective process that was contingent on deepening the client's self-understanding, his real motivation, his authentic direction, which is summarized in the concept of *kavvana*. The rabbis perceived human problems and symptoms as emanating from a distorted subjective experience and from unauthentic self-images and internal motivations. The rabbis tried to correct this distorted outlook so that their followers could more accurately experience what was going on in the real world. In this sense, the rabbis as counselors became very skillful in encouraging their clients to be authentic and in promoting honest self-disclosure. In this way, the rabbi's positive regard was earned, and the client could then regard himself in a more positive light.

By making the heart more consonant with behavior, by

making the client more true to himself and helping him to acknowledge what he is, the rabbis enabled the client to release what we now call "actualizing tendencies" that the client already possessed and that only needed to be triggered. Often, the counselor did not try to direct the counseling process, but instead offered himself as a willing, non-judgmental participant in the client's situation. In doing so, he served as a powerful role-model for the client to accept himself with all his faults, for his mentor, counselor, and teacher—the rabbi himself—was doing precisely that.

But the rabbis did not stop there. They were very much focused on problems and were action-oriented. They engineered specific outcomes and were not afraid to make a direct-action prescription.

The rabbis wanted to eliminate the dysfunctional, noxious, self-defeating behavior. They began with the symptom and used it effectively in the service of change. In this sense, what we have discovered in their stories is a powerful interaction between the person, the problem and the value context which together form a complex, integrated pattern by which the rabbis could help clients disrupt their malfunctioning. The rabbis rapidly gathered information and detailed the distortions in the client's situation.

As counselors, the rabbis were willing to use risky methods to establish rapport and engage the client in constructive activities. Their main objective in counseling was to help their followers resolve their problems in ways which restored their self-confidence and trust in God so that they could go on to become increasingly independent. In order to achieve this end, the rabbinical counselor could emphasize self-exploration and also develop action plans that led to the client's discovering his resources for attaining specific goals.

The rabbis got results, no question about that. Their flexible approach suggested different pathways for the continuing evolution of counseling through the stories as diverse clinical applications. They taught their followers to be independent and to look for answers in the mysteries of God and, ultimately, in themselves—this was the true "reality." But in order to achieve that reality they were not reluctant to prescribe rigorous actions to test their clients' mettle:

A Wanderer and Fugitive

After studying in Lublin and Rymanov for a time, Rabbi Shlomo Leib attached himself to the Yehudi, who said to him: "The most effective penance is to become a wanderer and fugitive." So Rabbi Shlomo decided in his soul to become a fugitive and wanderer.

Many years later, a Hasid who lived in Lentshno visited Rabbi Mendel of Kotzk. The rabbi asked him: "Did you see the Rabbi of Lentshno?"

"I took leave of him before coming here," answered the Hasid. "And was he cheerful?" asked the Rabbi of Kotzk. "Yes," replied the Hasid. "That's the way it is," the Rabbi of Kotzk said sorrowfully. "He who is first a wanderer and fugitive becomes cheerful afterward."

(*Buber, Late Masters, p. 199*)

In concluding this chapter on the role of the story in Hasidic counseling and education, we harken back to the central concept of *kavvana* in relation to God and the life of the people. The rabbis were basically concerned with a person's intention or motivation, the "reason" behind the reason for an action.

The metaphor for *kavvana* is the "heart" with all the connotations it has for us today. The Hasidim of old were very much like us in struggling to be straight and compassionate with each other and with themselves. What differentiates them from many of us today, however, is the love of God which pervaded their lives and which they struggled so hard to communicate to each other.

The Heart Remains

In his old age the Rabbi of Ger told this story:

"When I was still a student, Rabbi Shlomo Leib came up to me in the House of Study and said: 'Young man, you are known as the gifted Jew from Poland, so tell me why our sages commented on the verse in the scripture: "Thou shalt love the Lord thy God with all thy heart and with all thy soul," with the words: "Even if He takes your soul"; but failed to comment:

"Even if He takes your heart," concerning the other part of the verse which says we should love Him with all our heart.'

"I did not know what to say, for I did not consider his question a question at all. For to take one's soul simply means to take one's life. But what was the matter with me that I didn't even wish to know what he meant? The older I get, the larger his question looms before me. If God so desires, let Him take our life, but He must leave us that with which we love Him—he must leave us our heart."

(*Buber, Late Masters, p. 311*)

Part II

HASIDIC COUNSELING

INTRODUCTION

Probably the single most repeated story in psychological literature today is one told by Milton Erickson (Haley 1973), the great hypnotherapist, about a horse that wandered into his family's yard. No one knew where the horse had come from. Erickson mounted the horse and let the horse decide which way it wanted to go. He intervened only when the horse left the road to grazc. When the horse arrived at the yard of the owner several miles away, the owner asked Erickson, "How did you know that horse came from here?"

Erickson said, "I didn't know—but the horse knew. All I did was to keep him on the road."

Some 250 years ago in Sharigrod, in the Ukrainian province of Padolia, there lived Rabbi Jacob Joseph who "was very particular and quick to fly into a temper." Once this town was visited by the Baal Shem who so captivated the villagers with his storytelling that they forgot to go to the House of Prayer for the morning prayers. Martin Buber continues:

> In the meantime, the Baal Shem had finished his story and gone to the inn. There the servant of the House of Prayer found him and delivered his message. The Baal Shem immediately followed him out, smoking his pipe, and in this manner came

before the rav. "What do you think you are doing?" shouted the rav. "Keeping people from prayer!"

"Rabbi," said the Baal Shem calmly, "it does not become you to fly into a rage. Rather, let me tell you a story."

"What do you think you are doing?" was what the rav wanted to say, and then he looked at the man closely for the first time. It is true that he immediately turned his eyes away, nevertheless the words that he had been about to say stuck in his throat. The Baal Shem had begun his story, and the rav had to listen like all the others.

"Once I drove cross-country with three horses," said the Baal Shem, "a bay, a piebald, and a white horse. And not one of the three could neigh. Then I met a peasant coming toward me and he called: 'Slacken the reins.' So I slackened the reins, and then all three horses began to neigh." The rav could say nothing for emotion. "Three," the Baal Shem repeated. "Bay, piebald, and white did not neigh. The peasant knew what to do—slacken the reins—and they neighed." The rav bowed his head in silence. "The peasant gave good advice," said the Baal Shem. "Do you understand?"

"I understand, rabbi," answered the rav and burst into tears. He wept and wept and knew that up to this time he had not known what it was to weep.

"You must be uplifted," said the Baal Shem. The rav looked up to him and saw that he was no longer there.

(*Buber, Early Masters, p.* 57)

A feeling exists that across 250 years, the Besht and Erickson from two totally different cultures could understand each other perfectly! If there is a special division up there in applied psychology, they are exchanging stories right at this moment.

6

Pacing, Leading, and Identification

Two wonderful stories highlight the extraordinary affinity between the rabbis and their Hasidic followers. The rabbi and his Hasid were so in tune with each other, it was not necessary to communicate in words what each was thinking and feeling:

The Seer of Lublin and a Preacher

> A famous traveling *maggid* was once preaching in a city, when word came that the Rabbi of Lublin had arrived. And immediately all the *maggid's* audience left to greet the *tzaddik*. The preacher found himself quite alone. He waited for a little while, and then he, too, saw the Seer's table heaped with the "ransom-money" which petitioners and other visitors had brought him. The *maggid* asked: "How is it possible? I have been preaching here for days and have gotten nothing, while all this came your way in a single hour!"
>
> Rabbi Yitzhak replied: "It is probably because each wakens in the hearts of men what he cherishes in his own heart: I, the hatred of money, and you the love of it."
>
> (*Buber, Early Masters, p. 312*)

The story has a playful, paradoxical twist: Rabbi Yitzhak, the Seer of Lublin, is sincere—people believe he has their best interest at heart, uncontaminated by the need to make money. He, in fact, "hates" money (it is inconsequential), and he influences his followers also to believe it is not important; so, apparently, they are willing to part with it and give it to him.

And since the itinerant *maggid*, on the other hand, is concerned about money (he "loves" it), the same feeling is kindled in the people he addresses. They love money too, so they hold on to it and don't give him any!

A dark side to Hasidism begins to emerge here, i.e., the potential corruption of rabbis—a fact of life Hasidim were aware of and guarded against.

The rabbis of course were powerful role-models for their followers. The sensitivity of the rabbis in identifying with their Hasidim also meant that the Hasidim had excellent teachers and models for developing this same sensitivity. Rabbis tuned in quickly to their followers, but Hasidim just as swiftly tuned in to their rabbis:

The Rabbi of Lublin and the Iron Head

Rabbi Azriel Hurwitz, rav of the city of Lublin, who was also known by the name of Iron Head, kept plaguing Rabbi Yaakov Yitzhak, the Seer of Lublin, with constant objections and reproaches. Once he said to him: "You, yourself, know and admit that you are no *tzaddik*. Then why do you guide others to your way, and gather a community around you?"

Rabbi Yaakov Yitzhak replied: "What can I do about it? They come to me of their own free will, rejoice in my teaching, and desire to hear it."

Then the other said: "Tell all of them, this coming Sabbath, that you are not one of the great, and they will turn from you." The *tzaddik* agreed. On the next Sabbath, he begged his assembled listeners not to give him rank and honors that were not his due. As he spoke, their hearts were set aflame with humility, and from that moment on, they followed him even more fervently than before.

When he told Iron Head of his efforts and their results, the rav reflected, and then said: "That is the way you Hasidim are: You love the humble and eschew the haughty. Tell them that you are one of the elect and they will turn from you."

Rabbi Yitzhak replied: "I am not a *tzaddik*, but neither am I a liar, and how can I say what is not true!"

On another occasion, Rabbi Azriel Hurwitz asked the Seer: "How is it that so many flock about you? I am much more learned than you, yet they do not throng to me."

The *tzaddik* answered: "I too am astonished that so many should come to one as insignificant as myself, to hear God's word, instead of looking for it to you whose learning moves mountains. Perhaps this is the reason: they come to me because I am astonished that they come, and they do not come to you, because you are astonished that they do not come."

(*Buber, Early Masters, pp. 311–312*)

Rabbi Yaakov Yitzhak is conveying an important message: "Trust the people!" But he also speaks up strongly for humility and honesty.

Now comes a curious statement. The *tzaddik* is astonished that people come to hear one as insignificant as he rather than Iron Head, who is much more learned. Then he adds: "They come to me because I am astonished that they come, and they do not come to you because you are astonished that they do not come."

Very strange. Do the Hasidim come to the *tzaddik* because they see his humility in his surprise that they have come? Do they enjoy astonishing him with their presence? Or do they simply enjoy his astonishment as, for example, a parent does when playing peekaboo with a baby?

And so with Iron Head. Do the Hasidim enjoy surprising him by not coming and teaching him a lesson in humility? One can speculate endlessly. Whichever interpretation you choose, you will begin to realize how subtle, deep, and pervasive was the affinity between the rabbis and the Hasidim.

Humility and the importance of self-examination in achieving humility is emphasized not only in the last two stories, but in many others as well:

The Peg and the Crown

The Rabbi of Kobryn said: "He who is a leader of Israel must not think that the Lord of the World chose him because he is a great man. If the king chose to hang his crown on a wooden peg in the wall, would the peg boast that its beauty drew the king's gaze to it?"

(*Buber, Late Masters, p. 167*)

Humility

Rabbi Zusya and his brother Rabbi Elimelekh were once discussing the subject of humility. Elimelekh said: "If a man contemplates the greatness of the Creator, he will arrive at true humility."

But Zusya said: "No! A man must begin by being truly humble. Only then will he recognize the greatness of his Creator."

They asked their teacher, the *maggid*, who was right. He decided in this way: "These and those are the words of the living God. But the inner grace is his who begins with himself, and not with the Creator."

(*Buber, Early Masters, p. 243*)

The essence of humility for a leader is the realization that, despite the deference and honor given to him by others, he is still very human and subject to the limitations of all human beings. He certainly is not God; nor is he a special emissary endowed with superhuman powers. This is especially true of the modest help that the rabbi can give his Hasidim, and the point is made forcefully in the story, "The Limits of Advice," on page 9.

So, ironically, the sign of a true *tzaddik* is awareness of his severe limitations—that, in fact, he cannot solve the most pervasive problem plaguing everyone—unholy thoughts. And this 200 years before Freud!

What, then, can the rabbi-as-counselor do for his followers? There are two schools of thought on this matter, and they are clearly stated in the story, "Two Points of View" on page 77.

The thesis of this chapter is that the Hasidic rabbis in practice followed both points of view debated in the story. The first philosophy, followed by the overwhelming majority of psychologists today, is that qualified individuals can give useful counsel, and almost all of them agree that it takes special preparation to motivate the seeker of help to follow through on it.

The second philosophy, advocated by the Rabbi of Ger, is distinctively Hasidic and represents a unique contribution to psychology—one which is not widely reported in the literature. There is no doubt, however, that it is, in fact, extensively utilized, if our informed discussions with a variety of psychologists of different schools is a fair sample.

The key emphasis in each of the two approaches is different. In the first, which we will arbitrarily label "Pacing and Leading," the counselor calibrates the client's situation and problem, gathers information, develops rapport and lets the client know that he is with him, realizes the depth and seriousness of his problem, etc. Then, when the client is "ready," the counselor suggests to the client how he can use his own resources, often using a new strategy to resolve his problem.

The second point of view about the role of the counselor, supported by the Rabbi of Ger, has a very different emphasis. The Gerer Rabbi, in effect, is saying that the most useful contribution the counselor can make to a Hasid with problems is to share his own vulnerabilities, frailties and limitations and, by not denying them, but recognizing and accepting them, transcend them.

Lest the reader quickly dismiss this approach, he should realize that this is the basis of the most successful worldwide self-help movement, Alcoholics Anonymous, and all of its many affiliates. There is no doubt that many psychologists have confided at one time or another that they had a problem similar to the client's problem.

The Rabbi of Ger also warns the counselor against unduly separating himself from the Hasid with problems and creating a skewed subconscious gap between the dependent Hasid and the "expert" counselor—in effect, what Freud referred to as "counter-transference."

This second point of view, in which the counselor shares his limitations, we shall call "Identification." This is an extremely subtle, carefully crafted procedure which allows the counselor to mirror and feel within himself the Hasid's inner conflicts and limitations while at the same time acting as the rabbi-counselor for the Hasid.

PACING AND LEADING

Let us take a closer look at the differences between the two approaches. The Pacing and Leading method can be seen at work in a story wherein Rabbi Bunam tries, as a first step, to develop a relationship with a difficult charge:

In a Brothel

A lumber merchant once asked Rabbi Bunam to take his son, who was to attend to some business for him, to Danzig, and begged him to keep an eye on the youth.

One evening, Rabbi Bunam could not find him at the inn. He left immediately and walked along the street until he came to a house where he heard someone playing the piano and singing. He went in. When he entered, the song had just come to an end and he saw the lumber merchant's son leave the room. "Sing your best selection," he said to the girl who had been singing, and gave her a gulden. She sang, the door of the room opened, and the youth returned.

Rabbi Bunam went up to him and said, in a casual tone, "Oh, so there you are. They have been asking for you. How about coming right back with me?" When they reached the inn, Rabbi Bunam played cards with the youth for a while, and then they went to bed. The next evening, he went to the theater with him. But when they returned, Rabbi Bunam began to recite psalms and spoke with great force until he had extricated the youth completely from the power of materiality and brought him to the point of perfect turning [i.e., repentance, ed.].

Years later, the *tzaddik* once told his friends: "That time in the brothel, I learned that the Divine Presence can descend anywhere and if, in a certain place, there is only a single being who receives it, that being receives all of its blessings."

(*Buber, Late Masters, pp. 241–242*)

Apparently, the youth was deeply impressed by Rabbi Bunam's becoming his "pal," casually picking him up in the brothel, playing cards, going to the theatre with him—none of these exactly the favorite pastimes of a holy man. Unfortunately, we don't get much information about the youth's changing attitudes or what the "perfect turning" turned on.

The rabbi modestly disclaims any special powers of his own and attributes his success to the Divine Presence. The message of the story seems to be that God does not abandon the sinner who has descended to the lowest depths, but in fact gives him special attention.

In the next story we have a much more direct and intense engagement between a rabbi and his troubled disciple:

The Fiftieth Gate

> Without telling his teacher anything of what he was doing, a disciple of Rabbi Barukh's had inquired into the nature of God, and in his thinking had penetrated further and further until he was tangled in doubts, and what had been certain up to this time became uncertain.
>
> When Rabbi Barukh noticed that the young man no longer came to him as usual, he went to the city where he lived, entered his room unexpectedly, and said to him: "I know what is hidden in your heart. You have passed through the fifty gates of reason. You begin with a question and think, and think up an answer—and the first gate opens and to a new question! And again you plumb it, find the solution, fling open the second gate—and look into a new question. And on and on like this, deeper and deeper, until you have forced open the fiftieth gate. There you stare at a question whose answer no man has ever found, for if there were one who knew it, there would no longer be freedom of choice. But if you dare to probe still further, you plunge into the abyss."
>
> "So should I go back all the way, to the very beginning?" cried the disciple.
>
> "If you turn you will not be going back," said Rabbi Barukh. "You will be standing beyond the last gate: You will stand in faith."
>
> (*Buber, Early Masters, p. 92*)

In many ways, this story illustrates a model pacing of someone with intense conflict. First of all, Rabbi Barukh does not hesitate to go to the troubled disciple who has ceased coming to him. The rabbi surprises his disciple and engages him instantly by telling him that he knows "what is hidden" in his heart. Not only does this immediately gain great credibility for the rabbi in the disciple's mind, but it must also comfort him enormously to know that someone else knows the torture he is undergoing.

Rabbi Barukh then gets into an appropriately passionate dialogue, the first part of which perfectly mirrors the disciple's dilemma to the point of no return. The "nature of God" is a dangerous subject to pursue: If, at the end of the road, the disciple has the "answer," he may have resolved the problem of "freedom of choice"; and if he probes still further, the disciple could plunge "into the abyss," forever tormented by doubt.

The disciple is caught up in the rabbi's resumé of his own inner turmoil and cries out that he may have to start all over again, which is to say he may have reasoned faultily somewhere along the line. He still hopes to solve the problem rationally, logically.

Teacher and student are fully engaged and the teacher adeptly plays on the phrase "going back" and suggests instead a "turn," another direction: The way beyond the last gate is the path of faith—the "reason" beyond reason. No more need be said, and the story ends.

The story reveals, in rich detail, the rabbi pacing his student, gaining rapport with him, fully calibrating the point of impasse, and dramatically leading to a slight shift that is momentous for the disciple. A masterful demonstration of Pacing and Leading!

IDENTIFICATION

In contrast to Pacing and Leading, Identification carries the process of rapport, empathy, and engagement, one decisive step further: The rabbi-counselor absorbs within himself the inner conflict of the Hasid so the latter can "see" it objectified in someone else and look at it dissociated from himself. Identification is a special process somewhere between Pacing and Leading, that results in a "turning" for the Hasid.

The next two stories demonstrate this complex form of counseling. In the first, the Baal Shem Tov reveals his exquisite grasp of the psychology of behavioral change by utilizing the identification process.

Identification works especially well when it is done indirectly—in a familiar situation, bypassing the conscious and engaging the subconscious, and creating a point of identification with which the listener is compelled to compare himself. When the identification method is used with surgical precision, the transformation is often instantaneous:

The Scholars

> Moshe Hayyim Efraim, a grandson of the Baal Shem's, dedicated himself to study in his youth and became so great a scholar that this made him deviate somewhat from the Hasidic way of life. His grandfather, the Baal Shem, made a point of often walking with him beyond the town, and Efraim went with him, though with a hint of reluctance, for he begrudged the time he might have spent in studying.
>
> Once, they met a man coming from another city. The Baal Shem asked him about one of his fellow citizens. "He is a great scholar," said the man.
>
> "I envy him his scholarship," said the Baal Shem. "But what am I to do? I have no time to study because I have to serve my Maker." From this hour on, Efraim returned to the Hasidic way again with all his strength.
>
> (*Buber, Early Masters, p. 65*)

This is a model Identification. Let us recapitulate the story. The Baal Shem knows that his grandson is completely dedicated to study not only as a priority in his life, but as the only thing in his life. This goes against the grain of the Hasidim, who believed in a much more balanced way of life—a happy medium between study, care, and attention to other people on one hand, and, on the other hand, prayer and a general discovery of God in everyday, joyful existence. The Baal Shem maintained a close connection with his grandson and took periodic walks with him. Thus, despite the vast difference between the two, there was still an important relationship and ongoing communication. At the same time, the Baal Shem realized that his grandson was angry about the walks, because they took him away from his study. He was that diligent!

So they meet a man who tells them about another scholar. The kinship between this other scholar and the grandson is obvious. In the course of this natural situation, the Baal Shem has a wonderful opportunity to comment on "another" great scholar while he is really talking about his grandson, who also intends to become a great scholar. This is a subtle way of addressing his grandson indirectly.

The Baal Shem says that he envies this great scholar's scholarship, and then adds casually, as if it really weren't very important (and in a somewhat plaintive voice, I imagine), that he, the Baal Shem, cannot do what this great scholar is doing, even though he envies the scholar, because he has to serve his Maker.

What is happening here? On one hand the Baal Shem is saying that he envies the great scholar and that means that he also envies his grandson who is on his way to becoming a great scholar. No contest here. Nothing to resist here. Strong language. The Baal Shem envies them for their scholarship. Here is one of the greatest men of the era envying someone else because that person has something that he doesn't have—vast erudite scholarship. There could be no higher accolade from one person to another—one great man envying another great man.

And then comes the crushing blow: The reason the Baal Shem cannot do as the scholar does—namely, study all the time—is that the Baal Shem has dedicated his life to serving God rather than to studying books about Him.

What the Baal Shem has done here is to greatly magnify the conflict within his grandson and then show him a way of resolving that conflict—and all in a flash! The grandson is devoted to study. The Baal Shem is devoted to service. The Besht praises to high heaven both the scholar and his grandson. But hold on, there's something wrong here. There is a catch! The Baal Shem Tov can at one and the same time envy the scholar *and* not do what the scholar does, because suddenly there is revealed an even higher value—namely, serving God directly rather than through the study of His books.

It comes down to a question of the cost of all this scholarship. Is it worthwhile to become a renowned scholar to the point where study becomes an end in itself and God, and other people are secondary? Is that the way the grandson wants to live? Does he want to become a renowned scholar? Or does he want to serve God? Does becoming a great scholar in itself constitute a maximum service to God? Not according to the Besht.

There's a double message here that the Besht is sending to his grandson, and it reflects the latent conflict in the young man's soul. The Besht envies his scholarship, implying, "It's O.K. if you want to continue to be a great scholar. Do so, by all means. But at the same time realize that it is at the cost of a more rounded life of service to God." So the Besht perfectly sums up the evolving conflict within his grandson—scholarship versus service. The grandson begins a fundamental reordering of his priorities, making service first and scholarship secondary to it.

Now underlying all this is another important element—the vast humility of the Besht. The Baal Shem Tov shows his modesty when he admits that he does envy a great scholar and is sorry he is unable to be a scholar.

"The Scholars" is an artful example of the skill of the Hasidic rabbi in pacing his listener, taking advantage of a natural situation and involving himself totally in the situation.

At the heart of the intervention is a masterful use of *Potentiating Identification*, a process in which the Baal Shem perfectly mirrors his grandson: The Besht is obviously not as learned as the scholar and envies his scholarship; the grandson is becoming a scholar but is certainly not as learned as the scholar in question, so he also envies his scholarship and desires to be like him. (Remember, the grandson even chafed at taking time from his studies to walk with his grandfather.)

Now the Besht zeroes in on the latent conflict: He has no time to study—meaning he would love to—but he has to serve his Maker; this perfectly mirrors Efraim's struggle. The Besht decides first to serve his Maker, thus validating that there is, in fact, a conflict and that serving God has priority over study; Efraim returns to the Hasidic way.

Now, why does Efraim "return to the Hasidic way again with all his strength?" Has he been overcome with the realization that study carried to such an extreme interferes with serving God fully?

This "turn" by Ephraim was not a result only of seeing himself in the Besht's struggle; it is *also* a product of his identification with the Besht in all of the latter's humility and complete devotion to God. We call this process—the Hasid's seeing himself, or a significant part of himself, in the rabbi-counselor and *also* modeling himself after the rabbi—"Potentiating Identification." It is a unique contribution that the Hasidim have made to psychology and the healing process.

Incidentally, Efraim's return "to the Hasidic way again with all his strength" is in keeping with his character; he is the kind of person who goes all out in any endeavor, and now, having decided that he wanted to be like the Baal Shem Tov, he will put all his heart and soul into it.

In our second exmple of the identification method, the rabbi-counselor fully identifies with an innkeeper's "long years of sin":

Zusya and the Sinner

> Once, Rabbi Zusya came to an inn, and on the forehead of the innkeeper he saw long years of sin. For a while, he neither spoke nor moved. But when he was alone in the room which had been assigned to him, the shudder of vicarious experience overcame him in the midst of singing psalms, and he cried aloud: "Zusya, Zusya, you wicked man! What have you done! There is no lie that failed to tempt you, and no crime you have not committed. Zusya, foolish, erring man, what will be the end of this?" Then he enumerated the sins of the innkeeper, giving the time and place of each, as his own, and sobbed. The innkeeper had quietly followed this strange man. He stood at the door and heard him. First, he was seized with dull dismay, but then penitance and grace were lit within him, and he woke to God.
>
> *(Buber, Early Masters, p. 241)*

In this powerful story, Rabbi Zusya fully identifies with all the sins of the sinner as if they were his own: "There is no lie that failed to tempt you, and no crime you have not committed." How can this be? What is the "shudder of vicarious experience that overcame him"?

Rabbi Zusya obviously came to terms with his thinking about, or imagining or fantasizing these sins and crimes which can be as wicked for a holy man as actually committing them. By enumerating the sins of the innkeeper as his own, Zusya has forced the eavesdropping innkeeper to recognize his true self as reflected in Rabbi Zusya. This objectified revelation is now difficult to deny, and the innkeeper is "seized with dull dismay."

Rabbi Zusya, however, is not only revealing the innkeeper's sins, he is also admitting them openly and seeking repentance which arouses simultaneously repentance and a state of grace in the innkeeper.

One can only imagine the shock Rabbi Zusya's confession produced in the innkeeper. On one hand, he is amazed that such a holy man could be so grievous a sinner, just as he himself has been. On the other hand, he marvels at Zusya's courage in confessing to so many transgressions. The innkeeper's response is irresistible: "If he can do it, so can I!"

The rabbis developed a variety of forms through which they used the Identification mechanism. In the following tale, Rabbi Aaron Leib draws upon the story of King David, with whom he wishes an adulterous client to identify:

After He Had Gone in to Bathsheba

One day, Rabbi Aaron Leib of Primishlan was visited by a man on whose face he read the signs of having committed adultery. After he had talked to his caller for a little time, Rabbi Leib said to him:

"It is written: 'A Psalm of David: When Nathan the prophet came to him after he had gone in to Bathsheba . . .'

"What can this mean? It means that Nathan chose the correct way to influence David to turn to God. Had he confronted David publicly and as his judge, he would only have hardened his heart. But he censured David in secrecy and with love just as David himself had gone in to Bathsheba.

"And Nathan's censure went to the king's heart and melted and recast it, and from it mounted the song of one who had turned to God."

When Rabbi Aaron Leib finished speaking, the man confessed his sin and turned wholly to God.

(*Buber, Early Masters, p. 157*)

In this "isomorphic tale" we have parrallels between David and Bathsheba and the adulterer and his woman on one hand, and between David and Nathan and the adulterer and Rabbi Leib on the other.

Rabbi Leib immediately recognized that the man was scared stiff about public exposure. The David story was told to allay his fears.

The rabbi reframes the adulterer's sin by praising him for committing the adultery in secrecy and with love, just as David had done with Bathsheba. Just as the two adulterers had protected the women from public exposure, so both Nathan and Rabbi Leib protected the confidentiality of the adulterers. Here is another example of how, even with a most objectionable sin, the rabbi is still able to find some positive values through reframing the transgression.

This positive approach and the assurance of confidentiality combine to melt any resistance that the adulterer might have had to confronting his sin. In the absence of negative judgments, he is able to confess his sin and "turn wholly to God."

In this chapter we have spelled out the great affinity of feeling, thinking and judging between rabbi and Hasid. The rabbi knew his Hasid intimately, inside-out so to speak, just as the Hasid knew his rabbi. The rabbi used this intuition to enter the very soul of his Hasidic follower, and the subsequent revelation to the Hasid of his own fears and conflicts, minus any cover-ups, led to a significant "turning" in the Hasid's life.

As "the healer of the soul's diseases," the rabbi-counselor above all individualized every person who came to him. The rabbi did not work by formula—rather, he carefully considered every individual as unique:

The Healer of the Soul's Diseases

Said the Bratzlaver: "No physician can heal unless he is well acquainted with the physiology and anatomy of the body. In the same way, no healer of those sick in soul can cure them unless he thoroughly understands what particular spiritual remedy will furnish solace and comfort to every particular disease of the soul. He must know what the soul lacks before he can cure it. One man may be cured by reading ethical books; another, by practicing more hospitality; a third, by the reading of Psalms; a fourth, by engaging in profound learning; a fifth, by performing deeds of kindness; a sixth, by doing communal work."

(*Newman, Maggidim and Hasidim, p. 66*)

7

Reframing

INTRODUCTION

The single most pervasive psychological technique that the Hasidim use in their stories is *reframing*. Their stories abound in this technique, and they demonstrate how close our own psychological thinking today is to their work.

Reframing is a universal process that you use every single day of your life. It changes the meaning of an act so that its significance, for you and for others, is fundamentally transformed.

Suppose you lose ten dollars. You can be very angry or disappointed with yourself for being so careless as to lose the money, but you can also change the meaning of the loss. You can say to yourself: "How lucky I am to have lost only ten dollars and to have done this now, because it will make me be more careful and prevent me from losing a lot more money." So the loss becomes useful and helpful rather than negative and saddening.

What we have done here is to separate the meaning of behavior from the behavior itself. Every act has this dual component: the behavior itself and the meaning of the behavior. Losing the money is the behavior; its meaning is changed from a sad, or even depressing, event to a useful one, because it is seen in a positive light: It will prevent you from losing even more money by teaching you to be more careful.

Some experienced drivers use a quick reframe instinctively whenever they have a close shave driving their cars. Usually, this happens because they have become a mite careless. "I look at the near miss in avoiding an accident as a positive event," says one driver. "It is actually a blessing, because it immediately makes me more alert and careful about driving. Instead of castigating the other person or myself, I quickly change it into a positive incentive to be a more careful driver. I take fewer chances."

As can be seen, one can turn a loss into a positive event by analytically separating the meaning from the behavior and viewing the outcome as positive. Another frequently used method of reframing is to accept all behavior as useful in *some* context. In the second type of reframing, the task is to identify the context in which the behavior *is* appropriate and to attach the behavior there. For example, we could ask ourselves in what context would losing ten dollars be a useful act. If a starving person or someone who had lost all of his money found the ten dollars, the loss can be seen as most useful, especially if helping needy people is important to the loser of the money.

A HISTORICAL REFRAME OF REFRAMING

The widespread use of reframing can be seen historically in the gap between people's rising expectations and what they are actually able to achieve. Reframing is related to the psychological concept of "cognitive dissonance," the idea that people have to deal with all kinds of discrepancies between what they think they ought to have and what they actually do have.

In literature there are, of course, numerous examples of reframing as a central plot device from—*Aesop's Fables,* to Hasidic stories to Mark Twain's Tom Sawyer manipulating other boys to paint a fence for him.

Historically, reframing has been used to produce an extremely negative connotation. For example, Marx's phrase, "Religion is the opiate of the people," refers to religion as something that, by offering some spiritual pie in the sky, distracts people from changing the economic reality of their lives. Here is a classic Hassidic story along these lines:

The Want

In early life, Rabbi Yehiel Makhal lived in poverty, but not for an hour did happiness desert him.

Someone once asked him: "Rabbi, how can you pray day after day, 'Blessed be, Thou . . . who has supplied me every want?' Surely, you lack everything a man has need of."

He replied: "My want is, most likely, poverty, and that is what I have been supplied with."

(Buber, Early Masters, p. 138)

What we like most about this story is the phrase, "My want is, most likely, poverty." We like the idea that there is some smidgen of doubt about living in poverty. Even the great Mikhal leaves open the possibility that his want really is not poverty and that he might also live with happiness not deserting him for an hour if he were a little better off. Meanwhile, he is content to live happily with what he has. He reminds us of the rabbi who, when asked whether he had what he needed, replied, "What I need is what I have."

The one war the Hasidim were forever waging was the one between reason and faith. God, of course, gave man both, but they were not equal; and the Hasidim were always discovering ways by which faith could "trip up" man's reason:

Reason and Faith

Rabbi Makhal once said to one of his five sons, Rabbi Wolf of Zbarazh:

"When I had risen in prayer and was standing in the hall of truth, I begged God to grant me that my reason might never proceed against His truth."

(Buber, Early Masters, pp. 150–151)

This is a paradoxical reframe of a rabbi's faith wherein the rabbi asks God to curb his reason when it comes to God's

Truth, which is equated with a man's faith and its possible subversion by his reason. In other words, man is asking God to help his faith against his reason.

Through his prayer, Rabbi Makhal is asking God to reinforce his faith, which can reveal God's truth; the obstacle in his way is his own reason. Seeking support for his own faith through prayer is a meta-prayer, that is, a prayer that seeks to reinforce the efficacy of prayer and faith in the titanic struggle against doubt and skepticism, which are the hallmarks of reason. Reason is evil when it is against God's truth, and God's truth is essentially faith.

This is another practical demonstration of *kavvana*, the inner motivation and direction of a Hasid, which requires going beyond the surface to probe the heart, because that's where one's true belief lies. The Hasidim were keen observers and "readers" of this conflict between what one says and does, and what he believes in his heart. In brief, when someone says "I really don't care," the "really" in the statement is a dead give-away that underneath the surface confidence lurks a doubt, a conflict within the individual's soul.

Reframing became an integral part of the Hasidic way of thinking and relating to the world. Underlying this concept is the idea of finding something good in every person and every situation. This was not always apparent and sometimes required a protracted search, but for the Hasidim it was always there. When a central concept takes hold of a people, it generates support by going back into its history for verification. The Hasidim were not averse to reinterpreting the Bible in terms of modified reframes, as the following story shows us:

Find the Good

> Rabbi Bunam said: "Jacob ordered Joseph to go and see whether it was well with his brothers (Genesis 37:14).
>
> "Jacob used to hear from Joseph 'evil reports of his brothers' and therefore instructed him not to persist in looking for their misconduct, but rather to find the good in them."
>
> (*Newman, The Hasidic Anthology, p. 111*)

The wheel turns round and round. A few years ago, a book on instant management was published and one of its three main principles was "to catch someone doing something right." Most managers were bent on finding what their employees did wrong, and of course they criticized them for it. Rarely did they find good things that they were doing, and even more rarely did they give them praise for doing things right. The Hasidim were somewhat ahead of today's managers.

FRAMING AN EVENT

The Hasidim were keenly aware of how individuals can differ in framing an event. In typical rabbinical fashion, this difference in framing styles is reframed into a moral lesson:

Let Us Not Be Children

> Said the Mezeritcher: "A father lifted up his little son who had fallen and, noting a splinter in the boy's foot, he extracted it, unmindful of the lad's cries of pain. He then said: 'If you are not more careful in your play, you will suffer again the pain you felt a moment ago.' Both were in fear: the father, that infection would attack his son's foot; the boy, that he might again undergo the pain of having a splinter extracted. The father feared the wound, the son the cure. Likewise, God punishes us in order to cure us of our sins. He fears the harm to our souls, we fear the punishment which is the cure. Let us no longer be children, but let us understand that which truly inspires fear within us."
>
> (*Newman, The Hasidic Anthology, p. 116*)

One reframed message in this story is that we should be adults and see the longterm consequences of an event and not be impatient or shortsighted like children. This is then further reframed to say that whatever happens to us should not be feared compared to what "ought truly inspire fear within us." For the Hasidim that was a logical progression and an opportunity to set the record straight about the most important of all subjects—our relationship to God.

A healthy fun reframe is the following metaphorical play on words with numberless connotations:

To Open

> Rabbi Shlomo of Karlin said to someone: "I have no key to open you." And the man cried out: "Then pry me open with a nail." From that time on, the rabbi always said words of warm praise about him.
>
> (*Buber, Early Masters, p.* 277)

Our interpretation is that the man is crying out: "Don't be so gentle, subtle, considerate, tactful, conscientious, perfectionistic, or careful. Instead, take me head-on, rough me up, get to the problem and don't worry about my feelings." Your interpretation may be quite different—and equally valid!

REFRAMING "EVIL"

One of the games the rabbis often liked to play was the reframing of what most people saw an unmitigated evil. The rabbis would see very positive qualities in, for example, the sinner, the thief, the gambler:

The Merry Sinner

> In Lublin lived a great sinner. Whenever he wanted to talk to the rabbi, the latter readily consented and conversed with him as if with a man of integrity and one who was a close friend.
>
> Many of the Hasidim were annoyed at this, and one said to the other: "Is it possible that our rabbi—who has only to look once into a man's face to know his life from first to last, to know the very origin of his soul—does not see this fellow as a sinner? And if he does see it, that he considers him worthy to speak to and associate with?"
>
> Finally, they summoned up courage to go to the rabbi

> himself with their questions. He answered them: "I know all about him as well as you. But you know how I love gaiety and hate dejection. And this man is so great a sinner! Others repent the moment they have sinned, are sorry for a moment, and then return to their folly. But he knows no regrets and no doldrums, and lives in his happiness as in a tower. And it is the radiance of his happiness that overwhelms my heart."
>
> (*Buber, Early Masters, pp. 315–316*)

This was no run-of-the-mill sinner. He was not only merry with "the radiance of his happiness that overwhelms my heart," but also honest and a "great sinner"—whatever that means. (Some psychologists today would consider his sinning psychopathic, since it is so ego-symptonic.)

Intoxicated with life, the Hasidim were attracted to gaiety and happiness as moths are to light. Sins did not blind them to the positive qualities of a particular sinner. Not only were they impressed with the "good" in the bad, they also learned from it:

The Hopeful Thief

> The Berditchever traveled from town to town seeking to gather money for a worthy cause, but he met with only moderate success. He regretted the waste of time, and resolved not to undertake a similar enterprise in the future. On returning home, he saw a policeman beating a thief who had been caught red-handed. The rabbi paid the thief's fine and, upon his release, inquired if he had not been taught a lesson to abstain from thievery henceforth.
>
> The thief replied: "What if I was beaten! This time my luck was poor, but next time it will be better."
>
> "I must bear this reply in mind," thought the Berditchever. "My own success this time was meager, but I must not abandon a good deed because of setbacks. Next time I may have better fortune."
>
> (*Newman, The Hasidic Anthology, pp. 335–336*)

Finally, what the rabbis were to discover inevitably is not only the good and the admirable in "evil," but also how that in turn could serve God even more faithfully:

The Gamblers

A Hasid complained to Rabbi Wolf that certain persons were turning night into day, playing cards. "That is good," said the *tzaddik*. "Like all people, they want to serve God and don't know how. But now they are learning to stay awake and persist in doing something. When they have become perfect in this, all they need do is turn to God—and what excellent servants they will make for him then!"

(*Buber, Early Masters, p. 161*)

What is common to the last three stories is the rabbi's rejection of any all-encompassing stereotype of a sinner or a gambler, and his seeing positive qualities within the negative. The desire for change that the rabbis always generated would expand the positive side so that it would eventually overcome the "wickedness":

Tolerating the Sinner

Rabbi Zusya was seated in the reception room of the Mezeritcher *Maggid*. A man known for his evil ways entered the room to seek the *maggid's* presence. He came over to the *maggid* and with characteristic brazen-facedness stated his wish. Rabby Zusya could not restrain himself and shouted at the sinner:

"How dare you approach this holy rabbi without a sense of shame for your transgressions?"

When the man had left, Rabbi Zusya sought the *maggid's* forgiveness for his interference. The *maggid* said:

"Learn from me, Rabbi Zusya, to tolerate the sinner. Ignore the wickedness in him and endeavor to elicit the good."

This became Rabbi Zusya's habit, and when he would encounter a sinner, he would blame himself for being a sinner and tearfully implore the Lord for pardon. This self-accusation always moved the real sinner to repentance, and he would beg the rabbi to instruct him in the ways of self-betterment.

(*Newman, The Hasidic Anthology, p. 50*)

The extremely positive and optimistic outlook of the Hasidim and their mania for self-improvement prompted them to seek hints and clues for self-betterment everywhere. What, for example, can a young rabbinical disciple learn from a smith?

The Smith

When Rabbi Yaakov Yitzhak, the Yehudi, was young and had board and lodging in the house of his father-in-law, his next-door neighbor was a smith. The smith got up very early in the morning and struck hammer on anvil until the sound roared like thunder in the ears of the sleeping youth. Yaakov Yitzhak woke up and thought: "If this man tears himself away from sleep so early for worldy work and profit, shall I not be able to do the same for the service of the eternal God?"

The following morning, he rose before the smith, who, as he entered his smithy, heard the young man reading in a low tone. This irritated him: "There he is at work already, and he doesn't need to! I certainly won't let a fellow like that get ahead of me!" On the following night he got up before the Yehudi. But the young rabbi took up the challenge and won the race. In later years he used to say: "Whatever I have attained I owe first and foremost to a smith."

(*Buber, Late Masters, p. 225*)

Very few things were beyond the rabbis' ingenuity to reframe into a useful lesson:

Playing Checkers

On one of the days of Hanukka, Rabbi Nahum, the son of the Rabbi of Rizhyn, entered the House of Study at a time when he was not expected and found his disciples playing checkers, as was the custom on those days. When they saw the *tzaddik*, they were embarrassed and stopped playing. But he gave them a kindly nod and asked: "Do you know the rules of the game of checkers?"

When they did not reply for shyness, he himself gave the answer: "I shall tell you the rules of the game of checkers. The first is that one must not make two moves at once. The second is that one may move only forward and not backward. And the third is that when one has reached the last row, one may move where he likes."

(*Buber, Late Masters*, p. 73)

Even modern inventions could be used to teach something useful:

Of Modern Inventions

"You can learn something from everything," the Rabbi of Sadagora once said to his Hasidim. "Everything can teach us something, and not only everything God has created. What man has made can also teach us something."

"What can we learn from a train?" one Hasid asked dubiously.

"That, because of one second, one can miss everything."

"And from the telegraph?"

"That every word is counted and charged."

"And the telephone?"

"That what we say here is heard there."

(*Buber, Late Masters*, p. 70)

The rabbis often enjoyed reframing. For example, when miracles were "getting out of hand," one rabbi simply reframed the attitude toward miracles:

Miracles

The Rabbi of Kobryn said: "We paid no attention to the miracles our teachers worked, and when sometimes a miracle did not come to pass, he gained in our eyes."

(*Buber, Late Masters*, p. 154)

THE CLASSICAL REFRAME

What is a "classical reframe"? It is a shift in the meaning of a framing which significantly alters the way a person sees, feels, hears, interprets—in short, actually experiences—what he has been doing and thinking.

The following story is archetypical:

In a Hurry

> The Rabbi of Berditchev saw a man hurrying along the street, looking neither right nor left. "Why are you rushing so?" he asked the man.
>
> "I am after my livelihood," the man replied.
>
> "And how do you know," continued the rabbi, "that your livelihood is running on before you, so that you have to rush after it? Perhaps it is behind you, and all you need do to encounter it is to stand still—but you are running away from it!"
>
> (*Buber, Early Masters, p. 226*)

The Berditchever's reframe is an artful play on words that changes the meaning of the man's behavior. Rushing after something is a useful strategy, but it is probably counterproductive when it is the only one. The man-in-a-hurry has lost all perspective. Most things in life involve a balance between chasing after and "standing still" and absorbing:

What You Pursue

> Rabbi Pinhas used to say: "What you pursue, you don't get. But what you allow to grow slowly, in its own way, comes to you. Cut open a big fish, and in its belly you will find the little fish lying head down."
>
> (*Buber, Early Masters, p. 129*)

A similar message about the flow and ebb of life experiences is expertly depicted in the following story. Note how artfully the Baal Shem Tov reframes a disciple's occasional separation from feeling close to God. It is a masterful use of metaphor to explain to the disciple how something which appears to be negative is really positive, in fact, enriching:

Near and Far

> A disciple asked the Baal Shem: "Why is it that one who clings to God and knows he is close to Him, sometimes experiences a sense of interruption and remoteness?"
>
> The Baal Shem explained: "When a father sets out to teach his little son to walk, he stands in front of him and holds his two hands on either side of the child, so that he cannot fall, and the boy goes toward his father between his father's hands. But the moment he is close to his father, he moves away a little, and holds his hands farther apart, and he does this over and over, so the child may learn to walk."
>
> (*Buber, Early Masters, p. 65*)

This is an excellent example of how the Baal Shem changes the meaning of an act from what the disciple thought was negative to a positive significance: Having doubts about God is good, even necessary! It's not bad. It's normal. The disciple is compared to a child learning how to walk who stays close to his father and is guided by him. But as he gains in strength and ability, the child moves away from his father. Paradoxically, this enables the youngster to become even stronger and to strengthen, at the same time, his faith and love for his father.

There are layers of meaning in this story about the importance of having doubts and feeling removed from God. This is much preferable to an unquestioning, naive, unwavering faith in God. Doubt strengthens belief. Light can enter only where darkness has been. Refusing support in different situations strengthens both children and grownups. The lesson to be learned from this metaphor is that, instead of weakening, the disciple's bonds to God are actually strengthened through questioning and doubt. This is exemplified in many biblical stories, where the hero challenges God and ends up being closer to Him.

The Baal Shem was an extreme nonconformist. He frequently skipped school and spent time in the woods communing with nature. Nonconformity can lead to a renewal of faith at a deeper level. It all depends on the perspective; a slight shift in the meaning of behavior can have enormous consequences:

The Thieves

One night, thieves entered Rabbi Wolf's house and took whatever they happened to find. From his room, the *tzaddik* watched them but did not do anything to stop them. When they were through, they took some utensils, among them a jug from which a sick man had drunk that very evening. Rabbi Wolf ran after them. "My good people," he said, "whatever you have found here, I beg you to regard as gifts from me. I do not begrudge these things to you at all. But please be careful about that jug! The breath of a sick man is clinging to it, and you might catch his disease!"

From that time on, he said every evening before going to bed: "All my possessions are common property," so that in case thieves came again, they would not be guilty of theft.

(*Buber, Early Masters, p. 161*)

Hasidim also reframed feelings so that they could be more useful. One Hasid was counseled by his rabbi not to be anxious about something he did in the past, but to transfer his anxiety to the future and use its energy there. Any feeling has this potential for being reorganized by someone changing context, often from the past to the present or the future, and utilizing the energy associated with that feeling in a more positive direction. Anxiousness, uncertainty, and even fear can be useful in energizing a person and "psyching him up" to a positive action. One Hasid was told to pocket his anger and use it on an appropriate occasion.

Of all the hundreds (literally) of reframes that we looked at and considered for inclusion in this chapter, it is our belief that the following is the most powerful in its widespread universal connotations and applications to many diverse situations and experiences:

It Is the Beloved Who Are Loving

A Hasid from Poland, who went up to the Holy Land and settled in Jerusalem, found himself unable to adjust to conditions of life there. Accordingly, he decided to return to Poland. Before leaving the Holy City he went to take his leave of Reb

Simha Bunam of Vorki, the son of Reb Menahem Mendel of Vorki, who then lived in Jerusalem.

When he had explained his reason for leaving, the *tzaddik*, sighed from the depths of his heart and said: "I feel very sorry for you. It seems that you did not find favor in the eyes of Jerusalem, for if you had found favor in her eyes, she would have found favor in yours."

These words trickled into that Hasid's heart. He thought over his decision, and to the end of his days remained a loved and loving son of the Holy City.

(*Zevin, A Treasury of Hasidic Tales on the Festivals, Vol. I, p. 468*)

The lesson here is super-simple and one that all of us know in our hearts and yet forget so often! The message is clear: "If you hate Jerusalem, Jerusalem will hate you!" Or, putting it positively, "If you *had* found favor in her eyes, she would have found favor in yours."

How true this is in so many situations, with so many people. We are the cause, most often, of some place, person or thing "liking" us. The rabbis were keenly aware of the interactional causal relationship.

This story can stay with us as a striking image of our role in not liking something, and it gives us pause to consider whether it is in "it" or in us that we do not like each other and do not get along. And will this message "trickle" into our hearts?

Very often, we are not aware of our own strengths and positive qualities. One important function of reframing is to reframe our underestimation of ourselves and the significance of our own actions:

Nothing More Ambitious

Reb David Moshe of Chortkov told the story of a difficult moment in the life of his grandfather.

"When my grandfather, Reb Shalom of Probisht, was once at the home of his father-in-law Reb Nahum of Chernobyl," he said, "it so happened that while Reb Nahum was leading his congregation in the last *minha* service of the outgoing year with his accustomed ecstasy, my grandfather sensed that he himself had suddenly slipped from the lofty levels of divine service to which he had raised himself over the years. He found it quite impossible to worship in the way that a *tzaddik* commonly worships. He was sorely grieved. Why should this have befallen him at a moment like this, when every other Jew was now praying with his highest degree of devoutness? He made every effort to recapture his accustomed fervor, but in vain. Finally, after prodigious exertion, he succeeded somehow in making his way through the prayers with nothing more ambitious than a consistent attentiveness to the meaning of the words he was uttering—just as every other ordinary worshiper does.

"As soon as he reached the end of his prayers, Reb Nahum approached him and exclaimed: 'My son! What eloquent reverberations you set up in the heavens just now with your afternoon prayers! Do you know that thousands of erring souls were elevated through your words?'"

(*Zevin, A Treasury of Hasidic Tales on the Festivals, Vol. I, p. 29*)

REFRAMING THE REFRAME

We use the term "reframing the reframe" to refer to a situation in which a person consciously or subconsciously changes the meaning of an action and then has another change take place (caused by himself, or others, or God) which alters the original change of meaning:

The Sigh

Silently the *maggid's* wife held the hungry child. It was too weak to cry. Then, for the first time, the *maggid* sighed. Instantly the answer came. A voice said to him: "You have lost your share in the World-to-Come."

"Well then," he said, "the reward has been done away with. Now I can begin to serve in good earnest."

(*Buber, Early Masters, p. 99*)

This story illustrates the extraordinary power of introspection by the *maggid* in which a moment of weakness is revealed to him simply by a "sigh." The sigh indicates a break in faith, questioning God why he, his wife, and especially his hungry child, should be in such dire straits. The *maggid* instantly "knew" that his situation had drastically changed: "You have lost your share in the World-to-Come," which means that now he was being punished for his doubt about faith in God. The *maggid* was then able to take this insight and immediately reframe it into an even more powerful moral position: "I can now serve God with all my heart because I have no expectation of a reward in the World-to-Come."

This is one of the most powerful stories that we have read which sets forth unambiguously that God strikes no bargains; there is no *quid pro quo* for suffering or good deeds. How well we know this truth today!

This central concept is sharply expressed in the following metaphor, in which one word drastically alters the meaning of an experience in relation to one's faith in God:

Bitter, Not Bad

The Rabbi of Kobryn taught:

"When a man suffers, he ought not to say: 'That's bad! That's bad!' Nothing that God imposes on man is bad. But it is all right to say: 'That's bitter!' For among medicines, there are some that are made with bitter herbs."

(*Buber, Late Masters, p. 163*)

On a much lighter note, the following story tells us how a rabbi sees through a deceptive frame and reframes it in a "positive" way:

The Penitent Who Felt Ashamed

A sinner came to the Rabbi of Roptshitz to atone and learn what penance to do. He was ashamed to confess all his sins to the *tzaddik*, and yet he had to disclose each one, otherwise the rabbi could not prescribe the proper form of atonement.

So the sinner said that one of his friends had done such and such a thing, but had been too ashamed to come in person

> and had commissioned him to go and find out for him the purification for every one of his sins.
>
> Rabbi Naftali looked smilingly into the man's sly and intense face. "Your friend," he said, "is a fool. He could have easily come to me himself and pretended to represent someone else who is ashamed to come in his own person."
>
> (*Buber, Late Masters, p. 196*)

The double message exposing the sinner's reframe is right on the mark. On one hand, the rabbi is saying "Your friend is a fool," and the "friend" of course, is the sinner himself. On the other hand, the rabbi is in effect telling the sinner that he sees right through his deception, which is niftily revealed in the sentence, "Rabbi Naftali looked smilingly into the man's sly and intense face."

The next story is about a Hasid who reframed the meaning of his charity-giving and was hoist by his own petard with the "help of God," who accepted the reframe in slightly altered form, with disastrous consequences for the "charitable" Hasid:

The Recipient

> A man who lived in the same town as Rabbi Zusya saw that he was very poor. So each day he put twenty pennies into the little bag in which Zusya kept his phylacteries, so that he and his family might buy the necessities of life. From that time on, the man grew richer and richer. The more he had, the more he gave Zusya; and the more he gave Zusya, the more he had.
>
> But once he recalled that Zusya was a disciple of the Great Maggid, and it occurred to him that if what he gave the disciple was so lavishly rewarded, he might become even more prosperous if he made presents to the master himself. So he traveled to Mezeritch and induced Rabbi Dov Baer to accept a substantial gift from him.
>
> From then on, his means shrank until he had lost all the profits he had made during the more fortunate period. He took his trouble to Rabbi Zusya, told him the whole story, and asked him what his present predicament was due to. For had not the rabbi himself told him that his master was immeasurably greater than he?

> Zusya replied: "Look! As long as you gave and did not bother to whom, whether to Zusya or another, God gave to you and did not bother to whom. But when you began to seek out especially noble and distinguished recipients, God did exactly the same."
>
> *(Buber, Early Masters, p. 238)*

The cleverest reframe can be found is the following story, which is unsurpassed for sheer wit:

A Diplomatic Answer

> An adherent of the Lizensker *Tzaddik* left him and became a follower of the Lubliner Rabbi. The Lizensker soon after was passing through the town where his former Hasid resided, and he asked him the reason for his departure. The clever Hasid responded: "You were too lofty of mind, Rabbi, for my understanding. It seemed to me wise first to climb upon the shoulders of your disciple, and from this point, to make the attempt to reach your heights."
>
> *(Newman, Maggidim and Hasidim, p. 10)*

THE ROLE OF GOD IN REFRAMING

Hasidism's emphasis on *kavvana* (intention as a crucial element of religious life and service to God) has been described in considerable detail. This is one reason why Hasidim became extraordinarily adept at reframing every act to discover within it positive (divine) connotations. In every Hasidic interaction, God is either a vocal or a silent partner. He participates in every event and is the lodestar to the reframe. God represents the Hasid's higher self, his soul, and so in every action it is important to discover one's soul, which is connected to the Divine Spirit. Obeying and following God means leading the best possible moral life, and this is done by attributing to *all* behavior God's presence and guidance. The Hasid can thus discover within the most sinful, destructive, painful, or suffering behavior a positive manifestation of God.

Faith and trust in God constitute a constant support for the Hasid on which he can always lean. God is always there. Knowing that He is always there for you spills over into having faith in yourself. And that faith is critical for overcoming obstacles and getting on in life. Modern secular man has eliminated this "shepherd" and has only the "self," on which he never ceases working. So it is through God that the Hasid perfects his higher self and purifies his motives, and it is God on Whom he leans for support:

Abuse and Forbearance

> The Kobriner Rabbi related that in his boyhood a year of famine had occurred, and the poor wandered from village to village to beg food from the Jewish residents. A number of them came to his mother's home, and she prepared the oven to bake for them. Some of the beggars, growing impatient, began to abuse her with their words, and the distressed woman started to weep. Her small son, the future rabbi, said to his mother:
>
> "Why should you be troubled by their abuse? Does not this help you to aid them with a pure heart, and perform a good deed in perfection of spirit? On the other hand, had the poor praised and blessed you, the good deed would be less praiseworthy, since you might have performed it to gain their praises, and not entirely in obedience to the Lord's command and for the sake of His service."
>
> (*Newman, The Hasidic Anthology, p. 9*)

This little tale is a paradigm of the Hasidic story, for it stresses a fundamental Hasidic belief: that people ought to behave and think and feel as if they are serving the Lord and carrying out His commandments. What happened here is that the poor and hungry were becoming more and more ill-tempered at having to wait for a meal that was being prepared for them. It is difficult for people who have lived under conditions of extreme deprivation for a long time not to become upset in this situation. At the moment when a deprived person seems closest to getting long-neglected needs fulfilled, any delay becomes intolerable and the deprived person becomes even more distraught and angry, like a prisoner who is about to be freed but is not.

The woman who is preparing food for the poor wanderers becomes very upset at their abuse. Her son, however, reframes that abusive behavior by refocusing his mother's attention away from the abuse she is receiving to the godly service she is performing. He supports her by telling her the abuse makes her service purer and more praiseworthy. Don't take the abuse personally. God is with you even more solidly!

The young man, who is to become a renowned rabbi, goes even further in helping his mother reframe the abusive behavior. Now the abusive behavior becomes a very positive act because it helps his mother to aid the poor with a purer spirit. How can this be? The danger lurking here is that, in helping the poor, she might have been praised instead of abused by them and, being praised, could have changed the meaning of her charitable act, turned it into something based on the desire to get praise rather than the need to do it solely because it is carrying out God's will despite the praise (or the abuse). Carrying out the good deed is morally right in itself, and has its own reward.

So here we have an excellent example of how abuse, a bad thing, is converted into something positive with a little shift in focus (and help from God). It cannot be stressed too often that, from the Hasidic point of view, exchanges between people and between Hasid and God, are not based on calculated *quid pro quos*. One does not expect any return for a good deed. One learns to act morally as an end in itself, because that is what God wants. That is why reframing is knitted into so much Hasidic teaching and behavior. It is the psychological mechanism for transforming the motivation for behavior from a narrow focus on rewards received to a larger framework of faith and service to God and, by natural extension, to other people as a good in itself that requires no reward:

For Himself in the World-to-Come

The Neshchizer Rabbi related the following: "Late at night, a man came to the home of Rabbi Liber in Berditchev and asked for lodging. Rabbi Liber extended him a gracious welcome and began to arrange a bed for the guest. The man asked him: "Why do you trouble yourself to arrange my bed?"

Rabbi Liber replied: "It is not for your sake, but for my own that I am doing this."

(*Newman, The Hasidic Anthology, p. 185*)

The Hasidic method of reframing is to enlarge the way one sees behavior and events, to move away from a view based on mundane calculation rooted in base human concerns toward one that places the divine presence (often implicitly) at the center of every event. This enlargement redirects the individual away from egotistical intentions and reasons for doing anything and toward the higher motivation of serving God. Fundamentally, this means that the moral responsibility of concern for others comes first, and self-interests are a secondary consideration:

A Cow's Ascension to Heaven

Before Rabbi Mayer Premishlaner became known as a "rebbe," he was exceedingly poor, and his livelihood was obtained from a cow whose milk he sold among the neighbors. It was the rabbi's unvarying custom to save money each week and to distribute it for Sabbath among the poor.

Once he was unable to save anything. Without hesitation, he slaughtered the cow and gave away the meat to the poor. His wife arose in the morning and could not find the cow. She ran to Rabbi Mayer crying bitterly that the cow was missing.

Rabbi Mayer answered: "The cow is not missing; she has gone up to Heaven."

(*Newman, The Hasidic Anthology, p. 134*)

From a broader philosophical point of view, we can see that at the heart of the Hasidic use of framing is the struggle between the sacred and the profane. This was Hasidism's way of elevating every action and its meaning from calculated *quid-pro-quo* phenomenon to one that transcended self-concern and centered about concern for God and, through God, for others. In a very significant way, the Hasidim recognized the tremendous drive, encouraged by capitalism, for egotistical expansion at the cost of less devotion to God and fulfillment of His commandments. The purpose of the reframe was to reorient the Hasid toward his higher self, which was always performing God's service to the fullest.

How the Hasidim used reframing on themselves to reorient themselves more fully to God is beautifully revealed in this brief story:

Without the World-to-Come

> Once the spirit of the Baal Shem was so oppressed that it seemed to him that he would have no part in the World-to-Come.
>
> Then he said to himself: "If I love God, what need have I of a coming world!"
>
> (*Buber, Early Masters, p.* 52)

That, in a nutshell, is the whole Hasidic enterprise! "If I love God, what need have I of anything else?" To love God is to be like God; and to be like God is to live according to your higher self, your soul, which has a direct main-line connection to God and His spirit. This is the Hasidic answer to ontological anxiety: "I love God." All concerns, doubts, fears and egotistical strivings can be overcome by viewing the picture of one's life in the proper godly frame. Any event which brings out the worst in you becomes an opportunity for creating the best frame of all: a greater appreciation of God and a more humane you!

To the Hasid, love of God means conducting one's life with a heart full of joy and love and concern for others. Thus, the art of reframing is central among the Hasidim for connecting man and God. Faith in God leads to faith in oneself and this in turn leads to the confidence to be able to achieve what one wants in life. This refers not only to individuals, but to a people as a whole. Whenever there is a loss of faith in God, there is a loss of confidence in oneself. The two are inextricably intertwined: Faith in God leads to faith in oneself, lack of faith in God leads to self-doubt. The Hasidic outlook on man's relation to God can be interpreted as man's relation to his higher self; that is, to the virtuous, moral person one wants to be in life and to the laws according to which he wants to conduct his life.

This idea of looking to God first—for the individual as well as the whole people—whenever there is a breakdown in self-confidence or morale is beautifully illustrated in the following story:

The Battle against Amalek

Once Rabbi Pinhas of Koretz felt confused about his faith in God, and could think of no way to help himself except to travel to the Baal Shem. Then he heard that the master had just arrived in Koretz. Full of happiness, he ran to the inn. There he found a number of Hasidim gathered about the Baal Shem Tov, and he was expounding to them the verse in the Scriptures in which the hands Moses held up in the hour of struggle against Amalek are spoken of as being *emuna*, that is, trusting and believing. "It sometimes happens," said the Baal Shem, "that a man grows confused about his faith. The remedy for this is to implore God to strengthen his faith. For the real harm Amalek inflicted on Israel was to chill their belief in God through successful attack. That was why Moses taught them to implore God to strengthen their faith, by stretching to Heaven his hands which were, in themselves, like trust and faith. And this is the only thing that matters in the hour of struggle against the power of evil." Rabbi Pinhas heard, and his hearing of it was in itself a prayer, and in the very act of this prayer he felt his faith grow strong.

(*Buber, Early Masters, p. 60*)

This is another example of the extremely strong bias of Hasidism toward the motivational or psychological aspect of behavior rather than toward the results of behavior. The analogy to Moses and the struggle of the Israelites against Amalek, is made to show that the outcome—in this case a defeat—is always secondary to the impact of the event upon the individual's and the nation's spirit. Any defeat can be dealt with, as long as one recognizes that one needs to maintain faith and confidence in oneself.

At the beginning of the story Rabbi Pinhas was confused about his faith and didn't know what to do about his confusion. This is what the Baal Shem had to dissect and heal. The Hasidic faith in God is the fundamental ground upon which all Hasidic values and behavior are premised. One first turns to God with problems, defeats, confusion, doubt, etc. It is not the outcome itself but the meaning of an action that is the key. And this is what Rabbi Pinhas had forgotten. The worst thing that can happen to anyone as a result of a loss or a feeling of confusion is to be immobilized to the point where he cannot reassert his faith in God. This is the key.

When one begins to doubt the fundamental tenet of faith in God, there is no way to resolve the doubt, except by strengthening one's faith. When a crisis in faith leads to an individual's questioning whether he can restore his faith simply by demonstrating more faith in God, then that person is in deep, deep trouble. What he needs then is precisely what the Baal Shem prescribed.

Rabbi Pinhas's crisis was caused by his failure to draw upon his reserves to overcome his breakdown of faith. The Baal Shem enables him to "see" this by drawing upon the story of Moses and Amalek. Here the attention is drawn away from the military defeat toward the much more dangerous defeat of the faith in God. The danger for Rabbi Pinhas lay in creating a vicious circle that only would deepen his crisis and hasten his personal breakdown.

The story implies another way to overcome one's confusion about faith in God and escape the closed loop. That way is to associate with those who have faith. Active passionate listening to another person's prayer is in itself "a prayer" and a way to return to God and faith. When someone is in trouble, what he can get most from someone else is a feeling of confidence through a faith in God. That is why it is so important to have a *minyan*, a quorum of ten, for worship. Self-confidence through faith in God leads the individual to secure the necessary technical help and resources required to get on with life in a way that is commensurate with that person's highest ideals.

Reframes, then, were used by the Hasidic rabbis to return man to God. They would take the most ordinary situation and, through striking metaphors and images, show that nothing is what it appears to be; that what is really lacking is not enough devotion, faith and heartfelt prayer to God.

The rabbis strove mightily to counter the rising pursuit of material wealth with the "logically" superior richness of the spiritual life:

Why the Pious Are Poor

The Besht was asked why the pious are poorer than the impious. In reply he narrated the following parable:

"A king desired to please his loyal courtiers and announced that each would be granted his particular wish. Some asked for honors; others asked for wealth. But one of them said: 'My wish is to speak to the king three times a day.'"

"We, the pious, prefer communion with the Lord thrice daily above all honors and riches, and God grants us our wish."

(*Newman, The Hasidic Anthology, p. 323*)

Profit and Enjoyment

Said the Besht: "The man who anticipates the gain of a large profit finds little enjoyment in his food. Likewise one who appreciates spiritual riches will find no pleasures in worldliness."

(*Newman, The Hasidic Anthology, p. 514*)

Joy in Poverty

Said the Porissover: "If a man is poor and meek, it is easy for him to be joyful, inasmuch as he has nothing to guard against losing."

(*Newman, The Hasidic Anthology, p. 324*)

The Choice of Poverty

Said Rabbi Nahum Chernobyler: "Between poverty and wealth, I always choose poverty. It is the best shield against egotism and against every evil of the spirit. It is the least costly, the most easily attainable; it need not struggle against jealousy and competition; it need answer no questions or suspicions; it is understood without comments and without explanations. I beg of you, my good friends not to deprive me of this great treasure."

(*Newman, The Hasidic Anthology, p. 324*)

Many of the early Hasidic rabbis literally practiced what they preached. On Friday, after providing for the basic necessities, the Baal Shem would distribute to the poor all the remaining money in his household.

The rabbis also militated against the profanation of the spiritual life:

The Crowded House of Prayer

Once, the Baal Shem stopped on the threshold of a House of Prayer and refused to go in. "I cannot go in," he said. "It is crowded with teachings and prayers from wall to wall and from floor to ceiling. How could there be room for me?" And when he saw that those around him were staring at him and did not know what he meant, he added: "The words from the lips of those whose teaching and praying do not come from hearts lifted to heaven cannot rise; they fill the house from wall to wall and from floor to ceiling."

(*Buber, Early Masters, p. 73*)

This story points to another important function of the reframe: to show how behavior can mask the lack of wholehearted meaningfulness. Since behavior is not as important for Hasidim as the intention behind it, they always went beyond the surface of an issue; and they were never fooled by the appearance of some act that seemed right but lacked inner conviction.

What could be more holy than a crowded synagogue full of praying people? But one has to listen to how the prayers are being said and how the service is communicated to God. Saying the words of the prayer is not the same as reaching to God with one's heart. Ritual certainly can help in bringing out heartfelt feelings to God, but ritual can also serve as a mask for unauthentic feelings and intentions. The Baal Shem in this story objectifies this split between ritual and its lack of inner conviction and commitment by pointing out that this prayer is not going anywhere (literally and figuratively). All of this prayer has remained down below, because God will neither listen to nor accept prayers which are not from the heart. So it is impossible for the Baal Shem Tov to go into the synagogue because it is all stuffed up with "profane" prayers that have nowhere to go. This reframe redirects the congregants away from complacently mimicking the words of prayer without inner commitment and faith and makes them pay attention to the Divine Presence in the prayers.

Reframing, as we see in this tale, is a very powerful psychological device by which the rabbis reenergize their followers to overcome the discrepancy between mechanical ritual and heartfelt faith and to make the service to God a vibrant, meaningful encounter.

A vast area of reframing is concerned with reframing the meanings of prayers and biblical passages to reinforce key Hasidic values. One such value we have emphasized throughout this book has been self-fulfillment. The Hasidim were staunch believers in individualism, self-reliance, and "God helps those who help themselves." They emphasized the uniqueness of each individual:

Themselves

> The Baal Shem said:
>
> "We say: 'God of Abraham, God of Isaac, and God of Jacob,' for Isaac and Jacob did not base their work on the searching and service of Abraham; they themselves searched for the unity of the Maker and His service."
>
> (*Buber, Early Masters, p. 48*)

Finally, the supreme importance of a person's integrity is no more beautifully expressed than in the following reframing of one of our oldest commandments:

Thou Shalt Not Delude Thyself

The first time that Reb Yehiel Meir of Gostynin went to study at the feet of Reb Menahem Mendel of Kotzk, it was Shavuot, when the Ten Commandments are read from the Torah and expounded.

On his return home his father-in-law challenged him: "Do you think it was really worth going all the way to Kotzk? Why, did they receive the Torah differently over there?"

"Of course," replied the young man.

"How is that?" asked his father-in-law.

"You tell me," returned Reb Yechiel Meir. "How were you taught to interpret the commandment, 'You shall not steal'?"

"Simply and literally," said his father-in-law. "It means that a man must not steal from his fellow."

"But with us in Kotzk," said Reb Yehiel Meir, "this commandment means something else: 'You shall not steal *from yourself*!'"

(*Zevin, A Treasury of Hasidic Tales on the Torah, Vol. II, p. 431*)

8

Confusion Techniques and Trance

God's Back

Concerning the verse in the Scriptures: "And thou shalt see My back; but My face shall not be seen," the Rabbi of Kotzk said: "Everything puzzling and confused people see, is called God's back. But no man can see His face, where everything is in harmony."

(*Buber, Late Masters, p. 275*)

INTRODUCTION

Like every people on earth, Jews value the familiar and the strange, the old and the new, the established and the original. All of us need stability and security; the problem arises when that becomes the end-all and be-all of life. Many of us, unfortunately, lead lives of weary, superficial redundancy. The rabbis were constantly confronted with the challenge of making the familiar strange, and the strange familiar. Often they simply shocked their followers in order to extricate them from stale outlooks and routines.

THE APPRECIATION OF THE NEW AND THE ORIGINAL

Jews have to be surprised by a new twist to an old problem, idea or strategy. It adds zest to life and is so highly valued in itself that it has accrued considerable status, even though it can also be impractical and even threatening. The story, "In His Father's Footsteps" (see page 22), offers a novel response to the unsolvable paradox of being imitative and original at the same time. When asked why he does not do as his father, the *tzaddik*, did, Rabbi Noah replies: "I do just as my father did: He did not imitate and I do not imitate."

Rabbi Noah artfully crafted his response in a way which his followers "could not refuse:" Rabbi Noah was following his father; his father did not imitate others; Rabbi Noah was following his father and not following his father; doing his own thing and following his father at the same time. Rabbi Noah was teaching his disciples a powerful lesson: that the way to follow him was to imitate him in this very important respect—namely, *not to imitate him*!

The principle of individual creativity is so important that Hasidic rabbis have gone out of their way to avoid giving specific answers to problems presented to them by their followers. It was more important to respond in a way that forced the seeker of help to go inside himself and find his own strategy for solving the problem. The single most important part of that strategy is building up the faith in yourself, so that you have the resources to resolve your problem creatively. And this is communicated to a person with a problem by the rabbi's insisting on not telling him what to do.

In countless ways, the rabbis confronted their followers with the idea that, fundamentally, everyone must solve his own problems:

The Power of "Falsehood"

A Hasid was asked by the Kobriner: "Where is your aged father?"

"On the way to Kobrin," replied the Hasid.

"How old is he?" asked the rabbi.

"Seventy years old," was the response.

"How far is it from your city to Kobrin?" asked the rabbi.

"Sixty miles," said the Hasid.

The rabbi turned to his disciples and said: "Observe how great is the power of falsehood. It attracts a man of seventy years to walk sixty miles to visit me!"

(*Newman, The Hasidic Anthology, p. 489*)

From One Another

A Hasid who was an intimate of the Alexanderer, asked him why he did not admit the Hasidim who came to him until many hours had elapsed. The rabbi replied: "As long as they wait in the vestibule, they talk among themselves on *Hasidut,* and they learn from one another. But what can they learn from me?"

(*Newman, The Hasidic Anthology, p. 271*)

Reading Our Soul

The true spiritual leader need not read the souls of his adherents. He should instruct them so that they can read their own souls and eject all that is spurious.

(*Newman, Maggidim and Hasidim, p. 99*)

Comprehension Will Follow

Said the Hafetz Hayyim: "If you have commenced a study that is worthwhile and do not comprehend the theme of your research, do not fail to continue your application, for in the end comprehension will come. Does the storekeeper who has sold nothing on one day fail to open his store the next day?"

(*Newman, Maggidim and Hasidim, p. 175*)

A Habitual Visitor

Said Rabbi Isaac Ziditchover: "When a man visits me for the first time, I give him my blessing and I bid him farewell. When he visits me a second time, I allow my gaze to penetrate his inmost being, and I scrutinize him thoroughly. When he visits me a third time, I carry him on my shoulders."

(*Newman, Maggidim and Hasidim, p. 243*)

The point of view stressed in the stories above cannot be emphasized too strongly. From the rabbis' point of view, it was much more important for their followers to struggle to define *their own* problems and find *their own* answers than for a rabbi to find *the* answer. And that is why so many of the Hasidic stories seem so strange to our ears—we are so accustomed for advisors to give all kinds of solutions and answers to someone seeking help. The Hasidim looked down upon the *eitzeh geber*—the advice-giver. The *eitzeh geber* was often looked upon as an arrogant and lofty person who felt superior to the one he was giving advice to. Today, we know that giving advice helps the person giving the advice and rarely the person to whom advice is given. And the reason for this is that we know that the "solution" is not so much getting a specific formula or answer, but emerges from the individual struggling with different strategies based on his own experience for working through his problems.

CONFUSION: THE IMPORTANCE OF GETTING STUCK

One of the most important tools in the kit of techniques used by psychologists today is to confuse the client so that he/she begins thinking about more ideas and ways to resolve the confusion and get onto a new track for working on the problem. Light can enter only where darkness has been. Of course, one must be careful with clients so as not to confuse them to the point where they are so bewildered that they become paralyzed.

Confusion techniques are used to obtain three main results:

- They derail the client from using his usual methods of seeing the world and working at his problems.
- They prompt a person to dig into himself for new connections and come up with fresh approaches to old troubles.

- They shake up the client in such a way that it is hard for him to give up thinking about his problem or to stop figuring out different ways to solve it.

RIGHT BRAIN-LEFT BRAIN

Contemporary right brain-left brain theory helps explain how we react to mysteries and puzzles and confusion generally. The left brain works by logic and in sequence, in a digital, one-two-three fashion. Its hallmark is the syllogism. Most of us spend a great deal of our working time utilizing the left side of the brain to arrange and order the day and do our work efficiently.

The right side of the brain works more with pictures, and its archetypical mode of functioning resembles the putting together of a picture puzzle: that is, working from the parts to the whole and suddenly getting a glimpse of what the composite picture is and how the various parts fit into one another. The function of the right side of the brain is to put together complex bits very quickly, like a street person sizing up another individual and trying to find out what makes him tick: He notes the other fellow's tone of voice, gestures, the way *he* looks back, etc., and quickly assembles a picture of what that fellow is and how he can best deal with him. Fantasy, dreams, musings, going off into space—all kinds of trances—are manifestations of the right side of the brain at work.

Now this split brain theory emphasizes that, although the left side of the brain would like to deal with all issues in a digital, logical, sequential way and is a "bully" over the right brain, it can be overcome when it gets "puzzled." Then, it seems, one switches to the right side of the brain and it begins to make all kinds of associations to try to figure out a way to resolve the puzzle. The idea behind all this is that, in the process of discovering new ways of thinking, feeling, and acting, one first gets stuck—which forces the right brain to take over and make every possible association until some new path "pops" into your head.

Characteristically, the rabbis framed this concept in a religious context:

Our Final Aim

Said Rabbi Bunam: "Two merchants go to the Leipzig Fair. One goes by a direct route, another by an indirect, but both reach the same destination. Likewise, the aim of service to God is to attain holiness, and to arrive at the point where we make God's will our own. Hence, as long as we reach this point, it makes no difference how long we have served the Lord. One may die young or in the prime of life and become just as holy as one who has died in old age. We are taught by the Talmud: 'It is the same whether one does much or little, so long as he has aimed to do God's will.'"

(*Newman, The Hasidic Anthology, p. 171*)

Depend upon Yourself

Said the Hafetz Hayyim: "There are two kinds of heat: the heat of the fire, and the heat of an object near the fire. The latter will grow cold if it is removed from proximity to the fire. From this we can learn that a man should not depend upon his rabbi to kindle his warmth of devotions; he should be a rabbi by virtue of his own enkindlement, and he should maintain his religious observances even in the absence of a rabbi."

(*Newman, Maggidim and Hasidim, p. 262*)

The Hasidic stories reveal a great many puzzles, mysteries, magical events and sheer shock—all of which seem to upset the rational left side of the brain and "free the juices" to flow to the right side of the brain. Here is a good example of a story that is guaranteed to get you stuck and start you figuring out a "new" solution:

The Teaching of the Soul

Rabbi Pinhas often cited the words: "A man's soul will teach him," and explained these words: "There's no man that is not incessantly being taught by his soul."

One of his disciples asked: "If this is so, why don't men obey their souls?"

"The soul teaches incessantly," Rabbi Pinhas explained, "but it never repeats."

(*Buber, Early Masters, p. 121*)

This is a story to ponder; it could lead to as many interpretations as people who think about it. This story forces you to make all kinds of associations as you wonder: What does it mean that one's soul is incessantly talking to oneself but never repeats itself? What does it mean to have a soul talk to you? And how does a soul teach? And what does it mean that the reason we don't obey the soul is that the soul teaches us only once, despite its incessant teaching?

If the soul is always telling us something that we don't know consciously, then the problem is not so much that we have a soul that talks to us, but that we resist listening to our soul (and our subconscious!). Part of this difficulty with listening to our soul may be that it never stops talking—it runs on and on and on and on. To obey the soul is to listen and understand what another part of us may not want to hear—that we must apply the teachings of the soul to our actual behavior.

What Rabbi Pinhas is telling us, in the broadest sense, is that learning is not only going over what you have already read or heard. True learning also involves developing new associations and combinations—what we call today creativity, innovation, inventiveness, originality. Many scientists, artists, and scholars have talked about solutions to their problems coming from an unconscious part of themselves. It works its way mysteriously through the person and suddenly presents him with a new way of seeing or thinking or feeling. What Rabbi Pinhas is saying here is: Open yourself up to these ideas and thoughts that are coming from your unconscious mind, your soul. Pay attention! It is always telling us some new idea. Discovering a new path is not the problem as much as putting it into action, that is, "materializing" the thought or feeling. And it only tells you once!

Without Hearing or Feeling

Rabbi Dov Baer of Mezeritch said: "When I am discoursing on a subject of Torah I neither hear nor feel the words I am speaking. They issue from my mouth without my knowledge or help. As soon as I hear myself talking, I stop."

(*Newman, Maggidim and Hasidim, p. 207*)

THE REALITY OF THE UNREAL

The Hasidic belief that the inner world of feelings and motivations is as real as manifest reality (and perhaps even more important) became the basis for teaching about spirituality in contradictory, paradoxical, confusing and sometimes humorous ways that "made sense":

Through the Hat

Once, Rabbi Mikhal visited a city where he had never been before. Soon some of the prominent members of the congregation came to call on him. He fixed a long gaze on the forehead of everyone who came and then told him the flaws in his soul and what he could do to heal them. It got around that there was a *tzaddik* in the city who was versed in reading faces and could tell the quality of the soul by looking at the forehead. The next visitors pulled their hats down to their noses. "You are mistaken," Rabbi Mikhal said to them. "An eye that can see through the flesh can certainly see through the hat."

(*Buber, Early Masters, p. 142*)

The importance of not achieving a goal is especially important in divine matters. Note how beautifully the Yehudi paces his student and gains his support as he reframes "a not-finding" into a compelling demonstration of how one may discover a much larger truth:

The Road to Perfection

Once, the Yehudi was asked to examine thirteen-year-old Hanokh (later the Rabbi of Alexander), in the Talmud. It took the boy an hour to think over the passage which had been assigned to him before he could expound it. When he had done,

> the *tzaddik* cupped his hand around Hanokh's cheek and said: "When I was thirteen, I plumbed passages more difficult than this in no time at all, and when I was eighteen, I had the reputation of being a great scholar in the Torah. But one day, it dawned on me that man cannot attain to perfection by learning alone. I understood what is told about our father Abraham: that he explored the sun, the moon, and the stars, and did not find God, and how in this very not-finding the presence of God was revealed to him. For three months, I mulled over this realization. Then I explored until I, too, reached the truth of not-finding."
>
> (*Buber, Late Masters*, p. 224)

Not-finding God makes one's faith in God much more compelling—as is true with every unfulfilled fantasy!

A very clever pun on "nothing," a topic that preoccupied the Hasidic mind, is used in the following story:

Nothing at All

> They asked Rabbi Aaron what he had learned from his teacher, the Great *Maggid*. "Nothing at all," he said. And when they pressed him to explain what he meant by that, he added: "The nothing-at-all is what I learned. I learned the meaning of nothingness. I learned that I am nothing at all, and that I am, notwithstanding."
>
> (*Buber, Early Masters*, pp. 198–199)

Rabbi Aaron certainly learned a lot by learning "nothing at all." Confusing? Not at all! What does he mean when he says he learned "I am nothing at all"? He learned something priceless—humility—that he has no need to boast or be conceited, that he need not be self-aggrandizing because "I am!" What a lucky man!

Hasidim are quick learners, perhaps too quick. After they had mastered the unseen world, they were carried away by the use of abstractions that were thought of as actual, concrete, manifest. This led often, but never exclusively, to their ignoring the importance of the other powerful root of Hasidism—

nature, primitive reality, the everyday mundane objects and events of the world that are every whit as divinely inspired as the spiritual realms:

What He Prayed With

> The Rav once asked his son: "What do you pray with?" The son understood the meaning of the question, namely on what he based his prayer. He answered: "With the verse: 'Every statute shall prostrate itself before Thee.'" Then he asked his father: "And with what do you pray?" He said: "With the floor and the bench."
>
> (*Buber, Early Masters, p. 269*)

A very puzzling story that weaves the real into the unreal and compels the reader to go inside himself for some "solution" is the following:

Playing with a Watch

> A Hasid of Rabbi Pinhas of Kinsk, a grandson of Rabbi Yerahmiel, once came into the master's room and found him lying down and playing with his watch. He was surprised because it was almost noon and the rabbi had not yet prayed. Just then, Rabbi Yerahmiel said to the Hasid: "You are surprised at what I am doing? But do you really know what I am doing? I am learning how to leave the world."
>
> (*Buber, Early Masters, p. 234*)

Now what on earth (or Heaven) is the rabbi doing? He is "lying down . . . playing with his watch . . . had not yet prayed"—and this is helping him "learn how to leave the world"?

Howard Polsky says: "What happened with me and the story 'Playing with a Watch' is that I was puzzled for several days and kept mulling over the relationship between Rabbi Pinhas leaving the world and playing with a watch. Then came the 'aha,' the most elegant resolution imaginable to me: 'Leaving the world' is another way of saying 'time is running out,' and what more obvious aid is possible than a watch which keeps track of 'running' (and 'running out') time. A watch, of course, captures time and is also its eventual victim—there certainly may be some connections, leads—perhaps solutions?

"I liked the idea that Rabbi Pinhas was playing with his watch while he was thinking about such a portentous subject. This juxtaposition of the concrete and the playful, the abstract and the serious makes marvelous spiritual sense."

As the rabbis became more adept at interweaving fantasy and reality, the supernatural and the natural, the outrageous and the logical, the stories began to veer into legends which seemed strangely credible! This was because the phantasmagoria was embedded in a perfectly logical context.

The following two stories are excellent examples of this unique genre, which is a product of the Hasidic penchant for being quite logical about the fantastic:

At the Pond

After the Great *Maggid's* death, his disciples came together and talked about the things he had done. When it was Rabbi Schneur Zalman's turn, he asked them: "Do you know why our master went to the pond every day at dawn and stayed there for a little while before coming home again?" They did not know why. Rabbi Zalman continued: "He was learning the song with which the frogs praise God. It takes a very long time to learn that song."

(*Buber, Early Masters, p. 111*)

Refusal

Those in Heaven wanted to reveal to Rabbi Shlomo of Karlin the language of birds, the language of trees, and the language of the serving angels. But he refused to learn them before finding out of what importance each of these languages was for the service of God. Not until after he had been told this, did he consent to learn them, and then he served God with them also.

(*Buber, Early Masters, p. 275*)

One of the most puzzling aphorisms in the Hasidic literature, a saying by the Kotzker, gave us a lot of mixed pleasure as we mulled over it:

What Cannot Be Imitated

> The Rabbi of Kotzk said:
>
> "Everything in the world can be imitated, except truth. For truth that is imitated is no longer truth."
>
> (*Buber, Late Masters, p. 284*)

This is one of the finest Hasidic expressions of the supreme value of individual autonomy and creativity. The Kotzker's aphorism tells us that, no matter how impressive or compelling any "truth" is that we have read about or heard from others, that truth is, in the end, someone else's, the truth of the person who first conceived it.

Another person's truth cannot be yours, unless you choose to "imitate" it. Then it "is no longer truth."

What a marvelous lesson for us, to find our own "truth," by examining, altering, mending, varying, heightening everything others have told us and making it our own. What a difficult standard to meet for being truthful!

Here is a story with another perplexing aphorism, one that touches on another subject. It is a superb formulation of the essence of prejudice and bigotry:

Infirmity

> A man came to the Rabbi of Kotzk and told him his trouble. "People call me a bigot," he said. "What kind of an infirmity are they ascribing to me? Why a bigot? Why not a pious man?"
>
> "A bigot," the rabbi answered him, "converts the main issue of piety into a side issue, and a side issue into the main issue."
>
> (*Buber, Late Masters, p. 281*)

Modern theories of bigotry stress that the bigot seizes upon some small piece of truth and distorts it out of all proportion. The bigot's strategy is to expand one element so that it overshadows others, while he ignores other, more important elements so that all elements are out of focus.

The Rabbi of Kotzk said all of this with considerable wit: "A bigot converts the main issue in piety into a side issue and a side issue into the main issue." What does this mean?

A bigot is someone who is so obstinately attached to some creed, opinion, or practice as to be illiberal or intolerant of others. A pious person faithfully performs religious duties, but "faithful performance," can be stretched out of proportion by the bigot into rigidity, inflexibility, and inability to compromise, while heartfelt emotional dedication is down played.

Thus the Kotzker has tried to expand his follower's understanding of what has taken place, and perhaps he encouraged his follower to examine his own practices to see whether he who thinks of himself as pious may not be unduly pietistic. The Hasidic rabbis were shrewd, and they knew that what often seemed to be a problem caused by others was actually produced (at least in part) by the behavior of the complaining Hasid.

PARADOXICAL INTERVENTIONS

A paradox is a special kind of contradiction. A paradox, as we will be using the term, is an assertion or sentiment or belief that is seemingly self-contradictory and opposed to common sense and yet may be true "in fact" (i.e., "common-sense fact" rather than proven fact).

At a metaphysical level, paradoxes can be solved by simply stating the apparently contradictory question:

His Heart

> Once Rabbi Bunam was asked: "Have you ever known a *tzaddik* whose heart was broken and crushed and yet sound and whole?" Rabbi Bunam replied. "Yes, I did know such a *tzaddik*. It was Rabbi Moshe of Sasov."
>
> (*Buber, Late Masters, p. 95*)

No paradox apparently is worth worrying about:

Against Worrying

Rabbi Mordecai of Lekhovitz said: "We must not worry. Only one worry is permissible: A man should worry about nothing but worry."

(*Buber, Late Masters, p. 154*)

In other words, don't worry about resolving this riddle; worry only when you begin worrying about resolving it. Thus, as soon as you become aware of worrying, you will recognize how foolish it is and why "only one worry is permissible."

A good example of paradoxical assertion that is immediately solved is the following story:

The Ear That Is No Ear

Rabbi Pinhas said: "In the book, *The Duties of the Heart*, we read that he who conducts his life as he ought should see with eyes that are no eyes, hear with ears that are no ears. And that is just how it is! For often, when someone comes to ask my advice, I hear him giving himself the answer to his question. And that is the way it ought to be."

(*Buber, Early Masters, p. 126*)

This story has a number of interpretations. One is that ideally one "sees" and "hears" with his heart, not his eyes and ears. Another meaning is that, in addition to consulting his own heart (and one does not need eyes and ears to do that), one also consults the supplicant's heart and "listens-in" to the answers he is giving himself. The rabbi is a listener to the Hasid's heart and encourages him to do the same.

The rabbis' extraordinary sensitivity to how their message is received is very modern. Nowadays, every teacher is aware who among his/her students is listening and when. The inner feelings of interest, motivation, and desire are much more important than the physical act of hearing:

Those Who Are to Hear, Hear

Once a great throng of people collected about the Rabbi of Apt to hear his teachings.

"That won't help you," he cried to them. "Those who are to hear, will hear even at a distance; those who are not to hear, will not hear no matter how near they come."

(*Buber, Late Masters, p. 115*)

In general, the creation and solution of paradoxes is a captivating way to involve participants in discovering insights into themselves and others.

A paradox is an apparent contradiction. One part of us, the "left brain," likes order: People and situations and relationships should be neatly categorized as black or white, one thing or another, with as little overlapping as possible. Life, however, is for the most part all mixed up, as are most of us.

In the following story, we like the natural way in which the "contradiction" was neatly resolved with a keener understanding of how we relate, or perhaps should relate to others:

The Window and the Curtain

When young Rabbi Eleazar Koznitz, Rabbi Moshe's son, was a guest in the house of Rabbi Naftali of Roptshitz, he once cast a surprised glance at the window, where the curtains had been drawn. When his host asked the cause of his surprise, he said: "If you want people to look in, then why the curtains? And if you do not want them to, why the window?"

"And what explanation have you found for this?" asked Rabbi Naftali.

"When you want someone you love to look in," said the young rabbi, "you draw aside the curtain."

(*Buber, Late Masters, p. 177*)

"Very discerning," you will say. "Very penetrating and a very wise comparison." The analogy is rather simple, but it is true nevertheless: Each of us has a window and a curtain, and, of course, we reveal ourselves to people we love. That is how love is nourished and grows. Lovers have mutual open windows of vulnerability. Perhaps nations will learn that truth someday.

THE PARADOX AS A NORMATIVE METAPHOR

We have spoken before of paradox as a contradictory situation, idea, or statement which is opposed to common sense, but may nevertheless, be true. The Hasidim became enormously clever at stating initially confusing relationships and suddenly "clearing them up" in a *coup de grace* conclusion:

Gifts

> Rabbi Bunam said to his Hasidim:
>
> "He among you who is concerned with nothing but love is a philanderer; he among you who is nothing but devout is a thief; he among you who is nothing but clever is an unbeliever. Only he who has all these three gifts together can serve God as he should."
>
> (*Buber, Late Masters, p. 250*)

Again, we are back to balance, the golden mean, and what one has turned one's mind into. Any obsession is bad, William Blake notwithstanding. Too much love or sex results inevitably in trifling with others; it is flirtatious. The "nothing but devout" person we see as very hidebound and divorced from others, a "thief" who takes but doesn't give. The "nothing but clever" person is perilously close to becoming a skeptic or worse, a cynic. Qualities that are very self-limiting, even destructive when practiced alone and obsessively, become virtues when practiced together with others.

In this story and the next two, we find an underlying pattern based on the assumption that the reader, along with the characters in the story, have to pick one of two or more alternatives or they will be in an untenable and contradictory situation which they will not be able to maintain.

Usually, the contradiction is resolved through the discovery of a new angle, principle, or insight that satisfactorily encompasses both sides of the contradiction. Sometimes, this resolution is in the story, sometimes it is not. A good example of the resolution of a paradox in a Hasidic tale is the one about Rabbi Noah (p. 22) who was not imitative, yet imitated his father—who did not imitate anyone else.

Often however, two points of view are set up in a way that impels the reader at first to identify with two mutually exclusive viewpoints. More careful consideration, however, leads the reader to reject the either/or position and declare it essentially nonsensical.

The use of contradictions and paradoxes, often uttered in pithy statements, was often quite dazzling. Here are some of our favorites:

Learning Torah

A young man was asked by the Gerer Rabbi if he had learned Torah. "Just a little," replied the youth.

"That is all anyone ever has learned of the Torah," was the Rabbi's answer.

(Newman, *The Hasidic Anthology*, p. 478)

It May Be Harmful

The Hafetz Hayyim once overheard a man's reply to the query addressed to him: "How are things with you?" The man said: "Not bad, but it would not harm me if they were better." The rabbi commented: "How do you know it would not harm you, if things were better with you?"

(Newman, *Maggidim and Hasidim*, p. 106)

Self-Instruction

A man of piety complained to the Besht, saying: "I have labored hard and long in the service of the Lord, and yet I have received no improvement. I am still an ordinary and ignorant person."

The Besht answered: "You have gained the realization that

you are ordinary and ignorant, and this in itself is a worthy accomplishment."

(*Newman, The Hasidic Anthology, p. 429*)

A Greater Offense

Said the Koretzer: "A wise man was asked by his disciples for instruction on how to avoid sin. He replied: 'Were you able to avoid offenses, I fear you would fall into a still greater sin—that of pride.'"

(*Newman, The Hasidic Anthology, p. 354*)

A Man of Wonders

The Lentzner Rabbi declared that the Sassover Rabbi was a man of wonders: He was broken of heart and whole of heart at one and the same time.

(*Newman, The Hasidic Anthology, p. 261*)

Now we may be overstepping the permissible limits of interpretation by suggesting the possibility that in the following story the rabbis are poking fun at the creation of differences that, in the long run, really do not make much of a difference:

The Difference

While the quarrel between the Hasidim of Kotzk and those of Radoshitz was in full swing, Rabbi Yisakhar Baer of Radoshitz once said to a Hasid from Kotzk: "What your teacher believes in is: 'If you can't get over it, you must get under it,' but what I believe in is: 'If you can't get over it, you must get over it anyway.'"

Rabbi Yitzhak Meir of Ger, a disciple and friend of the Rabbi of Kotzk, formulated the difference in another way when a Hasid of the Radoshitzer visited him after his master's death. "The world thinks," said he, "that there was hatred and quarelling between Kotzk and Radoshitz. That is a grave mistake. There was only one difference of opinion: in Kotzk they aimed

> to bring the heart of the Jews closer to their Father in Heaven; in Radoshitz they aimed to bring our Father in Heaven closer to the heart of the Jews."
>
> (*Buber, Late Masters, p. 286*)

An explicit interpretation of the two points of difference might reveal a basic difference of philosophy or technique. Trying a new task *is* different from trying harder with the old method. The implication in the Gerer Rabbi's statement is that bringing God closer to the people means relaxing somewhat the stringent application of religious rules and rituals; bringing the heart of Jews closer to God implies giving them more support to carry out all the commandments.

We now raise a deeper question about these differences: Why is this an either/or proposition? Why is it not possible to alternate or even synthesize the differences? In other words, we are raising the whole question of "false paradoxes" and the importance of challenging the apparent differences as hardly mutually exclusive and therefore not irreconcilable.

In contrast to the above story, which incidentally we found to be applicable to every conflict we could think of, (see Chapter 17, "A Story for All Occasions"), the following story (first cited in the Introduction) is a legitimate paradox that has an insightful resolution:

How to Become Spiritual

> In the days of the Great *Maggid*, a well-to-do merchant, who refused to have anything to do with Hasidic teachings, lived in Mezeritch. His wife took care of the shop, and he himself spent only two hours a day in it. The rest of the time he sat over his books in the House of Study.
>
> One Friday morning, he saw two young men in the House of Study whom he did not know. He asked them where they were from and why they had come, and he was told they had journeyed a great distance to see and hear the Great *Maggid*. The well-to-do merchant decided he would also go to his house. He did not want to sacrifice any of his study time for this, so he did not go to his shop on that day.

> The *maggid*'s radiant face affected the merchant so strongly that, from then on, he went to his home frequently and ended up attaching himself to the *maggid* altogether. From that time on, he had one business failure after another, until he was quite poor.
>
> The merchant complained to the *maggid* that he had become impoverished since he had become his disciple. The *maggid* answered: "You know what our sages say: 'He who wants to grow wise, let him go south; he who wants to get rich, let him go north.' Now what shall one do who wants to grow both rich and wise?"
>
> The man did not know what to reply. The *maggid* continued: "He who studies makes of himself nothing and grows spiritually, and spirit does not occupy space. He can be north and south at the same time."
>
> These words moved the merchant's heart, and he cried out: "Then my fate is sealed."
>
> "No," said the *maggid*. "You have already begun."
>
> (*Buber, Late Masters, pp. 108–109*)

How is the reader to understand this? Here we have a merchant who becomes so involved in study and the teachings of the *maggid*, that he neglects his business and becomes poor. The merchant-turned-scholar complains that he is now poor.

The *maggid* answers him with a riddle. A man who wants to be wise goes south, a man who wants to be rich goes north. Is it then required of a person to choose either wisdom or riches? How is it possible to go in two directions at the same time? How is it possible to use your time so that at one and the same time you can continue to be rich—tend to your business—and grow wiser, spend time with studies? It would seem that "either/or" is perfectly applicable here, as long as one remains at the everyday, mundane level of thinking and believing that one cannot do both. It would not be possible to be in the store and in the House of Study at the same time. Apparently, the way to transcend the contradictions of the everyday world is to turn to the spiritual world, since anything is possible there.

What does it mean to turn spiritual and be able to be in two places at the same time? One explanation is that what is important is what's going on within a person, no matter what space the person is occupying physically. If one is spiritual, he will be so whether he works in his shop or sits in the House of Study. If one is not spiritual then, as the Hasidim see it, he will not be fulfilling a proper service to himself and to God.

There is another profound lesson underneath this. To become spiritual also means to become "nothing," much in the same way that we learned in numerous stories that God comes from nothing, is nothing and therefore is everything. The merchant's complaint that he was becoming poor meant that he had considerable ego left. From the Hasidic point of view, "poverty is a state of mind." "If a poor man realized the great good he acquires from his poverty, he would dance with joy." The merchant certainly must have had enough wealth, but he was worried about losing material things and the *maggid's* answer was for him to become more spiritual, perhaps lose everything and, by becoming nothing, become more spiritual and gain everything. Once he was spiritual, he could be everywhere at the same time.

This point is made dramatically in the last sentence. The merchant still does not quite understand what the *maggid* is talking about. What the merchant sees ahead of him is more poverty, because he is so preoccupied with his studies. The message continues to escape the merchant, who has not as yet, attained a level of learning which is spiritual. The *maggid* realizes that and assures him that now he is beginning to understand what it means to be a spiritual learner, not merely gathering more information, but learning so that the spirit of God enters his soul.

The *maggid* reassures him this has already begun, because he is now beginning to grapple with it. This is another fundamental Hasidic tenet: It is not as important to master any riddle or problem as it is to continue to struggle with it. And now, since the words of the *maggid* have entered "the merchant's heart," that means they will now gradually affect his actions and his soul. He is definitely on his way, because now he is struggling with the issue of how to be spiritual, which is tantamount to transcending himself. The path to God is strewn with obstacles and difficulties and failures, and the end is more struggle. The true journey to God never ends, and since the struggle is the end, the struggle never ends.

PARADOXICAL INTERVENTION

Up to this point in our discussion of confusion techniques, we have used primarily verbally confusing challenges that were met by transcending the apparent contradictions with verbal reformulations. The Hasidim took great delight in these verbal pyrotechnics.

However, the Hasidim were also very action-oriented and valued highly people who did not dilly-dally, believed in what they were doing and got things done. They believed words often covered up and postponed meaningful actions; and they were extremely suspicious of anyone who spoke too well. Taking action, doing things, was as important as study and prayer:

Credit Account

> A man came to Reb Yisrael of Ruzhin and said: "I am a sinner and want to repent."
>
> "So why don't you?" asked the *tzaddik*.
>
> "Because I don't know how to," said the other.
>
> "So how did you know how to sin?" asked the *tzaddik*.
>
> "First I acted," said the man, "and only later I found out that I had sinned."
>
> "So do the same thing now," said the *tzaddik*. "Repent now, and the accounting will come later."
>
> (*Zevin, A Treasury of Hasidic Tales on the Festivals, pp. 81–82*)

It has often been noted that when someone is encouraged to take a particular action affecting an issue or a problem, he will change his attitude, frequently in line with the action that has been taken. Taking a new action often leads to revelations of new information, which may influence attitudes and subsequent behavior.

Taking action—doing things—is emphasized over and over:

Most Important

Soon after the death of Rabbi Moshe, Rabbi Mendel of Kotzk asked one of his disciples:

"What was most important to your teacher?"

The disciple thought and then replied: "Whatever he happened to be doing at the moment."

(Buber, Late Masters, p. 173)

Now every teacher is well aware of the technique of getting a troubled student busy to distract him from being obsessed with his troubles. The rabbis were also acquainted with this simple technique of reorienting a troubled student or adult:

Look into the Book

A Hasid came to Rabbi Hanokh and wept and complained about some misfortune which had overtaken him.

"When I was in elementary school," the rabbi replied, "and a certain boy began to cry in class, the teacher said to him: 'He who looks into his book stops crying.'"

(Buber, Late Masters, p. 313)

In recent years, psychology has taken giant strides in the development of action prescriptions which are much more artful and deceptive (or "tactfully resourceful," if the latter word disturbs you) and are designed to "break open" problematic behavior by confusing the client and presenting choices that are readily accepted and therapeutic.

Hundreds of years ago, Hasidic rabbis were already utilizing techniques that we have only recently begun to name, define and codify. One of these important techniques is the therapeutic double bind or paradoxical intervention. This is a method of confusing an individual and thereby lowering his conscious resistance and opening up possibilities of new learning, insights and behavior. The paradoxical intervention involves giving an "instruction" to someone to do something or not to do something in such a way that, whether the person does or does not do what the counselor or rabbi has told him, he will still be fulfilling the counselor's prescription.

Let us give you a very homely example of how this technique works. Howard Polsky is an experienced teacher and, like many teachers whose classes are held first thing in the morning, he always had some students who came late repeatedly. He reports: "I used various techniques to stop the latecoming, including interrupting the class and saying hello to them in a wry or sarcastic way. Nothing worked. Those who were regularly late kept coming in late.

"Recently, I tried a paradoxical intervention. When three students came in late together, I announced to the class that I had reconsidered this whole problem of tardiness and now saw it in a whole new light. I told the class that coming late is really an indication of how important the class is to the latecomers, and I mentioned their names. They knew that they would be publicly pointed out and censured and yet, despite that, were willing to weather my caustic remarks and come in late. This means that the class is really important to them, because they are willing to subject themselves to public censure and still come. So I congratulated them for their willingness to come late because that meant that the class was really important to them and I said I would like them to continue coming late because that would be an indication of their commitment to the class and to the work. Of course, everyone laughed about this, including the three latecomers.

"Now the paradoxical bind that I put them in was as follows: They could continue to come late and thereby show their dedication to the class; or they could stop coming late, which would also be showing their dedication to the class. So I had them in this double bind, sometimes referred to as a 'therapeutic double bind,' which means that whatever the person does, the outcome is favorable. Both student *and* teacher can only win."

What this further does is cut down the resistance and rebelliousness that exists in all of us. We all have the urge to be a little deviant and rebellious. The therapeutic double bind reframes this behavior by showing that underlying that behavior is an intention which is just as authentic as nondeviant behavior. In other words, in the above sample, "coming late" now has as much virtue as coming on time because both are indications of a commitment to the class. And that is the important issue.

The three students who were constantly late suddenly stopped coming late and were on time for the rest of the semester. What this meant was that they no longer had an investment in challenging the teacher and resisting him by continuing to rebel.

Most people to some degree resist the controls that others may impose on them. Control and power is part of every relationship and the Hasidic rabbis realized this. They were extremely sensitive to the danger of creating a power conflict about who was in control and thereby losing the opportunity to influence another person's behavior. The rabbis, in all their wisdom, were adept in overcoming resistance to change by bypassing it on a conscious level and addressing the subconscious.

In the pages that follow, we will give many examples of paradoxical interventions used by rabbis, many of which entailed setting up or accentuating internal conflict by taking or not taking a specific course of action. Instead of a conflict between two courses of action, an internal struggle is intensified within the Hasid as a result of his taking a paradoxical course of action.

The following story is a modified paradoxical intervention—perhaps "induced contrast" would be a more apt phrase—for intensifying sensitivity to poor people. The intervention is surprising and psychologically sound:

Rich People's Food

A rich man once came to the Koznitzer *Maggid.*

"What are you in the habit of eating?" the *maggid* asked.

"I am modest in my demands," the rich man replied. "Bread and salt, and a drink of water are all I need."

"What are you thinking of!" the rabbi reproved him. "You must eat roast meat and drink mead, like all rich people." And he did not let the man go until he had promised to do as he said.

Later, the Hasidim asked him the reason for this odd request. "Not until he eats meat," said the *maggid,* "will he realize that the poor man needs bread. As long as he himself eats bread, he will think the poor man can live on stones."

(*Buber, Early Masters, p. 222*)

Because the rabbis were so attuned to the reality of their followers' inner worlds, interventions such as this made considerable psychological sense. The rabbis fully understood that lasting change in behavior could occur only if it were backed up by a psychodynamic change of feeling and values and understanding as well as behavior:

A Novel Penance

"Whatever penance you prescribe, rebbe! Fasts, self-mortification, ascetic exercises, anything—as long as I can atone for my sins!" insisted a certain penitent who had just confessed his long list of transgressions in the hearing of Reb Mordecai of Lekhovitch.

"And will you, in fact, undertake everything I instruct you to do, without turning left or right?" asked the *tzaddik*.

"Every single word!" exclaimed the penitent.

"In that case," said Reb Mordecai, "make sure that every morning you make your breakfast of fine white bread, roast chicken, and a casserole of meat and vegetables. Wash it down with a bottle of good wine—and do exactly the same in the evening. See to it that you sleep in a bed that has a cozy eiderdown, and don't even contemplate undertaking (God forbid!) anything resembling self-mortification. When you have done this for a whole year, come along here and we'll see then what to do next."

The penitent was wonderstruck. He had prepared himself to hear a forbidding list of fasts, and ritual immersions, and ascetic exercises such as rolling in the snow and who knows what else—and here the *tzaddik* had ordered him to wallow in the luxuries of this world! Was it possible that he would ever atone for his sins through such a penance? But there was no alternative: He had to obey the *tzaddik*.

Back at home, he discovered that, whenever he sat down to his rich repast, he was tortured by the same thought: "Here I am, a sinner who has repeatedly rebelled against his Maker;

I have dragged my soul from its heavenly source down into the mire of impurity. How, then, can I delight in the pleasures of This World and pamper myself with choice delicacies? What I deserve is to bite on a mouthful of gravel, to chew bitter herbs!"

At every meal, he would go through this torment, shedding bitter tears and finding no peace. And though he had been a man of robust build, by the time the year was over he had shrunk to a wretched skeleton. Barely did he have the strength to make the long journey to Lekhovitch.

The *tzaddik* took one look at him and said: "Enough."

He then prescribed a different lifestyle for him, and the man completed his days in joy and serenity.

(*Zevin, A Treasury of Hasidic Tales on the Festivals, Vol. 1, pp. 77–78*)

As the reader can readily attest, we have modified the concept of paradoxical intervention and defined it more broadly as an action which is applied to a problematic situation but seems contrary to perceived opinion or opposed to the usual common-sense reaction. And it works!

The following touching story is an example of this kind of paradoxical intervention:

The Rod

Moshe Leib's father was bitterly opposed to the Hasidic way. When he learned that Moshe Leib had left the house without his knowledge and gone to Rabbi Shmelke's House of Study in Nikolsberg, he flew into a rage. He cut a vicious rod and kept it in his room against his son's return. Whenever he saw a more suitable twig on a tree, he cut a new rod which he thought would be more effective and threw the old one away. Time passed and many rods were exchanged. In the course of a thorough house-cleaning, a servant once took the rod up to the attic.

Soon afterward, Moshe Leib asked his teacher's leave to absent himself for a short while and went home. When he saw his father jump up at the sight of him and start on a furious search, he went straight up to the attic, fetched the rod, and laid it down in front of the old man. The latter gazed into the grave and loving face of his son and was won over.

(*Buber, Late Masters, pp. 81–82*)

In this beautiful story, Moshe Leib by his action intensifies the latent conflict in his father which is covered over with rage. The son does not challenge his father's authority, but dramatically reaffirms it; he demonstrates by his action that he is not deceiving him; he shows courage in his willingness to be punished for his disobedience. Above all, the son shows his trust and faith that his father will temper his discipline with love. And finally, the young man displays remarkable psychological insight in weighing the danger of his risky action in choosing love over fear.

The most extreme paradoxical intervention is the use of shock. A shock certainly disturbs one's equilibrium and is unsettling for varying periods of time, depending on a number of variables, including the person's readiness and the severity of impact. Shock is not only physically upsetting, but disturbing to a person's emotional and intellectual faculties.

It seems that the shock most often does not directly produce change, but the resulting instability derails the recipient and opens up new avenues for change. Because it is so risky and may backfire, it is not often used. Nevertheless, it is present in the rabbis' arsenal of techniques. Consider, for example, the following uncanny story:

Of a Hidden Tzaddik

This story is told:

A Hasid of the Rizhyner had a daughter who was afflicted with serious eye trouble which no doctor knew how to cure. Time and again, he begged the rabbi to help him, but no help was granted him. Finally, when the girl was stricken blind, the *tzaddik* said to him, unasked: "Take your daughter to Lvov, and when you get there, wait for the vendors who go about the streets and call out their wares, each with his own singsong cry, for instance: 'Fine pretzels, fresh pretzels!' He whose cry you like best is the one who can heal your daughter."

The Hasid did as he was told and soon discovered the man who sang out his wares most to his liking. He bought a pretzel from him and asked him to bring some to the inn the next day. When the vendor entered his room, the Hasid locked the door, and repeated the words of the Rabbi of Rizhyn. The vendor's eyes snapped, and he shouted: "You let me out of here, or I'll make a heap of bones of you, along with your rabbi." The Hasid opened the door in terror. The man disappeared, but the girl was cured.

(*Buber, Late Masters, p. 65*)

Martin Buber's title, "Of a Hidden *Tzaddik*," intrigues us. The medicine is quite strong, but what is more important is that a cure was effected. Is the pretzel vendor the hidden *tzaddik*? Is the Rabbi of Rizhyn the hidden *tzaddik*? Is the rabbi the vendor *and* the hidden *tzaddik*? In the true spirit of legend, the man disappeared after the miracle. We are left with the awe of the mysterious and, in the words of a story cited earlier in this chapter, it is sufficient to know that the *tzaddik* is hiding to know that he exists.

And if perchance, dear reader, you are still confused, the same principle that applies to what is hidden from you (which, you know now, really is not), can be used to dispel confusion:

In the World of Confusion

They tell this story:

To Rabbi Yisakhar of Volborzh there came a dead man whom he had once known when he was alive and prominent in his community, and he begged the rabbi's help, saying that his wife had died some time ago and now he needed money to arrange for his marriage with another.

"Don't you know," the *tzaddik* asked him, "that you are no longer among the living, that you are in the world of confusion?"

When the man refused to believe him, he lifted the tails of the dead man's coat and showed him that he was dressed in his shroud.

Later, Rabbi Yisakhar's son asked: "Well, if that is so—perhaps I too am in the world of confusion?"

"Once you know that there is such a thing as that world," answered his father, "you are not in it."

(*Buber, Late Masters, p. 182*)

TRANCE

Trance is a phenomenon that appears in many Hasidic stories explicitly and implicitly. It is an altered state of consciousness, actually a subconscious level of functioning. The rabbis and the Hasidim were well aware of the various manifestations of trance in everyday life:

The Scroll of the Torah

Once, a new Torah Scroll was being dedicated in the House of Prayer. Rabbi David Moshe held it in his hands and rejoiced in it. But since it was large and obviously very heavy, one of his Hasidim went up to him and wanted to relieve him of it. "Once you hold it," said the rabbi, "it isn't heavy anymore."

(*Buber, Late Masters, p. 76*)

All of us have experienced in school, synagogue, and other settings our minds drifting off thousands of miles from the matter at hand:

The Absent Ones

Once, after he had recited the Eighteen Benedictions, the Rabbi of Berditchev went up to certain persons in the House of Prayer and greeted them, saying: "Peace be with you," several times over, as though they had just come back from a long journey. When they looked at him in surprise, he said: "Why are you so astonished? You were far away, weren't you? You in a marketplace, and you on a ship with a cargo of grain, and when the sound of praying ceased, you returned, and so I greeted you."

(*Buber, Early Masters, p. 214*)

Not seeing with your eyes open is an everyday parlor-trick effect that any hypnotist can easily induce, but it was somewhat more arcane 200 years ago:

With Open Eyes

Once, Rabbi Levi Yitzhak told the *Maggid* of Koznitz, whose guest he was, that he intended going to Vilna, the center of the opponents of Hasidic teachings, in order to debate with them. "I should like to ask you a question," said the *maggid*. "Why do you go contrary to the custom, in that you recite the Eighteen Benedictions with open eyes?"

"Dear heart," said the Rabbi of Berditchev, "do you think that when I do this I see anything at all?"

"I know very well," the *maggid* replied, "that you see nothing whatsoever, but what will you say to those others when they ask you this question?"

(*Buber, Early Masters, p. 214*)

For athletes today, trance may take the form of "being in the zone"—total concentration and absorption in the action, so that the player and stroke are one. Eugen Herrigel describes this in *Zen and the Art of Archery*. It took six years of practice shooting an arrow six to eight hours a day before the archer merged with the arrow so that they both shot together. This altered state of consciousness was not at all foreign to the Hasidim:

The Perfect Swimmer

When the Rabbi of Lentchna's son was a boy, he once saw Rabbi Yitzhak of Vorki praying. Full of amazement, he came running to his father and asked how it was possible for such a *tzaddik* to pray quietly and simply, without giving any sign of ecstasy.

"A poor swimmer," answered his father, "has to thrash around in order to stay up in the water. The perfect swimmer rests on the tide and it carries him."

(*Buber, Late Masters, p. 199*)

Trance was highly valued as a special gift of grace and harmony:

The Piece of Sugar

It is told:

When Rabbi Shlomo drank tea or coffee, it was his custom to take a piece of sugar and hold it in his hand the entire time he was drinking. Once his son asked him: "Father, why do you do that? If you need sugar, put in in your mouth, but if you do not need it, why hold it in your hand!"

When he had emptied his cup, the rabbi gave the piece of sugar to his son and said: "Taste it." The son put it in his mouth and was very much astonished, for there was no sweetness at all left in it.

Later when the son told this story, he said: "A man, in whom everything is unified, can taste with his hand as if with his tongue."

(*Buber, Early Masters, p. 276*)

One trait that we find most charming among the Hasidim is the ability to poke fun at everything, from the most mundane to the most serious and sacred. In the following story, the disciple who is boasting about his trance capability is gently put in his place by his teacher:

In Youth

Rabbi Mendel once boasted to his teacher, Rabbi Elimelekh, that evenings he saw the angel who rolls away the light before the darkness, and mornings the angel who rolls away the darkness before the light. "Yes," said Rabbi Elimelekh, "in my youth I saw that too. Later on, you don't see those things anymore."

(*Buber, Late Masters, p. 125*)

We believe there are four critical elements in trance which, singly and together, abound in Hasidic stories:

The unquestionable belief in the transcendental, the supernatural, the spiritual—an extraterrestrial world which is quite compatible with and includes altered states of consciousness that are the natural vehicles to and from this "real" other world:

Hasid and Mitnaged

A Hasid of the *tzaddik* of Lekhovitz had a business partner who was a *mitnaged.* The Hasid kept urging him to go to the rabbi with him, but the *mitnaged* was obstinate in his refusal. Finally, however, when they happened to be in Lekhovitz on business, he let himself be persuaded and agreed to go to the *tzaddik*'s for the Sabbath meal.

In the course of the meal, the Hasid saw his friend's face light up with joy. Later, he asked him about it. "When the *tzaddik* ate, he looked as holy as the high priest making the offering!" was the reply. After a while, the Hasid went to the rabbi, much troubled in spirit, and wanted to know why the other had seen something on his very first visit which he, the rabbi's close friend, had not.

"The *mitnaged* must see, the Hasid must believe," answered Rabbi Mordecai.

(*Buber, Late Masters, p. 156*)

A total absorption comes from within the individual with a real or projected phenomenon, be it an image, activity, object, to the point where person and the external phenomenon completely merge. For the Hasidim this, of course, was God:

Between

Concerning the verse in the Scriptures: "I stood between the Lord and you," Rabbi Mikhal of Zlotchov said: "The 'I' stands between God and us. When man says 'I' and encroaches upon the word of his Maker, he puts a wall between himself and God. But he who offers his 'I'—there is nothing between him and his Maker. For it is to him that the words refer: 'I am my beloved's and his desire is toward me.' When my 'I' has become my beloved's, then it is toward me that his desire turns."

(*Buber, Early Masters, p. 149*)

A feeling of self, call it "soul" or "spirit," is able to detach itself from the body and material reality and learns to have an ethereal autonomy of its own. There are many stories about this widespread, culturally-shared phenomenon, of which the following is quite characteristic:

Transformation

Rabbi Shalom's elder brother once asked him: "How did you happen to attain to such perfection? When we were quite young, I learned more quickly than you."

"This is how it happened, brother," the Rabbi of Belz replied. "When I became Bar Mitzva, my grandfather, Rabbi Eleazar of Amsterdam, of blessed memory, came to me one night in a vision and gave me another soul in exchange for mine. Ever since that time I have been a different person."

(Buber, Early Masters, p. 206)

Finally, it appears that, while one is in a trance, he becomes very suggestible, easily influenced by outside directions and prescriptions, as long as they are compatible with his values and intentions. This influence is considerably enhanced when a group or mass of people are under the same trance:

A Hand's Breadth Higher

When Rabbi Shlomo of Karlin was in the little town of Dobromysl (near Lozhny, where his former companion, Rabbi Schneur Zalman, was living at that time), he went to the Dobromysl House of Study. On Friday, Rabbi Zalman said to some Hasidim who had come to him in Lozhny: "Now I am not the rabbi. The holy *tzaddik*, our master Rabbi Shlomo, is within my district, so now he is the rabbi. You must go to Dobromysl and stay with him over the Sabbath."

They did so, and ate the three Sabbath meals at the table of the Rabbi of Karlin. And though he spoke no word of teaching, as their own teacher did on these occasions, their spirit beheld the holy light, and it was incomparably more radiant than ever before.

> At the third Sabbath meal, Rabbi Shlomo preceded the saying of grace with the brief psalm which begins, "His foundation is in the holy mountains," and ends, "All my springs are in thee," which he translated: "All my *springing* is in thee." And instantly, the springs of their spirit gushed forth. The spirit possessed them so utterly that, until long after the Sabbath they did not know the difference between day and night.
>
> When they returned to Rabbi Zalman and told him what had happened to them, he said: "Yes, who can compare to the holy Rabbi Shlomo! He knows how to translate. We cannot translate. Who can compare to the holy Rabbi Shlomo! For he is a hand's breadth above the world!"
>
> (*Buber, Early Masters, p. 283*)

The Hasidim were also quite clear that a trance suggestion will not work when it is imposed upon an individual or group that is opposed to it:

Failure

> Once, the Great *Maggid* concentrated all the force of his being on the coming of redemption. Then a voice asked from Heaven: "Who is trying to hasten the end, and what does he consider himself?"
>
> The *maggid* replied: "I am the leader of my generation, and it is my duty to use all my strength for that purpose."
>
> Again, the voice asked: "How can you prove this?" "My holy congregation," said the *maggid*, "will rise and testify for me."
>
> "Let them rise!" cried the voice.
>
> Then Rabbi Dov Baer went to his disciples and said: "Is it true that I am the leader of my generation?" But all were silent. He repeated his question, and still no one said, "It is true." Not until after he had left them, did the numbness leave their minds and tongues, and they were startled at themselves.
>
> (*Buber, Early Masters, pp. 110–111*)

THE STORY AS A TRANCE

In the chapter that follows on the Baal Shem Tov, we will show in detail how he utilized trance to influence his followers to cleave to the path of serving God. Trance is often implied in the follower as a result of spirited discussions, or unusual experiences, or simply the presence of a magnetic rabbi reputed to possess special powers of incantation. Such a figure was the Besht. His transpersonal experiences are recounted in many legends, and his believing followers expected to partake in them by giving themselves over to the Besht. In the next story, the Besht, who most often is very indirect and gentle in his prescriptions, very sharply confronts an unfeeling disciple who cannot empathize with a sinner. The disciple enters an altered state of consciousness.

The next two stories (especially the second one) have trance elements. The first one begins: "There was once a man" and can be quite absorbing. When a story is engrossing, the listener becomes involved in the plight of the characters and is very much influenced subconsciously by the engrossing action and the message of the narrative. The first story is an action-packed adventure with which every Hasid could easily identify:

Heavy Penance

There was once a man who had desecrated the Sabbath against his will because his carriage had broken down, and although he walked and almost ran, he did not reach the town before the beginning of the holy hours. For this, young Rabbi Mikhal imposed a very harsh and long penance on him. The man tried to do as he had been told with all his strength, but he soon found that his body could not endure it. He began to feel ill, and even his mind became affected.

About that time, he learned that the Baal Shem was traveling through this region and had stopped in a place nearby. He went to the Besht, mustered his courage, and begged the master to rid him of the sin he had committed.

"Carry a pound of candles to the House of Prayer," said the Baal Shem, "and have them lit for the Sabbath. Let that be your penance." The man thought the *tzaddik* had not quite understood what he had told him and repeated his request most urgently. When the Baal Shem insisted on his incredibly mild dictum, the man told him how heavy a penance had been imposed on him.

> "You just do as I said," the master replied. "And tell Rabbi Mikhal to come to the city of Khvostov, where I shall celebrate the coming Sabbath." The man's face had cleared. He took leave of the rabbi.
>
> On the way to Khvostov, a wheel broke on Rabbi Mikhal's carriage, and he had to continue on foot. Although he hurried all he could, it was dark when he entered the town, and when he crossed the Baal Shem's threshold, he saw he had already risen, his hand on the cup, to say the blessing over the wine to introduce the day of rest.
>
> The master paused and said to Rabbi Mikhal, who was standing before him numb and speechless: "Good Sabbath, my sinless friend! You have never tasted the sorrow of the sinner; your heart has never throbbed with his despair—and so it was easy for your hand to deal out penance."
>
> (*Buber, Early Masters, p. 142*)

The following story entrances us every time we read it or tell it to others. It has great emotional impact: For some, it brings back memories of how a parent, a teacher, or a mentor once related to them; for others, it stirs up feelings about how they would want a loving parent to relate to them:

Conversion

> Rabbi Aaron once came to the city where little Mordecai, who later became the rabbi of Lekhovitz, was growing up. His father brought the boy to the visiting rabbi and complained that he did not persevere in his studies. "Leave the boy with me for a while," said Rabbi Aaron. When he was alone with little Mordecai, he lay down and took the child to his heart. Silently he held him to his heart until his father returned. "I have given him a good talking-to," Rabbi Aaron said. "From now on, he will not be lacking in perseverance."
>
> Whenever the rabbi of Lekhovitz related this incident, he added: "That was when I learned how to convert men."
>
> (*Buber, Late Masters, p. 156*)

For Hasidim, God essentially is Unity, Oneness: "Hear O Israel, the Lord our God, the Lord is One." The world, of course, is quite fractured, but the Hasidim delighted in showing that beneath all the apparent contradictions is a world as unified as God. They saw every contradiction leading to a more powerful unity:

Twofold Character

The Ladier Rabbi said: "A man should so master his nature that he can habituate himself to both the positive and negative aspects of every character trait. For example, he should be both a conservative and a progressive; a man without fear and yet a man of peace; a man of strong personality, and yet a meek one."

(*Newman, Maggidim and Hasidim, p. 18*)

This need to unify taxed Hasidic ingenuity:

The Worthy Man

Rabbi Bunam said: "The man of learning is frequently a heretic; the good-hearted man is often a lover of the pleasures of the flesh; the pious man is usually an egotist."

"What then constitutes the worthy man?" the rabbi was asked.

"To be all of these together," was the reply.

(*Newman, The Hasidic Anthology, p. 494*)

Needless to say, the ultimate unity of God and man will come with the arrival of the Messiah:

Messianic Tribulations: Signs and Portents

Rabbi Bunam said: "Before the Messiah will come, there will be rabbis without Torah, Hasidim without Hasidism, rich men without riches, summers without heat, winters without cold, and grainstalks without grain."

(*Newman, The Hasidic Anthology, p. 253*)

9

From Story to Legend: The Psychological Skills of the Baal Shem Tov

INTRODUCTION

In recent years, it has become popular to talk about a "man for all seasons," a phrase celebrated in legends, books, plays and movies. How will we celebrate a "man for all ages"?

If

> Rabbi Leib, son of Sarah, the hidden *tzaddik*, once said to some persons who were telling about the Baal Shem: "You ask about the holy Baal Shem Tov? I tell you: if he had lived in the age of the prophets, he would have become a prophet, and if he had lived in the age of the patriarchs, he would have become an outstanding man, so that just as one says: 'God of Abraham, Isaac, and Jacob,' one would say 'God of Israel.'"
>
> (*Buber, Early Masters, p. 86*)

We are convinced that *if* the Baal Shem had lived in the age of Eric Berne, Milton Erickson, Virginia Satir, and Nathan Ackerman, he would have become a great psychologist.

It is our sincere intention to fully document in painstaking detail this bold assertion in the pages that follow. If anyone had the right—based on miraculous powers mostly quite understandable today—to be called a "legend in his own time" it certainly was the Baal Shem Tov! We can understand why his followers found it so easy to embroider with wild exaggeration his considerable powers and to turn his exploits into supernatural events.

Our purpose is to establish the hard base of actual psychological skills and healing powers upon which the legends grew. It is our firm belief that the Baal Shem Tov, who lived during the first half of the eighteenth century, was the first truly *modern* psychologist. And if he were alive today, he would be the first to pooh-pooh all the legends about himself and would appreciate this modest naturalistic examination of his psychological achievements.

The Baal Shem was the quintessential outsider. The following story aptly summarizes his renegade beginnings:

Vain Attempts

> After the death of Israel's father, the people looked out for the boy for the sake of Rabbi Eliezer, whose memory was dear to them, and sent his son to a *melammed.*
>
> Now, Israel studied diligently enough, but always only for a few days running. Then he played truant and they found him somewhere in the woods and alone. They ascribed his behavior to the fact that he was an orphan without proper care and supervision, and returned him to the *melammed* over and over. But over and over, the boy escaped to the woods until the people despaired of ever making an honest and upright man of him.
>
> (*Buber, Early Masters, p. 36*)

Four important consequences flowed from this outsider role: The first and most obvious consequence is that he enjoyed and was acutely sensitive to the strange, the different, the unnatural, the unparalleled. Since his early life was off the beaten track, he appreciated the capricious, the eccentric, and the odd—even the outlandish:

Obstacles to Blessing

The Baal Shem once asked his disciple Rabbi Meir Margaliot: "Meirle, do you still remember that Sabbath, when you were just beginning to study the Pentateuch? The big room in your father's house was full of guests. They had lifted you up onto the table and you were reciting what you had learned?"

Rabbi Meir replied: "Certainly I remember. Suddenly my mother rushed up to me and snatched me from the table in the middle of what I was saying. My father was annoyed, but she pointed to a man standing at the door. He was dressed in a short sheepskin, such as peasants wear, and he was looking straight at me. Then all understood that she feared the Evil Eye. She was still pointing at the door when the man disappeared."

"It was I," said the Baal Shem. "In such hours, a glance can flood the soul with great light. But the fear of men builds walls to keep the light away."

(*Buber, Early Masters, p. 42*)

The Baal Shem himself had insight into his preference for the strange, the new, and the unique—in short, the truth:

Truth

The Baal Shem said: "What does it mean, when people say that Truth goes over all the world? It means that Truth is driven out of one place after another, and must wander on and on."

(*Buber, Early Masters, p. 71*)

A second important consequence of the Besht's outsider status was his closeness to nature and to his solitary self via deep meditation and self-induced trance. There are many stories about his self-hypnosis which imperceptibly slide into legend:

Fasting

When Rabbi Elimelekh of Lizhensk once said that fasting was no longer service, they asked him: "Did not the Baal Shem Tov fast very often?"

"When the Baal Shem Tov was young," he replied, "he used to take six loaves of bread and a pitcher of water at the close of the Sabbath, when he went into seclusion for the entire week. On a Friday, when he was ready to go home and about to lift his sack from the ground, he noticed that it was heavy, opened it, and found all the loaves still in it. He was very much surprised. Fasting such as this is allowed!"

(*Buber, Early Masters, p. 45*)

Trance is a good example of how people's fascination with the mysterious excites wonder, baffles natural explanation, and spontaneously results in a supernatural solution to close the gap. The lack of understanding leaves one feeling hopeless and defeated. Trance, in our society, is still largely unnatural and conducive to supernatural solutions:

The Helpful Mountain

The summits of the mountain on whose gentle slopes Israel ben Eliezer lived are straight and steep. In hours of meditation he liked to climb these peaks and stay at the very top for a time. Once he was so deep in ecstasy, he failed to notice that he was at the edge of an abyss and calmly lifted his foot to walk on. Instantly a neighboring mountain leaped to the spot, pressed itself close to the other, and the Baal Shem pursued his way.

(*Buber, Early Masters, p. 41*)

Trance phenomena, which now can be produced readily in the experimental laboratory using trained Eastern mystics, were seen by the Hasidim as manifestations of the Besht's special relationship to God and were woven into stories which eventually became legends. The following two stories of modest paranormal phenomena are typical:

Trembling

Rabbi Jacob Joseph of Polnoye told:

"Once, a large water-trough stood in the room in which the Baal Shem was praying. I saw the water in the trough tremble and sway until he finished."

Another disciple told:

"Once, on a journey, the Baal Shem was praying at the east wall of a house at whose west wall stood open barrels filled with grain. Then I saw that the grain in the barrels was trembling."

(*Buber, Early Masters, p. 50*)

When the Sabbath Drew Near

The disciples of a *tzaddik* who had been a disciple of the Baal Shem Tov were sitting together at noon, before the Sabbath, and telling one another about the miraculous deeds of the Baal Shem. The *tzaddik*, who was seated in the room which adjoined theirs, heard them. He opened the door and said: "What is the sense of telling miracle tales! Tell one another of his fear of God! Every week, on the day before the Sabbath, around the hour of noon, his heart began to beat so loudly that all of us who were with him could hear it."

(*Buber, Early Masters, p. 50*)

The third consequence of the Baal Shem's outsider role coupled with his singular upbringing and involvement with psychic phenomena, particularly trance, was the interaction with the "insiders," who transformed him into a seer. At first, the villagers were skeptical, even suspicious of this strange fellow, but once the "turn" was made toward acceptance, stories that could be very easily explained naturalistically began to be overlaid more and more with supernatural or spiritual associations.

It seemed natural that the Baal Shem, who spent so much time alone, would "not know how to talk to people," and that reciting psalms would be a good exercise for talking out loud. His followers took this "failing" a step further:

How Ahijah Taught Him

The Rav of Polnoye told:

"At first, the Baal Shem Tov did not know how to talk to people, so wholly did he cling and cleave to God, and he talked softly to himself. Then his God-sent teacher Ahijah, the prophet, came and taught him which verses of the Psalms to say every day, to gain the ability of talking to people without disrupting his clinging to God."

(*Buber, Early Masters, p. 51*)

Many miraculous interpretations were bestowed upon the Besht's behavior, some of which, if attributed to others in the same situation, would not receive special recognition:

The Master Dances Too

One Simhat Torah evening, the Baal Shem himself danced together with his congregation. He took the scroll of the Torah in his hand and danced with it. Then he laid the scroll aside and danced without it. At this moment, one of his disciples who was intimately acquainted with his gestures, said to his companions: "Now our master has laid aside the visible, dimensional teachings and has taken the spiritual teachings unto himself."

(*Buber, Early Masters, p. 53*)

Of such ambiguous stuff are legends built. The Besht, of course, was an original, but for reasons much more profound than the miraculous legendary exploits of "moving mountains".

The fourth consequence of the Baal Shem's outsider role is the special relationship he evolved with God—a major "turning" that had a far-reaching impact upon the Jewish people throughout Europe during the eighteenth and nineteenth centuries and, in our own century, upon non-Jews as well as Jews.

According to legend, the Baal Shem's special relationship to God was foreseen by his father:

His Father's Words

Israel's father died while he was still a child.

When he felt death drawing near, he took the boy in his arms and said: "I see that you will make my light shine out, and it is not given me to rear you to manhood. But dear son, remember all your days that God is with you and that, because of this, you need fear nothing in all the world."

Israel treasured these words in his heart.

(*Buber, Early Masters, p. 36*)

Israel indeed "treasured these words in his heart" in the most consistently intense singular fashion possible. There are two sides to the ecstatic communion between the Besht and God. On one side nothing, absolutely nothing, could stand between the direct immediate love of the Besht for God in the here and now. Even the hope for a place in the World-to-Come could not interfere with this love. "If I love God," asked the Besht, "what need have I of the World-to-Come?" (See page 130).

It also followed (as already illustrated in Chapter 7 on reframing) that nothing on earth is all evil. Quite the contrary, there is much to learn from evil and wickedness. In fact, everything on earth has some virtuous quality:

The Dilgence of Satan

Said the Besht: "When you perceive the Satan diligently seeking to persuade you to commit an evil deed, understand that he is endeavoring to fulfill his duty as he conceives it. Learn from him diligence in performing your bounden duty—namely, to battle and overcome his persuasion."

(*Newman, The Hasidic Anthology, p. 82*)

But the most significant shift by far in the "new" relationship to God was the clear, overwhelming supremacy of service, of virtuous actions, of deeds (and prayer) over learning:

Knowledge

The Baal Shem said:

"When I reach a high rung of knowledge, I know that not a single letter of the teachings is within me, and that I have not taken a single step in the service of God."

(*Buber, Early Masters, p. 52*)

In our opinion, Hasidism was an enormously liberating and progressive theology for its time. It signaled an emancipation from desiccated teachings that had very little practical meaning for a bustling people coping with the onslaught of industrialization, commercialism and modernity. The Baal Shem opened up a whole new relationship between the people and God, Torah, good deeds and prayer. The rabbis could begin to deal directly with their followers' experiences and be helpful in their daily troubles and tribulations and, yes, supportive of their joys and achievements.

The Besht signaled a return to the ordinary people and rediscovery of their extraordinary powers. In "The Busy Man's Prayer," the story on page 52, he speaks of a man so occupied with business that he forgets God. But when this man remembers that he has to pray, and he regrets the time spent on vain matters, "God holds him very dear, and his prayer pierces the firmament."

The Besht elevated matters of the heart to the same or perhaps even a higher level than the intricacies of learning and thought. Expressions of spontaneous guileless feelings became a direct route to God:

The Axe

Once, the Baal Shem had his disciple Rabbi Wolf Kitzes learn the *kavvanot* of blowing the ram's horn so that, on New Year's Day, he might announce before him the order of the sounds. Rabbi Wolf learned the *kavvanot* but, for greater security, noted everything down on a slip of paper which he hid in his bosom. This paper, however, dropped out soon after and he never noticed it. They say that this was the work of the Baal Shem.

Now, when it was time to blow, Rabbi Wolf looked for his slip in vain. Then he tried to remember the *kavvanot*, but he had forgotten everything. Tears rose to his eyes and, weeping, he announced the order of sounds quite simply without referring to the *kavvanot* at all.

Later, the Baal Shem said to him: "There are many halls in the king's palace, and intricate keys open the doors, but the axe

> is stronger than all of these, and no bolt can withstand it. What are all *kavvanot* compared to one really heartfelt grief!"
>
> (*Buber, Early Masters, p. 64*)

There was one great difference between the rabbi as a paragon of learning and as a practical psychologist. The rabbi as scholar could clearly show his superiority by his vast erudition and powers of reasoning. The Besht was shrewd enough to realize and to warn his followers about the inherent limitations of the rabbi as an "applied psychologist." In the story on page 9, "The Limits of Advice," the Besht makes the point forcefully. If a learned rabbi advises people how to keep unholy thoughts from disturbing them in prayer, he is "of no account." For he does not understand the eternal struggle of man with the extraneous.

The Baal Shem Tov had to invent a "social work" and a "psychology" for directly serving the people. It is our thesis that this "new practice" was based, first and foremost, on the Besht's absolute and direct identification with God; and the Baal Shem Tov's faith not only motivated a matchless devotion to his people, but it figured prominently in his psychological powers of healing.

What is important here is that the Besht was liberated to use all of his imagination and cunning to help people with real problems. His faith in God was not hidebound, not obstinately and narrowly confined to reinterpretation of hundreds of years of Talmudic interpretations of the Bible piled upon each other. The heartfelt faith in God really meant that the Besht could trust *himself*: The genius within could now be sprung.

It is critical to distinguish between a faith that is doctrinaire, one governed by accumulated abstract rules and principles, and a theology that essentially bypasses the codified doctrine in favor of pragmatic and "humanistic" utilization of laws and rituals to deal with the troubles and suffering of ordinary folk. In the Besht's time, the Hasidim were, relatively speaking, within a religiously orthodox frame. With his idiosyncratic perceptiveness and creative intuition, the Baal Shem "humanized" religious practice by paying much more attention to people's specific needs and directly counseling them with increasingly sophisticated psychological techniques.

The more general question about belief in some "Power" beyond the natural and rational is an extremely important issue in psychology today. The parallel to the Baal Shem in our time is the influential hypnotherapist, Milton H. Erickson, who "never solved a problem in an old way." Analogous to the Besht's belief in God was Erickson's belief in the unconscious. One time, Erickson was asked at the last minute to deliver a lecture, and he had a lot of other things to do before he went to the auditorium. However, Erickson was not concerned, because (Rosen 1982) "I knew I could talk, and I knew I could think and I knew that I'd learned much in the course of the years."

Rosen adds the following note:

> Erickson models an attitude of trust in one's long-term memories and in unconsciously stored knowledge. He underlines the fact that the unconscious mind is a repository of memories and skills that can be called upon after many years.

The Baal Shem had exactly the same liberating attitude toward God which could be substituted for the "unconscious mind": "When I weld my spirit to God, I let my mouth say what it will." And that is why the Baal Shem, like Erickson, "never solved a problem in an old way."

THE BAAL SHEM'S PSYCHOLOGICAL SKILLS

The best way to comprehend the Baal Shem's highly effective psychological skills is to outline the four main factors in Hasidic counseling and then demonstrate (in the section immediately following) the unique forms in which they are integrated.

The four key psychological skills the Besht evolved were as follows:

- The ability to accurately size up the Hasid's situation and the central (often "hidden") problem. We have referred to this process before as "gathering information."

- A knack for gaining rapport with the person who has a problem and winning his or her trust and confidence. We have referred to this process as "pacing."
- The use of the rabbi's own self as a mirror of the Hasid's conflict ("identification"), so that the Hasid can "see" his situation dissociated from himself and in a more clear and objective way. This process also seems to develop a positive relationship between Hasid and rabbi.
- A specific practical intervention that (a) intensifies the inner conflict and initially confuses or surprises the recipient, and (b) leads to the emergence of a latent subconscious resolution that results in a significant "turning" of the Hasid onto a new path, with fresh options and strategies.

Each of these skills is illustrated in Hasidic tales. We will let the stories tell this "story."

SIZING UP THE SITUATION

Intuition is a kind of knowing without recourse to explicit references or reasoning. Often described as "innate" or "instinctive" knowledge, it is a gathering of information by quick and ready instantaneous comprehension:

The Money That Stayed in the House

The Baal Shem never kept money in his house overnight. When he returned from a journey, he paid all the debts which had accumulated in his absence and distributed whatever he had left among the needy.

Once, he brought a large amount of money back from a journey, paid his debts, and gave the rest away. But in the meantime, his wife had taken a little of the money so that she might not have to buy on credit for a few days. In the evening, the Baal Shem felt something impeding his prayer. He went home and said: "Who took the money?" His wife confessed it was she who had done so. He took the money from her and had it distributed among the poor that very evening.

(*Buber, Early Masters,* p. 51)

The "something impeding his prayer" is a negative vibration felt by the Besht that things were askew. This bespeaks exceptional powers to divine and to discern what has occurred and is now transpiring below the surface of reality. We believe this occurs when the diviner has trained himself to pick up inferentially slight clues that inspire him to see underlying connections:

The Jug

Once the Baal Shem said to his disciples: "Just as the strength of the root is in the leaf, so the strength of man is in every utensil he makes, and his character and behavior can be gauged from what he has made." Just then, his glance fell on a fine beer-jug standing in front of him. He pointed to it and continued: "Can't you see from this jug that the man who made it had no feet?"

When the Baal Shem had finished speaking, one of his disciples happened to pick up the jug to set it on the bench. But the moment it stood there it crumbled to bits.

(*Buber, Early Masters, p. 73*)

GAINING RAPPORT

In the stories that follow we will show the different methods that the Baal Shem used to gain the trust, confidence, *and* cooperation of his followers. Foremost among the techniques for gaining rapport was doing things together, in addition to carrying on spirited discussions.

The Besht's skill in addressing a group of Hasidim and simultaneously speaking to each one individually (the goal of every speaker) is highlighted in the following story:

The Address

Every evening after prayer, the Baal Shem went to his room. Two candles were set in front of him and the mysterious

> Book of Creation put on the table among other books. Then all those who needed his counsel were admitted in a body, and he spoke with them until the eleventh hour.
>
> One evening, when the people left, one of them said to the man beside him how much good the words of the Baal Shem had done him. But the other told him not to talk such nonsense, that they had entered the room together and from that moment on the master had spoken to no one except himself. A third, who heard this, joined in the conversation with a smile, saying how curious that both were mistaken, for the rabbi had carried on an intimate conversation with him the entire evening. Then a fourth and fifth made the same claim, and finally all began to talk at once and tell what they had experienced. But the next instant, they all fell silent.
>
> (*Buber, Early Masters, p.* 55)

"But the next instant they all fell silent." Did they realize suddenly that they were engaging in a stupid competitive contest? Did they all marvel over the Besht's incredible powers? Did they realize that, instead of fighting over whom the Besht was really talking to, it would be more productive to think about what the Besht had said to each one? Choose your own interpretation or, better, make up your own.

IDENTIFICATION

"Identification" is a process that involves two or more people in the sharing of a specific trait, characteristic peculiarity, problem, conflict, etc., or, in some cases, even a broader characterological configuration. That "sharing" can be emotional, perceptual, informational, and behavioral or all of them in combination. The identity can be a distinctive quality or utterly banal, and most often it is made up of rather mixed traits.

Almost all schools of psychology since Freud have emphasized that the client's identification with his therapist is a repetition of his relationship with his parents, the first, and most influential, authority in one's life.

What is extraordinary among the Hasidim, beginning most noticeably with the Besht, is the conscious reversal of this process, with the rabbi absorbing the Hasid's conflict to help the Hasid apprehend his conflict "outside" of himself and to give the rabbi a better "inside" grasp of the Hasid and his problem.

The Besht was so skilled at this process that he was able to "future-pace" a potential conflict his followers would experience. He did this by posing a question about his successor that would stimulate them to find someone who possessed *the* essential quality of character to succeed the Besht and carry on his work:

The Succession

> Before the Baal Shem died, his disciples asked him who was to be their master in his stead. He said: "Whoever can teach you how pride can be broken shall be my successor."
>
> After the Baal Shem's death, they first put the question to Rabbi Dov Baer. "How can pride be broken?"
>
> He replied: "Pride belongs to God—as it is written: 'The Lord reigneth; He is clothed in pride.' That is why no counsel can be given on how to break pride. We must struggle with it all the days of our life." Then the disciples knew that it was he who was the Baal Shem's successor.
>
> (*Buber, Early Masters, p. 100*)

SURGICAL INTERVENTION

In Chapter 5, "The Story's Role in Counseling and Education," the point was developed that counseling and teaching were not really separate departments. Nowadays, we differentiate between therapy and counseling; the first refers to treating someone who is ill, and the second is regarded as preventive treatment, promoting and reinforcing mental health. This notion is foreign to the Hasidim who thought of both processes as occurring simultaneously.

Frequently, thc Besht reinforces a key Hasidic value by identifying with someone and demonstrating how to convert an apparent "aberration" into a virtue:

The Court Sweeper

Once, just before New Year's, the Baal Shem came to a certain town and asked the people who led the prayers there during the Days of Awe. They replied that this was done by the *rav* of the town. "And what is his manner of praying?" asked the Baal Shem.

"On the Day of Atonement," they said, "he recites all the confessions of sin in the most cheerful tones."

The Baal Shem sent for the *rav* and asked him the cause of this strange procedure. The *rav* answered: "The least among the servants of the king, he whose task is to sweep the forecourt free of dirt, sings a merry song as he works, for he does what he is doing to gladden the king."

Said the Baal Shem: "May my lot be with yours."

(*Buber, Early Masters, p. 70*)

In this section we have described and illustrated four major psychological skills that the Besht honed in serving his followers: sizing up the situation and the problem; gaining rapport; identifying emotionally with the help-seeker; and prescribing strategies commensurate with the Hasidic capacities and spiritual resources.

But parts do not a whole make. Is there a design, a particular pattern to the Besht's counseling, which "never solved a problem in an old way"? Is the pattern one of no-set-pattern, which after all is a pattern? We think so, except for one caveat: the willingness to take more risks with each intervention, because, after all, were not his words "bound to their root in Heaven"?

THREE FABULOUS STORIES ABOUT THE BESHT

When we use the term "fabulous" to describe these stories, we by no means imply the impossibility of their occurrence. Quite the contrary. We do believe they did, in fact, occur, but the sophistication of the integrated psychological techniques used by the Besht leaves each of us muttering to himself. The reader will judge for himself, but we are convinced that no living psychologist is more sophisticated than the Baal Shem Tov as he is seen in the following three stories.

In the first story, the Besht "counsels" a student by mirroring precisely his conflict about becoming the Besht's disciple:

Losing the Way

Rabbi Yehiel Mikhal, later the *Maggid* of Zlotchov, did, indeed, seek out the Baal Shem while he was quite young; but he was not sure whether or not he should become his disciple. Then the *tzaddik* took him with him on a journey to a certain place. When they had been driving for a while, it became evident that they were not on the right road. "Why, rabbi!" said Mikhal. "Don't you know the way?"

"It will make itself known to me in due time," answered the Baal Shem, and they took another road; but this, too, did not take them to their destination. "Why, rabbi!" said Mikhal. "Have you lost your way?"

"It is written," the Baal Shem said calmly, "that God 'will fulfill the desire of them that fear him.' And so he has fulfilled your desire to have a chance to laugh at me."

These words pierced young Mikhal to the heart, and without further arguing or analyzing, he joined the master with his whole soul.

(*Buber, Early Masters, p. 61*)

Mikhal is traveling with the Baal Shem on a journey to a certain place which the Besht is not sure of finding. This in itself bespeaks the Besht's willingness to take risks. And when Mikhal challenges him with, "Don't you know the way?" the Besht presciently replies and seeds his legitimacy in Mikhal's subconscious: "It will make itself known to me in due time."

The Besht continues to lose his way, prompting Mikhal to scorn the Besht and treat him as an object of ridicule.

Mikhal's inner conflict is externally objectified by derisively confronting the Baal Shem when he loses his way. Mikhal's ambivalence about the Baal Shem is openly revealed. The shared experience has made the ambivalence much more real than any abstract discussion of the disciple's inner conflict could have done. The negative side of the ambivalence is brought out in the disciple's impatience with the Baal Shem in losing the way.

The Baal Shem's response is nothing short of genius. He reframes the contemptuous put-down in very positive terms. Explicitly bringing the Third Partner to every encounter, the Baal Shem reframes the disciple's mocking put-down of himself as an act of God: Mocking the Besht is actually an indication of Mikhal's fear of God and his powerful relationship with God, since God has fulfilled his desire to laugh at the Besht, which is, of course, one side of young Mikhal's ambivalence.

In other words, the Baal Shem is telling Mikhal: "It's o.k. for you to mock me. Even more than that, it shows how much God is with you when you ridicule me." So mocking the rabbi is o.k. But giving the disciple permission to do so, and even reinforcing him positively for mocking him "takes away" the rebelliousness that every student feels vis-à-vis his mentor. Mikhal wants to learn *and* be on his own. Mikhal's ambivalence is in part an indication of his desire to strike out on his own and become his own master, which is a very positive attribute among the Hasidim.

At the same time, removing the rebelliousness enables Mikhal to see that he still has very much to learn from his rabbi. The conflict is eliminated because he no longer has to resist the Baal Shem covertly. The Besht tells Mikhal that he is really terrific and has a right to put him down. Once he has that right, it is no longer a rebellious act.

The removal of one side of the ambivalence, namely the need to resist and rebel, enables the disciple to look more dispassionately at what he really wants and to decide whether he can learn more from the Baal Shem.

The problem of control and resistance to change is at the very heart of contemporary counseling and psychotherapy. In fact, there is a general rule in therapy which says, in effect, that first you have to deal with resistance to get anywhere with your client. As long as Mikhal resists, the struggle is centered around Mikhal's rebelliousness, and his ability to cope with the problem is negated by the conflict between him and the Baal Shem. As long as it remains in this "transference" stage, the chances of the individual learning and gaining insight into his own inner conflict are considerably diminished.

The rabbis were acutely sensitive to this. They didn't want conformity as such. They wanted their disciples to learn from them, but also to be independent, to be critical and skeptical. The rabbis knew that they were far from perfect and that their disciples could also see through them, especially when they had mastered the psychological skills that they had learned from their rabbis. They would, in turn, use those skills upon their teachers and mentors.

"Losing the Way" illustrates the Besht's supersensitivity to the disciple's need for resistance and rebellion and to the rabbi's need to foster it appropriately, so that the disciple can become truly independent. The use of the double bind, which dissolves the struggle between the rabbi and the disciple, results in the disciple's struggling within himself over his own inner questions and doubts instead of displacing them on the relationship between himself and his mentor.

This story reveals to other rabbis who listen intently to Hasidic stories how they, in turn, can deal effectively with the transference problem by paradoxically giving their blessing to rebellion and reframing it through seeing its positive connotations. Ultimately, what is important is the "whole soul," "wholeheartedness," and that cannot emerge without working through the questions of power and control that every person has vis-à-vis authority.

Lurking within a disciple's heart is the idea that he is following a rabbi with authority because he is afraid to let go and go out on his own. The Baal Shem takes the opposite track, a very different track from one that a typical person in authority will take. The conventional authority will try to impose his legitimacy over his follower by impressing him with his learning or skill or power. In a very paradoxical way, the Baal Shem puts himself down and says to his disciple: "Look, I'm very human, I've got a lot of foibles. In fact, I am inadequate in some respects; for example, I lose my way. And I can also help you lose your way. That's how ordinary I am."

Now an ordinary person would never admit his ordinariness. By admitting his, the Baal Shem shows how extraordinary he really is. This conveys to the student that he does not have to be conflicted about the Baal Shem's "super" authority, because the Besht is denying his infallibility. Young Mikhal can make a decision based on what he can actually learn from the Baal Shem, not because of the master's power over him.

By his behavior, the Baal Shem is also showing his disciple how he should deal with authority when he becomes a full-fledged rabbi. We are told that Mikhal fears the Lord, and that is the main thing: to fear God and not man, whatever his authority is. By using himself as an example, by reversing the roles and assuming a disciple role toward Mikhal, who now becomes the "authority," he is demonstrating how Mikhal could also counsel his disciples (when his term as rabbi-counselor comes) in a way which will foster nonconformity and doubt and challenge to authority. This is another example of the profound compassion and wisdom of the Baal Shem, whose spiritual identification with God enabled him to maintain a perspective which fostered faith in God and skepticism of all earthly authority—including his own. In this way, faith in God is constantly renewed.

Here we want to be precise about the "therapeutic double bind" that confronted Mikhal. The double bind is a situation in which a client is first healed by accepting or rejecting the counselor's assertion about him and his problem, but without being able to deny the assertion. The Besht tells Mikhal:

> God fulfills the desires of them that fear Him.
> You fear God, so He fulfills your desires.
> You, Mikhal, desire to laugh at me.
> God has fulfilled your desire to laugh at me.

The psychological logic is flawless. How can Mikhal respond?

1. Yes, my desire was to laugh at you and God supports me. (*Great!*)
2. No, it really is not nice to laugh at anyone—certainly, not at a revered rabbi. (*Not nice at all!*)
3. You are mistaken about God supporting me. (*But it does make sense.*)
4. I'm really all confused. All mixed up. I have even greater appreciation of your healing wisdom, Baal Shem, for seeing into and piercing my confusion and my heart. I do,

> indeed, have much more to learn from you and now, without any reservations, I join you with my "whole soul." (*And so it was.*)

* * *

In the second story about the Baal Shem, all his psychological skill is manifested in the way he gets to the heart of the problem and its resolution by suggesting what he says to himself when he is in an identical situation and frame of mind:

In the Hour of Doubt

> In the city of Satanov there was a learned man whose thinking and brooding took him deeper and deeper into the question of why what is, is, and why anything is at all. One Friday, he stayed in the House of Study after prayer to go on thinking, for he was snared in his thoughts and tried to untangle them and could not. The holy Baal Shem Tov felt this from afar, got into his carriage and, by dint of his miraculous power which made the road leap to meet him, he reached the House of Study in Satanov in only an instant. There sat the learned man in his predicament. The Baal Shem said to him: "You are brooding on whether God is; I am a fool and believe." The fact that there was a human being who knew of his secret, stirred the doubter's heart and it opened to the Great Secret.
>
> (*Buber, Early Masters, pp. 70–71*)

The introduction is sheer elegance—both rich and refined. We know from many other stories that the Besht was wont to ponder the imponderable and was able to extricate himself by a leap of faith. It is no wonder, then, that the Baal Shem was eager to talk to this learned man in his predicament and healed him "in only an instant"!

This is another example of the Besht's perfectly mirroring a troubled scholar's state of mind. First of all, for the Hasidim the only significant "theoretical" problem is God's existence when one's faith is shaken. Now let's dissect the Besht's intervention.

"I am a fool,"—perhaps not as learned as you, but not a dummy; and when it comes to the mysteries of God's being—that certainly is beyond me.

". . . and believe in God." Listen here, I may not know—no, I *certainly don't* know all the scholarly arguments, and I believe. There is no contradiction here at all. In fact, faith can take on all of reason's formidable powers. My Great Secret is to know that I don't know, and that, indeed, may make me a fool for still believing. And that's O.K. too, and I believe."

We are told in the story that the Besht "knew his secret," which, in view of the Besht's statement, may refer to the scholar's thinking himself a fool, something that the Besht accepts in his search for a greater truth. The "Great Secret" is a teaser, one which, from our vantage point, seems to be that faith encompasses doubt and thrives on it, as long as doubt is not lcft alone to "take the field."

* * *

The third and last story takes us to a whole new dimension in the recurrent struggle between knowledge and faith in the Hasidic outlook. The Baal Shem's task was intricate and difficult. Rabbi Baer was essentially a scholar and oriented to the world through academic learning. He had read the mystical writings of the Kabbala but evidently interpreted them through his study of the formal, legalistic Talmudic discipline. The Besht "knew" that Rabbi Dov Baer would be his heir, but only at the cost of a titanic struggle:

His Reception

> Rabbi Dov Baer, the Great *Maggid*, was a keen scholar, equally versed in the intricacies of the Gemara and the depths of the Kabbala. Time and again, he had heard about the Baal Shem and finally decided to go to him, in order to see for himself if his wisdom really justified his great reputation.
>
> When he reached the master's house and stood before him, he greeted him and then—without even looking at him properly—waited for teachings to issue from his lips, that he

might examine and weigh them. But the Baal Shem only told him that once he had driven through the wilderness for days and lacked bread to feed his coachman. Then a peasant happened along and sold him bread. After this, he dismissed his guest.

The following evening, the *maggid* again went to the Baal Shem and thought that now, surely, he would hear something of his teachings. But all Rabbi Israel told him was that once, while he was on the road, he had no hay for his horses, and a farmer had come and fed the animals. The *maggid* did not know what to make of these stories. He was quite certain that it was useless for him to wait for this man to utter words of wisdom.

When he returned to his inn, he ordered his servant to prepare for the homeward journey; they would start as soon as the moon had scattered the clouds. Around midnight it grew light. Then a man came from the Baal Shem with the message that Rabbi Baer was to come to him that very hour. He went at once. The Baal Shem received him in his room. "Are you versed in the Kabbala?" he asked. The *maggid* said he was. "Take this book, *The Tree of Life*. Open it and read." The *maggid* read. "Now think!" He thought. "Expound!" He expounded the passage that dealt with the nature of angels. "You have no true knowledge," said the Baal Shem. "Get up!" The *maggid* rose. The Baal Shem stood in front of him and recited the passage. Then, before the eyes of Rabbi Baer, the room went up in flame, and through the blaze he heard the surging of angels until his senses forsook him. When he awoke, the room was as it had been when he entered it. The Baal Shem stood opposite him and said: "You expounded correctly, but you have no true knowledge, because there is no soul in what you know."

Rabbi Baer went back to the inn, told his servant to go home, and stayed in Medzibozh, the town of the Baal Shem.

(*Buber, Early Masters, pp. 99–100*)

The Baal Shem begins altering Rabbi Baer's mind-set by recounting extraordinarily simple, mundane events that were utterly banal: Once, on a journey, he lacked the bread to feed his coachman, and a peasant happened along and sold him some bread; and the second time he was on the road, he had no hay for his horses, and a farmer came and fed the animals. What could be more ordinary? Why waste time thinking about them? Rabbi Dov Baer is mystified, terribly confused. What is his response? Instead of accepting the two stories as mysteries or puzzles to ponder, he dismisses them. He was not accustomed to being told trivialities; he was used to the abstruse and esoteric scholarly disquisitions of the Talmudic academies.

This "confusion" technique completely throws Dov Baer off his track and unsettles his usual way of thinking. The Baal Shem was perspicacious enough to see that, even though Rabbi Baer rejected dealing with these ordinary events, he was confused about their significance. Rabbi Baer could not handle ordinary life experiences. His mind was separate from his body and heart and totally encapsulated in the Talmud in a way which did not include everyday experiences. He could not respond to a simple event.

By rejecting the mystery in the ordinariness, by rejecting these simple events, Rabbi Baer refused to deal with the mysteries of everyday life—things not mentioned in the Talmud. His heart could not reach beyond his mind to grasp the divine wonders of everyday life situations. Rabbi Baer was clearly uncomfortable, frustrated, and confused.

Having not yet succeeded in reorienting Rabbi Baer, but perhaps opening him up to becoming "positively" unsettled and thereby opening his heart, the Baal Shem probes a subject that is more familiar to Rabbi Baer and with which he is more comfortable. He asks him to read from a Kabbalistic book and to explain what he had read. The passage was not simple, because it dealt with angels—mystical stuff, not dealt with easily by the Talmudic mind.

Finally, perhaps in exasperation, the Baal Shem tells the *maggid* that he does not have "true knowledge." In telling him this, however, the Baal Shem goes to a whole different level of discourse and explanation that works not only with the mind but the spirit. And this is done through a personal demonstration.

The Baal Shem reads the same passage that Rabbi Baer had read, but in such a way that the reader and the text "explode" and the entire room goes up in flames with angels surging through it. This is obviously too much for Rabbi Baer to handle, and he goes into shock.

Finally, Baal Shem is able to tell him: "You have no true knowledge, because there is no soul in what you know."

Putting this in modern psychological terms, powerful circuits need powerful circuit-breakers. Rabbi Baer was caught in a loop in which he interpreted his world exclusively through the mind. The Baal Shem was trying to explain to him that true knowledge goes beyond the mind to the body and spirit as well. In several different ways, the Baal Shem tries to break up Dov Baer's preset, stereotyped thinking, and he succeeds in upsetting Rabbi Baer to the point where he is ready to undergo a spiritual transformation.

The last story goes to the heart of the Hasidic revolution started by the Baal Shem Tov: "There is no soul in what you know."

Our world remains polarized on this fundamental issue: Can the unknown, the mysterious, the incomprehensible become known through reasoned knowledge? Or, alternatively, is faith in God an indispensable belief for probing the unknown, especially the intangible spiritual side of man?

One conclusion is inescapable: The Baal Shem Tov's distinctive and original contributions to psychology and understanding of the human heart are proof that one hypothesis is not more productive than the other. If one judges by results, it is quite clear that the psychological methods pioneered by the Besht and his successors were stunningly successful!

THE BAAL SHEM TOV'S SOCIAL LEGACY

We would be terribly remiss to conclude this chapter on the Besht without commenting on the powerful "democratic" social legacy he left behind for his successors.

Previously, we emphasized the Baal Shem's outsider status in his youth and, in many ways, throughout his life. He was extremely suspicious of all authority and accurately foresaw the corruption of his democratic legacy:

Like Locusts

Rabbi Mikhal of Zlotchov told:

"Once when we were on a journey with our teacher, Rabbi

> Israel Baal Shem Tov, the Light of the Seven Days, he went into the woods to say the Afternoon Prayer. Suddenly we saw him strike his head against a tree and cry aloud. Later we asked him about it. He said: "While I plunged into the holy spirit I saw that, in the generations which precede the coming of the Messiah, the rabbis of the Hasidim will multiply like locusts, and it will be they who delay redemption, for they will bring about the separation of hearts and groundless hatred."
>
> (*Buber, Early Masters,* p. 67)

His antidote to this "poison" was for the people to take charge of their own lives. Below is his stirring message, strongly reminiscent of Joshua's battle cry, "Have I not commanded thee? Be strong and of good courage; be not affrighted, neither be thou dismayed; for the Lord thy God is with thee wherever thou goest" (Joshua 1:9). Certainly, the Besht had this in mind, even though he quoted another passage from the Bible and deduced from it a democratic imperative:

Happy Is the People

> Concerning the verse in the psalm: "Happy is the people that knows the joyful shout; they walk, O Lord, in the light of Thy countenance," the Baal Shem said: "When the people do not depend upon heroes but are themselves versed in the joyful shout of battle, then they will walk in the light of Your countenance."
>
> (*Buber, Early Masters,* p. 67)

The Baal Shem Tov is one of the most enigmatic and baffling figures in Jewish history. In many respects, he is inexplicable because of his contradictory qualities. We think he would have liked, best of all, for us to say this about him: He was always coming up with surprises. He not only "never solved a problem in an old way," but he was always learning from experience and was unafraid to take new social risks.

Our lingering impression of the Besht is that of someone who was close to the ordinary people from whom he derived his enormous powers:

To One Who Admonished

The Baal Shem said this to a *tzaddik* who used to preach admonishing sermons: "What do you know about admonishing? You yourself have remained unacquainted with sin all the days of your life, and you have had nothing to do with the people around you. How should you know what sinning is?"

(*Buber, Early Masters, p. 71*)

Ultimately, the Baal Shem Tov knew that only his connection with people and their connections with one another offered an antidote to mankind's most pressing psychological problem—that of loneliness:

The Bird Nest

Once, the Baal Shem stood in the House of Prayer and prayed for a very long time. All his disciples had finished praying, but he continued without paying any attention to them. They waited for him a good while, and then they went home. After several hours, when they had attended to their various duties, they returned to the House of Prayer and found him still deep in prayer. Later, he said to them: "By going away and leaving me alone, you dealt me a painful separation. I shall tell you a parable.

"You know that there are birds of passage who fly to warm countries in the autumn. Well, the people in one of those lands once saw a glorious many-colored bird in the midst of a flock which was journeying through the sky. The eyes of man had never seen a bird so beautiful. He alighted on the top of the tallest tree and nested in the leaves. When the king of the country heard of it, he bade them fetch down the bird with his nest. He ordered a number of men to make a ladder up the tree. One was to stand on the other's shoulders until it was possible to reach up high enough to take the nest. It took a long time to build this living ladder. Those who stood nearest the ground lost patience, shook themselves free, and everything collapsed."

(*Buber, Early Masters, pp. 54–55*)

Part III

HASIDIC TEACHING

INTRODUCTION

Out of their intense community living, the Hasidim evolved a set of values—preferred ways of conducting one's life—that came to be known as Hasidism. A special cultural heritage was the precipitate of the Hasidim's shared life and their projections of the ideal way to live and die.

We have already spoken of the Hasid's zest, joy, spirit, individuality, compassion, love, and fear of God. These and other values will be explored more fully in this section. Now, underlying all of these values is a value—perhaps we can call it "meta-value"—that ties all the other values together. It is sometimes called "wisdom": an essential understanding of oneself, other people, and situations, as well as exceptional judgment in relating to others. There are different kinds of wise people because they live in different cultures and prize different values. We leave open the question of whether there is a substratum of universal values most, or even all, "sane" cultures would subscribe to.

A people's culture includes values which are quite prominent and frequently and openly announced. For example, in our society the proclaimed values are independence, democracy, freedom, and individual responsibility. So it is in the world of Hasidism. However, underlying the obvious shared Hasidic values is a more subtle, informal system of values that displays great intellectual *and* experiential depth, complexity and profundity and yet, paradoxically, has an elegant simplicity. We will attend to this deeper layer as well in this section and would like to give you one example of what we mean before we depart for Chapter 10.

A good way of highlighting important Hasidic values is to use contrast. "The Watchman Who Brooded" (see 26) is one of the funniest stories in Martin Buber's collection as well as one that gives us important insights into one type of character the Hasidim made great fun of.

Too much of a good thing was always suspect among the Hasidim. They ridiculed the uptight, obsessive individual who compulsively narrowed his life by concentrating excessively on one thing. Also at issue here is the total lack of flexibility and the fundamental lack of understanding that life has a rhythm, an ebb and flow as fundamental as the tides and the waning and expanding of the moon.

This latter philosophy is beautifully captured in Rabbi Pinhas's remark: "What you pursue, you don't get. But what you allow to grow slowly, in its own way, comes to you." (See page 119, "What You Pursue.")

The stories in this section grew slowly in their own way into our hearts and gradually became a part of our philosophy of life.

10

Merging with God

The Hasid and the German Jew

Once, a frail, short, slightly-built Hasid and a big, burly German Jew were playing golf together. The Hasid was superb—holes-in-one, 40 foot putts and finally, a score of six below par.

The husky German Jew, meanwhile, was huffing and puffing, missing very easy shots and, finally, he came in with a score of 145, more than double par.

The two met afterwards in the clubhouse for a *schnapps.*

"I don't understand," finally confessed the German Jew. "I've taken years of instruction from the best pros . . . nothing. You were great. Did you ever take lessons?"

"Nope," replied the Hasid and his eyes rolled heavenward, "God be blessed, I pray every morning in a very good *shul.*"

"And that's it?" marveled the German Jew. "That's it," replied the Hasid, "prayer every morning."

The next week, the two met again for a round of golf. The Hasid danced over the course and did even better than the week before. The German Jew did far worse.

Back in the clubhouse, the sweaty German Jew complained to the Hasid: "I don't understand. I went to temple every morning this last week."

"Where did you go?" asked the Hasid.

"The big Temple Emmanu-El, on 5th Avenue and 65th Street."

"Oh no," cried the Hasid, "that's not right. That temple is for tennis!"

This very contemporary joke speaks to the omnipresent fantasy of an all-powerful Father, Mother, Big Brother or Sister, Friend, Teacher, Rabbi—God—who will watch over us and take care of us and fulfill our grandest wishes. And all we have to do is be good or pray or be "us" and magically, everything we want to be, do and become will transpire:

The Choice of a Soul

Rabbi Hayyim Meir Yehiel once said to his Hasidim:

"I know a man who as a boy was removed to the upper world on the night he became Bar Mitzva, and there they allowed him to choose a soul to his own liking. And so he selected a great soul. But he did not reach any high rung after all, and he remained a little man."

The Hasidim realized that he had been speaking of himself.

(*Buber, Late Masters, p. 80*)

We found this story very touching: ". . . a great soul . . . a little man." Is this another story about great dreams and underachievement? Or is it a tale that teaches that God does not provide solutions? Only you, big or little, can do that. God provides the dream, and only you can make it real. An old Yiddish witticism puts it wryly: "God will provide. If only God would provide until He provides" (Ayalti 1949).

Many Hasidic stories speak about how God receives from His people but never "pays back." That is not allowed, however devoutly it may be deserved or desired. There is no *quid pro quo* with God. God takes all and gives capriciously, with no rhyme or reason that we mere mortals can discern:

Suffering

A man who was afflicted with a terrible disease complained to Rabbi Israel that his suffering interfered with his learning and praying. The rabbi put his hand on his shoulder and said: "How do you know, friend, what is more pleasing to God, your studying or your suffering?"

(*Buber, Late Masters, p. 60*)

By definition, unconditional love asks nothing in return. Serving God to receive a reward is blasphemous, self-degrading:

A Saying of the Fathers

A disciple told this story:

"My master, Rabbi Simha Bunam, once drew my head toward him with his holy hand until his lips touched the inside of my ear. Three times he whispered to me the words from *The Sayings of the Fathers*: 'Be not like servants who minister to their master on condition that they receive a reward.' My brain seemed to split with the holy and awesome breath of his mouth."

(*Buber, Late Masters, p. 252*)

To the untutored Hasid this "law of noncompensation" had to be explained over and over again, which the rabbis did, using the simplest and most homely metaphors that they could think of:

Like the Ox

A Hasid complained to the Rabbi of Ger: "I have worked and toiled, and yet I have not the satisfaction of a master-craftsman who, after twenty years of effort, finds some result of his labors in his work: Either it is better than it was at first, or he can do it more quickly. I see nothing at all. Just as I prayed twenty years ago, so I pray today."

The *tzaddik* answered: "It is taught in Elijah's name: 'Man should take the Torah upon himself as the ox takes the yoke and the ass his burden.' You see, the ox leaves his stall in the morning, goes to the field, plows, and is led home, and this happens day after day, and nothing changes with regard to the ox; but the plowed field bears the harvest."

(*Buber, Late Masters, p. 304*)

The rabbis had to find or invent metaphors that would clarify the idea that giving to God is really taking from Him, that in the giving is the taking and that's *it*: The prayer is God:

He Is Your Psalm

Concerning the words in the Scriptures: "He is the psalm and He is thy God," Rabbi Pinhas said the following:

"He is your psalm and He also is your God. The prayer a man says, the prayer, in itself, is God. It is not as if you were asking something of a friend. He is different and your words are different. It is not so in prayer, for prayer unites the principles. When a man who is praying thinks his prayer is something apart from God, he is like a supplicant to whom the king gives what he has begged from him. But he who knows that prayer in itself is God, is like the king's son who takes whatever he needs from the stores of his father."

(*Buber, Early Masters, p. 125*)

In fact, it is not achieving an object or an end, but the seeking of God that is man's joy and purpose in life:

The Joy of the Quest

The Apelier Rabbi made the following comment on the verse "Let the heart of them rejoice that seek the Lord" (I Chronicles 16:10): "When one seeks a certain object, he feels no gladness in his heart until his quest is successful. But when one seeks the Lord, the very act of seeking Him rejoices the heart of the seeker."

(*Newman, The Hasidic Anthology, p. 419*)

Indeed, man was created for that one purpose:

To What Purpose Was Man Created?

Rabbi Mendel of Kotzk once asked his disciple Rabbi Yaakov of Radzimin: "Yaakov, to what purpose was man created?" He answered: "So that he might perfect his soul."

"Yaakov," said the *tzaddik*, "is this what we learned from our teacher, Rabbi Bunam? No, indeed! Man was created so that he might lift up the heavens!"

(*Buber, Late Masters, p. 276*)

The rabbis reframed suffering, poverty, illness, misfortune, and death as tests for maintaining trust and faith in God. This theme is developed in countless Hasidic stories:

Living in Paradise

The Bratzlaver said: "The knowledge that whatsoever occurs to you is for your good, raises you to the heights of living in Paradise."

(*Newman, The Hasidic Anthology, p. 97*)

Accepting the World

One of Rabbi Moshe's Hasidim was very poor. He complained to the *tzaddik* that his wretched circumstances were an obstacle to learning and praying.

"In this day and age," said Rabbi Moshe, "the greatest devotion, greater than learning and praying, consists in accepting the world exactly as it happens to be."

(*Buber, Late Masters, p. 166*)

"Accepting the world" is accepting God; after all, it is God's world. He created it in the first place.

The rabbis fostered a direct unmediated relationship between Hasid and God. It proceeds from a single person and is intensely private and not intended to be known publicly:

Modest Piety

The Kozmirer Rabbi visited Rabbi Akiya Eger of Posen. The latter asked him to define a Hasid. The Kozmirer replied: "A Hasid is one of whose Hasidut or piety, only he and his Creator know."

(*Newman, The Hasidic Anthology, p. 270*)

When the Hasid specifically directs his attention to God, as in prayer, he is complete, in a state of plenitude:

What You Get out of Life

The Rabbi of Tzans told the following story and accompanied his words with gestures that conjured up a picture:

"People come to me who ride to market every day of the week. One such man approached me and cried: 'My dear rabbi! I haven't gotten anything out of life. All week I get out of one wagon and into another.' But when a man stops to think that he is permitted to pray to God Himself, he lacks nothing at all in the world."

(*Buber, Late Masters, p. 210*)

In the very complex story that follows, Rabbi Shlomo once again steps into the breach and subtly and gently makes so fine a distinction about what God really wants that the story must be reread several times to absorb its full import:

Out of Travail

Once, at the close of the Day of Atonement, when Rabbi Shlomo was in a gay mood, he said he would tell each Hasid what he had asked of Heaven on these holy days, and what answer was intended for his request. To the first of his disciples who wanted to be told, he said: "What you asked of God was that He should give you your livelihood at the proper time and without travail, so that you might not be hindered in serving Him. And the answer was that what God really wants of you is not study or prayer, but the sighs of your heart, which is breaking because the travail of gaining a livelihood hinders you in the service of God."

(*Buber, Early Masters, p. 280*)

The Hasid wants the security of an adequate livelihood to serve God. Sound familiar? How many of us have "sold their souls" to make money to enable us to be free to do what we really want to do? The question, of course, is rhetorical.

Rabbi Shlomo's response is sublime—spiritually, intellectually and morally. It inspires awe and implies an exaltation beyond ordinary human comprehension. It is a resplendent reframe, precisely because of its quiet, unassuming, evanescent, scarcely audible presence that threatens to dissipate unnoticed: ". . . the sighs of your heart. . . ."

What is Rabbi Shlomo saying? "Certainly you have to make a living! And while you are doing so, your heart is breaking at the waste of time and energy and soul in such mundane activity, and God hears!" God is where your heart is; and nowhere is this message more piercingly presented than in the last story.

THE REVOLUTIONARY IDEA OF GIVING WITHOUT RECEIVING ANYTHING IN RETURN

It is difficult for the modern secular mind to fathom the revolutionary moral idea of giving without receiving something in return. At the heart of every modern human relationship is an exchange of material, emotional, or symbolic values: Parents "sacrifice" for children with the expectation that their success in the future will reflect on them; a teacher gives knowledge and, in addition to pay, receives approval, recognition, and admiration; a manager guides a subordinate, the latter helps achieve departmental goals, and this redounds to the manager's benefit.

This exchange process is so universal today that a major school of social psychology developed originally by George C. Homans has as its central premise the idea that every relationship is built on an implicit and/or explicit calculus of cost-benefit analysis of the exchange partners. Modern behavior theory is essentially constructed on the same "What's in it for me?" premise.

Nine out of ten Americans believe that the best philosophy is to "give and take," and every relationship should include both. In fact, most people would regard anyone who gave without getting anything in return as masochistic, a martyr, a saint, a holy man, an angel, a wimp, insecure, a sufferer, dependent, lacking in self-esteem, and so forth.

And yet this is precisely what the Hasidic God requires—absolute, open-ended, endless, one-way fealty:

Why People Go to the Tzaddik

Rabbi Mordecai said: "People go to the *tzaddikim* for many different reasons. One goes to the *tzaddik* to learn how to pray with fear and love; another to acquire strength to study the Torah for its own sake. Still another goes because he wants to mount to a higher rung of spiritual life, and so on. But none of these should be the true purpose of going, for each of them can be attained, and then it is no longer necessary to toil for it. The only, the true purpose, should be to seek the reality of God. No bounds are set to this, and it has no end."

(*Buber, Early Masters, p. 164*)

If, indeed, there is no *quid pro quo* for the Hasid's devotion to serving God, then the serving itself is both the giving and taking. And because there is no return after the "end" of a service to God, serving God has no ending, and all the satisfaction lies in continuous service.

This continuous giving without any receiving, except in the giving itself, is an awesome moral act. It goes entirely against the grain of individual competitiveness and achievement: Whenever you do anything worthwhile, some reward is expected and most often given; without that incentive the activity ceases.

In human relationships, any person who gives unstintingly of himself to others is considered a saint, a guru, or a holy person. That designation is a "reward." A mother, perhaps, is close to such a relationship with her baby.

Search back into your memory to recall people who were "givers" without the need to get something in return. What you'll discover is a trait common to all of these people: They enjoy the giving, which they do not see as taking something from themselves, but as an end in itself. Winning or receiving something in return was considered secondary or, most often, not considered at all.

These were very special people who turned the secular culture of self-aggrandizement on its head. They are quite extraordinary in that they discovered the contentment and happiness, even the joy and strange self-empowerment in getting by giving and letting the commonly accepted end-result be damned, especially if it impeded in any way the fullness of giving.

We are not speaking of martyrs or saints or masochists. The givers we are speaking of are accomplished in their fields of endeavor and are strong personalities. We do not even believe their giving is the result of a thought-through philosophy. They simply give out of the plenitude of their infinite souls, always getting more by giving, and thoroughly enjoying themselves.

Now there is one mighty, one might say "almighty" difference between these givers and the Hasidim who give to God. The people the secular givers give to are real and may subliminally signal cues of appreciation, admiration, respect, even awe, which are picked up by the givers. That may be. We still believe the givers are largely oblivious to these appreciative reactions and give because they enjoy the act of giving.

Hasidim, however, give to God. And God is not a person. God is everywhere, of course (and nowhere), and certainly in the Hasid's imagination. So while the Hasid is serving (and/or praying to) his Maker, some manifestation of his Maker is being created that is the recipient of all this selfless giving.

And that is precisely the point! The giving is literally selfless; there is no regard for the self, except for the giving it over to someone outside of oneself. By giving oneself away to God, one enters an altered state of consciousness, an entrancement with the created image of a Divine Presence and by partaking of this divinity becomes divine himself—even if it may be through the most minute instantaneous spark that is quickly swallowed up by the night.

Thus, the Hasid goes one decisive step further than the secular person who gives of himself to other people. The Hasid quite literally in the trance gives his self away to God. But we must backtrack here a bit; it is not the giving away of the self that is joyous, but the act of giving away itself.

What an enormous irony, and what an impossible task the rabbis set for themselves! The Hasid's fantasy was to be taken care of; story after story attests to this deeply ingrained desire. Indeed, Hasidim are coerced, wheedled, cajoled, challenged, commanded, and confounded into giving their all to God with no expectation whatsoever of any reward!

Ultimately, we believe, there is an implicit promise here of the joyous life on earth. God is a bridge, a model transition to the appropriate moral life among people, however fantastic an ideal it may be. The best way to live is to act selflessly and enjoy thoroughly the act of giving, because that is all you will ever be fully entitled to do. This is the powerful lesson the Hasidim and their rabbis have taught us in countless parables, aphorisms and stories. It is not the giving of something, but the giving and caring that is divine:

Where to Find God

> A merchant once came to Rabbi Meir Shalom, a son of Rabbi Yehoshua Asher, and complained of another merchant who had opened his shop right next door to him. "You seem to think," said the *tzaddik*, "that it is your shop that supports you, and you are setting your heart upon it instead of on God, who is your support. But perhaps you do not know where God lives? It is written: 'Love thy neighbor as thyself: I am the Lord.' This means: 'You shall want for your neighbor what he needs, just as you do for yourself—and therein you will find the Lord.'"
>
> (*Buber, Late Masters, p. 235*)

In their endless one-way giving to God, the Hasidim, one might argue, were simply carried away. To give to God without return, to give to others without return—these are understandable. But to give to one's enemies as well, even the most precious of all your possessions?

Love for Enemies

> Rabbi Mikhal gave this command to his sons: "Pray for your enemies that all may be well with them. And should you think this is not serving God, rest assured that more than all prayers, this is, indeed, the service of God."
>
> (*Buber, Late Masters, p. 156*)

For those who think this is some abstract, fanciful notion that is not practiced, the following incident should remove any doubts:

For the Joy of Others

> The *mitnagdim* were making fun of the Rabbi of Lekhovitz on another occasion. But when they laughed, he did nothing but smile and say: "God has not created a single creature that does not give joy to others. So I, too, have been created for the joy of others, for those who are near to my heart because my nearness is pleasing to them, and for you because you mock me." The *mitnagdim* listened and grew silent and gloomy.
>
> (*Buber, Late Masters, p. 156*)

Giving to God without expectation of any reward focuses the interaction between God and Hasid on the process of serving Him. Thus, many Hasidic stories dwell on four interrelated themes: finding God; communicating with God; the Hasid–God relationship; the side-effects of serving one's maker.

FINDING GOD

Hasidic stories about finding God always begin with a misunderstanding about where to look, a misapprehension which is always clarified when the Hasid discovers that God is not elusive, but the seeker does not trust himself to find Him. Ordinarily, when someone is hiding, the searcher uses his legs and eyes to find the hiding place. To find God, the preferred (or perhaps the only) organ that is of any use is the heart!

Alfred North Whitehead called thinking about abstractions as real things "the fallacy of misplaced concreteness." It is a case of mistaken identity. An abstraction is an expression of a quality apart from any object. An abstraction is a generalization, the theoretical consideration of a subject apart from any specific concrete manifestation: truth, honesty, *kavvana*, God.

The most common way of seeing, thinking of, or visualizing God is as a super-person—first cause, creator, maker, author, beloved, king, master, lord, judge (supreme court), or, more modestly, as a shepherd, teacher, father.

Now just as giving to God entails no object, no end and no return, finding God consists of no place, no time and no object. And yet we are inexorably compelled to think about the search for God as looking for a treasure. This mistaken analogy of seeking God as a concrete metaphor rather than an abstract metaphor was a source of endless Hasidic speculation. They knew the Bible's references to that search:

> "Canst thou by searching find our God?" (Job 11:7).

> "If I ascend up into heaven, Thou [God] art there; if I make my bed in hell, behold, Thou art there" (Psalms 139:8).

There is a widespread belief, not unknown to the Hasidim, that a child's innocence is close to God. The hide-and-seek game of childhood is a natural metaphor for the Hasid's search for God:

Hide-and-Seek

> Rabbi Barukh's grandson Yehiel was once playing hide-and-seek with another boy. He hid himself well and waited for his playmate to find him. When he had waited for a long time, he came out of his hiding-place, but the other was nowhere to be seen. Now Yehiel realized that his friend had not looked for him from the very beginning. That made him cry and, crying, he ran to his grandfather and complained of his faithless friend. Then tears brimmed in Rabbi Barukh's eyes, and he said: "God says the same thing: 'I hide, but no one wants to seek me.'"
>
> (*Buber, Early Masters, p. 97*)

Children have a distinctive cleverness, because they are only partially socialized into adult culture and its accepted cliches and still see life "fresh":

Where Does God Live?

When Rabbi Yitzhak Meir was a little boy his mother once took him to see the *maggid* of Koznitz. There someone said to him: "Yitzhak Meir, I'll give you a gulden if you tell me where God lives!" He replied: "And I'll give you two gulden if you tell me where He doesn't!"

(*Buber, Late Masters, p. 303*)

Always, the main thrust for finding God was to literally redirect the Hasid's search for God's hiding place. And this is the heart of the matter: God is to be found in the Hasid, not somewhere outside of himself. To be even more precise, He is to be found in the Hasid's heart. But it is no simple task to discover God there, even though the Hasid knows He is hiding there. It takes a deliberate act of will to find God in one's heart:

Upon Thy Heart

Rabbi Mendel of Kotzk said:

"'And these words which I command thee this day shall be *upon* thy heart.' The verse does not say: '*in* thy heart.' For there are times when the heart is shut. But the words lie upon the heart, and when the heart opens in holy hours, they sink deep down into it."

(*Buber, Late Masters, p. 278*)

God's Dwelling

"Where is the dwelling of God?"

This was the question with which the Rabbi of Kotzk surprised a number of learned men who happened to be visiting him. They laughed at him: "What a thing to ask! Is not the whole world full of His glory?"

Then he answered his own question:

"God dwells wherever man lets Him in."

(*Buber, Late Masters, p. 277*)

The enigma of where and when God is, is part and parcel of what and who God is. God, indeed, may be only a blessed name, but this never sufficed for the ordinary Hasid villager who was forever trying to "get a handle" on the God epiphenomenon. Among themselves, the rabbis' search was much more esoteric, because of their ability to play with abstractions in a logical way:

God Is Nothing and Everywhere

> The Rav asked a disciple: "Moshe, what do we mean when we say 'God'?"
>
> The disciple was silent.
>
> The Rav asked him a second and a third time and then inquired: "Why are you silent?"
>
> "Because I do not know."
>
> "Do you think I know?" said the Rav. "All I can say is that He is definitely there, and except for Him nothing is definitely there—and this is He."
>
> (*Buber, Early Masters, p. 269*)

Although this sounds, initially, a bit abstract, it is also concrete and specific. The only way to think about God is to contrast Him with everything that is. So God is everywhere and everything on one hand, and He is also everything in-between where everything is, and everything that everything is not.

The Hasidim loved to play these games of imagining the unimaginable. The point about God being nothing is, of course, a big joke, and yet it is also very serious. Why is this? We think what is happening here is that the rabbis had as one of their objectives to de-anthropomorphize God as the image of man, in the way man is the image of God. This was far too mundane for them. The Hasidim envisioned God in a much more subtle, mysterious, and strange way and got away from the idea of Him as some sort of superhuman being. The Hasidic answer to anthropomorphism was to shroud God in a mysterious form of nothingness. This certainly contributes to the feelings of awe and profound ecstasy that Hasidim experienced in their romance with God, precisely because He was so elusive and difficult to imagine, and in the nothingness void they were forced to pour in more of themselves. What it came down to, ultimately, was imagining Him by imagining the unimaginable through very simple basic elements of things and not things, place and nowhere:

The Palace Treasures

Said the Besht: "Two persons went into the royal palace to see the king. At the entrance, they were informed that the king would not see petitioners on that day. One left immediately, but the other obtained permission to view the beautiful paintings and other valuable objects in the palace.

"In the same fashion, since mortals cannot comprehend God, there are some teachers and philosophers who declare that there is no need to study and to keep the Torah and its commandments: no matter, they affirm, how much a man may study, he cannot know God. This is wrong. Even if we do not behold the King face to face, we may view His treasures in His palace, and enjoy them through observing the prescribed regulations. That is to say, we may study God's world, God's Torah, God's creatures, and thereby at least be near to His presence."

(*Newman, The Hasidic Anthology, p. 160*)

Recognizing that except for Him there is nothing, a somewhat more mundane realization of God is to accept His creation "exactly as it happens to be," including all of its afflictions (See "Accepting the World," on page 209.):

Afflictions from Love

Said the Porissover: "Some Hasidim are so proud of their piety that they cannot believe the Lord sends them hardships in order to awaken in them penitence for their sins. They affirm: 'I am a perfect Jew, and I will accept these hardships as 'afflictions from love.' But afflictions from love are not sent in vain; they are intended as a means to arouse penitence. When the Rizhiner was imprisoned, he wept. He was asked: 'Why do you not accept this affliction as intended, in love?' He answered: 'When God sends bitterness, we ought to feel it.'"

(*Newman, The Hasidic Anthology, p. 485*)

Still another version of God is that His world is in a continuous process of change and creation:

Eternal Creation

Rabbi Bunam taught:

"This is how we must interpret the first words in the Scripture: 'In the beginning is God's creation of the heaven and the earth.' For even now, the world is still in a state of creation. When a craftsman makes a tool and it is finished, it does not require him any longer. Not so with the world! Day after day, instant after instant, the world requires the renewal of the powers of the primordial word through which it was created, and if the power of these powers were withdrawn from it for a single moment, it would lapse into *tohu vavohu* [i.e., chaos]."

(*Buber, The Hasidic Anthology, p. 259*)

COMMUNICATING WITH GOD

When God is "found" and the Hasid commences to communicate with Him to evolve his unique relationship, there occurs, Hasidim believe, a sort of spontaneous combustion—the self-ignition of a combustible heart.

Communication with God is controlled and directed internally. It arises from within, without external constraints. It is not contrived, manipulated, deliberated, or even planned. It is natural and impulsive, complete and intense. It is ingenuous, innocent, simple, naive. It is a spirit that arises naturally from the Hasid's heart without any special cultivation.

The communication with God ideally lacks artificiality and self-consciousness. It openly and fully and directly expresses the Hasid's deepest feelings and intentions. No special training is required, because communicating with God is artless—a naturalness that flows from releasing the feelings in the heart without censorship, cliches, and calculation; it is devoid of accountability for the effect it is producing. In short, the best communication with God is the spontaneous combustion of the heart.

The rabbis endlessly counseled their followers to avoid substituting strict mechanical observance of rituals for the natural and occasional "erring" of the heart:

Against Pious Thoughts

On a certain Purim, when the Rabbi of Mogielnica was reading the scroll of Esther, a young man stood nearby and said to him when the reading was over: "I fear I did not listen closely enough and perhaps skipped over one word or another while I was silently reciting the scroll with you."

Later, the rabbi said to his friends: "There's your super-pious man! All he cares about is doing exactly what is prescribed. But he whose soul is directed toward doing the will of God within the commandment, and clings wholly to God's will, may very possibly fail to do something of what is prescribed, but it does not trouble him. For it is written: 'In thy love for her wilt thou err constantly.'"

(*Buber, Late Masters, pp. 180–181*)

The Whistle

The story goes that one Day of Atonement, when the Jews were gathered in the synagogue, and all the rabbis were there, among them the Besht, one ignorant farmer brought his son with him to the services. The son, who could not read a word of the ritual, had with him a whistle which he used ordinarily when watching the cattle. He was exceedingly fond of this whistle which he used frequently at home. During the Neilah prayer, which marks the climax of the holyday, the boy took out his whistle and blew it. The Besht jumped up and congratulated the Jews: God had opened the gates; the Rabbis, with all their prayers and their learning, could not prevail with God, as had the young herdsman in his ignorance, by his simple desire to serve God.

(*Newman, The Hasidic Anthology, p. 520*)

The following deeply affecting story has all the psychological, dramatic and hypnotic qualities of the best Hasidic stories:

Tears and Laughter

A man once confessed a sin to the Rabbi of Apt and told him with tears how he had atoned for it. The *tzaddik* laughed. The man went on to tell what more he intended doing to atone for his sin; the rabbi went on laughing. The man wanted to speak on, but the laughter robbed him of his speech. He stared at the *tzaddik* in horror. And then his very soul held its breath, and he heard that which is spoken deep within. He realized how trivial all his fuss about atoning had been, and he turned to God.

(*Buber, Late Masters, p. 118*)

Powerful circuits need strong circuit-breakers. The confessor is entangled and trapped by procedure and ritual which he has substituted for listening to his own heart. How familiar this is to our ears. Carrying out the letter of the form totally violates the spirit of the activity. And the Hasid was so caught up in the outward form that he took it for the genuine way to act. He believed utterly in his own self-deception. This is another example of super-piety.

The rabbi laughs at the crying man. That is heavy. That takes great compassion—not to be seduced by tears. The *tzaddik*'s laughter completely derails the Hasid, because he was describing his automatic, ingrained way of atoning for his sin. The Hasid goes into shock and is literally "all shook up," which opens up new paths for insight into and feelings about what he is doing. He was at a breaking point where "his very soul held its breath," a very serious and precarious state.

Then, finally, came an insight, a message, an impulse from deep within which had not been affected by all his outward pretense, and he arrives at the realization that the ritual is only the outward wrapping of the heart's stirrings and when the latter is missing, all the atonement is just so much empty gesturing. With that realization, God enters his heart and he makes "the turn."

As the following story attests, all that is required for the Hasid to find God is to go in the right direction and use ritual as a *guide*, not an end:

Offering the First Part

Said the Lekhivitzer: "The Torah begins with the word '*bereishit*' [Gen. 1:1], which may be translated: 'for the sake of the first' the Lord has created the world. All that the Creator demands is that a man make a beginning in the right direction; thereafter, He will help him to continue in the right path. To symbolize this, He ordained that we should devote to the Lord the first fruits; the first stalks of grain; the firstborn cattle; and the Law of Tradition commands us to devote the first part of every day to prayer."

(*Newman, The Hasidic Anthology, p. 61*)

The idea that there are many ways to serve God is fundamental to Hasidic thought. The act, the actual behavior, live prayer or a good deed, can be separated from the way the doer's heart feels about it. This is a very important distinction. For the Hasidic rabbis, the different external ways one showed devotion to God were only of secondary interest, as long as the devotion was heartfelt. This point is reiterated in many stories by the rabbis—to each other, and to their followers:

The Way

Rabbi Baer of Radoshitz once said to his teacher, the Rabbi of Lublin: "Show me one general way to the service of God." The *tzaddik* replied: "It is impossible to tell men what way they should take. For one way to serve God is through the teachings, another way through prayer, another through fasting, and still another through eating. Everyone should carefully observe what way his heart draws him to, and then choose this way with all his strength."

(*Buber, Early Masters, p. 313*)

This story highlights the Hasidic emphasis upon the meaning behind the act that drives the act and makes secondary the activities by which people can worship God. This illustrates the entirely unified perspective of the profane and the secular, praying in the synagogue and eating at home—all of these can be filled with God's spirit through man's soul and heart. Once your heart is in the right place *every* activity is filled with God, and you can enjoy life to the fullest:

The Alphabet

> An ignorant villager, having heard it is a good religious deed to eat and drink on the day before Yom Kippur, drank himself into a stupor. He awoke late at night, too late for Kol Nidrei services. Not knowing the prayers by heart, he devised a plan. He repeated the letters of the alphabet over and over, beseeching the Almighty to arrange them into the appropriate words of the prayers. The following day he attended the Kotzker synagogue. After Neilah,[1] the rabbi summoned him to inquire the cause of his absence at Kol Nidrei. The villager confessed his transgression and asked whether his manner of reciting the prayers could be pardoned. The rabbi responded: "Your prayer was more acceptable than mine because you uttered it with the entire devotion of your heart."
>
> (*Newman, Maggidim and Hasidim, p. 97*)

We have stressed that the hallmark of the Hasidic way of life was the great importance that it attached to the meaning of an act and the feeling that a person has about it, rather than the act itself. The act is the outward form of *kavvana*, its spiritual significance comes from the heart and makes the external behavior authentic. The rabbis were not hesitant to share their own lack of understanding at times of this principle and how they were taught by their followers to appreciate the heart's melody, rather than merely the words:

Babbling Sounds

> Rabbi Levi Yitzhak once came to an inn where many merchants were stopping on the way to market their wares. The place was far from Berditchev and so no one knew the *tzaddik*. In the early morning, the guests wanted to pray, but since there

[1]Closing service on Yom Kippur.

was only a single pair of phylacteries in the whole house, one after another put them on and rattled off his prayer and handed them on to the next. When they had all prayed, the rabbi called the young men to him, saying that he wanted to ask them something. When they had come close, he looked gravely into their faces and said: "Ma-ma-ma; va-va-va."

"What do you mean?" cried the young men, but he only repeated the same meaningless syllables. Then they took him for a fool.

But now he said: "How is it you do not understand this language which you yourselves have just used in speaking to God?"

For a moment, the young men were taken aback and stood silent. Then one of them said: "Have you never seen a child in the cradle, who does not yet know how to put sounds together into words? Have you not heard him make babbling sounds, such as 'ma-ma-ma; va-va-va'? All the sages and scholars in the world cannot understand him, but the moment his mother comes, she knows exactly what he means."

When the rabbi heard this answer, he began to dance for joy. And from that time on, whenever on the Days of Awe he spoke to God in his own fashion in the midst of prayer, he never failed to tell this answer to Him.

(*Buber, Early Masters, pp. 214–215*)

So the rabbi can also learn new ways to appreciate the magic and the power of the inner spirit and how it can be confused by external expression. Even babble is spiritual when it is uttered from the heart. And that is why the rabbi danced for joy—he found how miraculous man and God's spirit are in that they can express themselves in the most meaningless sounds and still be understood. This is the power of faith and spirit in man, in oneself, and in God.

THE HASID–GOD RELATIONSHIP

The most full-blown metaphor of the relationship between God and human is that of the lovers in the Song of Songs. The ideal relationship to God is ecstasy—a loss of self, both spiritually and physically in the relationship:

The Original Meaning

This is what Rabbi Moshe said to an author who put questions to him concerning the Kabbala, the secret teachings, and the *kavvanot*, the mystical concentrations, which are directed toward superhuman effects: "You must keep in mind that the word *Kabbala* is derived from *kabbel*: to accept; and the word *kavvana* from *kavven*: to direct. For the ultimate significance of all the wisdom of the Kabbala is to accept the yoke of the Kingdom of God, and the ultimate significance of all the art of the *kavvanot* is to direct one's heart to God. When a man says: 'The Lord is my God,' meaning: 'He is mine and I am His,' must not his soul go forth from his body?" The moment the rabbi said this, he fell into a deep faint.

(*Buber, Late Masters, p. 166*)

Underlying the transcending relationship (perhaps even preceding it) is the spontaneous expression of feeling. The Hasidim were extraordinarily wary of intellectualizing the relationship between man and God. Unalloyed, direct, spontaneous feeling was the genuine expression of man's relationship to God; that feeling was incapable of being untruthful and therefore was to be regarded highly as, for example, in two Hasidic stories about fear and love:

Fear

The Rabbi of Kotzk asked one of his Hasidim:

"Have you ever seen a wolf?"

"Yes," he replied.

"And were you afraid of him?"

"Yes."

"But you were aware of the fact that you were afraid?"

"No," answered the Hasid. "I was simply afraid."

"That is how it should be with us when we fear God," said the rabbi.

(*Buber, Late Masters, p. 279*)

Our Test

The Yehudi said:

"Everything can be tested in some particular way to discover whether it is any good. And what is the test for the man of Israel? It is the love of Israel. When he sees the love of Israel growing in his soul day after day, he knows that he is ascending in the service of God."

(*Buber, Late Masters, p. 236*)

The exile theme was frequently reframed to demonstrate that God was even closer to the Jews because of it. The next story is typical:

In Exile

The *Maggid* of Mezeritch said: "Now, in exile, the holy spirit comes upon us more easily than at the time the Temple was still standing.

"A king was driven from his realm and forced to become a wayfarer. When, in the course of his wanderings, he came to the house of poor people, where he was given modest food and shelter but received as a king, his heart grew light and he chatted with his host as intimately as he had done at court with those who were closest to him.

"Now, that He is in exile, God does the same."

(*Buber, Early Masters, p. 103*)

The following moving story is the most piercing expression of the apocalyptic and apodictic relationship between humanity and God. We found it hard to hold back the silent dry tears that welled up within us. God is forever and we are for a moment, and how full, joyous and loving that moment on earth can be for two strangers:

The Two Strangers

In Psalm 119, the psalmist says to God: "I am a sojourner on the earth, hide not Thy commandments from me."

Concerning this verse, Rabbi Barukh said: "He whom Life drives into exile and who comes to a land alien to him, has nothing in common with the people there and not a soul he can talk to. But if a second stranger appears, even though he may come from quite a different place, the two can confide

> in each other, and live together henceforth, and cherish each other. And had they not both been strangers, they would never have known such close companionship. That is what the psalmist means: 'You, even as I, are a sojourner on earth and have no abiding place for Your glory. So do not withdraw from me, but reveal Your commandments, that I may become Your friend.'"
>
> (*Buber, Early Masters, p. 89*)

Finally, the Hasidim were unflinching in facing all possibilities, even, horror of horrors, denying the existence of God. The following story merges with being a parable as it is demonstrated that one can show in his act that he believes in God even though he says he doesn't:

When It Is Good to Deny the Existence of God

> Rabbi Moshe Leib said:
>
> "There is no quality and there is no power of man that was created to no purpose. And even base and corrupt qualities can be uplifted to serve God. When, for example, haughty self-assurance is uplifted, it changes into a high assurance in the ways of God. But to what end can the denial of God have been created? This, too, can be uplifted through deeds of charity. For if someone comes to you and asks your help, you shall not turn him off with pious words, saying: 'Have faith and take your troubles to God!' You shall act as if there were no God, as if there were only one person in all the world who could help this man—only yourself."
>
> (*Buber, Late Masters, p. 89*)

Whatever eschatology you ultimately choose or fall into, the Hasidim insist we love each other now, this moment; let us make a divinity of love and compassion and justice of our relationship and whether you believe in God or not, we are serving Him in all of our plenitude when we are fulfilling our highest ideals—and it is never too late:

The Change in the Work

When Rabbi Hirsh returned from his wife's funeral and went up the stairs to his room, he was heard saying to himself: "Up to now I have accomplished holy unification by marriage here below, now I shall try to accomplish unification by marriage up above."

Two weeks later, he died.

(*Buber, Late Masters, p. 218*)

SIDE EFFECTS OF SERVING ONE'S MAKER

The Hasidim insist that serving God is the reward. The recompense is in the giving. Whatever your creation of God and your relationship with Him is, there are definitive side effects and epiphanies which continually and cumulatively enlarge you by magnifying His presence in your life.

We will briefly take up four side benefits in the ongoing intimate relationship of Hasid and God:

- The cultivation of a sense of mystery and creativity
- Living up to the ideal morality that is projected onto God
- Relating to all people universally in the Name of a Universal God
- Constantly making oneself better in order to serve God better.

THE CULTIVATION OF A SENSE OF MYSTERY AND CREATIVITY

God's mystery is heightened when death approaches:

Seeing God

On a day shortly before his death, the Rav asked his grandson: "Do you see anything?"

The boy looked at him in astonishment.

Then the Rav said: "All I can see is the Divine Nothingness which gave life to the world."

(*Buber, Early Masters, p. 271*)

A person approaching death is close to God. The paradoxical idea of God as nothingness is that He is something that came from and is also nothing. Another way of putting it is that wherever there is something, at one time there was nothing. This nothingness gave birth to something. Thinking of God as nothing is what gave birth to wonderful creations. Akin to the idea that God is nothing and therefore everything, is the idea that anything that cannot be explained in ordinary terms emanates from God. Creativity is the unfathomed process by which humanity is renewed. The rabbis realized that to go beyond oneself entails opening up oneself to miraculous phenomena whose symptoms include an indwelling soul's pounding of the heart, an involuntary shudder, a mere glance.

Anyone who has ever created a poem or a story, a drawing or a painting, a beautiful relationship, a piece of jewelry, a tennis stroke—whatever—and has reflected on its creation cannot but marvel at the process of something emerging from "nothing." What is not there, and then is there in a very jumbled and chaotic mess, suddenly takes on a ravishing and inevitable form. Nietzsche was certainly right when he said that we have chaos and a dancing star in ourselves and one gives birth to the other.

The Hasidim were forever discussing these miraculous events in a godly frame, and they modeled their thoughts after the way God created the universe:

The Last Miracle

The *Maggid* of Mezeritch said:

"The creation of Heaven and earth is the unfolding of Something out of Nothing, the descent from above to below. But the *tzaddikim*, who in their work disengage themselves from what is bodily and do nothing but think about God, actually see and understand and imagine the universe as it was in the state of nothingness before creation. They change the

> Something back into the Nothing. This is more miraculous: to begin from the lower state. As it is said in the Talmud: 'Greater than the first miracle is the last.'"
>
> (*Buber, Early Masters, p. 104*)

What is truly astounding, however, is the rabbis' explanation of the creative process. In the following story, the Maggid of Mezeritch formulated some 200 years ago a theory of creativity which has not been improved upon since his time.

Every artist, scientist, athlete, and mystic who has written about the creative process has inevitably commented upon some intermediate sort of chaotic period or stage that must be undergone in passing from a lower to a *qualitatively* higher level of change. That is the price of change—undergoing a disorganized, disordered, confusing, muddled state that does, in a very strange way, have an "order" of its own, which means that its outcome is totally unpredictable. So people stick in there, hoping, believing and keeping the faith that a new order will emerge.

Nowhere, in our opinion, is this process more poetically and precisely described than in the following passage from the *Maggid* of Mezeritch:

The Between-Stage

> The *Maggid of* Mezeritch said:
>
> "Nothing in the world can change from one reality into another, unless it first turns into nothing, that is, into the reality of the between-stage. In that stage, it is nothing and no one can grasp it, for it has reached the rung of nothingness, just as before creation. And then it is made into a new creature, from the egg to the chick. The moment when the egg is no more and the chick is not yet, is nothingness. And philosophy terms this the primal state which no one can grasp because it is a force which precedes creation; it is called chaos. It is the same with the sprouting seed. It does not begin to sprout until the seed disintegrates in the earth and the quality of seed is destroyed in order that it may attain to nothingness which is the rung before creation. And this rung is called wisdom, that

> is to say, a thought which cannot be made manifest. Then this thought gives rise to creation, as it is written: 'In wisdom hast Thou made them all.'"
>
> (*Buber, Early Masters, p. 104*)

Wonderful! Wisdom is ". . . a thought which cannot be made manifest . . . and gives rise to creation." And it is true: The old must be destroyed to give way to the new, so that we can ever create anew. Everywhere, people are now recognizing that we are "in transition." Two hundred years ago, they called it "the between-stage," but it's the same concept!

Thank God for the Hasidim! They were always prepared to start anew, because they realized fully that the search is not finding someone or something at the end, but that the finding is in the seeking.

LIVING UP TO THE IDEAL MORALITY THAT IS PROJECTED ONTO GOD

This section could also have been titled: "The Education of the Rabbi of Apt." We are shaped by what we create. Once God becomes the accepted creation of all the people and there is consensus about all of His admirable superhuman qualities, then we all—*tzaddik*, rabbi, teacher, janitor, student, peasant, businessman, men and women, rich and poor alike—can hold one another accountable for deviations from an ideal that we can never attain and never cease striving to attain. We are fashioned by what we create:

The Turning Point

> A respected woman came to ask the advice of the Rabbi of Apt. The instant he set eyes on her, he shouted: "Adulteress! You sinned only a short while ago, and yet now you have the insolence to step into this pure house!" Then, from the depth of her heart the woman replied: "The Lord of the world has patience with the wicked. He is in no hurry to make them pay their debts, and He does not disclose their secret to any creature, lest they be ashamed to turn to Him. Nor does He hide His

face from them. But the Rabbi of Apt sits there in his chair and cannot resist revealing at once what the Creator has covered." From that time on the Rabbi of Apt used to say: "No one ever got the better of me except once—and then it was a woman."

(*Buber, Late Masters, p. 111*)

Powerful stuff. The woman, who is, unfortunately but typically, unnamed, is both passionate and eloquent. Obviously, she pierced the heart of the Rabbi of Apt, not because he saw that she was right and he was wrong, but because he apparently was able to utilize his new understanding to change his behavior:

The Proud and the Humble

Once, the Rabbi of Apt came to a city in which two men competed for the privilege of giving him lodgings. Both houses were equally roomy and comfortable, and in both households all the rules were observed with pious exactness. But one of the men was in ill repute for his many love affairs and other sinful doings, and he knew quite well that he was weak and thought little of himself. The other man, however, no one in the community could accuse of the slightest breach of conduct. With proud and stately steps he walked abroad, thoroughly aware of his spotless purity.

The rabbi selected the house of the man with the bad reputation. When he was asked the reason for his choice, he answered, "Concerning the proud, God says: 'I and he cannot live together in this world.' And if God Himself, blessed be He, cannot share a room with the proud, then how could I! We read in the Torah, on the other hand: 'Who dwelleth with them in the midst of their uncleannesses.' And if God takes lodging there, why shouldn't I?"

(*Buber, Late Masters, pp. 111–112*)

The Hasidim, rabbis and followers, were keenly aware that the ideal godly morality lay in *every* person as well as in the impediments to attaining the ideal. A stiff-necked people, they were not at all "ashamed" to put anyone "on the carpet" when he deserved it. God existed not to be found, but to be sought in our behavior toward each other!

RELATING TO ALL PEOPLE UNIVERSALLY IN THE NAME OF THE UNIVERSAL GOD

A Prayer

The Rabbi of Koznitz said to God: "Lord of the Universe, I beg of you to redeem Israel. And if you do not want to do that, then redeem the *goyim*."

(*Buber, Early Masters, p. 289*)

The ultimate test of the faith of an individual and a people is centered on loyalty to God, to a universal morality, as opposed to loyalty to family, friends, and countrymen, people with special connections of blood and common experiences.

A good example of the ethical conflict involved in this problem, referred to in sociology as "Universalism versus particularism," is an experiment where a student is assigned a monitoring role for fellow students who are taking an important final exam. The student-monitor's best friend cheats during the exam. What is the student-monitor to do? Should he turn him in to the school authorities because he has cheated (universal morality)? Or should he "forgive" the transgression and not turn in his best friend (particularistic loyalty)?

The rabbis were well aware of this conflict, and there are many stories about how they always chose the higher morality of truth—God—even though it was done at the cost of turning against their own loved ones. The rabbis did not believe in the principle "my country right or wrong." The following is a typical example of choosing a universal morality over expediency and loyalty to one's own:

The Servant

Rabbi Wolf's wife had a quarrel with the servant. She accused the girl of breaking a dish and wanted her to pay for the damage. The girl denied breaking the dish and refused to replace it. The quarrel became more and more heated.

Finally, Rabbi Wolf's wife decided to refer the matter to the Beit Din, the Jewish court, and she quickly dressed for a visit to the *rav* of the town. When Rabbi Wolf saw this, he too put on his Sabbath clothes.

When his wife asked him why he was going, he told her that he intended to accompany her. She objected to this on the grounds that this was not fitting for him and besides, she knew very well what to say to the court.

"You know what to say very well," the *tzaddik* replied, "but the poor orphan, your servant, on whose behalf I am coming, does not know how to deal with the court, and who except me is there to defend her cause?"

(*Buber, Early Masters, p. 159*)

Clearly, the Hasidic Jews would not have made good Mafia members. This is a beautiful example of how a belief in a universal morality that stems from a universal God is not to be compromised in practice. And it is only through behavior that the true morality of a people can be tested and shown. Hasidim would have made great whistle-blowers!

But the Hasidim were not fools. True, the Hasidic faith in God and faith in faith was so immense that it bordered on naivete. The idea that faith can bring any result has echoes in current evangelical T.V. ministers who promise everything from bucketsful of money to a place in Kingdom Come.

But the Jewish people were too pragmatic, too shrewd, too full of common sense to rely solely on faith to deliver the promised universal good life to them. They made fun of faithful, pious individuals who expected a utopian heaven on earth:

Thieves' Luck

With regard to Rashi's comment[2]: "He whose ear heard 'Thou shalt not steal' on Mount Sinai and then went and stole, his ear shall be pierced," Rabbi Shmelke said:

"Before God gave His commandments down from Mount Sinai, everyone took good care that his property was not stolen from him. And because the thieves knew this, they did not try

[2]Rashi is an acronym for Rabbi Shlomo Yitzhak of Troyes (1040–1105), the most popular Jewish commentator on the Bible and the Talmud.

> to steal. But after God spoke the words, 'Thou shalt not steal,' men felt secure and the trade of thieves began to thrive."
>
> (*Buber, Early Masters, p. 193*)

Whom is Rabbi Shmelke kidding? Were the Jews or the Hebrews so naive that they believed that everyone would religiously follow God's commandments and everyone therefore didn't watch out for his property and stimulated thieves to rob him? Our guess is that this is simply a naive bit of wishful thinking about God's commandment automatically being fulfilled in people's lives, and is a spoof on innocent righteous people who can't conceive of anyone disobeying God.

In a deeper sense, what's being said here is that it is precisely the simple-mindedness and naivete of believers in God that produce thieves. It's not God. It's people who take literally what God says that absolves God of creating thieves and places the blame on these simple-minded believers in faith.

Nevertheless, the key question remains: Do we need God to really understand and internalize the wisdom that when we give to someone else we are bountifully giving to ourselves, and when we hurt others we are destroying ourselves?

We remain more convinced than ever that true joy lies in the giving, and whatever you may get out of this book, we want you to know that we're having a wonderful time!

CONSTANTLY MAKING OURSELVES BETTER IN ORDER TO SERVE GOD BETTER

According to Ralph Waldo Emerson, "Every man contemplates an angel in his future self." A Jew, Hasidic or otherwise, cannot accept himself as he is because ultimately he can always improve his service to God, to others and to himself. This is the source of his historical and contemporary neurosis. There are always new wonders to create, behold and transmit both within and outside of ourselves!

Understanding of God, the cosmos and oneself is neverending! The wonder to be discovered in us matches the wonder in God and in nature. The key to all this unceasing improvement is faith. If you believe you can learn more to better serve God you will fulfill this prophecy. God never deceives us—we deceive ourselves. The Jewish God never confused the Jew's spiritual desire to learn more about Him with learning about himself. The search is literally endless. Quite the contrary. The Jew's kinship with God exalted the exalter.

The idea of working upon oneself to give better service to God radically influences what the Hasid will be working on to improve himself. It certainly is not to make more money, gain more power or recognition. We have said service to God is, above all, giving oneself to God without any expectation of a *quid pro quo.* The giving is in the giving. This is a difficult kind of working on oneself: to be more compassionate, caring, genuine, spontaneous, feeling, and humble. That indeed is a large, generous and impossible agenda that the rabbis and Hasidim grew increasingly to respect and appreciate.

The Rabbi of Zans is a case in point. (See the story "Resignation," on page 70.) "In my youth, fired with love for God, I thought I could convert the whole world." And he failed. Nor could he convert his town or his household. At last, he realized that he had to work on himself "to give true service to God. But even this I did not accomplish."

For the rabbis, the single biggest impediment was the sin of pride. They were always vulnerable because of the adulation of their followers. They needed all the help they could get from God:

Endless Struggle

> Rabbi Rafael, who was humble all of his days and avoided being honored, begged his teacher over and over to tell him how he could wholly fend off pride, but received no answer. Again he pressed his master: "O rabbi—pride, pride!"
>
> "What do you want?" said Rabbi Pinhas. "This is a piece of work with which a man must wrestle all his years, and which he can never finish. For pride is the garment of God, as it is written: 'The Lord is king; He is clothed in pride.' But God is boundless, and he who is proud, injures the garment of the

unbounded. And so the work of self-conquest is without bounds."

(*Buber, Early Masters, p. 128*)

It would be wrong to end this chapter on a cautionary note. We love the early Hasidim because of their zest for life, their incessant efforts toward self-improvement, their joy and, above all—their absorbing curiosity in the mystery of life:

> The secret things belong unto the Lord our God; but the things that are revealed belong unto us and to our children forever, that we may do all the words of this law.
>
> —*Deuteronomy 29:28*

11

Joy

He that is of a merry heart has a continual feast.

—*Proverbs 15:15*

A merry heart doeth good like a medicine.

—*Proverbs 17:22*

All Joys

Rabbi Pinhas said: "All joys hail from paradise, and jests too, provided they are uttered in true joy."

(*Buber, Early Masters, p. 135*)

"Thou shalt be joyous!" is not one of the Ten Commandments, but the central importance it assumes in Hasidic life could very well make it number eleven whenever we will summon the courage to make any additions. Perhaps it could be one of the Ten Commandments for children?

According to the Hasidim, we can learn the following from a child:

- He is merry for no particular reason.
- Never for a moment is he idle.
- When he needs something, he demands it vigorously.

Some of the satisfaction in experiencing joy in daily life, in addition to feeling good about feeling good, was the Hasidim's clandestine delight in upsetting their dour erstwhile antagonists, as the Rabbi of Lekhovitz did with *mitnagdim* who laughed at him. (See "For the Joy of Others," on page 215.) "All God's creatures give joy to others," said the rabbi, "and I am a source of joy to you who mock me."

Joy became a cardinal principle of holiness . . . a key element in giving service directly to God. And as the story below attests, the joy in lusting, eating and drinking was a master key for distinguishing the Hasidim from the *mitnagdim*:

Two Kinds of Tzaddikim

The Rabbi of Rizhin told how the people of Jassy sneered at the Rabbi of Apt after his sermons. He added: "In every generation there are people who grumble about the *tzaddik* and look askance at Moses. For the Rabbi of Apt is the Moses of his generation." He paused, and after a while he continued: "There are two kinds of service and two kinds of *tzaddikim.* One sort serves God with learning and prayer, the other with eating and drinking and earthly delights, raising all this to holiness. This is the kind the grumbling is about. But God has made them as they are because He does not want man to be caged in his lusts, but to be free in them. That is the calling of these *tzaddikim*: to make men free. Those others are the lords of the manifest, these are the lords of the hidden world. It is to them that secrets are revealed and the meaning of dreams unfolded, as it was to Joseph, who curled his beautiful hair and served God with the delights of this world."

On another occasion he spoke about the verse: "The heavens are the heavens of the Lord; but the earth hath He given to the children of men," saying: "There are two kinds of *tzaddikim.* Those of the one sort learn and pray the livelong day and hold themselves far from lowly matters in order to attain to holiness, while the others do not think of themselves, but only of delivering the holy sparks which are buried in all things back to God; and they make all lowly things their concern. The former, who are always busy preparing for Heaven, the verse calls 'the heavens,' and they have set themselves apart for the Lord. But the others are the earth, given to the children of men."

(*Buber, Late Masters, pp.* 53–54)

This story deserves close scrutiny, because it carefully distinguishes between two major eighteenth and nineteenth century religious lifestyles among Jews. According to the Hasidic Rabbi of Rizhin, the scholarly *mitnagdim* learn and pray all day and downgrade lowly matters of sex, food, and drink—they are above all that. The *mitnagdim* set themselves apart from the people with their erudition and, through their studies and exclusiveness, they prepare for Heaven:

Two Forms of Kabbala

Before the advent of the Besht, the Kabbala concerned itself with things spiritually divine, with objects in the higher spheres.

The Kabbala of the Besht, however, concerned itself with things materially divine, with objects in the lower strata.

The Kabbala before the Besht found God above us; the Kabbala of the Besht found God within and about us.

The Besht taught that the divine light descends directly into men's heart. This is called in the Kabbala: "The Inner Light."

(*Newman, Maggidim and Hasidim, p.* 95)

Here we have an intriguing proposition: that the Hasidim not only make all lowly things—sex, food, drink—their concern, but in those apparently mundane activities they find Godly sparks of holiness that are returned to Him. This quickly escalates into Hasidim as "lords of the hidden world," people to whom all kinds of secrets and mysteries, including the meaning of dreams, are revealed.

Now, this is a most peculiar juxtaposition: a delight in mundane, earthly things—not the magnificent creations of the intellect—and the discovery that these transitory, practical, ordinary, immediate, short-term, common, animalistic, vulgar, crude, primitive activities are full of divine sparks, are, in effect, certain manifestations of the Almighty Himself. How could this be?

The answer lies in the simultaneous cultivation of a vivid imagination bordering on the mystical and a strong faith that God is truly everywhere and therefore can be reached not only through Talmudic and Kabbalistic studies, but even more directly by the ordinary concerns and routines of everyday (not only holiday) life. It was not even necessary to see the divine sparks fly out every time. The important factor was to believe. The *tzaddik* of Lekhovitz put it very succinctly in "Hasid and Mitnaged" (p. 243).

In the mystic life, believing is essential and far more weighty than seeing. Believing determines seeing and, especially, the assumption of altered states of consciousness:

The Fool

> The Rabbi of Kobryn was asked: "Why is it that a cantor is always called a fool?"
>
> "You know," he replied, "that the world of music verges on that of the turning to God. When the cantor sings he is in the world of music and quite close to that other. How can he manage to keep from leaping over into it and giving himself up to the true turning? Is there any foolishness as foolish as that?"
>
> (*Buber, Late Masters, p. 168*)

We believe the Rabbi of Kobryn is being ironic here. Who would be so foolish as to refuse a true turning and a piece of Heaven?

The Hasidim used all activities to transcend themselves and their earthly existence. They made fun of the devout and pious because they followed empty ritual and accepted outward forms rather than sensuously experiencing and enjoying life. The acceptance of outward forms was a form of idol worship:

Sacrificing to Idols

> Rabbi Bunam was asked: "What is meant by the expression 'sacrificing to idols'? It is unthinkable that a man should really bring a sacrifice to idols!"

> He said: "I shall give you an example. When a devout and righteous man sits at table with others and would like to eat a little more but refrains because of what the people might think of him—that is sacrificing to idols."
>
> (*Buber, Late Masters, p. 256*)

Again we are impressed by the courage of the Hasidim in valuing what they can taste, see and feel rather than what people think they *should* revere. The Hasidic outlook consisted precisely in challenging and overcoming the worship of rituals and outer forms of veneration. There are many ways to experience God directly:

Hasid and Mitnaged

> The Kotzker said: "The Hasid has fear of the Lord, and the *mitnaged* has fear of the *Shulhan Arukh*."
>
> (*Newman, The Hasidic Anthology, p. 136*)

To be on the safe side, the Hasidim justified their belief in joy and rejection of sadness with appropriate interpretations and statements from the Bible:

God and Gladness

> Concerning the words in the Scriptures: "And it shall be, if thou shalt forget the Lord thy God," the Rabbi of Rizhin said: "It is well known that by every 'And it shall be' in the Scriptures, gladness is meant. Here we are told: 'If you forget gladness and fall into a depression, you are forgetting the Lord your God.' For it is written: 'Strength and gladness are in His place.'"
>
> (*Newman, Maggidim and Hasidim, p. 103*)

The rabbis went on to define sadness and dejection as well as joy and arrived at the major theoretical formulation that the purpose of suffering, failure and disappointment is to produce a downcast, dispirited and disheartening state within the person who has had negative experiences and who is in danger of letting sad experiences turn him into a melancholy person. Ultimately, for the Hasidim, dejection and melancholy "corrode" service to God:

Against Dejection

Rabbi Bunam expounded:

"In the psalm we read: 'Who healeth the broken in heart. . . .' Why are we told that? For it is a good thing to have a broken heart, and pleasing to God, as it is written: 'The sacrifices of God are a broken spirit.' But further on in the psalm we read: 'And bindeth up their wounds.' God does not entirely heal those who have broken hearts. He only eases their suffering, lest it torment and deject them. For dejection is not good and not pleasing to God. A broken heart prepares man for the service of God, but dejection corrodes service. We must distinguish as carefully between the two, as between joy and wantonness; they are so easily confused and yet are as far removed from one another as the ends of the earth."

(*Buber, Late Masters, p. 263*)

For the Hasidim, life is a celebration every single day, and the following story contains an appropriately joyous metaphor for this perspective:

The House of Weddings

Rabbi Hanokh told this parable:

A man from a small town moved to Warsaw. From a house near the one in which he had rented a room, he heard the sound of music and dancing. "They must be celebrating a wedding there," he thought to himself. But the next day, again, he heard the festive music, and the same thing happened on the day after that. "I wonder who the owner of that house can be," he said to friends he had in the city. "He seems to have a lot of sons he is marrying off." They laughed at him. "That house," they said, "is rented out every day for the purpose of celebrating weddings. Then the musicians play, and the guests dance. Because of this, we call it the house of weddings."

And then Rabbi Hanokh added: "This is why our sages compare this world to a house of weddings."

(*Buber, Late Masters, p. 314*)

It is time to shake ourselves loose from the idealistic vision of the world as a "house of weddings" and begin to ask the hard questions about how joy actually works. Is it enough to be spontaneously ourselves with good hearts? Will everything then fall into place? Is it truly enough to be joyous so that everyone will respond joyously and be joyous? Does joy beget joy? Is everything good, beautiful, right even when it is evil, ugly and wrong? In short, doesn't joy fly in the face of what is going on now in the world?

Given all the possible caveats in the above questions, would not most people regard anyone who is always joyous, or joyous at inappropriate times, as some sort of idiot? If that stops you from being joyous, you can fall back to the rationale Rabbi Bunam took:

The Story He Told

> Rabbi Bunam said:
>
> "Once, when I was on the road near Warsaw, I felt that I had to tell a certain story. But this story was of a worldly nature, and I knew that it would only rouse laughter among the many people who had gathered about me. The Evil Urge tried very hard to dissuade me, saying that I should lose all those people, because once they heard this story they would no longer consider me a rabbi. But I said to my heart: 'Why should you be concerned about the secret ways of God?' And I remembered the words of Rabbi Pinhas of Koretz: 'All joys hail from paradise, and jests too, provided they are uttered in true joy.' And so in my heart of hearts I renounced my rabbi's office and told the story. The gathering burst out laughing. And those who up to this point had been distant from me, attached themselves to me."
>
> (*Buber, Late Masters, p. 248*)

THE PRACTICE OF JOY

In this section we will tackle the nature, attributes and manifestations of joy. Like any other human quality, joy can be discussed in terms of acting, feeling, and thinking.

In general, the Hasidim, in contrast to their chief adversaries, the *mitnagdim,* were strong believers in being decisive, taking action immediately, and not dilly-dallying. It is better to learn from imperfect actions than to deliberate too long and miss "golden opportunities." Taking quick action is especially praiseworthy, as you can well imagine, in doing good deeds:

Three Characters

Said the Kotzker: "Three characters can be found in a man about to perform a good deed: If he says, 'I shall do it soon,' his character is poor. If he says, 'I am ready to do it now,' his character is of average quality. If he says, 'I am doing it,' his character is praiseworthy."

(*Newman, The Hasidic Anthology, p. 29*)

Being active soon became, for the Hasidim, their chief method of doing God's will:

The Vessel

A disciple of Rabbi Mendel told this story in his old age, shortly before he died:

"I shall tell you the first saying I heard from the rabbi. I heard many after that, but with this first he kindled my heart forever."

It was on a Sabbath eve, after the Benediction of Sanctification. The rabbi sat in his big chair, and his face was transformed as though his soul had left his body and was floating about him. He stretched out his arms with a gesture of great decision, poured water over our hands, spoke the benediction over the bread and broke the bread. Then he said:

"In the world there are sages, students, and thinkers. They all think of and study the mystery of God. But what can they find out about it? No more than they can grasp from their rung of reason. But the holy children of Israel have a vessel: it is to do God's will. And with this vessel they can hold more than is accorded their rung, they can grasp what is accorded on the rung of the ministering angels. That is what is meant by the words spoken at Sinai: 'We do, we hear.' It is with our doing that we grasp."

(*Buber, Late Masters, pp. 277–278*)

For the Hasid, the good or righteous man practiced in his life the Godly virtues. Sin was created by God to strengthen man's virtues and was to be expected. Light can enter only where darkness has been. At the same time, the Hasid believes that overcoming sin is always possible, and the sooner the better:

The Great Crime

Rabbi Bunam said to his Hasidim:

"The sins which man commits—those are not his great crime. Temptation is powerful and his strength is slight! The great crime of man is that he can turn at every moment, and does not do so."

(*Buber, Late Masters, p. 257*)

The task of mankind, said the *tzaddikim*, was to turn earth into a paradise:

To the Children of Men

When Rabbi Hanokh had said the verse in the psalms, "The heavens are the heavens of the Lord, but the earth hath He given to the children of men," he paused. Then went on to say: "'The heavens are the heavens of the Lord'—you see, they are already of a heavenly character. 'But the earth hath he given to the children of men'—so that they might make of it something heavenly."

(*Buber, Late Masters, p. 317*)

The Hasidic dedication to the fulfilling of their Godly objectives by the way in which they conducted their lives was a very creative transformation of the most mundane worldly behavior into spiritual acts. One of the most famous stories about this new spiritual way of feeling and thinking is the following story:

To Say Torah and to Be Torah

Rabbi Leib, son of Sarah, the hidden *tzaddik* who wandered over the earth, following the course of rivers, in order to redeem the souls of the living and the dead, said this:

"I did not go to the *maggid* in order to hear Torah from him, but to see how he unlaces his felt shoes and laces them up again."

(*Buber, Early Masters, p. 107*)

This story raises a host of imaginative possibilities when it comes to seeing all the mundane acts that make up the whole of life as holy, transcendental and meriting veneration. In this context, the following story is perfectably reasonable:

The Honest Sleep

It was the day before the New Year, and people from all over had come to Vorki and gathered in the House of Study. Some were seated at the tables studying, others who had not been able to find a place for the night were lying on the floor with their heads on their knapsacks, for many of them had come on foot.

Just then, Rabbi Mendel entered, but the noise those at the tables made was so great that no one noticed him. First he looked at those who were studying, and than at those lying on the floor. "The way these folk sleep," he said, "pleases me more than the way those others are studying."

(*Buber, Late Masters, p. 302*)

The performance of the most mundane and routine act could have monumental spiritual significance, but the manner, mode and feeling of the action were also important. For the Hasidim, it was not enough to be merely content or mildly happy—one had to be joyous! God meant us to be overjoyed at all the possibilities for serving Him.

How the Hasidim were able to square all this joyous living with sin, suffering, cruelty, pain, illness, pogroms, persecution, and hunger will be the subject of the section on how Hasidim view reality and reframe it.

THE FEELING OF JOY

The activitism of the Hasidim extended to making oneself and others joyous by acting joyously:

Sabbath Joy

Once, Rabbi Barukh was entertaining a distinguished guest from the Land of Israel. He was one of those who are forever mourning for Zion and Jerusalem, and cannot forget their sorrow for a single second. On the eve of the Sabbath, the rabbi sang: "He who sanctifies the seventh day . . ." in his usual manner. When he came to the words, "Beloved of the Lord, you who await the rebuilding of Ariel," he looked up and saw his guest sitting there as gloomy and sad as always. Then he interrupted himself and, vehemently and joyfully, shouted in the very face of the startled man: "Beloved of the Lord, you who await the rebuilding of Ariel, on this holy day of the Sabbath, be joyful and happy!" After this, he sang the song to the end.

(*Buber, Early Masters, p. 95*)

In a very important sense, the Hasidim were "behaviorists" in that they believed that doing the right thing often enough and long enough will produce the right feelings, intentions, and motivations.

Awakening the Heart

A Hasid said to the Bratzlaver: "You say that one should pray much and recite many psalms. But how can one compel his heart to be engrossed therein?" The rabbi replied: "The recitation of prayers and psalms has the virtue of awakening the heart. Make use of your lips, and your heart will follow their lead."

(*Newman, Maggidim and Hasidim, p. 127*)

How to Do Things with Your Heart in the Right Place

A storekeeper complained to the Kobriner that his business was meager whereas his neighbor's was flourishing.

The Kobriner replied: "I shall pray for you on the condition that you give thanks to the Lord and say: 'Blessed be the Lord who sends His abundance to a fellow Israelite.' First you will utter these words without the acquiescence of your old heart; later, however, you will sincerely mean them. Does not the Torah (Deut. 30:14) command us 'to do right with our lips and with our heart'?"

(*Newman, The Hasidic Anthology, p. 502*)

Today, we are well aware that it is much easier to change behavior than feelings and attitudes. Needless to say, a change in behavior may not lead to a change in attitude. "Going through the motions" is the term we use for those who may be doing the right thing but don't really mean it.

The rabbis were extraordinarily sensitive to this behavioral camouflage. Even for those sincerely motivated to change, a great deal of practice was required:

God's Fatherhood

Concerning the verse in the Scriptures, "But from thence ye will seek the Lord thy God, and thou shalt find Him," the *Maggid* of Mezeritch said: "You must cry to God and call Him father until He becomes your father."

(*Buber, Early Masters, p. 103*)

What we find amazing is the sophistication of the rabbis in recognizing the importance of behavioral programs when it comes to creating specific feelings and in their clever designing of "protocols":

The Sabbath Feeling

Week after week, from the coming of the Sabbath to the going, and especially when they ate the Sabbath meal among the Hasidim and spoke words of teaching, Rabbi Elimelekh and Rabbi Zusya were overcome by a feeling of holiness. Once, when they were together, Rabbi Elimelekh said to Rabbi Zusya: "Brother, I am sometimes afraid that my feeling of holiness on the Sabbath day may not be a true feeling, and that, in such a case, my service may not be the right service."

"Brother," said Zusya, "I, too, am sometimes afraid of that very thing."

"What shall we do about it?" asked Elimelekh.

Zusya replied: "Let each of us, on a weekday, prepare a meal which is exactly like a Sabbath meal. And let us sit with the Hasidim and say words of teaching. Then, if we have that feeling of holiness, we shall know that our way is not the true way. But if we do not have it, this will prove that our way is right."

And they did accordingly. They prepared a Sabbath meal on a weekday, put on Sabbath clothes and the fur caps they wore on the Sabbath, ate with the Hasidim, and spoke words of teaching. And the feeling of holiness overcame them just as on Sabbath. When they were alone together, Rabbi Elimelekh asked: "Brother, what shall we do?"

"Let us go to the *Maggid* of Mezeritch," said Rabbi Zusya. They went to the Mezeritch and told their teacher what was weighing upon them.

The *maggid* said: "If you put on Sabbath clothes and Sabbath caps, it is quite right that you had a feeling of Sabbath holiness. Because Sabbath clothes and Sabbath caps have the power of drawing the light of Sabbath holiness down to earth. So you need have no fears."

(*Buber, Early Masters, p. 24*)

The Hasidim trusted their feelings, encouraged and nurtured them, and schemed to release them. Feelings do not lie, as the mind can. Feelings, of course, can be wrong, but that is not by intention. Feelings, including faith, are truthful, while seeing is only believable. Everyone can learn the same page of a Talmud, but the way it enters a Hasid's heart is very individual. The heart sees what is invisible to the eye. The heart is the seat of emotions, and it is "half a prophet."

If feelings are more true and honest than thinking and acting, then the more intense the feeling the more exalted is the truth. Passionate feelings were admired and highly esteemed:

The Enemy

In his youth, Rabbi Moshe Teitelbaum had been an enemy of the Hasidic teachings, for he regarded them as rank heresy.

Once, he was staying with his friend Rabbi Joseph Asher, who was also opposed to these innovators. At just about this time, the prayer-book of the holy Rabbi Isaac Luria had appeared in print. When the volume was brought to the two friends, Rabbi Moshe snatched the heavy tome from the messenger, and threw it on the floor. But Rabbi Joseph Asher picked it up and said: "After all, it is a prayer-book, and we must not treat it disrespectfully."

When the Rabbi of Lublin was told of the incident, he said: "Rabbi Moshe will become a Hasid; Rabbi Joseph Asher will remain an opponent of the Hasidic way. For he who can burn with enmity can also burn with love for God, but he who is coldly hostile will always find the way closed." And so it was.

(*Buber, Late Masters, p. 189*)

The Hasidim recognized that their passion could sometimes "carry them away," but this was a small price to pay for the powerful thrust it gave to their actions:

The Fight

Rabbi Hanokh was asked why the Hasidim did not begin to pray at the set time.

"While soldiers are going to their training," he replied, "there is a certain set time for everything they have to do, and they must follow their schedule. But when they are in the thick of battle, they forget what was prescribed and fight as the hour demands."

"The Hasidim," the rabbi concluded, "are fighters."

(*Buber, Late Masters, p. 317*)

Passion is the most general term we have for intense feelings that are time-bound. To the extent to which strong feelings can be directed to some specific end, we call a person enthusiastic, or zealous, or full of fervor or ardor. All of those feelings were highly valued by the Hasidim. Nothing of true value, particularly service to God, could be attained without fervor. Passion in the service of God is joy.

And now we come to one of the most fascinating paradoxes about the individual Jew and the Jewish people as a whole: The more difficult the obstacles in the way of true service to God (and to others and to yourself), the greater the ardor and enthusiasm for overcoming them and reaching God (attaining your goal). The closer you are to achieving your goal and the less difficulty you have, the more your enthusiasm wanes and your fervor diminishes. It is almost as if God perversely releases the passion in man by placing obstacles between Himself and His creation, and then the closer man comes to God and overcomes all the obstructions, the easier his fervor dissipates. What a dilemma!

The Flame Goes Out

> A Hasid complained to the Rabbi of Kobryn that every time he set out to see him, his heart was aflame with fervor and he thought he would fly straight to Heaven the moment he stood before his teacher; yet every time he saw him face to face, the flame went out, and his heart felt more shriveled and cold than at home.
>
> The rabbi said: "Remember what David says in the psalm: 'My soul thirsteth for God,' and further on, 'So have I looked for Thee in the sanctuary.' David implores God to let him feel the same fervor in the holy sanctuary that he felt when he was 'in a dry and weary land where no water was.' For first, the all-merciful God wakens a man to holiness; but once he is kindled to act, the flame is taken from him, so that he may act for himself and of himself attain to the state of perfect awakening."
>
> (*Buber, Late Masters, p. 165*)

Yes, but what can a man do to keep the flame burning within himself, and how can he do it? How does he keep himself motivated and enthusiastic and joyously living an active life while pursuing his most desired goals?

One answer, which is discussed in the next section, forms the essential basis of many, if not most, of the Hasidic stories: If there were no obstacles to reaching God and your goals, you would have to invent them. There is no success without failure. Light can only enter where darkness has been. The Hasidim took this all-important concept one step further: When you are close to what you most desire, even when you achieve it, you become a candidate for a major tragedy. Is getting what you want, therefore, undesirable because the ardor and joy and enthusiasm are then extinguished? Or is the belief that anyone gets what he truly desires a figment of the imagination from the start? Is the only failure not trying again? "He that lies on the ground cannot fall" (Ayalti 1949).

One thing is clear: If you stand up again to go forward, there have to be more obstacles in the way:

Mastering Evil Desires

A villager lamented to the Krobiner that his evil desires constantly overcame him and caused him to fall into transgression.

"Do you ride a horse?" the rabbi inquired.

"Yes," answered the villager.

"What do you do if you happen to fall off?"

"I mount again," said the villager.

"Well, imagine the Evil Impulse to be the horse," remarked the rabbi. "If you fall, mount again. Eventually you will master it."

(*Newman, The Hasidic Anthology,* p. 431)

The great obstacle facing the Hasidim's promotion of joy as a way of life was how they would deal with all the inevitable tragedies facing man throughout his lifetime from loneliness and sickness to death.

THE THINKING IN JOY

Just as action can lead to the creation of specific feelings, so can it influence thought. Again, the psychological sophistication of the Hasidim shines through brilliantly in the way they were able to conceptualize the interplay of action and thinking:

Rich People's Food

A rich man once came to the *Maggid* of Koznitz.

"What are you in the habit of eating?" the *maggid* asked. "I am modest in my demands," the rich man replied. "Bread and salt and a drink of water are all I need."

"What are you thinking of?" the rabbi reproved him. "You must eat roast meat and drink mead like all rich people." And he did not let the man go until he had promised him to do as he said. Later, the Hasidim asked him the reason for this odd request.

"Not until he eats meat," said the *maggid*, "will he realize the poor man needs bread. As long as he himself eats only bread, he will think that the poor man can live on stones."

(*Buber, Early Masters, p. 292*)

Nowadays, the wealthy have no difficulty living lavishly, even ostentatiously, and new paradoxical strategies may be required. The principle, however, is sound: If the rich could truly enjoy themselves more, they might very well be willing to help others live a mite more comfortably. The obscene, ostentatious waste of food in the United States alone could feed all the starving adults and children in the world.

For the Hasidim, reality was mostly spiritual; but it also had a bedrock of materiality, of natural cause and effect. The taste of bread is the taste of bread, not God. The real world is not easy to live in, and one does not cope with it joyously every moment. Life, in fact, is dangerous, unpredictable, and definitely terminable.

There is also a reality within us, and this inner spiritual reality, say the Hasidim, powerfully imposes itself on the natural world. The Hasidim developed three main strategies for seeing, visualizing and defining their relationship to the real world:

1. Accepting (in the sense of recognizing) the reality of the real world
2. Reframing evil, either by denying its existence or by showing that it is an integral part of God
3. Using evil joyously and triumphantly to renew goodness

ACCEPTING THE REAL WORLD

There is something fantastically strengthening about accepting the world as it is. It seems that, in recognizing reality with all its multi-hued manifestations, we are able to appreciate the bright colors even more and joyously experience them. Everything becomes more dangerous and disappointing when reality is not clearly recognized. Wisdom and joy lie in reality, and despair and ignorance are in words that conceal it.

The Hasidim were solidly grounded in reality—in the action in the here-and-now:

Most Important

> Soon after the death of Rabbi Moshe, Rabbi Mendel of Kotzk asked one of his disciples:
>
> "What was most important to your teacher?"
>
> The disciple thought and replied:
>
> "Whatever he happened to be doing at the moment."
>
> (*Buber, Late Masters, p. 173*)

Recognizing and accepting reality is the way to serve God. The greatest sin is deception, especially of oneself. The Hasidim came to the profound conclusion that there could be no general homage to God, to others, or to oneself without recognizing and accepting the reality of one's intentions—*kavanna*—good or bad. Admitting your reality was a necessary first step and holy in itself, however unholy your inner state might be. Admitting what is, including your unholiness, is the first step toward God:

The Foolish Prayer

> At the close of the Day of Atonement, the Rabbi of Berditchev said to one of his Hasidim: "I know what you prayed for this day! On the eve, you begged God to give you the thousand rubles which you need in order to live and usually earn in the course of a year, all at once, at the beginning of the year, so that the toil and trouble of business might not distract you from

learning and prayer. But in the morning you thought better of it and decided that, if you had the thousand rubles all at once, you would probably launch a new and bigger business enterprise which would take up even more of your time. And so you begged to receive half the amount every half year. And before the Closing Prayer, this too seemed precarious to you, and you expressed the wish for quarterly installments, so you might learn and pray quite undisturbed. But what makes you think that your learning and praying is needed in Heaven? Perhaps what is needed there is that you toil and rack your brains."

(*Buber, Early Masters, pp. 215–216*)

Many Hasidic stories highlight accepting the world as the "greatest devotion" to God. In "Accepting the World" (see page 209), Rabbi Moshe says: "In this day and age, the greatest devotion, greater than learning and praying, consists in accepting the world exactly as it happens to be."

Is the world fundamentally good, and is the only way we can know that to have both the good and the bad? And are good and bad inextricably bound up with one another? Can there be good without the bad? And does the bad make the good better and joyous? Can we have wisdom, not to mention joy, without the spice of the bad and wickedness in the good? Can light enter only where darkness has been?

The Hasidim in fact saw good springing from evil (and vice versa):

The Greatness of Pharaoh

Rabbi Levi Yitzhak said:

"I envy Pharaoh! What glorification of the name of God did his stubbornness beget!"

(*Buber, Early Masters, p. 228*)

The fallback, or should we say the fallup, position for good arising from evil lay in the World-to-Come. Good and evil are deceptive. Spinoza pointed out that a good which prevents us from enjoying a greater good can be regarded as evil.

Be that as it may, the rabbis concluded that our abode is all right just as it is:

The Faithful Servant

Rabbi Nahum of Stepinesht once said this of his brother, Rabbi David Moshe of Tchortkov:

"When my brother David Moshe opens the Book of Psalms and begins to recite the praises, God calls down to him: 'David Moshe, my son, I am putting the whole world into your hands. Now do with it just as you like.' Oh, if he only gave me the world, I should know very well what to do with it! But David Moshe is so faithful a servant that when he gives the world back, it is exactly as it was when he received it."

(*Buber, Late Masters, p.* 75)

And part of the all-rightness of the world is its imperfection. What on earth would Hasidim (and the rest of us) do if indeed our world were Godly?

The End of Prayers

At the close of Psalm 72 are the words: "And let the whole earth be filled with His glory. Amen, and Amen. The prayers of David the son of Jesse are ended."

Concerning this, Rabbi Levi Yitzhak said: "All prayers and hymns are a plea to have His glory revealed throughout the world. But if once the whole earth is, indeed, filled with it, there will be no further need to pray."

(*Buber, Early Masters, p.* 216)

One crucial and very difficult reality to recognize and accept is the truth about one's own deceptions, flaws, and shortcomings. This is very difficult, but the rabbis were unflinching in their resolve to "tell it like it is":

Self-Mortification

To the *Maggid* of Koznitz came a man who, in order to mortify himself, wore nothing but a sack on his bare body and fasted from one Sabbath to the next. The *maggid* said to him: "Do you think that the Evil Urge is keeping away from you? It is tricking you into that sack. He who pretends to fast from Sabbath to Sabbath but secretly eats a little something every day, is spiritually better off than you, for he is only deceiving others, while you are deceiving yourself."

(*Buber, Early Masters, p. 291*)

The *maggid* offers us an elegant paradox about deceiving others and oneself. Far more serious than deceiving others is deceiving oneself. The faster who eats secretly would have great difficulty in fooling himself into believing that he is fasting, although that certainly is not beyond some charlatans. The faster who is trying to impress everyone or who is fasting for some egotistical or other external (not Godly) reason and does not cheat in his fasting is truly much more deceptive.

The Hasidim extended the principle of vigorous self-examination to groups and even to nations. Without self-criticism, there can be no redemption:

Concerning Joseph's Brothers

The Rabbi of Lelov said to his Hasidim:

"A man cannot be redeemed until he recognizes the flaws in his soul and tries to mend them. A nation cannot be redeemed until it recognizes the flaws in its soul and tries to mend them. Whoever permits no recognition of his flaws, be it man or nation, permits no redemption. We can be redeemed to the extent to which we recognize ourselves.

"When Jacob's sons said to Joseph: 'We are upright men,' he answered: 'That is why I spoke unto you saying: Ye are spies.' But later, when they confessed the truth with their lips and with their hearts, and said to one another, 'We are verily guilty concerning our brother,' the first gleam of their redemption dawned. Overcome with compassion, Joseph turned aside and wept."

(*Buber, Late Masters, pp. 187–188*)

Understanding the truth about yourself is crucial to overcoming self-delusions and living with your true self-image and with reality. There can be no power and no joy without insight into the true reality of the world of your own self. How that insight can open up new worlds is beautifully recounted in the following story:

So Be It

Rabbi Jacob Joseph, the Rav of Polnoye, was once invited to a circumcision which was to take place in a nearby village. When he arrived, one man was still lacking to make up the quorum of ten.

The *tzaddik* was very much annoyed that he was forced to wait. Waiting always displeased him. A heavy rain had been falling since early morning, and so they couldn't get hold of a passerby for quite a while.

At last, they saw a beggar coming down the street. When they asked him to attend the ceremony as the tenth man, he said: "So be it."

After the circumcision, they invited him to the meal and he gave the same reply. Finally his host asked him: "Why do you always say the same thing?"

The man answered: "For it is written: 'Happy is the people with whom it is so'" (Psalm 144:15).

And with that he vanished before the eyes of all.

That night the rav could not sleep. Over and over again, he heard the beggar say: "So be it," until it became manifest to him that it could have been no one but the prophet Elijah, who had come to reprove him for his tendency to get annoyed.

"Happy is the people that is in such a case," he whispered, and instantly fell asleep.

(*Buber, Early Masters, pp. 167–168*)

"Happy is the people with whom it is so." What is the "it"? "It" is reality, and the prerequisites for happiness are awareness and acceptance of reality—the starting point of every school of contemporary psychology and the foundation stone of Alcoholics Anonymous, the most successful self-help movement in the world today.

Acceptance of what is has a remarkable effect: It enables one to change reality and imparts the confidence and zeal to "move mountains" and "go North and South at the same time."

Acceptance of reality is self-and-God affirming, and it is basic to joyously experiencing the world. Joy is adversely related to guilt, defensiveness and illusion. It springs spontaneously from a whole heart.

But the reality of the world, in many places and at many times, stinks, to put it plainly. What do we do with this stinking reality? The Hasidim perfected a master technique not unlike the gardener's trick of using the foulest dung to produce the most beautiful, sweet-smelling flowers. Much depends on your interpretive framework. That technique is—again—"reframing"!

REFRAMING EVIL

Dreams, illusions, fantasies and paradises are full of joy. Imagination uses desire and joy to create visions of reality that make it bearable and even desirable. In our imagination, what is and what might be are often mixed up.

The Hasidim artfully reframed the world of pain, suffering and ugliness into a world filled with the sparks of the Divinity. His plenitude suffused the earth. We will show, step by step, the cumulative effect of turning the world into a place where man can live joyously in harmony with God's spirit and can use the contrary powers of evil to add to that joy.

The first step is to let God's light shine forth:

The Streets of Nehardea

Rabbi Shalom said:

"The Talmud tells of a wise man versed in the lore of the stars and relates that the paths of the firmament were as bright and clear to him as the streets in the town of Nehardea, where he lived. Now, if only we could say about ourselves that the streets of our city are as clear and bright to us as the paths of the firmament! For to let the hidden life of God shine out in this lowest world, the world of bodiliness, that is the greater feat of the two!"

(*Buber, Late Masters, pp. 50–51*)

A great problem, however, is the Evil Urge. How can we be safe and joyous with the Evil Urge always lurking about? Why do we need it in the first place? Obviously, there must be some good in the Evil Urge, and the Hasidim's ingenuity did not fail them in the search for it.

Ingeniously, Rabbi Mikhal redefines the Evil Urge as a mixed bag of evil and good. All man has to do is learn how to utilize the good side of the Evil Urge's ambivalence, so that the Evil Urge can enable man to serve God even better:

Man and the Evil Urge

This is what Rabbi Mikhal said concerning the verse in the Scripture: "Let us take our journey, and let us go, and I will go before thee."

"That is what the Evil Urge says to man secretly. For this urge is to become good and wants to become good by driving man to overcome it and to make it good. And that is Satan's secret request to the man he is trying to seduce: 'Let us leave this disgraceful state and take service with the Creator, so that I too may go and mount with you rung by rung, although I seem to oppose, to disturb and hinder you.'"

(*Buber, Early Masters, p. 145*)

The ingenuity of Rabbi Mikhal's formulation is breathtaking. The Evil Urge is not the Evil Urge but the Evil-and-Good-Urge; deep, deep down he is really a good guy, and all that seduction and deception are merely to test your mettle and faith! "I am merely mettlesome," says the Evil Urge, "to test your tenacity of faith and capacity for joy, but really I want to help you serve God!"

Hasidic ingenuity knows no bounds. Evil temptations can be graded from "petty" to "grave," with "superior" men, of course, receiving the most grave temptations and, by overcoming them, improving their "superiority":

Temptations

Rabbi Joseph Landau of Jassy, Rumania, had rejected a bribe offered him by a prominent member of his congregation whom he had opposed because the man had violated a religious law. Shortly after this, he visited the Rabbi of Apt and, with a self-satisfied air, told him how he had resisted temptation. When the *tzaddik* bade him farewell, he blessed him and expressed the hope that he would become an honest and God-fearing man. "I am delighted with the blessing of my teacher and master," said Rabbi Joseph Landau, "and what more could I ask? But why did you wish me this just at this time?"

The Rabbi of Apt replied: "It is written: 'Also unto Thee, O Lord, belongeth mercy; for Thou renderest to every man according to his work.' Those who expounded these verses asked themselves time and again why paying a hired man his proper wages should be called 'mercy.' But the truth of the matter is that God has mercy when He leads every man into the temptation befitting his inner level: the common man into petty, the superior man into grave temptation. The fact that you were exposed to so slight a temptation is a sign that you have not yet reached one of the upper rungs to perfection. That is why I blessed you, asking God to let you ascend to them and to be found worthy of a greater test."

(*Buber, Late Masters, pp. 110–111*)

If the Hasidim could so radically redefine the Evil Urge, other evil phenomena such as war, for example, do not require much more imagination:

The Birth of a Melody

The Rabbi of Tchortkov once said:

"Sometimes it happens that war breaks out between two kingdoms, and the war drags on for thirty years. Then, out of the groans of those who fell in battle and the cries of the victors, a melody is born so that it may be sung before the *tzaddik*."

(*Buber, Late Masters, p. 75*)

Robbery and thieving could be eliminated by declaring (reframing) that all of one's possessions are common property:

The Thieves

One night, thieves entered Rabbi Wolf's house and took whatever they happened to find. From his room the *tzaddik* watched them but did not do anything to stop them. When they were through, they took some utensils and among them a jug from which a sick man had drunk that very evening. Rabbi Wolf ran after them. "My good people," he said, "whatever you have found here, I beg you to regard as gifts from me. I do not begrudge these things to you at all. But please be careful about that jug! The breath of a sick man is clinging to it, and you might catch his disease!"

From that time on, he said every evening before going to bed: "All my possessions are common property," so that—in case thieves came again—they would not be guilty of theft.

(*Buber, Early Masters, p. 161*)

A proper reframe can enable an innkeeper to make money and be hospitable and serve God at the same time; money becomes the means, not the end of innkeeping:

Commandment and Money

Rabbi Yitzhak once praised an innkeeper who was eager to satisfy every wish of his guests. "How anxious this man is to fulfill the commandment to be hospitable!" he said. "But he takes pay for it," someone remarked. "He accepts money," answered the *tzaddik*, "so that it may be possible for him to fulfill the commandment."

(*Buber, Late Masters, p. 295*)

And one's enemy of many years' standing can be suddenly converted into a supporter:

The Good Enemy

The quarrel that broke out between Rabbi Bunam and Rabbi Meir of Stabnitz lasted for many years. When Rabbi Meir died, a Hasid of Rabbi Bunam's came and brought him the good news.

The *tzaddik* jumped up and struck his hands together. "That is meant for me," he cried, "for he was my support." Rabbi Bunam died that same summer.

(*Buber, Late Masters, p. 267*)

Not only did the Hasidim see evil as a part of goodness, they took the reframing of evil one decisive step further.

EVIL JOYOUSLY AND TRIUMPHANTLY RENEWS GOODNESS

Increasingly, the Hasidim began to see evil as a necessary force in the world to renew, refresh, and rejuvenate the good. After all, good can grow old and stale, like everything else on earth. Even the earth itself is not exempt from the ravages of time. Everything decays and finally disintegrates. Good can also be depleted. We all need refreshing, but how can we retain our youthful vigor in the face of time's merciless advance?

Evil can give you that new lease on life, and it should not be shunned or merely regarded as good, but joyously accepted and utilized to further goodness and to enhance service to God:

Poverty and Joy

> Said the Kobriner: "If a poor man realized the great good he acquires from his poverty, he would dance with joy."
>
> (*Newman, The Hasidic Anthology, p. 213*)

Envy

> Walking in the street, the Rabbi of Berditchev once went up to a man who held an important office and was as evil-minded as he was powerful, took hold of the hem of his coat, and said: "Sir, I envy you! When you turn to God, each of your flaws will become a ray of light, and you will shine with a great light. Sir, I envy you your flood of radiance!"
>
> (*Buber, Early Masters, p. 219*)

The turning for the Jewish people comes on the Day of Atonement. Rabbi Shmelke, in remarks which deserve careful (and joyous) scrutiny, sets the record straight about the Day of Atonement: "No joy is greater than the joy on this day, when it is granted to us to drive all evil impulses from our hearts through the power of turning."

A Sermon for Atonement

On the eve of the Day of Atonement, Rabbi Shmelke of Nikolsberg put on his prayer shawl and went to the House of Prayer. On his way from the entrance to the Ark, he called aloud the words of the Scriptures: ". . . for on this day shall atonement be made for you, to cleanse you," and after he quoted Rabbi Akiva's words from the Mishna: "Before whom do you atone, and who cleanses you: your Father in Heaven," all the people burst into tears.

When he stood in front of the Ark, he said: "Brothers of my heart, you must know that the core of turning is the offering up of life itself. For we are of the seed of Abraham who offered his life for the sanctification of the blessed Name and let them cast him into a lime-kiln; we are of the seed of Isaac who offered his life and laid his neck on the stone of the altar—they are surely pleading to our Father in Heaven in our behalf on this holy and awful day of judgment. But let us, too, walk in their tracks and imitate their works: let us offer up our own lives for the sanctification of the Name of Him who is blessed. Let us unite and sanctify His mighty Name with fervent love and with this as our purpose, let us say together: 'Hear, O Israel!'" And weeping, all the people said: "Hear, O Israel: The Lord our God, the Lord is one."

Then he went on to say: "Dear brothers, now that it was vouchsafed us to unite and sanctify His Name in great love, now that we have offered our lives, and our hearts have become cleansed for the service and fear of the Lord, we must also unite our souls. All souls come from one root, all are carved from the throne of His splendor, and so they are a part of God in Heaven. Let us be united on earth too, so that the branches again may be as the root. Here we stand, cleansed and pure, to unite our souls. And we take upon us the commandment: 'Love thy neighbor as thyself.'" And all the people repeated aloud: "Love thy neighbor as thyself." And he continued: "Now that it has been vouchsafed us to unite His Great Name, and to unite our souls, which are a part of God in Heaven, let the holy Torah plead in our behalf before our Father in Heaven. Once God offered it to all peoples and to all languages, but we alone accepted it and cried: 'All that the Lord has spoken will we do,' and only then did we say: 'We hear.' And so it is fitting that the Torah ask our Father in Heaven for mercy and grace for us on this holy and awful day of judgment." And he opened the doors of the Ark.

Then, in front of the open Ark, he recited the confession of sins, and all the people repeated it after him word for word, and as they did so, they wept. He took out the scroll and, holding it high in his hands, spoke to his congregation about the sins of man. But in the end he said: "You must know that the weeping we do on this day is unblest if it is filled with gloom, for the Divine Presence does not dwell in heaviness of heart, but only in rejoicing in the commandments. And, see, no joy is greater than the joy on this day, when it is granted to us to drive all evil impulses from our hearts, through the power of turning, to come closer to our Father in Heaven whose hand is outstretched to receive those who turn to Him. And so, all the tears we shed on this day, should be tears of joy, as it is written: 'Serve the Lord with fear, and rejoice with trembling.'"

(*Buber, Early Masters, pp. 186–187*)

Evil tests our capacity for joy in using it to restore goodness. Would it not seem strange for most outsiders to see a rabbi dancing after hearing that a friend has fallen ill?

The Dance of Healing

News was brought to Rabbi Moshe Leib that his friend, the Rabbi of Berditchev, had fallen ill. On the Sabbath, he said his name over and over and prayed for his recovery. Then he put on new shoes made of morocco leather, laced them up tight and danced.

A *tzaddik* who was present said: "Power flowed forth from his dancing. Every step was a powerful mystery. An unfamiliar light suffused the house, and everyone watching saw the heavenly host join in his dance."

(*Buber, Late Masters, p. 90*)

Joyful or ecstatic dance propels the dancer into an altered state of consciousness (and therefore closeness to God) which can even overcome pain:

Dancing and Pain

Every Sabbath, Rabbi Hayyim of Kosov, the son of Rabbi Mendel, danced before his assembled disciples. His face was aflame and they all knew that every step was informed with sublime meanings and effected sublime things.

Once, while he was in the midst of dancing, a heavy bench fell on his foot and he had to pause because of the pain. Later, they asked him about it. "It seems to me," he said, "that the pain made itself felt because I interrupted the dance."

(*Buber, Late Masters, p. 99*)

Not only does evil enlarge and multiply good, but good can also increase, joyfully, by reforming evil. In fact, that is why evil is also God-given and is, therefore, in no way alien to man. This is very modern: Love the wicked man and hate the wickedness—man is always reformable:

The Commandment of Love

A disciple asked Rabbi Shmelke: "We are commanded to love our neighbor as ourself. How can I do this if my neighbor has wronged me?"

The rabbi answered: "You must understand these words aright. Love your neighbor like something which you yourself are. For all souls are one. Each is a spark from the original soul, and this soul is wholly inherent in all souls, just as your soul is in all the members of your body. It may come to pass that your hand makes a mistake and strikes you. But would you then take a stick and chastise your hand, because it lacked understanding, and so increase your pain? It is the same if your neighbor, who is of one soul with you, wrongs you for lack of understanding. If you punish him, you only hurt yourself."

The disciple went on asking: "But if I see a man who is wicked before God, how can I love him?"

"Don't you know," said Rabbi Shmelke, "that the original soul came out of the essence of God, and that every human soul is a part of God? And will you have no mercy on him, when you see that one of his holy sparks has been lost in a maze, and is almost stifled?"

(*Buber, Early Masters, p. 190*)

There is a series of steps in the Hasidic reframing of evil: viewing evil as a part of good; using evil to enhance good; enhancing good by using it to reform evil; regarding evil and good as equal sparks of God; and, finally, the understanding that man was created "to strive against the evil in his soul with unalloyed joy," and that striving is the test of his faith in God:

The Two Generals

Rabbi Levy Yitzhak said: "Whether a man really loves God—that can be determined by the love he bears his fellow-men. I shall give you a parable:

"Once upon a time, a country was suffering from the ravages of war. The army, which was sent against the foe, was vanquished. The king discharged his chief general and put in his place another man who succeeded in driving out the invader. The first general was suspected of betraying his country. The king wondered whether there was any way to find out whether he really loved or hated him. He realized that there was one unerring sign which would discover the truth to him: If the man about whom he was in doubt showed friendship for his rival and expressed unalloyed joy at his success, he might be regarded as trustworthy; but if he plotted against his rival, his guilt would be proven.

"God created man to strive against the evil in his soul. Now there is many a man who does, indeed, love God, but is defeated in that bitter struggle. He can be recognized by his ability to share wholeheartedly and without reservation in the happiness of his victorious fellow-man."

(*Buber, Early Masters, p. 227*)

The Hasidic emphasis on feeling good or, better still, joyous, is justified, because God and life are basically good; and evil was created to make life and service to God better. For Jews, God ultimately has to be reasonable and that is why evil ultimately was discovered to be an agency of good. Morality is, after all, our interpretation of the world in terms of good and bad. The moral life is not dreary but full of joy, and Satan's challenges and tricks only make us appreciate God's world even more joyfully. The challenge to forego the forbidden is an adventure and adds gusto to life.

In short, the Hasidim had to deal with evil, it is so much with us and so tightly locked in combat with good. No man is all good or bad, but the interplay of good and bad has the potential for making us all better.

It is, of course, impossible to be joyous *all* the time. That is unreasonable, and the Hasidim, who were not fools, knew that some values are more important than joyousness—caring for others and helping them, for example:

The Two Caps

> Rabbi David Moshe, the son of the Rabbi of Rizhin, once said to a Hasid:
>
> "You knew my father when he lived in Sadagora and was already wearing the black cap and going his way in dejection; but you did not see him when he lived in Rizhin and was still wearing his golden cap." The Hasid was astonished. "How is it possible that the holy man from Rizhin ever went his way in dejection? Did not I myself hear him say that dejection is the lowest condition?"
>
> "And after he had reached the summit," Rabbi David replied, "he had to descend to that condition time and again in order to redeem the souls which had sunk down to it."
>
> (*Buber, Late Masters, p. 68*)

SOLIPSISM

Did the Hasidim go too far in using their vivid imaginations to reframe the real world? Did they take their spiritual vision too seriously? Did they eventually come to confuse the ideal heavenly world created in their imagination with the real world under their feet?

The Hasidim came perilously close to solipsism—the belief that the self (including God) is the only reality, and the self only knows and can know whatever it wants to know from within itself. The *tzaddik* of Neskhizh says this in so many words:

Seeing and Hearing

> A rabbi came to the *tzaddik* of Neskhizh and asked: "Is it true what people say, that you hear and see all things?"
>
> "Think of the words of our Sages," he replied, "'a seeing eye and a hearing ear.' Man has been so created that he can see and hear whatever he wants to. It is only a question of not corrupting his eyes and his ears."
>
> (*Buber, Early Masters, p. 165*)

Rabbi Barukh seems to be saying the same thing: The world is what you want to make it, one needs only sufficient inner resolve:

The Twofold World

> Rabbi Barukh once said: "What a good and bright world this is if we do not lose our hearts to it, but what a dark world, if we do!"
>
> (*Buber, Early Masters, p. 97*)

It is, actually, a very small step from reframing evil in the world to denying evil altogether:

Thanking for Evil

> A Hasid asked the Seer of Lublin: "To the words in the Mishna: 'Man should thank God for evil and praise Him,' the Gemara adds: 'with joy and a tranquil heart.' How can that be?"
>
> The *tzaddik* could hear that the question sprang from a troubled heart. "You do not understand the Gemara," he said. "And I do not understand even the Mishna. For is there really any evil in the world?"
>
> (*Buber, Early Masters, p. 318*)

In light of such observations, it becomes an increasingly moot point whether the beliefs in the following two stories are ridiculous or the end-result of a theological development that transformed a hard material reality into a spiritual world:

The Blessing

Rabbi Mikhal once said to his sons: "My life was blessed in that I never needed anything until I had it."

(*Buber, Early Masters, p. 156*)

The Want

Early in life, Rabbi Yehiel Mikhal lived in great poverty, but not for an hour did happiness desert him.

Someone once asked him: "Rabbi, how can you pray day after day, 'Blessed be Thou . . . who has supplied my every want?' For surely, you lack everything a man has need of!" He replied: "My want is, most likely, poverty, and that is what I have been supplied with."

(*Buber, Early Masters, p. 138*)

Was Hasidism in danger of sinking into a kind of quietism, a religious philosophy that maintains that the spiritual life is attained by the contemplation and absorption of God and his divine manifestations ("sparks") and the exorcism of reality? Does this religious system require the annihilation of the real world?

We are not competent to answer, or even speculate about such questions, but we do have a responsibility to report what Hasidic stories are telling us implicitly and explicitly, specifically and generally.

One thing we do know: Whatever the implications are for Hasidism as a movement, on a personal level its adherents practiced the theology of joy in ways that may never be surpassed until a truly sane world does evolve:

Why Lessen Their Joy?

Several Hasidim came to the Besht and said: "Our opponents, the sages of Brody, persecute us continually, and accuse us, Heaven forbid, of disobedience to the Law and irreverence towards the traditions of our forefathers. We can endure it no longer, and we must answer them."

"Our adversaries," replied the Besht, "do this certainly out of pious zeal. They believe they are performing a good deed, and they take joy in oppressing us. Why should we seek to deprive them of their joy?"

(*Newman, The Hasidic Anthology*, p. 88)

The Ultimate Joy

Soon after the death of Rabbi Mendel's wife, his daughter also died. People whispered to one another not to tell him of it just yet, but when his son-in-law entered the House of Prayer weeping while the rabbi was saying the Morning Prayer, he at once realized what had happened. He finished the Eighteen Benedictions, and said: "Lord of the world, you took my wife from me. But I still had my daughter and could rejoice in her. Now you have taken her from me too. Now I have no one left to rejoice in, except You alone. So I shall rejoice in You." And he said the Additional Prayer in a transport of joy.

(*Buber, Late Masters*, p. 137)

In the following complicated story we are led to believe that God indeed responds to our suffering, but at a terrible cost:

Suffering and Pangs

Once, the Rabbi of Sadagora sat at his midday meal and sighed, and did not eat. His sister asked him what was troubling him and repeated her question several times. At last he answered her with a question of his own: "Have you heard the reports about the sad condition of our brothers in Russia?"

"It seems to me," she answered, "that these sufferings might be the birth pangs that herald the coming of the Messiah." The *tzaddik* considered this. "Perhaps, perhaps," he finally said, "but when suffering is about to reach its peak, Israel cries out to God, saying it can bear it no longer, and God is merciful and hears them; he relieves the suffering and postpones redemption."

(*Buber, Late Masters*, p. 72)

Whatever the ultimate faith of the world may be, on an individual level the philosophy and practice of joyousness, when consistently upheld, has much to recommend it as a way to live a full, active life.

And it applies to death, also a part of life. Consider the response of the Rabbi of Ulanov, to the ultimate test each of us is fated to address:

Do Not Stop!

On the Day of Rejoicing in the Law, the Rabbi of Ulanov who was a dear friend of the Rabbi of Roptshitz, lay dying. In Roptshitz the Hasidim had just begun the great round dance in the court of the *tzaddik*'s house. He was standing at the window and looking down at them with a smile, when suddenly he raised his hand. Instantly they stopped and gazed up at him with faltering breath. For a while, he kept silent and seemed as someone who has been overcome by bad news. Then he signed to the Hasidim with his hand and cried: "When one of the generals falls to battle, do the companies scatter and take to flight? The fight goes on! Rejoice and dance!" Later it became known that the Rabbi of Ulanov had died that very hour.

(*Buber, Late Masters, p. 197*)

Rejoice and dance! Amen!

12

The Courage to Become One's Self

As he thinketh in his heart, so is he.

Proverbs 23:7

He that observeth the wind shall not sow; and he that regardeth the clouds shall not reap.

Ecclesiastes 11:4

Pride goeth before destruction, and a haughty spirit before a fall.

Proverbs 16:18

THE CONCEPT OF SELF

The courage to know one's self touches upon a perplexing question that must be addressed before examining how to attain this most desirable goal: What is one's self?

A Vain Search

Rabbi Hanokh told this story:

There once was a man who was very stupid. When he got up in the morning, it was so hard for him to find his clothes that at night he almost hesitated to go to bed for thinking of the trouble he would have on waking. One evening, he finally made a great effort, took paper and pencil, and as he undressed noted exactly where he put everything he had on.

The next morning, very pleased with himself, he took the slip of paper in hand and read: "Hat"—there it was, he sat it on his head; "pants"—there they lay, he got into them; and so it went until he was fully dressed.

"That's all very well, but where am I now myself?" he asked in great consternation. "Where in the world am I?" He looked and looked, but it was a vain search; he could not find himself.

"And that is how it is with us," said the rabbi.

(*Buber, Late Masters, p. 314*)

This Hasidic story makes great fun of the idea that a person's self is an object like his cap and pants. But this idea is true not only of Hasidim, but of all of us as well; each of us believes he has a unique inner self. This modern self is not as autonomous and individualistic as it makes itself out to be. Our sense of self is derived from what our culture prizes. Current expectations, norms, are that individuals should be maximally self-aware but also ironic, detached, and, above all, artful in presenting themselves to others. The modern ideal includes a casual, "cool," self-possessed self not unduly averse to taking whatever advantage he can of any situation by violating the spirit if not the letter of the law.

Of course, such values were derived by the Hasidim. They, too, believed in an inner self and in an inner life, in *kavvana*, the subjective self; but they could not possibly conceive of it as something separate from God. In fact, the Hasid had a direct line from his best self to God and he got into trouble every time that line was cut. But the Jews were, and apparently will always be, a stiff-necked people. Jews are forever taking shortcuts between their higher inner selves and God's Spirit. The rabbi's task was to constantly repair that line. So the rabbis became master repairmen!

What is this concept of the individual self? It means, of course, something subjective; one's self is not the same as one's body. The body is part of the physical natural world, while the self, although encased in the body of the individual, gets its meaning from our social and cultural life. The self is an idea that you hold about yourself and it is derived not only from self-reference, but from ideas other people and the culture as a whole hold about you.

This concept of the individual, responsible self becomes the powerful link between the Hasidic world and our contemporary society. The Hasidic concept of the inner self is captured by the term *kavvana*—intention or motivation. The idea behind *kavvana* is that every individual's act is judged by the subjective meaning the act has for the individual. *Kavvana* is an extraordinarily modern concept. It is not only what a person does, but how he does it and how much of the inner self is involved in the act.

Our modern selves can become quite complicated. The greatest contemporary ethnographer of the modern individual as an actor and impression-manager, is Ervin Goffman. He has demonstrated that the individual has layers upon layers and becomes adroit in pretense, which takes a lot of careful planning and effort, if it is to be carried off successfully. Goffman compares social life to a theater: On stage, people present idealized pictures of themselves, wearing the right clothes, making the right facial expressions and using the right words and gestures; backstage, people relax, are more themselves and prepare their new roles. Backstage is where people recover from being "on stage."

Is there a final self behind all these layers? Is it possible for an individual to strip away all of the different performances and come up with some kernel of an authentic individual self? Goffman does not think so. He believes that each person is composed of many different selves, individually manufactured to survive in different groups and social settings. Goffman thinks that one can peel away an infinite number of layers of the self without ever reaching a center.

The Hasidim disliked opportunists, people who could not make up their minds about what they wanted, and shifty people who were always making up reasons, after their actions, for doing one thing or another. They much preferred the person of resolve, a man of consistency, someone who tuned in to what his heart really wanted and went all out with that. The Hasid had great disdain for the person who was constantly second-guessing himself:

The Patchwork Rabbi

A Hasid of the Rabbi of Lublin once fasted from one Sabbath to the next. On Friday afternoon, he began to suffer such cruel thirst that he thought he might die. He saw a well, went up to it, and prepared to drink. But instantly he realized that because of the one brief hour he still had to endure, he was about to destroy the work of an entire week. He did not drink. He went away from the well.

Then he was touched by a feeling of pride for having passed this difficult test. When he became aware of it, he said to himself: "Better that I drink than let my heart fall prey to pride." He went back to the well, but just as he was about to bend down to draw water, he noticed that his thirst had disappeared.

When the Sabbath had begun, he entered his teacher's house. "Patchwork," the rabbi called to him, as he crossed the threshold.

(*Buber, Early Masters, p. 316*)

The rabbi instantly recognized that this kind of activity could drive a person crazy. One creates vicious loops of doubt: One does something and then reflects, and worries and questions what he has done, which makes the activity less certain, and, in turn, makes the individual more uncertain about what he is doing and then influences what he is doing in a negative way and makes him feel more alienated. The rabbis were great enough psychologists to be aware of this kind of negative feedback. This kind of "patchwork" person is always second-guessing what he is doing or about to do, and the uncertainty enters into his activity and creates not only a patchwork activity but a patchwork person as well. Such people exist today, as they did 200 and 300 years ago.

This is not to say that someone might not change his mind in midstream and decide not to go ahead with something that is perhaps no longer of great value, or whose cost is too high, for example. It is the constant nit-picking and examination of one's motives, often based on sheer convenience and a presumption of great nobility, that aggravated the rabbis. "Patchwork" is a very derogatory term for people who are always dragging in all kinds of extraneous and righteous explanations of what they are doing. A patchwork person is just the opposite of someone who makes a deliberate decision to do one task wholeheartedly.

HASIDIC VALUES

One of the greatest sins that anyone could commit, according to the Hasidim, was to shame another person. In the close, tight-knit *shtetl* life, where everyone knew everyone else and community norms were very powerful in regulating individual lives, a put-down could devastate a person's entire life. So this sensitivity to respecting another person's dignity and not shaming him before others was an extremely important subject of many Hasidic stories:

Putting to Shame

A poor schoolteacher once came to visit Rabbi Hayyim of Zans. "I suppose you are preparing for your daughter's wedding," said the *tzaddik*. "I don't know," said the other. Rabbi Hayyim looked at him inquiringly. "I still haven't the money to buy the bridegroom a prayer shawl and a fur cap, as custom demands," said the schoolteacher sadly.

Rabbi Yehezkel, the rabbi's son, who was listening to the conversation, interrupted at this point. "Father," he cried, "just a few days ago I saw this man buying both these things!" The teacher reddened and left the room in silence. "What have you done!" said Rabbi Hayyim. "Perhaps he was not able to pay for what he bought, or perhaps he needs money to have a dress made for his wife to wear at the wedding but does not want to say so. And now you have put a man to shame."

Rabbi Yehezkel ran into the street, caught up with the schoolteacher and begged his forgiveness. But the man refused to forgive him and insisted that the *tzaddik* should judge the matter. Soon they both stood before him.

"Don't forgive him," the old man said to the schoolteacher. "Don't forgive him until he has paid the entire cost of the wedding down to the last shoelace." And so it was done.

(*Buber, Late Masters, pp. 212–213*)

What is interesting in the above story is the relative value of the transgression and the repentance for it. On one hand, the teacher was so insulted and shamed that a simple apology rang hollow in his ears. He was still overcome with shame, and rightfully so. At this point, both the teacher and the rabbi are in an alliance on the seriousness of the sin of shaming: It is not to be taken lightly. Insulting someone, stripping away his dignity and, in effect, telling him that he's a liar and a cheat, are very destructive acts—and the severity of the reparation must be meted out accordingly.

The rabbi finds a penalty that fits the crime. The rabbi's son is required to pay for the entire wedding, not just for a small fraction of it, as the poor schoolteacher had originally requested. The rabbi continues to help the poor man, relatively speaking, in an honorable way without shame. The rabbi has to pay him!

This story can be understood fully, we believe, only if one understands the subtext. Shaming a person is going to that person's "heart" and destroying his entire character. Not only did the poor teacher say something wrong, but his intention was to lie as well—a calculated deception. The kind of accusation made by the son can so degrade someone that his whole life is reconstructed around the one defamatory remark and he may live out the rest of his life in utter shame.

So how does one repent? One repents, according to Rabbi Hayyim, by loading the other half of the scale to balance the degradation symbolically. In this case, enough can be done to ease the shamed person's degradation and to make the shamer more keenly aware of the seriousness of his sin. The shamer, it turns out, is far more sinful than the liar and the schemer!

The same theme is illustrated somewhat differently in the following story:

The Radish-Eater

At the third meal of the Sabbath, an intimate and holy gathering, the Hasidim at Rabbi Wolf's table carried on their conversations in low voices and with subdued gestures so as not to disturb the *tzaddik*, who was deep in thought.

> Now it was Rabbi Wolf's wish, and the rule in his house, that anyone could come in at any time and seat himself at his table. On this occasion, a man entered and sat down with the rest, who made room for him although they knew that he was an ill-bred person.
>
> After a time, this man pulled a large radish out of his pocket, cut it into a number of pieces of convenient size and began to eat with a great smacking of lips. His neighbors were unable to restrain their annoyance any longer. "You glutton," they said to him. "How dare you offend this festive board with your barroom manners?"
>
> Although they had tried to keep down their voices, the *tzaddik* soon noticed what was going on. "I just feel like eating a really good radish," the rabbi said. "I wonder whether anyone here would get me one?"
>
> In a sudden flood of happiness which swept away his embarrassment, the radish-eater offered Rabbi Wolf a handful of pieces he had cut.
>
> (*Buber, Early Masters, pp. 159–160*)

In this wonderful story we see two kinds of "deviant" actions and how Rabbi Wolf is able to resolve both of them. One one hand the newcomer, whose manners are crude, sits down and enjoys himself in a loud, vulgar way that may be disturbing the rabbi who is in deep meditation. The Hasidim, in turn, shame the newcomer—a less obvious deviation.

The rabbi sees instantly that the two "deviations" are not at all comparable. It may be that some of the radish-eater's behavior is gross and below the standards of the others, but to shame him is a more outrageous sin. The rabbi clearly makes an alliance with the radish-eater to teach the others a lesson: Whenever one "corrects" another in a way which degrades and shames him, the "correction" is far more reprehensible than the "sin." And this is what Rabbi Wolf is trying to teach here. The radish-eater may have been a bit ungentlemanly, but that is nothing compared to putting him down.

Thus we learn of the importance of respecting people and upholding their dignity. We are all extremely frail human beings and shame can engrave itself on one's heart and soul so deeply that it can last a lifetime. It can be very destructive, not only to the shamed person, but to the shamer giving it as well, especially when he becomes overly righteous. That is another reason why Rabbi Wolf very pointedly sided with the radish-eater. Shaming a person can be a greater sin than the naive "sin" of which that person is accused. It was only the total identification of the rabbi with the radish-eater that enabled the latter to sweep away his embarrassment. We are sure that Rabbi Wolf heartily smacked his lips as he wolfed down the radish pieces that the radish-eater gave him!

In the Hadisic community, everyone was obliged to balance his needs and self-interests with care for the needs of others. This was not always easy to do, but the fact that the Hasidim were always struggling with these competing needs turned them into a truly compassionate community:

In a Fur Coat

> The Rabbi of Kotzk once said of a famous rabbi: "That's a *tzaddik* in a fur coat." His disciples asked him what he meant by this. "Well," he explained, "one man buys himself a fur coat in winter, another buys kindling. What is the difference between them? The first wants to keep only himself warm, the second wants to give warmth to others too."
>
> (*Buber, Late Masters, p. 274*)

Nor was it enough to think solely about the welfare of one's family.

With the aid of an ingenious metaphor, the following story warns us about limiting our concern to our immediate family. The Hasidic outlook stressed sympathetic consciousness of the distress of others outside the family and the desire to alleviate the suffering:

The Stork

> The Yid was asked: "In the Talmud it says that the stork is called *hasida* in Hebrew, that is, the devout or the loving one, because he gives so much love to his mate and his young. Then why is he classed in the Scriptures with the unclean birds?"
>
> He answered: "Because he gives love only to his own."
>
> (*Buber, Late Masters, pp. 231–232*)

The rabbis were exceedingly optimistic about the possibilities of their followers transforming themselves. They did not believe that "character was fate"; quite the contrary, they believed that if a person could be engaged and set in motion, he could change and become a different person. Ultimately, of course, a person is transformed through faith in God:

The Chief Trait

After the death of Rabbi Uri Strelisker, one of the Hasidim came to Rabbi Bunam. The latter welcomed him and asked him what particular trait of character it was Rabbi Uri's main purpose to instill in his Hasidim. The Hasid replied: "I believe Rabbi Uri sought to make his Hasidim very humble. The rabbi would order a rich Hasid to draw water at the pump and to bring in the pail on his shoulder—a thing the man would never have done at home."

Rabbi Bunam remarked: "My way is different, I will explain it to you by a parable: Three men were convicted of a crime and were lodged in a dark dungeon. Two of them were men of intelligence, but the third was a witless person. When food was lowered in the dark, the witless one did not know how to take his share and would break the plate or cut himself with the knife. One of his fellow prisoners sought to aid him by rehearsing with him the necessary behavior, but the next day a different arrangement of the food would baffle him again.

"One of the prisoners then remarked: 'Why waste time teaching this fellow every time? Help me to bore a hole in the wall to admit light, and then he will know how to eat unaided.'"

Rabbi Bunam concluded: "Likewise, I attempt to admit into the soul of man the fear and the love of God. This is a light whereby a man can learn wise conduct in its entirety and not trait by trait."

(*Newman, The Hasidic Anthology, p. 30*)

The moral of Rabbi Bunam's parable is that changes are always possible if a man can be provided with the resources to try new strategies by himself. The rabbis add the *caveat* that it is possible to transform one's character constantly, but only as long as one trusts in God, which can also be translated into trust in oneself.

The Hasidic masters believed that finding God was an individual journey, unique to every person. There was no formula for finding God. And this, in turn, creates unique individuals:

By His Own Abilities

Said the Besht: "No two persons have the same abilities. Each man should work in the service of God according to his own talents. If one man tries to imitate another, he merely loses his opportunity to do good through his own merit, and he cannot accomplish anything by imitation of the other's service."

(*Newman, The Hasidic Anthology, p. 152*)

Themselves

The Baal Shem said: "We say: 'God of Abraham, God of Isaac and God of Jacob,' and not: 'God of Abraham, Isaac and Jacob,' for Isaac and Jacob did not base their work on the searching and service of Abraham; they themselves searched for the unity of the Maker and His service."

(*Buber, Early Masters, p. 48*)

The Besht here points up the individuality of every person *and* his special relationship to God, which is what makes every individual different. It is a unique way of expressing the concept of individuality within the framework of a common faith in God.

The Hasidim believed so strongly in action that preoccupation with study alone was thought to be wicked. Isolation from the real world leads to passivity. The best learning is through give-and-take with fellow human beings:

With Yourself

This is how Rabbi Barukh expounded the words in *The Sayings of the Fathers,* "and be not wicked by facing yourself only" (that is, do not think that you cannot be redeemed):

> "Every man has the vocation of making perfect something in this world. The world has need of every single human being. But there are those who always sit in their rooms behind closed doors and study and never leave the house to talk with others. For this they are called wicked. If they talked to others, they would bring to perfection something they are destined to make perfect. That is what the words mean: 'Be not wicked by facing yourself only.' Since you face yourself only, and do not go among people, do not become wicked through solitude."
>
> (*Buber, Early Masters, pp. 89–90*)

The rabbis were so enamored with this principle of activity that they were hesitant to stop the action an individual was engaged in. They taught their followers to follow through with their actions to the end, and any interference was detrimental to their own good:

Into the Inn

> Rabbi Shlomo asked his disciple, Rabbi Asher: "When did you come to prayer?"
>
> "At just the right time for the inn named 'Exult, O Ye Righteous,'" was his reply.
>
> "Well done," said the *tzaddik.* "If you drive, you drive, and if you stop, you look around to see if anything is wrong. For if you do stop midway, it is easy to fall behind."
>
> (*Buber, Early Masters, pp. 278–279*)

Do your thing with all the zest and confidence and consistency and persistence at your command. These two cardinal tenets of the Hasidic faith, to be oneself and to be active, are very modern principles. They help to overcome the doubts and fears that often stand in our way and stop us from doing what we want to do.

Here is a story that can be found (dressed up, of course, in modern garb) in many of the hundreds of diet books on the market. Every useful diet book stresses awareness of what and how you eat; the use of contrasting imagery to exaggerate both the bad and good patterns of thinking, feeling and acting, and the habit of doing things as if you will be doing them forever (self-fulfilling prophecy). On all three accounts the story below is superlative:

In the Bowl

Rabbi Yisakhar Baer was very poor in his youth. One year he had to fast after as well as before the Day of Atonement, and when the Feast of Booths drew near he did not have the wherewithal to celebrate it. So he stayed in the House of Study after prayer, for he knew that there was no food in his house. But his wife had sold a piece of jewelry she still had, without telling him about it, and had bought holiday loaves and potatoes and candles for the sum she received.

Toward evening, when the rabbi came home and entered the booth, he found a festive table awaiting him, and was filled with joy. He washed his hands, seated himself, and began to eat the potatoes with great gusto, for he had gone hungry for days.

But when Rabbi Yisakhar Baer grew aware of how preoccupied he was with eating, he stopped. "Berel," he said to himself, "you are not sitting in the festive booth; why, you are sitting right in the bowl!" And he did not take another bite.

(*Buber, Late Masters, p. 200*)

THE SELF-DECEPTION OBSTACLE

There is no possibility of true courage without the boldness to face and even court our own deficiencies and vices. We are much more skillful at lying to ourselves than to others. The rabbis' most challenging test lay precisely in peeling away the layers of concealment and disguise that cover up self-deceptions. This is especially true of the self-mortifier who denies himself pleasure for some allegedly moral purpose. The Hasidic rabbis utterly detested these people, as you can well imagine. The self-mortifier in Hasidic stories inevitably wants to let other people know about his self-sacrifices and martyrdom, which were particularly odious to the Hasidim. Self-denial, to a Hasid, was not at all virtuous, but proof that the flagellant was tormented by impious thoughts, or egotistical and vain or perhaps both.

One of the most finely crafted responses to a man undergoing mortification, but primarily suffering from a bad case of self-deception, is the following story, which we could not fully appreciate until the second or even third reading:

Result of Mortification of the Flesh

A man once told Rabbi Bunam: "Time and again I have mortified my flesh and done all I should, and yet Elijah has not appeared to me."

In reply the *tzaddik* told him this story: "The holy Baal Shem Tov once went on a long journey. He hired a team, seated himself in the carriage, and uttered one of the holy Names. Immediately, the road leaped to meet the straining horses, and hardly had they begun to trot when they had reached the first inn, not knowing what had happened to them. At this stop they were usually fed, but they had scarcely calmed down when the second inn rushed past them. Finally it occurred to the beasts that they must have become men and so would not receive food until evening, in the town where they were to spend the night. But when evening came and the carriage failed to stop, but raced on from town to town, the horses agreed that the only possible explanation was that they must have been transformed into angels and no longer required either food or drink. At that moment, the carriage reached its destination. The horses were stabled, given their measure of oats, and they thrust their heads into their feedbags as starved horses do.

"As long as you are in a like situation," said Rabbi Bunam, "you would do well to be content."

(*Buber, Late Masters, p. 254*)

In this very powerful story, mortification and self-deception are interlocked, so that in the "punch-line" both are thoroughly intermingled in one fell swoop.

The mortifier is compared to the horses. They were racing through the night driven by the holy Baal Shem Tov. Progress was swift, so they sped past the first inn where the horses were to be fed. The horses then rationalized that they had become men and would be fed that evening; but they kept going, so the horses reasoned that they were transformed into angels. But at that moment the carriage stopped, the horses were stabled and hungrily dug into their feedbags like normal horses—and apparently shed all of their illusions.

Rabbi Bunam tells the mortifier that he should be content, for he is in a situation similar to that of the horses. In other words, he is in the wonderful position where he can shed his illusions because Elijah has not turned up, and he can now heartily enjoy a good meal just as the starved horses did when they "thrust their heads into their feedbags."

What a marvelously isomorphic tale. It is universal, too, with its very thin, blurred, shifting line between ambition and pretension. Pretension suggests zealous desire for recognition of accomplishment without achieving it or actually possessing the requisite skills, ability or character to do so. Because independence, achievement, originality are so eagerly sought and so amply rewarded, many are tempted to claim more than they have actually attained. In the above story, Rabbi Bunam very artistically created a custom-made tale that fits precisely his follower's situation. The story can be adapted to any situation in which people make claims for recognition that is undeserved.

We can now begin to put together a picture of the ideal character the Hasid screws up his courage to become: The ideal Hasid is a person of moderation and joy, realistic, perfectible, caring and compassionate for others, and quiet, even taciturn. The development of these qualities is extremely important to the Hasidim. No matter how learned a person might be, without these qualities his brilliance was of little value:

A Good Man Is Like the Torah

> Rabbi Leib Saras said: "Of what avail is mere study of the Torah when he who learns it is contaminated by pride and temper? The good man should himself be the Torah, and people should be able to learn good conduct from observing him."
>
> (*Newman, The Hasidic Anthology, p.* 8)

Rabbi Leib's comparison of man to Torah is fetching. The Torah is a model creation of God. Man is also God's creation, but he is always tempted to be less divine than He is. One way for a person to become like God is to study His creations, such as the Torah, and through study achieve the righteous way. But for the Hasid it is not enough merely to study the Torah; one has to absorb it, so that the Torah enters him through the heart and is within him and he is in the Torah, and his character and the Torah become one.

The Hasidim took an extra step: They wanted study to become part of daily activity. The Torah affects the whole man. That, in essence, is the Hasidic point of view—Torah not only in the head, but in every part of the student and in his every activity.

In that sense, man is like the Torah itself—he is of one piece; and just as one reads the Torah to learn about God, so he can "read" or observe the Hasid, who is like the Torah, and discover the moral, just and good way of life.

As we have seen, the values the Hasidim most admire are the guidelines by which they judge one another's character. You are what your values are. Thus, one's character is never really set, but hammered out in experiences throughout a lifetime:

The Wise and the Wicked

> Said the Medzibozher: "As for the wise, what he is, he says; as for the wicked, what he says, he is."
>
> (*Newman, The Hasidic Anthology, p. 512*)

THE CORE PATTERN OF HASIDIC CHARACTER

One of the fundamental beliefs that all people maintain at different levels of awareness is the idea that, amidst the fluxion of reality, there are recurrent patterns that give meaning, coherence, and shape to life in the face of the constant battering change to which we are subjected. Of course, some people take very safe routes throughout life as a defense against the inevitable insecurity that accompanies the challenge of the new and unfamiliar.

We raise these issues because we have not yet zeroed in on the core values that constitute the ideal Hasidic personality, toward which the Hasidim daily struggled. Related to this is a beautiful story about finding a pattern in the strange and unfamiliar:

The Hidden Pattern

Once upon a time, an Ottoman Sultan decided to travel incognito among his people and experience life as an ordinary subject of the kingdom. It so happened that on his first day he was captured by bandits and, then and there, he decided to use his wits rather than his royalty to set himself free.

He persuaded his captors to purchase mats from which he could make exotic quilts that they could sell. He told the bandits that he was a master craftsman, and they should ask exorbitant sums of money for the quilts.

And so it transpired. One of the bandits went to the bazaar with a quilt, asked for a ridiculous amount of money, and was derisively laughed at. A Jewish wine-merchant was passing by and asked what all the commotion was about. He was told about the man who was trying to sell an ordinary reworked mat for a ridiculously high amount of money.

The Jew was curious. He carefully examined the mat and noticed a letter woven into it. He decided to buy the mat and was told he could buy one like it every day.

The Jew agreed, and by the fifth day he could tell by the progression of letters that indeed this was the name of the missing Sultan. The "salesman" was followed to the bandits' hideout, and the Sultan was freed.

As a reward, the Sultan decreed that the Jew and his seed would have special privileges including *carte blanche* admission to the palace at all times.

Several years later, the Jew was falsely accused of a crime, but the Sultan remembered and came to his rescue.

And they all lived happily ever after.

(*Polsky, after Zevin, Vol. II, 1980*)

"The Jew was curious." He went beyond the obvious and recognized a difficulty, an incongruity in the high price of an ordinary mat and the salesman's persistence in demanding it.

The Jew had to make some sense, find some pattern in this strange train of events.

On the other hand, the Sultan was clever enough to fashion an escape which included hiding a "pattern" that the bandits would not notice but one that a more sharp-witted person would detect. A hidden pattern figures importantly in the Sultan's overall plan for escape.

THE GLORY AND THE DANGER OF BEING ONESELF

If the Hasidic stories in Martin Buber's anthology were arranged by themes, "independence" and "conceit" would be among the largest entries. This is a curious phenomenon. It is as if the rabbis' program for fostering independence had become too successful, so that the self-reliant were tempted to overvalue themselves. Perhaps that is what underlies the two extremes that the rabbis abhorred; the dependent "wimp" who scarcely values himself at all, and the egotist who sets too great a value upon himself. Do independence and achievement lead men to enjoy honor and then seek it to confirm to themselves that they are truly important?

We found this juxtaposition of large numbers of stories about the values of independence and of humility to be a challenge: What is the relationship between the two themes? Can one find a common basis in Hasidism for both themes?

The two themes can be viewed from the vantage point of the Hasidic rabbi as a leader of the people and also as a creator of Hasidic stories. The stories can be read as cautionary tales, designed as a forewarning to the rabbis themselves to beware of the twin dangers of infantilizing their followers and making them dependent on the rabbis, and of the rabbis' taking to heart their self-importance, because so many Hasidim seek their help and pay them so much homage.

We see here two streams of independence and pride flowing into one river of self-importance accelerating into self-glorification. The two streams feeding this river are dependent followers and arrogant leaders. If that is true—and we believe we can document this thesis in the two sections that follow—

the stories stand as a remarkable monument of cautionary restraint to help the rabbis keep from becoming rescuers of lost souls or cynosures plagued with an excessive desire to win the notice and praises of others, based on often quite trivial attainments.

The rabbis required this constant warning because they fully believed one's worst enemy can't harm one as much as oneself. By making public in countless stories their vulnerability to these "traps," they also empower their Hasidic followers to check any excesses in being either too helpful or too lofty and removed.

At the end of this chapter we shall show how the two streams—independence and modesty (rather than "humility," which may imply undue self-deprecation, which can then be connected with "vanity")—come together to define the core of the ideal Hasidic character, and how that may be expressed in practical terms. But first, we shall examine the Hasidic programs for fostering self-actualization and appropriate self-esteem.

FOSTERING HASIDIC INDEPENDENCE AND THE COURAGE TO BE ONESELF

Independence and courage are powerfully intertwined. As we have seen, a sense of oneself is important in risking that self. The more confused one is about who he is and what he wants to do, the more he will avoid commitment and will fail to live up to minor challenges, much less ideal goals. The biggest failure in life is to fail to come to grips with oneself. The hedger's energies are all turned inward in ineffectual efforts to put his various parts together—like the "patchwork rabbi."

This section covers two main topics:

- What are the key qualities underlying courage and independence?
- By what process or stages does one become courageously independent?

WHAT ARE THE KEY QUALITIES UNDERLYING COURAGE AND INDEPENDENCE?

Assertiveness is critical to independence. The assertive person compels, in a nonaggressive way, recognition of his rights. He confidently states his position without the necessity to prove his legitimacy. Diffidence, coyness (assumed or affected shyness), timidity and modesty that implied lack of assertiveness were all severely reproved. "Go for it!" could well have been a Hasidic rallying cry:

The Spoon

> Rabbi Elimelekh's servant once forgot a spoon for Rabbi Mendel who was a guest at Rabbi Elimelekh's table. Everyone ate except Rabbi Mendel. The *tzaddik* observed this and asked: "Why aren't you eating?"
>
> "I have no spoon," said his guest.
>
> "Look," said Rabbi Elimelekh, "one must know enough to ask for a spoon, and a plate too, if need be!"
>
> Rabbi Mendel took the word of his teacher to heart. From that day on, his fortunes were on the mend.
>
> (*Buber, Late Masters, p. 125*)

Rabbi Mendel was a very fast learner, which meant taking the counsel "to heart" and taking charge of his life; naturally and immediately, "his fortunes were on the mend."

Through the stories, the rabbis persistently strove to encourage their followers to find a balance between running to them for counsel and solving their problems on their own. Trivial concerns that were brought to them were especially baneful:

The Pin in the Shirt

> Once, some women came to Rabbi Pinhas from a nearby town and bothered him with trivial concerns. When he saw them at his door again the following morning before prayer, he

fled to his son's house and cried: "If only the Messiah came, so that we might get rid of the *tzaddikim*, 'the good Jews.'" After a while, he added: "You think that it is the wicked who delay the coming of the Messiah? Not so—it is 'the good Jews' who are delaying it. A nail somewhere in the wall—what has that to do with me? But a pin sticking in my shirt—that's what pricks!"

(*Buber, Early Masters*, p. 133)

Aside from the lack of judgment about annoying the rabbis with trivial concerns (were these women perhaps seeking some contact and response?), the rabbis were concerned that their followers might be socialized into what we call today "learned helplessness." Over and over, the rabbis emphasized in their stories the need for Hasidim to rely on themselves. Even if they did consult a rabbi, ultimately they would have to help themselves:

The Morning Prayer

"There are *tzaddikim*," said Rabbi Naftali, "who pray that those in need of help may come to them and find help through their prayers. But the Rabbi of Roptchitz gets up early in the morning and prays that all those in need of help may find it in their own homes, and not have to go to Roptchitz, and not be deluded into thinking that the rabbi has helped them."

(*Buber, Late Masters*, p. 193)

The Hasidic rabbis set a goal of enlarging their followers' perspective by insisting on the very radical idea (quite current today) that they themselves were responsible for achieving anything worthwhile; and if they didn't do it with their own will, brains and skill, it was not worth doing:

First Prize

Rabbi Yehiel Meir, later the Rabbi of Gostynin, who was a poor man, went to his teacher, the Rabbi of Kotzk, with a beaming face and told him he had won the first prize in a lottery. "That wasn't through any fault of mine," said the *tzad-*

dik. Rabbi Yehiel went home and distributed the money among needy friends.

(*Buber, Late Masters, p. 285*)

The clear message here is that *anything* one gets through his own efforts is worthwhile whereas anything obtained without effort is worthless. Is this why, relatively speaking, there are today fewer lottery and casino players among Jews than in the general population? This point is pushed even further in the following story, namely, that what one gets without working for it, he doesn't even have, even if he has it:

Peasant Wisdom

Rabbi Yisakhar Baer once met an old peasant from the village of Oleshnye who had known him when he was young, but was not aware of his rise in the world. "Berel," the peasant called to him, "what's new with you?"

"And what's new with you?" asked the rabbi.

"Well, Berel, what shall I tell you," answered the other. "What you don't get by your own work you don't have."

From that time on, whenever Rabbi Baer spoke of the proper way to conduct one's life, he added: "And the old man of Oleshnye said: 'What you don't get by your own work, you don't have.'"

(*Buber, Late Masters, p. 203*)

Another obstacle against which the rabbis waged a relentless war was the dependent mentality. Dependency, conformity and lack of courage go together. And all three add up to a very low self-image. Dependency was abhorred, as was opting for secure, limited gains instead of longer-range, larger goals:

The Foolish Request

The Rabbi of Roptshitz told the following incident:

"During the siege of Sebastopol, Czar Nicholas was once riding along one of the walls when an enemy archer took aim at him. A Russian soldier who observed this from afar screamed and startled the emperor's horse so that it swerved to the side and the arrow missed its target. The Czar told the man to ask any favor he pleased. 'Our sergeant is so brutal,' the soldier faltered. 'He is always beating me. If only I could serve under another sergeant!'

"'Fool,' cried Nicholas, 'be a sergeant yourself!'

"We are like that: we pray for the petty needs of the hour and do not know how to pray for our redemption."

(*Buber, Late Masters, p. 194*)

The path the rabbis took to encourage nonconformity was to emphasize the multiple ways to serve God. That is a clear signal to the Hasid to be a person in his own right and to find his own path to God and to his total existence.

The rabbis in their wisdom were promulgating a norm, a point of view about the holiness of unconventionality. The hope and self-fulfilling prophecy was that it would be less difficult to be unconventional if to be unconventional were to become culturally conventional. The following stories strongly emphasize this point:

In Many Ways

Some time after Rabbi Shalom, the son of Rabbi Abraham, the Angel, had died, two of his disciples came to Lublin to study with the Seer. They found him out in the open, saying the blessing of the New Moon. Now, because he did this a little differently in some details from what their teacher had accustomed them to, they did not promise themselves much from Lublin and decided to leave the town the very next day. When they entered the rabbi's house shortly after, he spoke words of greeting to them and immediately added: "A God whom one could serve only in a set way—what kind of God would that be?" They bowed before him and became his disciples.

(*Buber, Early Masters, p. 313*)

Even if one is poor and highly dependent on others, he can be unconventional in not adopting a poor person's lowered self-esteem and image:

Assistance

While Rabbi Wolf was on a journey, a poor young Hasid came up to him and asked for financial assistance. The *tzaddik* looked in his purse, put back a large coin he had happened to find, fetched out a smaller one and gave it to the needy young man.

"A young man," he said, "should not have to be ashamed, but neither should he expect Heaven knows what." The Hasid went from him with bowed head.

Rabbi Wolf called him back and asked: "Young man, what was that you were just thinking?"

"I have learned a new way to serve God," the other replied. "One should not be ashamed and one should not expect Heaven knows what."

"That was what I meant," said the *tzaddik* and accorded him help.

(*Buber, Early Masters, p. 162*)

HOW DOES A PERSON BECOME COURAGEOUSLY INDEPENDENT?

How do you know that you are on the track to becoming courageously independent? A smart aleck once said that courage is doing the thing you are afraid of before you change your mind. On second thought, perhaps that is not so smart-alecky. As soon as you feel yourself doubting, procrastinating, fearing, uncertain, lacking confidence, distrusting yourself—any or all of these—that is precisely the moment to march into the breach. Meeting obstacles head on, especially the doubts and fears within yourself, is the surest way to fulfill the commandment to be courageous:

The Unredeemed Place

Once Rabbi Bunam was praying at an inn. People jostled and pushed him, but he did not go into his room. Later, he said to his disciples: "Sometimes it seems impossible to pray in a certain place and one seeks out another place. But that is not the right thing to do. For the place we have quitted cries out mournfully: 'Why did you refuse to make your devotions here with me? If you met with obstacles, it was a sign that it was up to you to redeem me.'"

(Buber, *Late Masters*, p. 256)

By far the single most courageous act a Hasid or rabbi could perform was to challenge superior rabbinical authority. You have to remember that a rabbi was not solely a teacher: He was a mentor, leader, religious authority, "parent," coach, model, and ideal human being, which many, if not most, of his followers aspired to become. Challenging such an authority was only two steps below challenging the Father of us all.

Yet to their everlasting credit, the rabbis told and retold stories in which their very own authority was challenged and the petitioners turned out to be right. That is the truest testimony to their affirmation of the value of individuality and nonconformity:

Refusal

The people of a certain city begged the Baal Shem Tov to induce his disciple, Yehiel Mikhal, to accept the position of rabbi, which they had offered him. The Baal Shem Tov urged him to accept, but he persisted in his refusal. "If you do not listen to me," said his master, "you will lose this world and the World-to-Come, too."

"Even if I lose both worlds," answered the disciple, "I shall not accept what does not befit me."

"Then, receive my blessing, my son," said the Baal Shem, "that you have withstood temptation."

(Buber, *Early Masters*, p. 141)

We are well aware today that it may be as much a problem for the parent or teacher to disengage from the child and student as it is for the latter to disengage from his guide. We recognize that there are symbiotic parents who cannot let go of their children. The following lovely fantasy teaches us about one disciple's effort to free himself of his master:

The Offer

> The story is also told that when his master had died and Rabbi Mendel was greatly troubled as to who would now be his teacher, the Yehudi appeared to him in a dream and tried to comfort him, saying that he was willing to continue to teach him. "I do not want a teacher from the other world," answered Mendel.
>
> (*Buber, Early Masters, p. 272*)

The meaning is quite clear. Rabbi Mendel is carrying his teacher within himself and is having trouble letting him go. In the story he boldly confronts his own subconscious and exorcises his teacher "from the other world."

Incidentally, the Baal Shem himself tells us how it is possible to foster autonomy and give support whether it be between God and man, between teacher and student, or between parent and child. In the lovely story "Near and Far" (page 120), he strikes just the right balance between support and letting go.

The following extraordinarily moving story is also one of the most poetically crafted, in the sense that it soars above and beyond the truth of history and nature into the truth of a timeless spiritual stratosphere:

The Judgment of the Messiah

> Many heads of families in Berditchev complained to the Rabbi of Rizhin that their sons-in-law had left wives and children in order to become his disciples, and when they asked him to persuade the youths to return home, he told them about a young man who had lived in the days of the Great *Maggid.* He had quit his father-in-law's house to go to the *maggid.* They had fetched him back, and he had pledged on a hand-clasp that he would stay at home. Yet shortly thereafter, he was gone. Now his father-in-law got the rav of the town to declare that this broken promise was a cause for divorce. The young man was thus deprived of all means of subsistence. Soon he fell ill and died.
>
> When the *tzaddik* had finished his story, he added: "And now, my good men, when the Messiah comes, the young man

will hale his father-in-law before this court of justice. The father-in-law will quote the rav of the town, and the rav will quote a passage from the commentary on the *Shulhan Arukh*. Then the Messiah will ask the young man why, after giving his hand on it that he would remain at home, he broke his promise just the same. And the young man will say: 'I just had to go to the rabbi!' In the end, the Messiah will pronounce judgment. To the father-in-law he will say: 'You took the rav's word as your authority and so you are justified.' And to the rav he will say: 'You took the law as your authority and so you are justified.'

"And then He will add: 'But I have come for those who are not justified.'"

(*Buber, Late Masters,* p. 57)

Is there truly a moral authority beyond one's father-in-law, the rav and the holy Torah itself? How is that justified? Can one break "laws" in this world, and still be justified on a higher (literally) moral plane? If ever there was a need for a Messiah or God, it may very well be as a legitimizing force against all fallible terrestrial judicial authorities.

Someone once said that the belief and trust in God means a willingness to take chances. But the idea that the Messiah will champion fighters for change and independence against established authority is really attributing a rebellious and even revolutionary role to His mission. This is a very important point, because it gives some support to deviation and nonconformity, without which a culture is bound to stagnate.

We fervently thank the Hasidim, and especially the Rabbi of Rizhin, for this creative insight into the Messiah as a revolutionary.

WILY PRIDE

The other major obstacle that stands in the way of a man's having the courage to be himself is vanity—undue or excessive pride in one's appearance or achievements. The vain person is so enamored of the need for recognition (and power) that substantive values he may have had shrivel into nothingness. Vanity suggests a lack of real substance, soundness and authenticity. Often, the vain or prideful assume an air of superiority. They always claim more for themselves than is warranted. Sometimes, pride can deteriorate into arrogance, contemptuous haughtiness, and intolerable insolence.

These developments, however, are patently too obvious, so pride will often slyly cover itself up in various guises which may not be readily apparent.

Vanity is a disease that afflicts superior people:

The Obstacle

> Once, Rabbi Jacob Yitzhak confidently expected salvation to come that very year. When the year was over, he said to his disciple, the Yehudi: "The rank and file of people either have turned completely to God, or can, at any rate, do so. They present no obstacle. It is the superior people who constitute a hindrance. They cannot attain humility, and therefore they cannot achieve the turning."
>
> (*Buber, Early Masters, p. 308*)

Among the superior people whom pride afflicts are the rabbis, and even the *tzaddikim*. In "The Two Lights" (page 11), Rabbi Mendel of Rymanov comments on this affliction and its effect upon the rabbis: "So it was in the days of our Sages: There was a whole skyful of stars, large stars and small stars, and they lived together in all brotherliness. Not so the *tzaddikim* of our day! Now no one wants to be a small light and bow to a greater. So it is better for each to have his own firmament all for himself."

This is truly a sad state of affairs. However, we think it took enormous courage on Rabbi Mendel's part to call a spade a spade. After all, the *tzaddikim* were the moral supermen of their time and to admit publicly to the all-too-human failing of vanity and conceit is both sorrowful and exhilarating. Again, the Hasidim were so far ahead of us that they put us to shame. We have exactly the same problem among contemporary leaders in every field of endeavor, but very, very few among them would openly indict their "own" for the same human shortcoming.

Pride and vanity subtly insinuate themselves into a person's character. Suddenly it's there—slipping slyly over the border from modesty and piety to self-righteousness:

Temptation

Rabbi Mikhal said: "When the Evil Urge tries to tempt man to sin, it tempts him to become all too righteous."

(*Buber, Early Masters, p. 153*)

One of the foxiest strategems employed by a vain person is for a notable person to recognize his accomplishments and worth. This seems to be the indispensable route to pride. As soon as you know you are good, it is difficult to avoid blowing yourself up beyond recognition. That seems to be the reason behind the following story:

In the Last Hour

On a certain New Year's night, the *Maggid* of Zlotchov saw a man who had been a leader in the city, and who had died a short time ago. "What are you doing here?" he asked.

"The rabbi knows," said the dead man, "that in this night, souls are incarnated anew. I am such a soul."

"And why were you sent out again?" asked the *maggid.*

"I led an impeccable life here on earth," the dead man told him.

"And yet you are forced to live once more?" the *maggid* went on to ask.

"Before my death," said the man, "I thought over everything I had done and found that I had always acted in just the right way. Because of this, my heart swelled with satisfaction and in the midst of this feeling I died. So now they have sent me back into the world to atone for my pride."

At that time a son was born to the *maggid.* His name was Rabbi Wolf. He was very humble.

(*Buber, Early Masters, p. 158*)

Sometimes one can fall quite innocently and unconsciously into the pit of conceit, and super-insight is required to become aware of one's deeply hidden haughtiness:

The Walls

On a business trip to Leipzig, Rabbi Bunam, together with a number of merchants who had accompanied him, stopped at the house of a Jew in order to say the Afternoon Prayer. But the moment he entered, he realized that he had come to an ill-smelling house; never had he prayed in such a room. He gave the others a sign and they left. The rabbi turned to go to the next house. But after a few steps he stopped. "We must go back!" he cried. "The walls are summoning me to judgment because I scorned them and put them to shame."

(*Buber, Early Masters, p. 240*)

In the next story, vanity assumes an artful momentary disguise that the sensitive rabbi instantly recognizes:

Self-Confidence

Rabbi Hanokh told this story:

"In the house of my teacher, Rabbi Bunam, it was customary for all his Hasidim to assemble on the eve of the Day of Atonement, and to recall themselves to him. Once, when I had settled the accounts of my soul, I was ashamed to have him see me. But I decided to go with the others, to remind him of me, and then leave hurriedly. And that is what I did. The moment he saw me getting ready to go, however, he called me to him. It flattered my vanity that the rabbi wanted to look upon me. But the very moment I felt flattered at heart, he said to me: 'Now there is no longer any need for it.'"

(*Buber, Late Masters, pp. 251–252*)

What's happening here? At first, Rabbi Hanokh is appropriately embarrassed about seeing his teacher after recounting all his sins of the year. Then he decides "to remind" his teacher about himself and leave "hurriedly." Rabbi Hanokh is getting ready to leave when his teacher summons him. He feels "flattered at heart" because he is singled out, but the rabbi tells him precisely what is going on within him. He accomplishes this by saying he no longer needs to see him. The silent additional message is, "As long as vanity has taken you over, whatever I have to say will not be worth anything!"

Finally, in this last story about wily pride, Rabbi Bunam artfully nails a follower who takes pride in not having any pride, but makes the fatal error of telling this to the acerbic rabbi:

Reluctant Honor

Someone said to Rabbi Bunam: "My case certainly proves the falseness of saying that honor will run after him who flees from her and will flee from him who runs after her. For I ran diligently away from her, but she did not take a single step to catch up with me."

"Evidently, she noticed that you were looking back at her," answered the rabbi, "and was no longer attracted by the game."

(*Buber, Late Masters, p. 255*)

TURNING THE TABLES ON PRIDE

Let us review some of the strategies by which the Hasidim countered the ceaseless insinuation of pride in their lives. One strategy devised by a naive disciple was to assume the discipline of silence, save in prayer and study:

Silence and Speech

A man had taken upon himself the discipline of silence, and for three years had spoken no words save those of the Torah and of prayer. Finally, the Yehudi sent for him. "Young man," he said, "how is it that I do not see a single word of yours in the world of truth?"

"Rabbi," said the other to justify himself, "why should I indulge in the vanity of speech? Is it not better just to learn and to pray?"

"If you do that," said the Yehudi, "not a word of your own reaches the world of truth. He who only learns and prays is murdering the world of his own soul. What do you mean by 'vanity of speech'? Whatever you have to say can be vanity or it can be truth. And now I am going to have a pipe and some tobacco brought for you to smoke tonight. Come to me after the Evening Prayer and I shall teach you how to talk."

They sat together the whole night. When morning came, the young man's apprenticeship was over.

(*Buber, Late Masters, p. 228*)

This is a case of the cure becoming more harmful than the disease. The Yehudi confirms that since the same words can be interpreted as vanity or as truth, one has to be exquisitely discriminating about himself. Vigilance and awareness are the price for avoiding this cunning enemy, not silence, which is also, incidentally, proof of lack of confidence and lack of courage.

A second strategy, implied in the preceding story, is made explicit in the following story: namely, the idea that pride can never really be overcome once and for all, but must be overcome day by day. The implication is that even "overcoming" pride can lead to pride. When Rabbi Dov Baer is asked ("The Succession," page 188), "How can pride be broken," he replies: "Pride belongs to God—as it is written: 'The Lord reigneth; He is clothed in pride.' That is why no counsel can be given on how to break pride. We must struggle with it all the days of our life."

A third strategy employed by Hasidim to combat pride is to take the initiative, upon receipt of any hint of recognition that they were persons of importance, and denouncing or denying it immediately:

Punishment

When the *maggid* realized that he had become known to the world, he begged God to tell him what sin of his had brought this guilt upon him.

(*Buber, Early Masters, p. 99*)

A typical counterthrust to placement on a pedestal:

The Threat

A prominent man threatened to thrust Rabbi Hanokh down from all the spiritual rungs he had attained at a single blow. He replied: "You could not thrust me down to a lowlier place than the one I am already in."

(*Buber, Late Masters, p. 313*)

A fourth, and the cleverest, strategy, is the opposite of flatly denying vanity. It consists in reframing pride and using it to one's own modest advantage. Since pride is always lurking around, ready to leap, invite it in, so to speak, so that you can in jujitsu fashion disarm it and render it impotent. The technique developed by Rabbi Mendel is quite ingenious:

The Heap of Cinders

Before leaving for the Land of Israel, Rabbi Menahem Mendel paid a visit to old Rabbi Jacob Joseph of Polnoye, the great disciple of the Baal Shem Tov. He arrived at the inn in a *troika*, and this in itself was enough to annoy the Hasidim in Polnoye, whose master insisted on a simple life. But when Rabbi Mendel left the inn and went to the *tzaddik*'s house hatless and beltless, a long pipe in his mouth, they all thought that Rabbi Jacob Joseph, who was known for his violent temper, would refuse to receive his guest because of his careless and lax behavior. But the old man welcomed him on the threshold with a great show of love, and spent several hours talking to him. When Rabbi Mendel had gone, the disciples asked their master: "What is there to this man who had the impudence to enter your house with only the cap on his head, with silver buckles on his shoes, and a long pipe in his mouth?"

The *tzaddik* said: "A king who went to war hid his treasures in a safe place. But he buried his most precious pearl, which he loved with all his heart, in a heap of cinders because he knew that no one would look for it there. And so that the powers of evil might not touch it, Rabbi Mendel buries his great humility in the cinder-heap of vanity."

(*Buber, Early Masters, p. 178*)

This is clever: One takes on the trappings of pride but not the whole content and foils one of pride's main tools, flamboyant public insouciance, by artfully assuming it but not really meaning it.

A related device for combating pride—and this is one of

the trickiest strategies of all—is to become so "normally" humble that it is not a big deal. This course is definitely not recommended for novices—the danger of flunking the maneuver is very high:

The Signature

> When Rabbi Menahem wrote letters from the Land of Israel, he always signed himself: "He, who is truly humble."
>
> The Rabbi of Rizhin once was asked: "If Rabbi Menahem were really humble, how could he call himself so?"
>
> "He was so humble," said the Rabbi of Rizhin, "that just because humility dwelt within him, he no longer regarded it as a virtue."
>
> (*Buber, Early Masters, p. 180*)

A final strategy, and the most difficult of all, is to accept as inevitable that pride—and vanity, conceit and its numerous conspirators—will succeed in conquering you; that is its role. But you can pick up the pieces afterwards. "A broken and humble heart can burst open all the gates and all the heavenly palaces." To a grieved disciple who wept with a broken heart because he had not prepared adequately for Rosh Hashana services, the Besht said: "In a king's palace there are many chambers, and each door has its own particular key. But there is one implement which can open all the doors, and that is the axe. The Kabbalistic *kavvanot* are the keys to the gates in the World Above, each gate requiring its own particular *kavvana.* But a broken and humble heart can burst open all the gates and all the heavenly palaces."

COURAGE

An interesting aspect of the idea of courage is that it is defined negatively in the sense of overcoming difficult obstacles: the mental and/or moral strength to resist opposition, danger, hardship. It implies fortitude, resilience, determination, tenacity, and unwillingness to acknowledge defeat—all admirable qualities.

We have tried to explore courage as a process; one is always becoming courageous, never attaining it. Courage is paradoxical in that you must learn to wish yourself to truly become yourself. And now we begin to get into the content of courage—the courage to be yourself. Courage is character in the sense that the character *is your own,* not imitated or borrowed from someone else. Courage in this sense demands only one feat—not to run away from yourself.

In this context the big challenge is to seek someone who can enable you to be yourself. Perhaps the greatest courage is needed to face unflinchingly that inexplicable stranger that is yourself:

Master and Disciple

Rabbi Hanokh told this story:

"For a whole year I felt a longing to go to my master Rabbi Bunam and talk with him. But every time I entered the house, I felt I wasn't man enough. Once though, when I was walking across a field and weeping, I knew that I must run to the rabbi without delay. He asked: 'Why are you weeping?' I answered: 'I am, after all, alive in this world, a being created with all the senses and all the limbs, but I do not know what it is I was created for and what I am good for in this world.'

"'Little fool,' he replied, 'that's the same question I have carried around with me all my life. You will come and eat the evening meal with me today.'"

(*Buber, Late Masters,* p. 251)

Perplexity about who you are and what you should do is the lot of man, and courage exists precisely in accepting your bewilderment and living with it to the end of your life. When we have learned to do that, our reward may very well be the advent of the Messiah himself:

The Hour

The Rabbi of Kotzk said:

"Generation after generation has toiled to bring the Messiah, each generation in its own way, and they have not succeeded. One cannot bring the Messiah. Some day, when the Jews are all busy with caring for their daily bread, and bewildered in spirit—he will come."

(*Buber, Late Masters, p. 287*)

Another way of accepting yourself is to be fully absorbed in what you are doing; that is a courageous act, no matter what enterprise you are involved in—to be so fully engaged in what you are doing that you and your task are one:

The Rope Dancer

Once, Rabbi Hayyim of Krosno, a disciple of the Baal Shem, was watching a rope dancer together with his disciples. He was so absorbed in the spectacle that they asked him what it was that riveted his gaze to this foolish performance. "This man," he said, "is risking his life, and I cannot say why. But I am quite sure that while he is walking the rope, he is not thinking of the fact that he is earning a hundred gulden by what he is doing, for if he did, he would fall."

(*Buber, Early Masters, p. 174*)

A sure sign that you are cultivating courage is the readiness to deal with obstacles that will stand in the way of achieving your goals. In fact, to the Hasidim obstacles are sent by God to enable you to become yourself in your choice of activities that represent and shape you. In the tale on page 297, "An Unredeemed Place," Rabbi Bunam continues to do what he has to do despite distractions. It was his time to say his prayers, and he intended to finish in the place where he had started the service.

In light of this incident, Rabbi Bunam sagaciously warned his fellow rabbis of their severe limitations in enabling each of their followers to fully discover himself:

All and Each

Rabbi Bunam once said:

"On a Sabbath, when my room is full of people, it is difficult for me to 'say Torah.' For each person requires his own

Torah, and each wishes to find his own perfection. And so what I give to all I withhold from each."

(*Buber, Late Masters, p. 248*)

And perhaps that is precisely why Hasidim look beyond their rabbis to the ultimate guide:

The Solitary Tree

Rabbi Bunam once said:

"When I look at the world, it sometimes seems to me that every man is a tree in the wilderness, and that God has no one in His world but Him, and that He has no one to turn to, save only God."

(*Buber, Late Masters, p. 256*)

The rabbis warn that, although we can gain considerable support from other people, there are severe limitations even to this source of comfort. The Rabbi of Rizhin cleverly introduces another strategy in the next story by suggesting to a disciple that he apply a method that has worked for him in one situation, to another more difficult situation. Note the clever use of "light" as a metaphor in pacing and counseling the young rabbi:

To Walk with One's Own Light

A young rabbi complained to the Rabbi of Rizhin: "During the hours when I devote myself to my studies I feel life and light, but the moment I stop studying it is all gone. What shall I do?"

The Rabbi of Rizhin replied: "That is just as when a man walks through the woods on a dark night, and for a time another joins him, lantern in hand, but at the crossroads they part, and the first must grope his way on alone. But if a man carries his own light with him, he need not be afraid of any darkness."

(*Buber, Late Masters, pp. 62–63*)

THE CROWNING ACHIEVEMENT

The rabbis formulated a powerful message for themselves and their followers. The problem is that this message has become a cliché today, a trite phrase, so hackneyed that it is summarily dismissed. We no longer fully grasp its worth, its significance and its momentous consequences.

If we could re-evaluate, even admit once again this absolutely critical quality that the Hasidic rabbis stress, we could at least express our gratitude. That quality, variously stated, is:

- Accept yourself.
- Be yourself.
- Look to yourself for all the untold treasures in the world.
- In yourself is everything of any worth.
- Without yourself you are nothing.

In a very deep and fundamental sense, this is what the Hasidic stories are all about. And this must be said over and over again, despite the danger that the message will become hackneyed. It is puzzling to find so many people nowadays who cannot grasp this personally redeeming, revolutionary point of view.

Let us turn to our stories for the novel ways the theme of finding yourself in yourself can be expressed:

World-Peace and Soul-Peace

> Rabbi Bunam taught:
>
> "Our Sages say: 'Seek peace in your own place.' You cannot find peace anywhere save in your own self. In the psalm we read: 'There is no peace in my bones because of my sin.' When a man has made peace within himself, he will be able to make peace in the whole world."
>
> (*Buber, Late Masters, p. 264*)

In one tale of this genre, the self is likened to a treasure trove:

The Treasure

Rabbi Bunam used to tell young men who came to him for the first time the story of Rabbi Eisik, son of Rabbi Yekel in Cracow. After many years of great poverty which had never shaken his faith in God, he dreamed someone bade him look for a treasure in Prague, under the bridge which leads to the king's palace. When the dream recurred a third time, Rabbi Eisik prepared for the journey and set out to Prague. But the bridge was guarded day and night, and he did not dare to start digging. Nevertheless, he went to the bridge every morning and kept walking around it until evening.

Finally, the captain of the guards, who had been watching him, asked in a kindly way whether he was looking for something or waiting for somebody. Rabbi Eisik told him of the dream which had brought him here from a faraway country. The captain laughed: "And so to please the dream, you, poor fellow, wore out your shoes to come here! As for having faith in dreams, if I had it, I should have had to get going when a dream once told me to go to Cracow and dig for treasure under the stove in the room of a Jew—Eisik, son of Yekel, that was the name! Eisik, son of Yekel! I can just imagine what it would be like, how I should have to try every house over there, where half of the Jews are named Eisik, and the other half Yekel!" And he laughed again. Rabbi Eisik bowed, traveled home, dug up the treasure from under the stove, and built the House of Prayer which is called "Reb Eisik's Shul."

"Take this story to heart," Rabbi Bunam used to add, "and make what it says your own: There is something you cannot find anywhere in the world, not even at the *tzaddik*'s, and there is, nevertheless, a place where you can find it."

(*Buber, Late Masters, pp. 245–246*)

Why is it so difficult for us to accept this simple precept and live by it? Do we really dislike ourselves? Would we demand too much of ourselves by unduly escalating the value of an achievement sought for and gained? Would it help to reiterate that we have vast untapped treasures within ourselves and can easily spend many lifetimes drawing them out from ourselves?

Or would it help to cite one of the most pious of the rabbis on this theme, that in actuality we have no alternative to being ourselves?

The Query of Queries

Before his death, Rabbi Zusya said: "In the World-to-Come, they will not ask me: 'Why were you not Moses?' They will ask me: 'Why were you not Zusya?'"

(*Buber, Early Masters, p. 251*)

13

Mentors and Disciples

INTRODUCTION

Education maintains and expands a culture from generation to generation. But is formal teaching the best way to educate the young and old? Is education, as the origin of the word suggests, a drawing out of what is latent in a person?

> Counsel in the heart of man is like deep water;
> But a man of understanding will draw it out.
>
> *Proverbs 20:5*

Do teachers do more than teach reading, writing and arithmetic? Should they also teach goodness, justice, compassion, beauty and virtuous action? And what about George Bernard Shaw's famous maxim: "He who can, does. He who cannot, teaches." And is the accumulation of knowledge more important than learning how to learn, so that you can become your own teacher in life after graduation? And what is the relationship between education and the good (or even saintly) person?

For the Hasidim, education was a total upbringing. A teacher was a mentor, father, and rabbi. And everyone learned from everyone, everywhere, all the time:

> I have learned much from my teachers, and from my colleagues more than from my teachers, and from my students more than from all.
>
> *Haggada, Palestinian Talmud*

The Hasidim carried this principle further than the Talmudic scholars did:

Learn from All

They asked Rabbi Mikhal: "In *The Sayings of the Fathers* we read: 'Who is wise?' He who learns from all men, as it is said, 'From all my teachers I have gotten understanding.' Then why does it not say: 'He who learns from every teacher'?"

Rabbi Mikhal explained: "The master who pronounced these words, is intent on having it clear that we can learn not only from those whose occupation is to teach, but from every man. Even from one who is ignorant, or from one who is wicked, you can gain understanding as to how to conduct your life."

(*Buber, Early Masters*, *p. 146*)

Many famous people have commented that anything wholly worth knowing cannot be taught. We believe this is especially true of Hasidic education. Learning from books is one kind of learning; learning from life experience is superior, because it is more fruitful:

Palm and Cedar

"The righteous (*tzaddik*) shall flourish like the palm tree; he shall grow like a cedar in Lebanon." Concerning this verse in the psalm, the *Maggid* of Mezeritch said: "There are two kinds of *tzaddikim.* Some spend their time on mankind. They teach them and take trouble about them. Others concern themselves only with the teachings themselves. The first bear nourishing fruit, like the date palm; the second are like the cedar: lofty and unfruitful."

(*Buber, Early Masters, pp. 101–102*)

Hasidic rabbis were extremely wary of abstract knowledge. They believed it often became an end in itself, removed both from direct service to God and from assistance to others. Superior knowledge, they thought, led to arrogance:

Books

> Once the [Rabbi of Kobryn] said:
>
> "If it were within my power, I should hide everything written by the *tzaddikim*. For when a man has too much knowledge, his wisdom is apt to be greater than his deeds."
>
> (*Buber, Late Masters, p. 161*)

Hasidic instruction ranged from pop-psychology advice, often tortuously derived from the Bible, to ecstatic mystical encounters that resulted in altered states of consciousness. The rabbi as mentor covered every conceivable experience as well as all legal works, Talmudic writings, and Kabbalistic visions.

For example, in the following story, the rabbi encourages his followers to learn how to take advantage of interruptions and regard obstacles as temporary resting places:

Up the Mountain

> Rabbi Yehiel Mikhal said: "It is written: 'Who shall ascend onto the mountain of the Lord? And who shall stand in His holy place?' For the sake of comparison, let us take a man who rides up a mountain in his carriage, and when he is half-way up, the horses are tired and he must stop and give them a rest. Now, whoever has no sense will, at this point, roll down. But he who has sense will take a stone and put it under the wheel while the carriage is standing. Then he will be able to reach the top. The man who does not fall when he is forced to interrupt his service, but knows how to pause, will get to the top of the mountain of the Lord."
>
> (*Buber, Early Masters, p. 153*)

In the following example, Rabbi Mikhal quizzically confronts a colleague about things that don't make any difference. The implication is "Who needs it?"

The Hair Shirt

Rabbi Yudel, a man known for his fear of God and the harsh penances he imposed on himself, once came to visit the *Maggid* of Zlotchov. Rabbi Mikhal said to him: "Yudel, you are wearing a hair shirt against your flesh. If you were not given to sudden anger, you would not need it, and since you are given to sudden anger, it will not help you."

(*Buber, Early Masters, p. 153*)

The Hasidim valued highly the direct presence of their rabbi. Because learning was essentially the development of character, rather than the accumulation of knowledge, the presence of the rabbi as a model with whom to identify was extremely important. The great rabbis of the past were highly revered; the stories about them were told and retold, but it was the living rabbi who embodied the "mystery of the Divine Presence in exile":

Not without the Garment of Flesh

Rabbi Hayyim Meir Yehiel told this story:

"When I was five years old I said to my grandfather, the holy *maggid*: 'Grandfather, you go to a rabbi, and my father goes to a rabbi. I am the only one who doesn't go to a rabbi; I want to go to a rabbi, too.' I began to cry.

"Said my grandfather to me: 'But I, too, am a rabbi.'

"Said I to him: 'Then why do you go to a rabbi?'

"Said he: 'What makes you think I go to a rabbi?'

"Said I: 'Because at night I see an old man with you, and you are seated before him as a servant before his master—so he must be your rabbi.'

"'My child,' said he, 'that is the Baal Shem Tov, may his merits shield us. When you are older, you will also be able to study with him.'

"Said I: 'No, I don't want a dead rabbi.'

"And I think the same to this very day. For I do not want the rungs of the spirit without the garment of flesh. When learning from a rabbi, the disciple must resemble his teacher at least in one thing—in having a garment of flesh. That is the mystery of the Divine Presence in exile."

(*Buber, Late Masters, p. 179*)

A Hasidic rabbi's teachings were not learned solely through the head, but rather passed from heart to heart:

Testimony of the Disciple

The Rabbi of Kalev once asked Rabbi Yehuda Zevi to tell him words of the teachings which he had heard from his teacher, Rabbi Uri. "The teachings of my teacher," said Rabbi Yehuda Zevi, "are like manna that enters the body but does not leave it." But when the Rabbi of Kalev would not stop pressing him, Rabbi Yehuda Zevi tore open the coat over his breast and cried: "Look into my heart! There you will learn what my teacher is."

(*Buber, Early Masters, pp. 148–149*)

Above all, the rabbi was a mentor, a trusted guide to the spiritual life. One important manifestation of climbing a rung or two on the spiritual ladder was assuming an altered state of consciousness, an action which was performed by Hasidic rabbis in the presence of their disciples and, as we have already seen, was utilized by the Baal Shem in his counseling and teaching.

Trance was *prima facie* evidence of spiritual communion with God:

The Original Meaning

This is what Rabbi Moshe said to an author who put questions to him concerning the Kabbala, the secret teachings, and the *kavvanot*, the mystical concentrations, which are directed toward superhuman effects. "You must keep in mind that the word Kabbala is derived from *kabbel*: to direct. For the ultimate significance of all the wisdom of the Kabbala is to accept the yoke of the Kingdom of God, and the ultimate significance of all the art of the *kavvanot* is to direct one's heart to God. When a man says: 'The Lord is my God,' meaning, 'He is mine and I am His,' must not his soul go forth from his body?" The moment the rabbi said this, he fell into a deep faint.

(*Buber, Late Masters, p. 166*)

Altered states of consciousness could be attained by *tzaddikim*, of course, but by Hasidim as well. It became a special badge of spirituality, because a brief loss of conscious control could easily be interpreted as the soul taking temporary leave, and could be connected with the realm of God's spirit:

Lighting the Pipe

A *tzaddik* told:

"In my youth I once attended a wedding to which the Rabbi of Lublin had also been invited. Among the guests were more than two hundred *tzaddikim*, as for the Hasidim—you could not even have counted them! They had rented a house with a great hall for the Rabbi of Lublin, but he spent most of the time alone in a little room. Once, a great number of Hasidim had gathered in the hall, and I was with them. Then the rabbi entered, seated himself at a small table and sat there for a time in silence. Then he rose, looked around and, over the heads of the others, pointed at me, standing up against the wall. 'That young man over there,' he said, 'shall light my pipe for me.' I made my way through the crowd, took the pipe from his hands, went to the kitchen, fetched a glowing coal, lit the pipe, brought it back into the hall, and handed it to him. At that moment, I felt my senses taking leave of me. The next instant, the rabbi began to speak and said a few words to me, and at once my senses returned. It was then that I received from him the gift of stripping myself of all that is bodily. Since then, I can do this whenever I want to."

(*Buber, Early Masters, pp. 306–307*)

As is well known in hypnosis and other trance-work, the most important factor is the subject's trust and will to believe in the one who induces the trance. Sometimes putting a group into a trance can be even more powerful than one-on-one:

Effect

A number of disciples once went to the *maggid*. "We are not going to stay," they said to one another. "We only want to look into his face." They told the coachman to wait in front of

> the house. The *maggid* at once told them a story which consisted of twenty-four words. They listened, bade him farewell, and said to the coachman: "Drive on slowly. We'll catch up with you." They walked behind the carriage and talked about the story they had heard. For the rest of that day and the whole of the night, they walked after the carriage. At dawn the coachman stopped, looked back, and said crossly: "Isn't it bad enough that yesterday you forgot the Afternoon and the Evening Prayer! Are you going to skip the Morning Prayer too?" He had to repeat this four times before they even heard him.
>
> (*Buber, Early Masters, p. 102*)

What, then, is the essence of the mentor–disciple relationship? Is there a way of summarizing or generalizing from this bewildering range of teaching and role-modeling experiences what the rabbi transmits to his disciples?

In typical mystical-puzzling fashion, Rabbi Moshe of Kobryn tries to explain that Hasidic education is not a matter of one person giving something and another person receiving it. It is not consciously attained. Although a rabbi may not put it that way, he would mean that the teaching grows organically within a person and is suddenly there; and we believe, too, that that is exactly the way it happens:

A Free Gift

> After Rabbi Yitzhak of Vorki's death one of his Hasidim went to Rabbi Moshe of Kobryn. "What do you hope to get from me, here in Lithuania?" asked the rabbi, "that you could not get just as much of, or even more, from any *tzaddik* in Poland?" "My teacher," the man replied, "often said that it was a sacred duty to learn to know the Rabbi of Kobryn because he spoke the truth that is in his heart. And so I decided to go to you and hoped you might teach me how to attain the truth."
>
> "Truth," said the Rabbi of Kobryn, "is not something that can be attained. God looks at a man who has devoted his entire life to attaining the truth—and suddenly He gives him a free gift of it. That is why it is written: 'You will give truth to Jacob.'"
>
> He took a pinch of snuff between two fingers and scattered it on the floor. "Look, even less than this!" Again he took

some snuff—only a few shreds of tobacco, "And it can be even less, if only it is the truth!"

(*Buber, Late Masters, pp. 166–167*)

As you can very well imagine, the rabbis had enormous authority and power in the Hasidic community. They were fully and keenly aware of Lord Acton's maxim: "Power tends to corrupt, and absolute power corrupts absolutely." Unlimited power is dangerous—not so much because of what it will do to the Hasidic followers, but because of its potential harm to the rabbis, the wielders of authority. How could the rabbis avoid becoming a coercive, tyrannical authority? And how could they model their ordinariness, which many genuinely felt and believed? The rabbis knew they had to define clearly the limitations of their authority. They had to curtail power severely, lest power beget more power.

The path the rabbis took was to appeal to the Ultimate Authority and to recognize that the pursuit of their vocation involves all the pitfalls facing any person doing his "job" and, to some extent, attaining his goals. The main pitfall is that success will go to his head, which is disastrous for anyone, including rabbis.

The rabbi in the following story, Rabbi Jacob Yitzhak, goes even further. It is inevitable that in climbing spiritual rungs, he becomes a "wrongdoer" as much as those greedy for gold or for honor. Greed is greed, even in the pursuit of spirituality! What a powerful warning the rabbis have addressed to themselves and their followers:

Payment

On one Friday evening, before the consecration of the Sabbath, the rabbi had retired to his room and locked the door. Suddenly, it opened and he came out. The house was full of his great disciples in the white satin robes the great *tzaddikim* used to wear in those days. The rabbi addressed them:

"It is written: 'and repayeth them that hate Him to their face, to destroy them.' This is what it means: He pays his haters for the good works they do in this world in spite of themselves, in order to destroy them in the World-to-Come. And so I ask you: Given that the wrongdoer is greedy for gold, well, then, he will receive his fill of gold; and given that the wrongdoer is greedy for honors, well then, he shall have his fill of honors. But now suppose the wrongdoer is not out for honors, and not for gold, but for spiritual rungs, or that he is out to be a rabbi—what then? Well then, he who is out for spiritual rungs, will mount them, and he who is out to be a rabbi, will become one—in order to be destroyed in the World-to-Come."

(*Buber, Early Masters, pp. 308–309*)

Perhaps the ultimate test of an authority that does not seek to become authoritarian and absolute is the willingness to poke fun at oneself. The following ironic put-down of the *tzaddik*, the super-rabbi with a special spiritual grace, is testimony that no human being, however saintly, is infallible:

The Greatest Lust

A learned man once said to the Rabbi of Rozdol: "It seems to me that the condition of being a *tzaddik* is the greatest of all lusts."

"That's how it is," the rabbi replied, "but to attain to it, you first have to get the better of all the lesser lusts."

(*Buber, Late Masters, p. 219*)

The strong experiential component of Hasidic education, combined with the culturally inherited didactic and moralistic emphasis, resulted in the development of a unique method of socialization. Teaching, in the sense of giving instruction on a specific subject, was only part of the whole process of mentoring, and not the most significant at that. Three main themes capture the essence of the Hasidic mentor-disciple relationship:

- Hasidic concept of growth, development, and internalization of new learning and values
- General teaching-learning principles
- Applied teaching in natural life-situations

THE HASIDIC CONCEPT OF GROWTH, DEVELOPMENT, AND INTERNALIZATION OF NEW VALUES

Everything takes time to develop. Anything really worthwhile takes time to ripen. Growth is life. Crawling comes before walking, and walking before dancing. In an exciting life, one is "born" many times. One word leads to another, except when we reach a dead-end and have to start over.

The Hasidim believed in organic growth—individuals developing in the manner of a living creature or plant:

The Growing Tree

> Rabbi Uri taught:
>
> "Man is like a tree: If you stand in front of a tree and watch it incessantly to see how it grows and to see how much it has grown, you will see nothing at all. But tend to it at all times, prune the runners, and keep the vermin from it, and—all in good time—it will come into its growth. It is the same with man: all that is necessary is for him to overcome his obstacles, and he will thrive and grow. But it is not right to examine him every hour to see how much has been added to his growth."
>
> (*Buber, Early Masters, p. 148*)

The Hasidim recognized that the whole was more than the sum of its parts. Development is a complex structure of interdependent parts whose relationships and growth are a function of the whole system. Life, the growth and development of a person, is possible only because of the autonomy of the person who, willy-nilly, must do his individual "thing."

It was also clear that growth was impossible without impediments along the way. Obstacles are necessary for men to thrive. The difficulties in your path are there to overcome, and the more challenging they are, the more valuable the goal and its end-products. Light can enter only where darkness has been.

It is possible, however, to assess growth and development by taking larger chunks of time and focusing on critical components of the growth process: for example, the evolving stages of the mentor-disciple relationship.

As teachers, mentors and surrogate parents, the Hasidic rabbis were very concerned about implanting the core values of their heritage into the minds and hearts of their disciples. They were keenly aware that this is a process. But what constituted this process?

A very modern theory of the stages in the internalization of values is brilliantly formulated in the following story:

The Faithful Servant

It is told in the Midrash:

The ministering angels once said to God: "You have permitted Moses to write whatever he wants to, so there is nothing to prevent him from saying to Israel: 'I have given you the Torah.'"

God replied: "This he would not do, but if he did, he would still be keeping faith with Me."

Rabbi Yitzhak of Vorki's disciples once asked him to interpret this. He answered by telling them a parable:

"A merchant wanted to go on a journey. He took on an assistant and let him work in his shop. He himself spent most of his time in the adjoining room from where he could hear what was going on next door. During the first year he sometimes heard his assistant tell a customer: 'The master cannot let this go for so low a price.' The merchant did not go on his journey. In the course of the second year he occasionally heard the voice next door say: 'We cannot let it go for so low a price.' He postponed his journey. But in the third year he heard his assistant say: 'I can't let this go for so low a price.' It was then that he started on his journey."

(*Buber, Late Masters, pp. 295–296*)

The relationship between the merchant and his assistant is an insightful and creative metaphor for the way relationships evolve among teachers and students, parents and children, mentors and disciples, trainers and trainees, and, apparently, God and his "messiahs."

Three stages are delineated in the rabbi's parable. In the first stage, *power-compliance,* the assistant carries out his master's instructions because he was told to, but dissociates himself from his employer, saying, "The master cannot let this go." The assistant has not internalized, that is, made his master's instructions a part of his own value system. The assistant carries out instructions in the most superficial way; if he doesn't do what the boss wants him to do, he could be fired—at this stage, sufficient reason to do his master's bidding.

In the second stage, *identification*, the assistant says: "*We* cannot let it go." Here the assistant fully identifies with his master. In other words, the motivation here apparently is that the assistant does what the master bids him because he now feels he is one with him and wants to do what the master would do in this situation. The master has been accepted fully as a model person to emulate. The assistant wants to be like his master and feels comfortable saying "we" because he so likes or admires and respects his master that he wants to do what he would do and also to become like him. But this is still, relatively speaking, an external reason for what he is doing, namely, just what his master would do. It is in sharp contrast to the third stage.

In the third stage, *internalization*, the assistant finally says, "*I* can't let this go." Here the assistant has fully internalized his responsibilities according to his master's instructions and has completely identified with the instructions. The instructions have entered into and become a part of the assistant's internalized value system. The assistant totally believes in the instructions because they are now a part of him, not because he has to (stage one), not because he wants to show his respect and admiration and be like his master (stage two), but because he wholeheartedly believes in the instructions and has made them part of his own belief system (stage three).

It is no wonder that the merchant "started on his journey" only when this stage was reached. This sophisticated understanding of the stages of internalization further attests to the closeness of the Hasidic rabbis to the experiences of their followers.

There is something even more amazing about this story: the ability of the rabbis to generalize, conceptualize and even theorize about such complex issues as internalization of values. Their conceptualization is based on careful, thorough, detailed observations that stand up under critical examination.

Life does not come to us in neat theoretical packages. We have to make them up, based on experiential data. Without theory we would not be able to penetrate the ongoing stream of life and realize what is important and how one thing leads to another. To take everything as it comes, without making head or tail of it, is to live stupidly, caged in by the ceaseless onrush of a jumbled mass of things, persons and processes mingled together without order or sense. The Hasidim were too intellectual to live in such a state of perpetual confusion.

GENERAL TEACHING-LEARNING PRINCIPLES

It is our conviction that the rabbis thought of themselves as professional educators. In fact, they were able to enunciate professional principles and "codify" them in many stories which developed and complemented them in a variety of ways.

For example, the crucial difference between a lay person and a "professional" is that the former says what he knows and the latter knows what he says: In other words, the professional not only states what he knows but weighs its impact on the listener. That is a crucial difference. It takes some degree of empathy to understand others and put oneself in their places. The Hasidic rabbis recognized that people must be studied and understood the way the *mitnagdim* studied the Talmud. We understand ourselves better by understanding others better, and vice versa. And because of their commitments to *kavvana*, knowing the motivation behind behavior, they had a complex multidimensional view of human nature, which they made use of in educating the young. Note, for example, how the father in this story maintains the child's interest:

Maintaining Interest

Said the Dubner: "A father once bought an excellent watch for his small son. Not wishing his son to lose interest in it, he began by teaching him how to tell the time. Later, he showed him that the longer hand indicated the minutes; then he pointed out the moving hand for the seconds. Finally, he opened the lid and, step by step, he showed him the various works inside. In this way, the lad continued to find the watch of engrossing interest."

(*Newman, Maggidim and Hasidim, p. 41*)

In many different ways, the rabbis patiently explained through their stories (often using the horse, their favorite animal, as an illustration) the importance of understanding their disciples and of checking to see that the disciple understood them:

With Animals

One Friday afternoon, Rabbi David was on a journey, when suddenly the horse stopped and refused to go on. The driver beat the horse, but the *tzaddik* objected.

"Rabbi," cried the driver, "the sun will soon be setting and the Sabbath is almost here."

"You are quite right," answered Rabbi David, "but what you have to do is to make the animal understand you. Otherwise, it will some day summon you to court in Heaven, and that will not be to your honor."

(*Buber, Late Masters, p. 187*)

By extension, the rabbis were opposed generally to corporal punishment, in favor of empathy, reason, discussion, and dialogue:

The Horses

When Rabbi Wolf drove out in a carriage, he never permitted the whip to be used on the horses. "You do not even have to shout at them," he instructed the coachman. "You just have to know how to talk to them."

(*Buber, Early Masters, p. 160*)

The Hasidim were well aware of the importance of speaking to others in what we call today the listener's "frame of reference."

The Chameleon

Rabbi Moses Sopher said: "We must not condemn a public leader if he seems to change his countenance like a chameleon that changes the color of its skin. To different people, the leader must know how to speak in different ways."

(*Newman, Maggidim and Hasidim, p. 99*)

The idea of thinking before you speak was thoroughly ingrained in the rabbis. They disliked thoughtless people who talked off-the-cuff or showed off what they knew without rhyme or reason:

The Fool and the Sage

Rabbi Bunam once said:

"If I were to set out to give learned and subtle interpretation of the Scriptures, I could say a great many things. But a fool says what he knows, while a sage knows what he says."

(*Buber, Late Masters, p. 256*)

The rabbis despised ostentation and pomposity. They were quick to put down any appearance of importance, justified or unjustified. And they were supersensitive to any hints of exaggerated display of self-importance:

Fine Words

One Sabbath, a learned man who was a guest at Rabbi Barukh's table, said to him: "Now let us hear the teachings from you, rabbi. You speak so well!" "Rather than speak so well," said the grandson of the Baal Shem, "I should be stricken dumb."

(*Buber, Early Masters, p. 94*)

If one reads Hasidic stories carefully, he will be impressed, time and again, with the subtle balance between giving support and letting the student struggle independently to discover *his* own truth.

Both alternatives were unacceptable: abandoning the student without support, or coddling him and robbing him of his struggle to master the material for himself. Note how carefully Rabbi Bunam formulates the philosophy of encouraging independent learning:

The Maze

Rabbi Bunam was told about *tzaddikim* who wore themselves out in the ecstasies of solitary service.

He replied: "A king had a broad maze with many intricate windings built around his palace. Whoever wanted to look upon him had to go through this maze where every step might lead into unending confusion. Those who dared enter because of their great love for the king were of two kinds. The one thought only of fighting their way forward bit by bit, the others left signs at the most puzzling twists and turns to encourage later comers to proceed on their way without, however, making the way any easier. The first submitted to the intention in the *orders* of the king; the second trusted in the purpose of his mercy."

(*Buber, Late Masters, p. 255*)

The Hasidic rabbis truly believed that every person has all the resources he needs to solve his problems. Therefore, the role of the rabbi as counselor or teacher is to remind the disciple that indeed he has all the means with which to solve his problems. Thus, rather than give answers, the rabbis originated ingenious ways for the help-seeker to go into himself and find the solution. When a young rabbi complained to the Rizhiner that he lost his *joie de vivre* the moment he stopped studying, the *tzaddik* replied: "That is like a man walking through the woods on a dark night. But if a man carries his own light with him, he need not be afraid of any darkness." (See "To Walk with One's Own Light," page 310.)

The beauty of the Rizhiner's reply lies in the confidence that the rabbi had in the younger rabbi. The younger man, by virtue of being a rabbi, was already able to solve many problems. Suddenly he was confronted with a situation he could not immediately handle.

The older rabbi's strategy was, in effect, to inform the young rabbi that he had a powerful "light" within him—that is, the understanding, experience and skill to resolve this difficulty just as he had resolved other problems. He was reminding the young rabbi of something he had temporarily forgotten, namely, that he was a resourceful person who had already solved many problems.

The technique of using a story within a story bypasses direct resistance from the help-seeker. A story leads the listener to go into himself and seek the connection between the story and what's going on now within him; to ask, "What is it that prevents me from resolving my problem?"

The focus of the Rizhiner's remark is not on the problem that the young man could not resolve, but on devising a strategy for solving it. It was not the problem, but the way in which he worked on it that troubled him, as the older rabbi saw immediately. The difficulty lay in a sudden lack of self-confidence. The rabbi wisely and gently reminded him that he has "his own light" to resolve his own problem:

Study Yourselves

> The Hafetz Hayyim said: "Do not say: 'and teach them (the words) to your children,' but say rather: 'and study the words yourselves.' No one can be certain that his children will maintain their father's eagerness to study and learn subjects of Torah."
>
> (*Newman, Maggidim and Hasidim, p. 139*)

The Hasidic rabbi was an exemplary model for his followers. It was not necessary for the rabbi to know everything, for he could learn from his followers as well as they from him. Long before today's "joint-participative learning," the rabbis were promulgating very similar ideas:

Looking for the Way

> In the month of Elul, when men prepare their souls for the days of judgment, Rabbi Hayyim was in the habit of telling stories to a tune that moved all his listeners to turn to God.

Once, he told this story: "A man lost his way in a great forest. After a while, another lost his way and chanced on the first. Without knowing what had happened to him, he asked the way out of the woods. "I don't know," said the first. "But I can point out the ways that lead further into the thicket, and after that let us try to find the way together."

(*Buber, Late Masters, p. 213*)

The following story captures the love of teaching and learning as a way of life, rather than as a method of imparting subject matter impersonally in a classroom. The rabbi as teacher is so caught up in learning in the story that he is learning simultaneously with his students—the best kind of teaching and teacher:

To Himself

In a sermon which Rabbi Mikhal once gave before a large gathering, he said: "My words shall be heeded." And he added: "I do not say, 'You shall heed my words.' I say: 'My words shall be heeded.' I address myself too! I, too, must heed my words!"

(*Buber, Early Masters, p. 143*)

Finally, in this section on teaching and learning, there is a brief but wonderful story that captures both the essence of learning and the role of the story in furthering learning:

How He Became a Hasid

Rabbi Mendel said:

"I became a Hasid because, in the town where I lived, there was an old man who told stories about *tzaddikim*. He told what he knew, and I heard what I needed."

(*Buber, Late Masters, p. 270*)

This is the summit of maturity for teacher and student. The teacher gives what he has learned, and the student takes what he needs, and both parties are delighted with the arrangement.

APPLIED TEACHING IN NATURAL LIFE SITUATIONS

The Hasidic rabbis were always drawing moral lessons from their own experiences and those of others. It was almost as if the very purpose of experience was that it taught us how to live better. In a profound sense, life experience was the teacher and the stories the textbook. In fact, a subtle competition began creeping into Hasidic life to see how clever one could be in creating analogies and metaphors between selected aspects of everyday life and lessons or generalizations:

Of Modern Inventions

"You can learn something from everything," the Rabbi of Sagadora once said to his Hasidim. "Everything can teach us something, and not only everything God has created. What man has made has also something to teach us."

"What can you learn from a train?" one Hasid asked dubiously.

"That because of one second one can miss everything."

"And from the telegraph?"

"That every word is counted and charged."

"And the telephone?"

"That what we say here is heard there."

(*Buber, Late Masters, p. 70*)

We learn the values of promptness from a train, accountability from the telegraph, and silence from the telephone. Not a bad haul in one story!

A profound statement about the whole of life can be gleaned even from the game of checkers:

Playing Checkers

On one of the days of Hanukka, Rabbi Nahum, the son of the Rabbi of Rizhin, entered the House of Study at a time when he was not expected, and found his disciples playing checkers, as was the custom on those days. When they saw the *tzaddik*, they were embarrassed and stopped playing. But he gave them a kindly nod and asked: "Do you know the rules of the game of checkers?" And when they did not reply, for shyness, he himself gave the answer: "I shall tell you the rules of the game of checkers. The first one is that one must not make two moves at once. The second is that one may move only forward and not backward. And the third is that when one has reached the last row, one may move wherever he likes."

(*Buber, Late Masters, p.* 73)

This story can be read as a metaphor for one's journey through life. In the beginning we take one step at a time, not two moves at once.

The middle phase of life requires direction—a forward movement is best. You know that your overall direction is forward, even though you may make contradictory moves from time to time. Consistency is important, despite diversions.

In the third and climactic phase, you have definitely peaked, and can move wherever you like. The world has opened up for you. From a careful, slower, more restricted movement you enter the freer traffic of an expansive, unrestricted and broader highway.

In short, this is a metaphor of the development of one's spirit—from a cautious, stumbling, one-step-at-a-time period to a time of looking ahead and deciding upon a direction you want to take in life and, finally, to the "freedom" to become a free spirit.

Evil, according to the Hasidim, was deliberately created to be overcome; for true believers, evil makes one stronger and more faithful. It is commonly believed that it is better not to succumb to evil in the first place, but that is totally unrealistic. Evil is often useful. You can also learn from evil:

The Diligence of Satan

Said the Besht: "When you perceive the Satan diligently trying to persuade you to commit an evil deed, understand that he is endeavoring to fulfill his duty as he conceives it. Learn from him diligence in performing your bounden duty—namely, to battle to overcome his persuasion."

(*Newman, The Hasidic Anthology, p. 82*)

The Diligence of Haman

Said the Besht: "From the diligence of Haman learn to perform with enthusiasm the will of Mordecai."

(*Newman, The Hasidic Anthology, p. 82*)

Evil can help you practice haughtiness, which on occasion can be useful:

Worthy to Obey

Shall men, then, always walk in meekness? Not so, say the *tzaddikim.* There are moments when haughtiness becomes a duty. When the Evil Inclination approaches, whispering in the ear: "You are unworthy to fulfill the Law," say: "I am worthy."

(*Newman, The Hasidic Anthology, p. 186*)

The Hasidic rabbis feared that if one commits too many evil acts, he may come to think of himself as an evil person. That would, indeed, be disastrous. For the Hasidim, prayer and repentance are urgently needed to make a turning. In an excellent metaphor, Rabbi Bunam finds an ingenious way to make this point during a game of chess:

The Wrong Move

Once, Rabbi Bunam was playing chess with a man he was particularly anxious to turn from his evil ways. He made a wrong move, and now it was the move of his opponent, who put him in a difficult position. Rabbi Bunam begged to be allowed to take back his move and the man consented. But when the same thing happened again, the other refused to give in to him a second time. "I let it pass once," he said, "but this time it must count."

> "Woe to the man," the *tzaddik* cried, "who has crept so deep into evil that prayer can no longer help him turn!" His fellow player stared at him, silent and motionless, his soul on fire.
>
> (*Buber, Late Masters, p. 239*)

The chess player was someone the rabbi "was particularly anxious to turn from his evil ways." Rabbi Bunam puts him in the position of refusing the rabbi a second chance to take back a wrong move. The chess player is tough with his opponent. At that point Rabbi Bunam turns the tables. Now the chess player is catapulted from "not forgiving" to the possibility that he will not be forgiven. The conflict is intensified within the chess player: His soul is "on fire." Time is running out for him, and he had better make a move toward a turning.

THE ACTION ORIENTATION OF HASIDIM

All the prayers, repentance and scholarly achievement can be outweighed by one good deed. Promises are cheap—the true test is taking action. All the learning of the Bible and the Talmud is meaningless without good actions.

A Hasid is best defined by his acts. To the Hasidim, good action is wisdom. Men of action were far more esteemed than preachers. Action, not thinking, ultimately resolves doubt. One of the biggest obstacles to taking action is trying to figure out in excessive detail all the specific steps to a goal. The step from knowing to doing could be fraught with too much knowledge and paralyze the doing, which annoyed Hasidim no end:

Blow!

> Once, when Rabbi Bunam honored a man in his House of Prayer by asking him to blow the ram's horn, and the fellow began to make lengthy preparations to concentrate on the meaning of the sounds, the *tzaddik* cried out: "Fool, go ahead and blow!"
>
> (*Buber, Late Masters, p. 252*)

This story, together with the next one, further emphasizes the point that too much scholarly and analytical study destroys spontaneity and the flow of action, which has its own internal dynamics generated in the doing.

Moreover, the Hasidim were not unaware of the psychological repercussions of excessive analysis without action. They would have understood Hamlet and his dilemma perfectly, and would have risen from their seats and yelled at Hamlet to stop "*dreyen ah kop*," which means, roughly, "Stop nit-picking and *do* something!"

Where Ignorance Is Bliss

The awesome moment had arrived. The rebbe was present—Reb Shlomo of Radomsk—but all eyes were focused on the pious and scholarly Hasid whom he had singled out for the sought-after responsibility of blowing the *shofar* for the whole congregation. Despite all his efforts, however, he could not muster one solitary blast. A young man was called up to substitute for him, and all the sounds came out melodiously, without a single hitch.

After the prayers, seeing that the would-be *shofar* blower looked somewhat crestfallen, Reb Shlomo called him over and said: "Here is a parable for you:

"In honor of the coronation of their new king, the people of a certain land fashioned him a magnificent gold crown. All that was now needed was to set it with precious gems, but no craftsman dared to undertake the delicate task, lest he damage the priceless crown. At long last, there arrived a master goldsmith who asked for one month in which to complete the work. Day after day and week after week, he sat and studied the crown from all angles, contriving in his imagination how best to bedeck it. Two days before his time ran out he made a great effort and determined to overcome his apprehension—but the moment he actually took the crown into his trembling hands, it slipped and fell. How was the work to be done?

"He called in his apprentice, who did not know that this was the king's crown, and gave him precise instructions as to how to set the gems. He himself was still so seized by anxiety that he left the workshop and waited outside until the work was completed. And, indeed, the young lad carried out his task in a craftsmanlike manner, without a single hitch."

(*Zevin, A Treasury of Hasidic Tales on the Festivals, Vol. I, p. 52*)

THE RABBIS' USE OF PERSONAL EXPERIENCES TO TEACH MORAL LESSONS

Throughout the Hasidic stories, the rabbis use personal experiences as core material. In writing about themselves, they are, to an outstanding degree, very frank about their own foibles and limitations. In fact, they teach the importance of openness, sharing, and self-criticism by recording their mistakes, misdeeds, pettiness, and seem to emphasize the bad things they have done—"Let this be a lesson to you!"—more than the good things.

At times, however, the rabbis were not too modest to recount their heroic deeds as well:

Zusya and the Birds

Once, Rabbi Zusya traveled cross-country collecting money to ransom prisoners. He came to an inn at a time when the innkeeper was not at home. He went through the rooms, according to custom, and in one saw a large cage with all kinds of birds. Zusya saw that the caged creatures wanted to fly through the spaces of the world and be free birds again. He burned with pity for them and said to himself: "Here you are, Zusya, walking your feet off to ransom prisoners. But what greater ransoming of prisoners can there be than to free these birds from their prison?" Then he opened the cage, and the birds flew out to freedom.

When the innkeeper returned and saw the empty cage, he was very angry and asked the people in the house who had done this to him. They answered: "A man is loitering about here and he looks like a fool. No one but he can have done this thing." The innkeeper shouted at Zusya: "You fool! How could you have the impudence to rob me of my birds and make worthless the good money I paid for them?" Zusya replied: "You have often read and repeated these words in the psalms: 'His tender mercies are over all His works.'" Then the innkeeper beat him until his hand grew tired, and he finally threw him out of the house. And Zusya went his way serenely.

(*Buber, Early Masters, p. 245*)

The charm of this story is totally captured in the very last word. How the storyteller must have relished that ending!

The rabbis were also not averse to sharing their mysterious brilliance and effectiveness:

Peacemaking

Rabbi David and his disciple Yitzhak, later the Rabbi of Vorki, were once on their way to a place Rabbi David had been asked to come to in order to make peace between two men who had a long-standing quarrel. On the Sabbath, he acted as the reader of the prayers. The two adversaries were present. After the close of the Sabbath, he ordered the horses harnessed for the journey home.

"But the rabbi has not carried out what he came for," said his disciple.

"You are mistaken," said Rabbi David. "When in the course of my prayer I said: 'He who maketh peace in His high places, may He make peace for us,' the peace was made." And it was really so.

(*Buber, Late Masters, p. 186*)

This is a wonderful self-fulfilling prophecy. The two quarrelers were placed in a therapeutic double bind. As worshipers, they are obligated to pray so that the prayers enter their hearts and guide their actions. They now face these alternatives: If they were attentive to the prayer, "He who maketh peace in high places, may He make peace for us," and took it to heart, they would have to make up. If they disregarded the prayer, they have sinned grievously against God. According to Rabbi David, this is not an alternative, so the peace had to be made. Harnessing his horses for the journey home was a neatly finessed maneuver for concluding his consultation and confirming the only viable alternative. Once the motivation to make peace was there, the petty mechanics of who gets what are routine and really don't require any more guidance.

Note how deftly and naturally Rabbi David teaches the Freudian concept of "displacement":

The Mistake

Rabbi Yitzhak of Vorki told this story:

"Once, when I was on the road with my holy teacher, Rabbi David of Lelov, and we stopped over in a town far from our home, a woman suddenly fell upon him in the street and began to beat him. She thought he was her husband who had abandoned her many years before. After a few moments, she saw her error and burst into a flood of tears.

"'Stop crying,' Rabbi David said to her. 'You were not striking me, but your husband.' And he added in a low tone: 'How often we strike someone because we take him for another!'"

(*Buber, Late Masters, p. 186*)

The rabbis not only puzzled their clients to get them to think more deeply about their problems, but they also placed puzzles upon themselves so that they could learn through the same method:

Lighter

The Rabbi of Lublin once said: "How strange! People come to me weighed down with melancholy, and when they leave, their spirit is lighter, although I myself" (and here he was going to say: "am melancholy," but then he paused and then continued:) "am dark and do not shine."

(*Buber, Early Masters, p. 308*)

Now this is a puzzle, indeed. What is the Lubliner questioning himself about? He says it is peculiar that people come to him to get cheered up and he himself is often in a dark, somber mood. He has very little "light" that others can take from him. He is able to empathize with others who are melancholy, because he has the same tendencies in himself. Others are probably comfortable with him because he understands what they are going through.

The point is, however, that the rabbi was able to confront himself with something that was askew, something that did not fit. It is enough to be curious and to pose a question to yourself, to have taken the first step toward wisdom. If you are willing to recognize and accept what is happening, there is always hope for a resolution. Light can enter only where darkness has been. The puzzling observation about himself helped lighten his spirit. This occurs with all puzzles that we are willing to confront; the delight lies in trying to figure out the answer, and in learning that for some puzzles there may, indeed, be more than one answer.

The preceding stories endow Hasidic life with a form with which Hasidim can identify and use to consolidate their core values and beliefs. The stories flow from Hasidic experiences and in turn contribute to shaping them.

Explicitly or implicitly, Hasidic tales have morals that are an integral part of their form. They are also a sort of documentary history of Hasidic life. Based upon selected episodes from the past, present, and future, they are the entertainment of eighteenth and nineteenth century *shtetl* life.

The final test of the stories' value is their durability. Clearly, they speak to us today. They are not only useful and enlightening and "conversation pieces," but also lovable. They are warm, funny and generous happenings with lessons on how we can live better lives right now—if we take them to heart.

When we read, tell or listen to a Hasidic tale, we enter a universe radically different in customs but remarkably similar in psychology to our own world. The story once took place, but our sharing it means it is also taking place right now. In that sense, it is contributing to our culture—the beliefs, values and morals by which we live.

The stories also give us an active opportunity to relive our past, to remake our present and project our future. The Hasid thought, felt, and acted differently because of these stories, and we find ourselves doing so as well. In the last analysis, the story itself becomes our own private mentor:

Folk Stories for the People

The Besht was narrating folk stories to his disciples. Noting their surprise, he told them the following parable:

"A king sent his son to take charge of a fortress situated near the frontier. He informed him that the enemy was planning an attack in the near future, and instructed him to store within the fortress all food procurable. If he could not secure food of superior quality, he was to fill every storehouse with food of poor grade. Though the king's counsel did not seem necessary to him, the prince obeyed. The siege of the fort continued a long time, and the coarse food in the end proved the safeguard against surrender.

"Likewise, my friends, store in your memory those common tales I narrate to you, as well as the teachings which seem to you profound. In your work among the people, everything will prove useful."

(*Newman, The Hasidic Anthology, p. 345*)

Part IV

STORYTELLING

INTRODUCTION

The whole point in telling stories is that they be relevant to the audience. This involves tinkering with Hasidic stories so that they work for your contemporary religious or nonreligious listener. This chapter will help you craft your story and hone your storytelling skills.

We want to stress the super-importance of modifying a story to make it work with your listeners. This is best accomplished by using stories as examples of your overall statement. Here is a story that makes our point nicely, although it is not a Hasidic tale:

The Marksman

The Gaon of Vilna asked his friend, the Dubner *Maggid*: "How do you find a parable suitable to any particular subject?"

The *maggid*, in accordance with his custom, responded with a parable:

"A student at a military academy was returning home after graduation. He stopped over at a village inn in order to give his horses a rest. In the barn, he noticed that circles had been chalked on the walls, with a bullet hole in the very center of each circle. He was astonished at such an exhibition of marksmanship and asked to see the marksman. A little barefoot boy came over to him and introduced himself as the person responsible. 'Where in the world did you learn to shoot so accurately?' inquired the military student. 'Nowhere,' was the boy's reply. 'I simply shoot at the wall and then encircle the hole.'

"It is the same with me," continued the *Maggid*. "When I hear or think out a good parable, I retain it in my memory. Then I strive to fit it to an appropriate subject."

(*Newman, Maggidim and Hasidim, p. 136*)

We have used the following story before, and now want to illustrate how we changed it while retaining its essential thrust:

How to Become Spiritual

In the days of the Great *Maggid*, a well-to-do merchant, who refused to have anything to do with Hasidic teachings, lived in Mezeritch. His wife took care of the shop. He himself spent only two hours a day in it. The rest of the time he sat over his books in the House of Study. One Friday morning, he saw two young men there whom he did not know. He asked them where they were from and why they had come, and was told they had journeyed a great distance to see and hear the Great *Maggid*. Then he decided that for once he too would go to his house. He did not want to sacrifice any of his study time for this, so he did not go to his shop that day.

The *maggid*'s radiant face affected him so strongly that from then on he went to his home more and more frequently and ended up attaching himself to him altogether. From this time on, he had one business failure after another until he was quite poor. He complained to the *maggid* that this had happened to him since he had become his disciple.

The *maggid* answered: "You know what our Sages say: 'He who wants to grow wise, let him go south; he who wants to grow rich, let him go north.' Now what shall one do who wants to grow both rich and wise?" The man did not know what to reply.

The *maggid* continued: "He who thinks nothing at all of himself, and makes himself nothing, grows spiritual, and spirit does not occupy space. He can be north and south at the same time." These words moved the merchant's heart and he cried out: "Then my fate is sealed!" "No, no," said the *maggid*. "You have already begun."

(*Buber, Early Masters, p. 108*)

One interpretation of this story is that if one is "spiritual," he can go in opposite directions at the same time. This spiritual person's latent destiny gradually becomes manifest (like most good things in life).

This story was retold (by Howard Polsky) to a university class to encourage students to be inquisitive and skeptical about everything they learn:

It is told:

A rabbi entered a room full of noisy disciples. He quickly got their attention by rapping his ruler on the table and asking the following:

"How can you go north and south at the same time?"

This was a sharp bunch of lads who loved puzzles, as befits any yeshiva student.

"Walk backward!"

"Ride backward!"

"Step back and forth over the North Pole!"

"Walk around the world!"

"Become a boomerang."

To all of these answers and to many more, the rabbi responded with a hearty "No!"

And suddenly the rabbi vanished.

The following day at exactly the same time, the rabbi reappeared and was showered with many more answers, to all of which he responded in the negative.

Suddenly everyone was silent.

The rabbi said: "You can go north and south at the same time by meditating on such questions such as how you can go north and south at the same time."

And the rabbi vanished.

14

A Story for [Almost] All Occasions

We now turn our attention to storytelling and the interaction between storyteller and audience. Storytelling can be divided into story-selection, crafting and telling the story, the role of the story in the social and cultural relationship between storyteller and audience, and the evolution of our cultural heritage.

A difficult task for many storytellers is selecting an appropriate story for a given situation. What if there were universal needs, cares and desires occurring everywhere, in all cultures? If there were no limits or exceptions and these universal concerns were operative everywhere, in societies as well as subcultures and formal and informal subgroups, would it not be advantageous to start with a story related to a universal need?

If so, it takes very little preparation, maneuvering and prompting to begin with a story related to the group's particular concerns and needs.

We must forewarn the reader that some of the stories in this section are repeats, and we ask you to greet them as welcome acquaintances to be appreciated from a new angle.

Every culture poses a question as to how we should serve God, which we extend to how we serve each other or, even more simply, what is the best way to live?

Among all the answers to this question on how to live life, we are willing to wager that the most generally accepted solution lies in the following story:

Walking the Tightrope

Once, the Hasidim were seated together in all brotherliness, when Rabbi Israel joined them, his pipe in his hand. Because he was so friendly, they asked him: "Tell us, dear rabbi, how should we serve God?" He was surprised at the question and replied: "How should I know?" But then he went right on talking and told them this story:

There were two friends, and both were accused before the king of a crime. Since he loved them he wanted to show them mercy. He could not acquit them because even the king's word cannot prevail over a law. So he gave this verdict: A rope was to be stretched across a deep chasm and the two accused were to walk it, one after the other; whoever reached the other side was to be granted his life. It was done as the king ordered, and the first of the friends got safely across. The other, still standing in the same spot, cried to him: "Tell me, my friend, how did you manage to cross that terrible chasm?" The first called back: "I don't know anything but this: Whenever I felt myself toppling over to one side, I leaned to the other."

(Buber, Late Masters, pp. 59–60)

This is a powerful metaphor on how to live life. It is inevitable that we will sometimes topple to one side or another in intense pursuit of a goal. Expect it. The remedy is right at hand—lean to the other side. How often we ignore this simple universal truth! Not only can this story be used in every group situation, but you can also use it on yourself and note the huge variety of personal situations to which it is applicable.

THIRTEEN UNIVERSAL CONCERNS FOUND IN (ALMOST) EVERY CULTURE

In addition to the tightrope story about how to live one's life, the thirteen stories that follow all have application to thirteen universal issues and concerns, both of groups and of individuals. The frequency and intensity of these concerns, of course, varies with each group and each culture, but they are all there, either lurking somewhere behind the scenes or boldly stepping forth on center stage:

- **Conflict.** Are conflict and differences among people inevitable, and if so, what is a constructive perspective on this issue?
- **Relationships.** What is the basis for an open, trusting, self-exposing relationship?
- **Me.** The desire to be someone else; what can I do about it?
- **Sin.** What is the best attitude toward this hardy perennial intruder?
- **Retirement.** When? Why? Alternatives?
- **Self-criticism.** How important is it?
- **Calamity.** One way of coping with distress caused by a major misfortune.
- **Tolerance.** How to encourage people to be sympathetic to beliefs and behavior differing from or conflicting with their own.
- **Teaching.** 250-year-old philosophy of teaching that is as valid today as it was then.
- **Change.** Why change is important for a paradisaical future.
- **Making up.** Two major contrasting consequences of settling differences.
- **Pains-in-the-Neck.** The ultimate put-down of a pain-in-the-neck.
- **Rebellion.** Why being different from other people is necessary.

CONFLICT

When one is in conflict with another person, many peculiar consequences result. One may become more uptight, more inflexible, more judgmental and negative about the opponent. It is as if the merits and demerits of the issue are transformed into the feeling that one is being personally attacked and that one's integrity is questioned.

It is against this curiously escalating "we-they" polarization that the following story warns us in a humorous way:

The Difference

While the quarrel between the Hasidim of Kotzk and those of Radoshitz was in full swing, Rabbi Yisakhar Baer of Radoshitz once said to a Hasid from Kotzk: "What your teacher believes in is: 'If you can't get over it, you must get under it,' but what I believe in is: 'If you can't get over it, you must get over it anyway.'"

Rabbi Yitzhak Meir of Ger, the disciple and friend of the Rabbi of Kotzk, formulated the difference in another way when a Hasid of the Rabbi of Radoshitz visited him after his master's death. "The world thinks," said he, "that there was hatred and quarreling between Kotzk and Radoshitz. That is a grave mistake. There was only one difference in opinion: In Kotzk they aimed to bring the heart of the Jews closer to their Father in Heaven; in Radoshitz they aimed to bring our Father in Heaven closer to the heart of the Jews."

(*Buber, Late Masters, p. 286*)

Jews love to make hair-splitting distinctions. Sometimes they may be important, but often they are ridiculous when examined more minutely, and then suddenly they can be seen as pretense and sham. The sham is in assuming one has to take one side or the other, not both sides or neither. How often we get caught up in these presumed differences, which have more to do with the contestants' egos than with substantial differences!

The Path of Moderation

Said the Hafetz Hayyim: "There are Jews today taking the right-hand road, which is too warm; these are the Hasidim. Others decide to take the left-hand road, which is too frigid. It is best to take the middle pathway, according to the custom of the Sages."

(*Newman, Maggidim and Hasidim, p. 122*)

Perhaps it is time to change the slogan from *vive la difference* to *vive la similitude.* With long live the difference, we might have a more sane and happy world. Nevertheless, the preceding story, which makes fun of differences that aren't very different, makes an important contribution to the cause of sanity!

RELATIONSHIPS

All of us are largely puzzles to others. Even when we get to know each other better, we can become more puzzling to one another.

Psychology today cannot tell us very much about how we can understand and love each other more. George C. Homans (1974) shocked many professionals not too long ago with his assertion that we have few strong propositions about how people develop meaningful and lasting relationships.

Homans himself enunciated one simple but profound principle about relationships: The more you interact with someone, the more you like that person; the more you like someone, the more you interact with that person. Now that rule has thousands of exceptions, such as two prisoners in the same cell who hate each other's guts. So the rule applies to situations in which people start off "neutral" to each other and, over time, depending on the frequency of interaction and depth of liking, the relationship becomes more intense or gradually withers away.

The practical way to apply this rule is for those who want to get to like someone more, or to have the other like them more, to increase the interaction. And vice versa: If you don't like someone, increase the distance until the relationship dies.

We believe the Hasidim have formulated a rule about relationships every whit as potent as Homans's proposition:

The Window and the Curtain

When young Rabbi Eleazar of Koznitz, Rabbi Moshe's son, was a guest in the house of Rabbi Naftali of Roptshitz, he once cast a surprised glance at the window, where the curtains had been drawn. When his host asked him the cause of his surprise, he said: "If you want people to look in, then why the curtains? And if you do not want them to, why the window?"

"And what explanation have you found for this?" asked Rabbi Naftali.

"When you want someone you love to look in," said the young rabbi, "you draw aside the curtain."

(*Buber, Late Masters, p. 177*)

The metaphor of the window and the curtains is a simple yet profound proposition about self-revelation and increasing love. This relationship makes complete sense: The more you like someone, the more you reveal about yourself; the more you dislike someone, the less you reveal.

The opposite is equally true. The more you reveal about yourself, the more you like the other person; the less you reveal, the less you like him. One problem with dynamic propositions like these is that they can be used by unscrupulous people. *Othello* immediately comes to mind because revelations and love are so intimately intertwined at every stage of the drama.

It is true! When we love someone, we do draw aside our curtains for that person to peer in, and what that person discovers may surprise us. That is why love is such a serendipitous adventure: The other person can help you discover hidden treasures within yourself! But first you have to let that person in!

ME

What am I, really? And must I be one thing or another? I know or sense that I must be myself, but who is that? Wouldn't you like to be completely you? Of course, once you have that inside view of who you are, you can become more or less of the same or change it completely.

The struggle to be yourself and no one else is impeded when you are not sure who you are. The more blurred is your image of who you are, the more likely you are to want to be like someone else who comes across in bold, decisive strokes. One resolution of that problem is *to be* someone else, a wish children often express, but also, possibly, many adults as well.

Ultimately, a maturity or wisdom achieved in many different ways recognizes the necessity of being what you are and not anyone else. Everyone is free to be himself, and Rabbi Bunam adds a pinch of salt to the value of being who you are. At any moment of your life, you are not only what you are, but also just a dash more:

Do Not Change Places

Rabbi Bunam once said:

"I should not like to change places with our father Abraham. What good would it do God if Abraham became like blind Bunam, and blind Bunam became like Abraham? Rather than have this happen, I think I shall try to grow a little over and beyond myself."

(*Buber, Late Masters, p. 256*)

Rabbi Bunam tells the story as if he could make himself be like Abraham, and then rejects the foolhardy notion by confirming his liking for himself by deciding to grow beyond what he is now, which is a very dynamic acceptance of oneself. In this sense, Rabbi Bunam becomes more himself by expanding himself. The place to go to outstrip yourself is to yourself—there lie the biggest impediments and richest resources for change. In sum, anyone who looks outside of himself to become himself is doomed to disappointment. Surely the world was created for each one of us—for me and for you:

True Humility

Rabbi Baruch of Leipnik heard that a rav in the neighborhood professed to be a greater scholar than himself. The rabbi smiled and said: "I do not doubt at all that there exists in the world a person greater than I am. Does it matter to me if this particular rav believes himself to be that greater man?"

(*Newman, Maggidim and Hasidim, p. 82*)

SIN

When the Hasidim speak of sin, they are referring not only to transgressions of the law of God, but infractions of law and rules in general. The rabbis had a very curious attitude toward sin, which one can glean by reading between the lines of a story. The brief story that follows tells us more by inference about the Hasidic approach to sin than by what is explicitly said:

The Great Crime

> Rabbi Bunam said to his Hasidim:
>
> "The sins which man commits—those are not his great crime. Temptation is powerful and his strength is slight! The great crime of man is that he can turn at every moment, and does not do so."
>
> (*Buber, Late Masters, p. 257*)

This story attests to the extraordinary realism of the rabbis. Sin is here to stay. It's got too much going for it to go away. It is too powerfully seductive. Sin may be pleasurable and profitable; often it is desirable precisely because it is forbidden. So sin has a lot going for it, and one expects to find people committing it again and again.

Man, apparently, does not have many effective resources or strategies for resisting the temptation to sin: "His strength is slight."

Another important inference in the story is that Hasidim cannot fool themselves into believing that they have not sinned if in truth they have. Jews have a hard time denying unpleasant realities. "Be sure your sin will find you out," says the Bible (Numbers 32:23).

So it's neither sinning nor denying the sinning that is the problem, but failure to turn away from it. Now we have a dilemma. We are told that committing a sin is not the "great crime," that temptation is strong and that man is weak, and that the "great crime" is not changing one's ways, which can be done at any time in one's life.

Does this make any kind of sense? Is it useful in any way to you and me? Precisely because it is puzzling, this approach is useful, because it makes us think about sin and re-evaluate it, see it in a new way.

What are the teaching assumptions seeded in the reader's mind after reading Rabbi Bunam's counsel?

First of all, the point of attack on sin is crucial. Don't fret, harass, or attack yourself incessantly to the point of desperation because you have sinned. It accomplishes nothing. What's done is done. There is no point in stewing over the past. Rather, look to the future.

The big thing is that you can change, make a turn, go in an entirely new direction. So turn your attention to *what you can do*, you have to be the one to do it and it's not a matter of regretting, praying or saying you won't do it again. What is required is to do something now and in the future.

That is the optimistic, forward-looking, self-fulfilling message: "Man can turn at every moment." It is well within his capabilities to change his ways radically. Therein lies his great crime—not to turn!

So the rabbis' role in all of this is clear. Their task is not to be entrapped by giving penances and counseling repentance and prayers for sins committed, but rather to help refocus the Hasid on *how to turn*—that is the key issue.

Thus, long before our current emphasis on behavioral strategies and behavioral modification, the rabbis over 250 years ago were directing their followers' attention to creating new behavior patterns for the future, instead of dwelling on the past:

Good and Evil

> The Gerer Rabbi said: "We are told by the psalmist first to leave evil and then to do good. I will add that, if you find it difficult to follow this advice, you may first do good, and the evil will automatically depart from you."
>
> (*Newman, Maggidim and Hasidim, p. 30*)

Perhaps the only major difference between the rabbis of 250 years ago and us is that we are far less moralistic. In fact, the word "moralistic" connotes today excessive concern with conformity to standards of human conduct from a narrow and conventional perspective. We are less certain today of what is good and right and how it affects our character and conduct. In fact, "virtue," moral excellence of character, seems old-fashioned, and "righteous" has become sanctimonious. And how many of us know of anyone who is "noble"—of moral eminence and devoid of petty, mean and dubious conduct? Perhaps we are all the losers in this modern de-emphasis of involvement in the difficult and subtle questions of good and just conduct?

Accordingly, instead of saying, "The great crime of man is that he can turn at every moment but doesn't," a modern psychology text would say: "The great *challenge* to man is that he can turn." By becoming less moralistic, we have become both richer and poorer, and the implications of that ambiguous assertion will take a lot of sorting out.

RETIREMENT

The extreme activist orientation of the Hasidim is nowhere more clearly stated than in the following story:

Extension

> In his old age, Rabbi Israel said: "There are those *tzaddikim* who—as soon as they have accomplished the task appointed to them for their lives on earth—are called to depart. And there are those *tzaddikim* who—the moment they have accomplished the task appointed to them for their lives on earth—are given another task, and they live until that, too, is accomplished. That is the way it was with me."
>
> (*Buber, Early Masters, p. 298*)

We like the implications embedded in this story. We believe, like the Hasidim, that there is no graceful exit, no appropriate time to quit an intense engagement with every moment we are blessed with life.

All of us have witnessed at firsthand the scourge of purposelessness, the vacant stares and random, directionless movements of retirees who live more and more in the past without any road ahead. They walk about with increasingly aimlessness, lacking determination and purpose.

The story above beautifully captures the two possible adaptations to *older* age and retirement. The bite in the story is precisely the idea that when you finish your "task," you might as well depart; if you pick up another task, you will have more to live for and will live longer, with yet another task, even longer—perhaps forever?

What good is all that wisdom, accumulated over the years, if it is not tested in still another project? Continual doing is the best preparation for the next world. When there is a thing to be done, our body and soul ignite. The Hasidim were fervent believers in doing rather than preaching about doing things. Holiness is action. In the battle for priority between knowledge and action, the Hasidim invariably and overwhelmingly chose action, even with its inevitable mistakes. Mistakes help us go forward again.

It is from this activist perspective that a Hasid is constantly tested, even when it may be socially proper to withdraw from the daily battle. To the Hasid, becoming less active is tantamount to accepting death, and that reality is not embraced except in the last hours of life.

SELF-CRITICISM

We have already touched upon self-criticism, but to comment briefly on the following story:

Concerning Joseph's Brothers

The Rabbi of Lelov said to his Hasidim:

"A man cannot be redeemed until he recognizes the flaws in his soul and tries to mend them. A nation cannot be redeemed until it recognizes the flaws in its soul and tries to mend them. Whoever permits no recognition of his flaws, be it man or nation, permits no redemption. We can be redeemed to the extent to which we recognize ourselves.

> "When Jacob's sons said to Joseph: 'We are upright men,' he answered: 'That it is I spoke unto you saying: Ye are spies.' But later when they confessed the truth with their lips and with their hearts and said to one another: 'We are verily guilty concerning our brother,' the first gleam of their redemption dawned. Overcome with compassion, Joseph turned aside and wept."
>
> (*Buber, Late Masters, pp. 187–188*)

In telling this story today, we would stress that a nation reveals most clearly its insecurity when it hides its flaws, refuses to recognize them except through deception, and therefore does not deal with them. Instead of using the term "redemption," with its connotation of atonement or expiation, a kind of liberation from the bondage of sin in the broadest context, we would say that without facing one's faults, a person impedes his own progress. And the *quid pro quo* is probably correct: The more you can face yourself squarely, both the good and the bad, the more liberated and productive and ultimately content with yourself you can be. The less need anyone has to distort reality, especially regarding oneself, the more productive and happy he can be. Today we call this "congruency"—being in touch with the reality of yourself, because basically you accept yourself, "warts and all."

But there is something deeper and more emotional about "redemption" through "owning up" to past "sins," and it crops up in the preceding story: The "sin" of harming someone in your own family is so grave that the pain and suffering are almost beyond endurance. To admit to such a grievous and onerous sin against someone in one's own family is to invite a loss of esteem and severe humiliation, the dishonoring of one's name, extreme contempt and, eventually, overwhelming feelings of guilt and remorse.

Now, of course, in the heat of a sin it can be rationalized every which way. However, in retrospect the feelings of remorse, self-reproach, and guilt can become overwhelming. It may very well be that with our heightened cynicism today, with the belief that human conduct is motivated wholly by self-interest, it is difficult to value the depth of anguish and unavailing remorse in the admission, "We are verily guilty concerning our brother. . . ." But we can begin to understand the power and depth of this admission through Joseph who, "overcome with compassion . . . turned aside and wept."

Now we can begin to understand the terrifying dynamics of the admission of sin as it affects the relationship between sinner and wronged. The sinned against finds it virtually impossible to forgive and then perhaps to forget without the sinner's sincere admission and recognition of what he has done. That is why Joseph wept, not only tears of sorrow at what his brothers had done to him, but also tears of joy because reconciliation had become possible.

Self-criticism is a healing process within individuals and between them, and also within nations and between them. The more grievous the sin, the more powerful the redemption and the more demonstrative the weeping for the sorrows of the past and the joys of the future.

CALAMITY

A calamity is an extraordinarily grave event marked by a great loss and lasting distress, affliction and misery. There is always a major (often sudden) misfortune or loss followed by a subjective reaction of distress. The misfortune is palpable, real, objective: It happened and its consequences exist.

The subjective reaction is also real, but in a different way. Attitude matters here, how you perceive and react, based on internal personality factors. Each subjective reaction is peculiar to a particular individual, although groups of people can share a common reaction.

The Hasidim were very much attuned to inner feelings and drives. As we have seen, they were experts in reshaping reality by reshaping and reframing perceptions of real events and thereby altering feelings of poignant sorrow, dread and deep, inconsolable misery brought on by a calamity:

Concentrated Anxiety

Rabbi Leib Dimimles of Lantzut was a wealthy merchant, and very learned in the Torah. It happened that he lost his

> money and was reduced to poverty. Rabbi Leib paid no heed to this calamity and continued his studies. His wife inquired: "How is it possible for you not to show the least anxiety?" The rabbi answered:
>
> "The Lord gave me a brain which thinks rapidly. The worrying which another would do in a year, I have done in a moment."
>
> (*Newman, Maggidim and Hasidim, p. 127*)

Now this may sound flippant. "Come now," you might say, "it's not that simple or easy to overcome a sudden tragedy of giant proportions." You could be right!

A closer examination of the story, however, gives us some clue that this may not be merely a case of someone trying to be clever-by-half. Rabbi Leib is both a wealthy merchant and very learned. Perhaps his self-image was mostly related to his scholarly role, which is very absorbing. If so, he can continue to pursue his main interest even more assiduously. The idea of using his learning ability to evoke a rapid emotional release to overcome his worry is actually quite fascinating. NLP (Neurolinguistic Programming) has a whole battery of techniques through which feelings can be changed by slowing or speeding them up, changing their colors, enlarging or diminishing them and so on. Here again, we can see the ingenuity of the Hasidim in their discovery of comparable techniques over 200 years ago!

TOLERANCE

At one time or another we are all short-tempered with other people and sometimes even with ourselves! We also have some capacity to endure and adapt to behavior and situations that annoy us. Tolerance is a sympathetic regard for beliefs or practices differing from our own. Tolerance means living with deviations from standards set by the individual as well as conventional society. We use "tolerance" in the positive sense of successfully overcoming the need to have others be like us or the urge to denigrate those of different beliefs, habits, appearance or life-styles.

Tolerance is living with people as they are, however different, as long as they cause you no harm, and it is much preferred to the odious task of trying to make everyone the same. Tolerance is most manifest in the patience we show to people who "turn us off." That's the rub! When do idiosyncrasies and eccentricities become major aberrations, which are downright infuriating? What does one do about tolerance then? How much tolerance should we tolerate?

Love, of course, supplies one answer. In loving someone, we learn to tolerate a lot! We also learn to tolerate what we can do nothing about, or what we fear. Tolerance is one of the best approaches for overcoming differences: namely, accepting and living with others.

In the next story, still another strategy is proposed for learning how to live with behavior that is annoying:

The Harpist

In the very act of praying, the Rabbi of Lublin would occasionally take a pinch of snuff. A most diligent worshiper noticed this and said to him: "It is not proper to interrupt the prayer."

"A great king," answered the Rabbi of Lublin, "was once walking through his chief city and heard a ragged old street singer singing a song and playing the harp. The music pleased him. He took the man into his palace and listened to him day after day. Now the minstrel had not wanted to part with his old harp, and so he often had to stop and tune it in the middle of playing. Once, a courtier snapped at the old man: 'You really might see to the tuning of your instrument beforehand!' The harpist answered: 'In his orchestras and choirs, our king has lots of people better than I. But if they do not satisfy him and he has picked out me and my harp, it is apparently his wish to endure its peculiarities and mine.'"

(*Buber, Early Masters, pp. 317–318*)

This approach to living with annoying aberrations for the sake of the greater good enlarges the "tolerator's" perspective and is a wonderful way to view bothersome behavior. It also enlarges one's empathy for living with all kinds of behavior, which serves others and annoys you, but may, in the end, contribute to the value of your relationships with them.

TEACHING

No other story of the more than 5,000 tales we have read about the Hasidim equals the clear ring of modernity of "Near and Far." It is not only about teachers and students but about all relationships, including those with the Lord in Heaven:

Near and Far

> A disciple asked the Baal Shem: "Why is it that one who clings to God and knows he is close to Him, sometimes experiences a sense of interruption and remoteness?"
>
> The Baal Shem explained: "When a father sets out to teach his little son to walk, he stands in front of him and holds his two hands on either side of the child, so that he cannot fall, and the boy goes toward his father between his father's hands. But the moment he is close to his father, he moves away a little, and holds his hands farther apart, and he does this over and over, so that the child may learn to walk."
>
> (*Buber, Early Masters, p. 65*)

In one fell swoop, the Baal Shem has presented a method whereby every teacher, parent, spouse, and others can care for and support another person *and* still give the person the space to grow by oneself.

Both are necessary: the guiding, caring love and the letting go. And this universal human need to grow is divinely inspired, because that is precisely how He relates to all of us.

The Baal Shem adds the wise caution that this supporting and letting go is sometimes experienced as abandonment . . . which is why pacing is important. The distortion occurs because we are all not perfect—yet.

CHANGE

The only eternal law for us and our earth is that everything is changing and in a state of flux. Time presupposes change. Of course, there are changes and changes. There is a world of difference between passing from age 50 to 51 and passing from life to death—even though both occur in a second. Change is ceaseless and perpetual, but qualitative changes occur in larger chunks of time.

If everything changes all the time and leaps unpredictably in qualitative change, we would do best to think, feel and act in changeful ways. The only constant is change. The Hasidim did not believe in mere flux and random change. They knew their end-goal—communion with God—and were always striving to deepen that relationship. But they also believed in changing fundamentally themselves and their relations with others in addition to coming ever closer to God:

A New Zest

> Said the Besht: "A king enjoyed immensely the playing by a certain musician, and he invited him to play before him daily. After a time, however, the king observed that the musician had wearied of playing before the same listener constantly. Therefore, the astute king invited fresh guests daily to listen with him. The musician responded by displaying his skill with a new zest. In the same way, God enjoys hearing new interpretations in theology offered by a Sage. But He sends to the interpreter new disciples in order to awaken a new zest in him in giving form to the fruit of his intellect."
>
> (*Newman, Maggidim and Hasidim, p. 125*)

The Hasidim believed in fundamental qualitative leaps of change—what they called "a turning." This was a combination of insight and behavioral change and occurred episodically for true believers.

Change is challenging because every venture into the new and unknown is accompanied by some foreboding. It is hard for many of us to "welcome a stranger," but that is precisely what the Hasidim set up as an ideal. It is almost as if, by encouraging, stimulating, and advancing change, we are preparing ourselves for a most awesome transformation:

Today as Yesterday

> The Rabbi of Rozniatov, Rabbi Eliezer Lippmann, persistently inquired from Rabbi Mendel of Kossov why the Messiah had not come and why the Redemption promised by the prophets and sages has not been fulfilled.
>
> Rabbi Mendel answered: "It is written: 'Why has the son of Jesse not come either today or yesterday?' The answer lies in the question itself: 'Why has he not come?' Because we are today just as we were yesterday."
>
> (*Newman, Maggidim and Hasidim, p. 247*)

In light of the foregoing commentary, this story makes good sense. How will we be able to handle the Messiah, if we cannot create the ordinary, mundane changes of day-to-day living?

The challenge here is formidable: to change from one day to the next. "How to" is another matter. But to pose the question is ninety percent of the solution. There are so many ways to change deliberately, and in addition we have this ultimate, stunning and glorious incentive: the coming of the Messiah.

There is also the hidden implication in Rabbi Mendel's remarks that change is vital, even though you may be uncertain as to where you are going. Change shakes up the old habits and routines and opens up new vistas.

It occurs to us that a kind of death occurs when one day is pretty much the same as the day before. The story suggests that as long as there is change there is hope for transformation, and as long as there is transformation there is a possibility for the greatest transformation of all! Even an attempt to change which does not succeed is a change—for it requires some alteration in past routines.

Another deep meaning to the story is that it essentially echoes the famous passage in Ecclesiastes (1:9): "There is no new thing under the sun". This then would be a rather pessimistic and cynical interpretation: Compared to what it could be, all of human change does not amount to much. That is why the Messiah has delayed his arrival.

We believe the Hasidim were too activist, optimistic, self-possessed and confident in God, themselves and the future ever to despair of changing themselves fundamentally. We feel the story should be read as a challenge to begin thinking about change in relation to one's own life, and the possibility that it may give us a glimpse into a world that has been joined by the Messiah!

MAKING UP

As long as we continue to have differences and conflicts, we will also have accords, adjustments, settlements, and reconciliations. We can make up, or separatc, or continue to be angry with each other after a disagreement. Making up is a universal human need.

In the next story, we have an insightful distinction regarding the quality of a covenant between the Israelites and the Philistines. It can be applied to agreements among any two parties:

The Covenant with the Philistines

Rabbi Bunam once had the horses harnessed and drove to Warsaw with several of his Hasidim. When they arrived there, he told the coachman to stop at an inn. They entered and sat down at a table. At a corner table near theirs sat two porters who were drinking schnapps and talking. After a while, the first asked: "Have you already studied the weekly portion of the Torah?"

"Yes," answered the second.

"I too have learned it," said the first, "and I found one thing hard to understand. It is the passage about our father Abraham and Avimelekh, the king of the Philistines, where it says: '. . . and they two made a covenant.' I asked myself: Why say 'they two'? That seems utterly superfluous."

"A good question!" cried the second. "But I wonder what answer you will find to it."

"What I think," said the first, "is that they made a covenant, but still they did not become one; they remained two."

> Rabbi Bunam rose and left the inn with his Hasidim. "Now that we heard what these hidden *tzaddikim* had to tell us," he said, "we can go back home."
>
> (*Buber, Late Masters, pp. 263–264*)

This is a marvelous distinction, certainly a worthy contribution by a "hidden *tzaddik*." It makes such practical eminent sense that it stands out prominently, readily perceivable, and understood by all. Certainly, that is what happens when two people try to make up. If one side remains basically distrustful and separate, they remain two parties with an agreement.

When they are prepared to go beyond the "agreement" and reconciliation has entered each party's heart, to use Hasidic terminology, they are on their way to becoming one—a new unity!

This is a powerful piece of knowledge. Sometimes it is possible to conclude an agreement only with the two parties remaining essentially divided. The danger lies in confusing the two types of agreement. And the challenge is to move towards more harmony, with the possibility of reaching a true unity.

Is not this unity the kind of agreement we desperately need today among the nations of the world? And, incidentally, isn't that why the Messiah has delayed his arrival?

PAINS-IN-THE-NECK

A nuisance persists in annoying, unpleasant and even obnoxious talk and behavior. A pain-in-the-neck is an accomplished nuisance who gets to you emotionally, makes you feel guilty and upset, and interferes with whatever you are trying to accomplish.

The pain-in-the neck's wailing does not cease even after you have commiserated and expressed your deepest concern for his/her plight. The pain-in-the-neck wants more than sympathy and tears—he wants your blood. And he also wants your repentance, and more and more and more of a share of you and what you can give him.

On what basis can the pain-in-the-neck make such demands on your time, energy and possessions? A careful random survey by the authors of this book reveals that nine out of ten times the pain-in-the-neck believes that you have not treated him fairly and have unjustly favored others over him (the tenth person felt that he gave too much to others and that they had not properly reciprocated).

Now, whether one is fair to another may be entirely in the eye of the beholder. From a very early age, children make assessments about how they are not treated fairly compared to siblings or children in other families. This continues with regard to peers, teachers, rabbis, family, spouses, colleagues, employers, and even counselors and therapists.

The pain-in-the-neck feels he is not getting a fair deal. His feeling is based on a belief that is widespread not only in our society but also in the world of the Hasidim: "Life should be fair. Others are unfairly getting more than I am."

Of course, there is enough bias, prejudice, and irrational hostility in the world to support the pain-in-the-neck's vexatious provocations.

Nevertheless, the recipient of such irritating persistent attacks may reach the end of his tether and strike back:

The Gift to His Adversary

A Jew from Kosov, who was known to be opposed to the Hasidic way, once came to Rabbi Mendel and complained that he was about to marry off his daughter and did not have the money for her dowry. He begged the rabbi for advice on how to earn the sum he needed. "How much do you need?" asked the Rabbi. It came to a few hundred gulden. Rabbi Mendel opened a drawer in his desk, emptied it, and gave the money to the man.

Soon after, the *tzaddik*'s brother learned what had occurred. He took the *tzaddik* to task, saying that whenever something was needed in his own house, he said he had no money to spare, yet now he had given such a large sum to an adversary. "Someone was here before you," said Rabbi Mendel, "and said exactly the same thing, except that he expressed himself much better than you."

"Who was it?" asked his brother.

Rabbi Mendel replied: "It was Satan."

(*Buber, Late Masters, p. 98*)

That is pretty powerful medicine for a pain-in-the-neck who is also one's brother! But perhaps it is not. For all the reasons cited, Satan has given the pain-in-the-neck a solid basis for his objectionable behavior. Strong circuits need strong circuit-breakers.

We also want to suggest another strategy for dealing with the pain-in-the-neck. It is beautifully summed up in an Arabic proverb:

> The dogs bark, but the caravan moves on.[1]

REBELLION

Rebellion is necessary for growth and development. Everyone, at one time or another, renounces, resists or disobeys someone of authority or in control of his life. Rebellion now and then is as necessary as salt or pepper to a bland dish.

It is true that the urge to rebel in all of us needs occasional releases; it is an integral part of our character. But disobedience does more than contribute to one's character. It also is the motor for change directed at the establishment and a spur and model for less courageous persons to emulate. There is no progress without rebellions, large and small.

The founder of Hasidism, the Baal Shem Tov, was a heretic who stuck to his own ideas despite initial ostracism by the Jewish establishment of his time. This dissent was dangerous. Who changes long-established beliefs easily? No one could stop the unruly and obstreperous young man from doggedly pursuing his rebellious path, and he was eventually joined by millions of followers.

Hasidism's insurrectionary origins are securely and permanently recorded in countless Hasidic tales and legends. Perhaps that is why rebellion always had such a warm reception among the early Hasidim. Only a vibrant culture could tolerate heretical challenges to its core belief system. Of course, heresy is meaningless if it does not challenge set beliefs. The ability of

---

[1]*The International Thesaurus of Quotations,* compiled by Rhoda Thomas Tripp (New York: Thomas Y. Crowell Co., 1970).

the early Hasidim to absorb heterodox views is testimony to its vitality. Among the dead there is no dissent.

The importance of dissent, disobedience and "doing one's own thing" is beautifully captured in the following story, actually a fable—a tale which includes animals that speak and act like human beings and is intended to support and confirm a practical truth:

The Hen and the Ducklings

Rabbi Shalom Shakhna, the son of Abraham the Angel, lost both his parents when he was very young and grew up in the house of Rabbi Nahum of Chernobyl, who gave him his granddaughter to wife. However, some of his ways were different from Rabbi Nahum's and unpleasing to him. He seemed to be very fond of show, nor was he constant in his devotion to the teachings. The Hasidim kept urging Rabbi Nahum to force Rabbi Shalom to live more austerely.

One year during the month of Elul, a time when everyone contemplates the turning to God and prepares for the Day of Judgment, Rabbi Shalom, instead of going to the House of Study with the others, would betake himself to the woods every morning and not come home until evening. Finally, Rabbi Nahum sent for him and admonished him to learn a chapter of the Kabbala every day, and to recite the psalms as did the other young people at this season. Instead, he was idling and loafing in a way, particularly ill-becoming to one of his descent.

Rabbi Shalom listened silently and attentively. Then he said: "It once happened that a duck's eggs were put into a hen's nest and she hatched them. The first time she went to the brook with the ducklings they plunged into the water and swam merrily out. The hen ran along the bank in great distress, clucking to the audacious youngsters to come back immediately lest they drown. 'Don't worry about us, mother,' called the ducklings. 'We needn't be afraid of the water. We know how to swim.'"

(*Buber, Late Masters, p. 49*)

Surely, many Hasidim must have remembered that it was the Baal Shem Tov's heretical rebellion that eventually established a new community that was open to the idea of rebellion and dissent as expressed in this story.

15

Ten Best Stories Times Two

If there is one lesson that Hasidism teaches us above all others, it is simply this: "Trust yourself!" Self-trust is the basis for gaining the capacities to accomplish what you desire. Does self-confidence lead to ability or does ability lead to self-confidence? Often, but not always, they are married to each other.

The basis of trust in yourself is the faith that you *can*, indeed, trust yourself. However you achicvc it, the foundation of constantly remaking yourself in these fast-changing times is the confidence you have in yourself.

One way to build self-trust is to begin to make choices. Choosing, selecting, discriminating are ways to create yourself, like yourself, and trust yourself.

In this chapter the authors select the ten stories that had the most influence on their lives. The selection will tell you much about each of us.

Why are we doing this exercise? To illustrate the powerful proposition that what works for me will also work for you. You are what you choose. You are the stories that you like best, and be assured that others will like them also. Trust your instincts, and you will be so delighted with the results that you will want to sharpen them further. Trust your instinct at the beginning, in the middle, at the end, and when you start over again. At every juncture and crossroad, instinct paves exciting new paths.

Thus, you are both parent and child of each story you select, first for yourself, then for others. Each story you select passes through the prism of your perspective on life. You reflect a part of the world and then project it for others to reflect upon.

This selection of ten stories is our best bet for today, this moment; tomorrow it may be different. We will not be, as we hope you will not be, confined by critical choices that cannot be changed. That would be making you a prisoner of your first choice(s). Follow your own direction, especially when you have to contradict your own past.

The important point is to decide: Even if you could reach your goal on another person's path—would reaching that goal be worth such an *ersatz* effort? The Hasidim definitely thought that anything worth attaining must be achieved through your own efforts.

Every activity you engage in is yours—it belongs to you. Storytelling begins with selecting a story. In the previous chapter we cited thirteen common human needs and situations, from making up to rebellion. Since these needs are always present, overtly or latently, you can ignite any occasion with a story related to whatever people are conversing about. Or you can be a leader and innovator by uncovering a hidden subject, idea, or feeling that people are concerned about subconsciously but cannot discuss openly. Whenever you can invigorate a group by raising to a conscious level implicit thematic concerns, you will be called "brilliant."

Pick *your* favorite stories and, as you practice telling them with more and more confidence and panache, you will enrich the lives of your listeners and enliven your own culture. In this process you will come to know and like yourself better. The stories give us a heightened awareness of what we ought to be and how to get there, and they shed light on who and where we are now. The stories help us understand the meaning of our lives. When you speak truly about yourself, you are speaking to others about themselves. Only if your achievements are truly your own will others want to share your discoveries:

The Philosopher's Counsel

> Said the Besht: "A king was told that a man of humility is endowed with long life. He attired himself in old garments, took up his residence in a small hut and forbade anyone to show reverence before him. But when he honestly examined himself, the king found himself to be prouder of his seeming humility than ever before. A philosopher thereupon remarked to him: 'Dress like a king; live like a king; allow the people to show due respect to you; but be humble in your inmost heart.'"
>
> (*Newman, The Hasidic Anthology, p. 90*)

HOWARD POLSKY'S TEN BEST STORIES

I decided to select stories that touched me in a very personal way and in which, in one way or another, I saw myself. The stories uncorked hidden springs within me. They not only gave me insights into a better way to live, but also showed *how* to attain it.

I recognized that I would have to think not only about selecting stories that were powerful and effective but, more important, think through why these ten stories were special to me.

Every time you have to decide what values are important to you, you are recreating yourself. I decided to select stories that changed me. I know they have changed me because I find myself habitually meditating upon them. These stories have entered my soul.

The phrase "ten best" begs the question: "Best about what?" This forced me to frame criteria for my selections. The values underlying the criteria are intrinsically useful and desirable to *me*. I hold certain qualities in high esteem, and so each of the ten stories is the one best suited to reflect one specific quality. Each one is to me personally the most . . .

- Provocative
- Amusing
- Liberating
- Wise
- Ridiculous

- Moving
- Challenging
- Helpful
- Ethical
- Simple—and, for an encore—
- Puzzling

THE MOST PROVOCATIVE

The following story is best told in a relaxed atmosphere with time on your hands and everyone in a mood to *shmooze.* Sometimes, I introduce it by posing the question: "Has any one of you known someone who is a real giver, a strong, well-defined person who gives freely without measuring what he will get in return? He just gives and, at least on the surface, does not need admiration, approval, or thanks. Apparently, the giving itself is his gratification."

And then I tell the following story:

For Himself in the World to Come

> The Neshchizer Rabbi related the following:
>
> "Late at night, a man came to the home of Rabbi Liber of Berditchev and asked for lodging. Rabbi Liber extended to him a gracious welcome and began to arrange a bed for the guest. The man asked him: 'Why do you trouble yourself to arrange my bed?'
>
> "Rabbi Liber replied: 'It is not for your sake, but for my own that I am doing this.'"
>
> (*Newman, The Hasidic Anthology, p. 185*)

Two audience responses immediately occur when this story is told. One is a challenge to the concept that (except for saints, martyrs or masochists) there are people who give because they get satisfaction from giving. Some will argue that our greedy, materialistic, individualistic and opportunistic culture conspires against producing such people.

The other audience response, often after only a moment of reflection, is a semi-reverie about very giving persons. Remembering, audience members glow as they recount incidents from an inexhaustible fount of tales about giving without the need to get back. Such an account makes the giver seem awesome! The teller is so moved that others in the audience are also moved, and they recall comparable events from their own experiences. A celebration begins to take place, a ceremony set off as special, away from routine lives and daily activities. Everyone is deeply affected.

I sometimes lead off a workshop with this story and the ensuing discussion evokes a mellow and warm feeling that lasts throughout the day. In relaxed circumstances, it brings everyone closer together, as if recalling the spirit of these special givers made us more giving and loving.

THE MOST AMUSING

Hasidic humor tends to be witty, dry, ironic, factual, low-key and full of puns and sparkling repartee. It's not so funny or comical as to make you laugh hilariously and fall out of your seat.

Hasidim have their own peculiar sense of humor. But they also share the universal dynamics of the comic sense, and they will laugh when a pompous ass slips on a banana peel, or when the "bad guy" is hoist by his own petard. The Hasidic joke, however, most often contains a subtle spiritual element. The Hasidic jest is sometimes used to put a brash aggressor in his place. Jokes are often exaggerated or even caricatured reflections of truth and, like humor everywhere, the Hasidic brand is not always tasteful.

These points are illustrated in the following story, which I can envisage being told by Hasidic stand-up comic in a large ballroom at Grossinger's full of Hasidim, working it around the theme of why they all came, *davke*, to Grossinger's:

On the Way to Karlin

A Hasid was on his way to visit the Karliner Rabbi. A rav met him, and said: "Can't you find a rabbi nearer than Karlin?"

"No, I cannot," answered the Hasid. "I read the thoughts of all the rabbis, and find them to be spurious."

"If you read thoughts," said the rav, "then tell me what I am thinking now."

"You are thinking of God," answered the Hasid.

"No, your guess is incorrect; I am not thinking of God."

"There you have it," remarked the Hasid. "You yourself stated the reason why I must go to Karlin."

(*Newman, The Hasidic Anthology, p. 255*)

As a second choice, here is another Hasidic tale with a similar humorous twist:

Go up to Heaven

When Rabbi Abish became Rabbi of Frankfurt, the most desirable rabbinical post at the time, he was informed that a minority of congregants were opposed to his selection. He invited the members of the opposition to his home and addressed them as follows: "Gentlemen, you may ask me three questions: 'How has it transpired that so lowly a rav as myself should presume to accept so lofty a post? How did such a superior community come to elect me? Why was it the will of Heaven that I should become rav of Frankfurt?' My answer to the first question is as follows: I was elected, and therefore I accepted the call. My answer to the second question is: The community elected me because it was the Will of Heaven. The third question I answer thus: In order to know why it was the Will of Heaven that I be elected Rabbi of Frankfurt, go to Heaven and ask them there."

(*Newman, Maggidim and Hasidim, p. 75*)

THE MOST LIBERATING

Liberation is a special condition, a necessary one for finding yourself. Without it, you are doomed to life imprisonment by your own prejudices. The distinctive mark of liberation is the freeing of your imagination to host new possibilities in coping with your situation. Liberation begets new choices; it frees you from compulsively acting the way you always have and thereby deepening your misery.

Perhaps the most important function of the Hasidic stories is to liberate the Hasidim from constraints and obligations that confine them to behavior and ideas that ensnare them in vicious cycles of despondency.

Every time I think of the following story, I radically shift my attention away from the bad things that I have done and toward the positive things I can do to get on with my life. It is a tickler that reminds me not to be trapped by what I have done, and to do what I can do to live better this moment. In this sense, the story is liberating to me:

Sin and Despondency

> A Hasid complained to the Rabbi of Lublin that he was tormented with evil desire and had become despondent over it. The rabbi said to him: "Guard yourself from despondency above all, for it is worse and more harmful than sin. When the Evil Urge wakens desires in man, he is not concerned with plunging him into sin, but with plunging him into despondency by way of sinning."
>
> (*Buber, Early Masters, p. 315*)

THE WISEST

Wisdom lies not in knowing what is right, but in acting right. Wisdom is practical knowledge—understanding in action. A person who acts wisely is wise. A wise person is not necessarily learned, but learning can't do any harm either.

A wise person deals with a situation in a way that makes him better and wiser, whatever the outcome. But we hasten to add that wise people are not losers. A wise man prefers making new mistakes to repeating old ones. That is why he is sometimes an adventurer, sometimes a fool. If knowledge is in the head and understanding is in the heart, then wisdom is in the hands and feet.

It has often been asserted—without basis whatsoever, I

might add—that wisdom, in contrast to knowledge, cannot be communicated. This is not true. Wisdom prefers to express itself through stories. What we want from wisdom is how to act in the shorter term, with an eye out, to be sure, for the longer-range consequences.

The next story expresses the essence of wisdom to me, and proof of that flabbergasting assertion lies in the tale's universality:

Walking the Tightrope

Once, the Hasidim were seated together in all brotherliness, when Rabbi Israel joined them, his pipe in his hand. Because he was so friendly, they asked him: "Tell us, dear rabbi, how should we serve God?" He was surprised at the question and replied: "How should I know!" But then he went right on talking and told them this story:

"There were two friends, and both were accused before the king of a crime. Since he loved them, he wanted to show them mercy. He could not acquit them, because even the king's word cannot prevail over a law. So he gave this verdict: A rope was to be stretched across a deep chasm, and the two accused were to walk it, one after the other; whoever reached the other side was to be granted his life. It was done as the king ordered, and the first of the friends got safely across. The other, still standing in the same spot, cried to him: 'Tell me, my friend, how did you manage to cross that terrible chasm?' The first called back: 'I don't know anything but this: whenever I felt myself toppling over to one side, I leaned to the other.'"

(*Buber, Late Masters, pp. 59–60*)

The wisest comment I have found on how to fulfill my role as a teacher (after twenty-eight years at the Columbia University School of Social Work) is in the following brief encounter:

To Learn versus to Be

Rabbi Samuel Shinager came to Rabbi Bunam for the first time and introduced himself. Rabbi Bunam said: "If it is thy

10

29 What does God do?

Tzedaka

59 79-

60

64

67 101

68 154

69

70 Howl

89 153

92

> wish to be a good Jew, thy coming was for naught; but if thou wishest to learn to be a good Jew, it is well that thou hast come to me."
>
> (*Newman, The Hasidic Anthology, p. 458*)

The distinction is crucial for all teachers, counselors and mentors, who at most are guides for travelers who ultimately choose their own paths.

THE MOST RIDICULOUS

> A man's worst enemy can't wish him what he thinks up for himself (Ayalti 1949).

There is a type of wish-obligation that Hasidim place upon themselves and that completely turns me off. It often begins "If I—" and concludes with the assumption of an unbearable burden. It is ridiculous because it is unrealistic. It is a built-in, self-fulfilling prescription for bankruptcy and self-ruin. I hate it:

If I Knew

> Rabbi Moshe once said:
>
> "If I knew for sure that I had helped a single one of my Hasidim to serve God, I should have nothing to worry me."
>
> Another time he said:
>
> "If I knew I had said 'Amen' just once in the way it ought to be said, I should have nothing to worry me."
>
> (*Buber, Late Masters, p. 172*)

Here is an even sadder demonstration of this unbearable sanctimonious self-obligation:

His Own Suffering

> Whenever the Rabbi of Sasov saw anyone's suffering, either of spirit or of body, he shared it so earnestly that the

other's suffering became his own. Once, someone expressed his astonishment at this capacity to share in another's troubles.

"What do you mean 'share'?" said the rabbi. "It is my own sorrow; how can I help but suffer it?"

(*Buber, Late Masters, p. 86*)

I also place the following story in my category of ridiculous tales. The goal it presents is impossible to achieve:

Loving Thy Neighbor

Rabbi Israel Baal Shem Tov interpreted the commandment, "Love thy neighbor as thyself," in the following manner: "Love thy neighbor, despite all his shortcomings and displeasing habits, in the same way that thou lovest thyself with all thine own shortcomings and undesirable ways."

(*Newman, Maggidim and Hasidim, p. 127*)

THE MOST MOVING STORY

We have commented before about the following story (see page 173), but I still find it devastates me every time I read it:

Conversion

Rabbi Aaron once came to the city where little Mordecai, who later became the Rabbi of Lechovitz, was growing up. His father brought the boy to the visiting rabbi and complained that he did not persevere in his studies. "Leave the boy with me for a while," said Rabbi Aaron. When he was alone with little Mordecai, he lay down and took the child to his heart. Silently he held him to his heart until his father returned. "I have given him a good talking-to," he said. "From now on, he will not be lacking in perseverance."

Whenever the Rabbi of Lechovitz related this incident, he added: "That was when I learned how to convert men."

(*Buber, Early Masters, p. 200*)

I think I can zero in on why this story so strongly affects me: Little Mordecai "did not persevere in his studies," and the only "lesson" Rabbi Aaron "taught" him was that he loved and understood him.

Now I will offer a formula so simplistic that I will be banned forever from academia: Every time you want someone to do something, understand and love him instead. And if he does not grow up to be a doctor, leave him alone; *you* go to see a therapist instead!

Thank you, Rabbi Aaron, for reminding us, and thank you, Rabbi of Lechovitz, for remembering this incident!

THE MOST CHALLENGING

"Go for it" is the rallying cry for anyone who ultimately has to take a chance and risk what he has, to obtain what he has not:

What the Mouth Will

> The Baal Shem said: "When I weld my spirit to God, I let my mouth say what it will, for then all my words are bound to their root in Heaven."
>
> (*Buber, Early Masters, p. 51*)

The Baal Shem's marvelous comradeship with God sustained his courage to "go for it." Frankly, I don't have such an intimate relationship with God. What, then, sustains me?

I'm afraid I have a much more prosaic answer—a plain, practical and unimaginative scheme which sustains me. I search my experiences and ruminate through my mind for associations with the story above, and dredge up from my subconscious an organizing theme—like "going for it" and the support that it requires—and then I "go for it." In other words, I hedge my risks with some organization; but how I build on the early organization is fairly free and spontaneous, taking advantage of all surprises along the way.

This may not always work, but it sure is a lot of fun. My "root" is in the organizing theme most intuitively felt. Proceeding this way is dangerous and adventurous. When I come out o.k., I am a hero. But win or lose, it is an exciting way to live.

And, incidentally, it is the best way I know to learn about yourself as well as the subject at hand. So . . .

Go for it!

THE MOST HELPFUL

Nearly all of the Hasidic stories are helpful to some degree—that is their primary function. So on what basis have I selected the most helpful among many helpful stories? Very simple. The frequency with which I call upon a story to help me.

I use the following story so often that I recall it automatically whenever I am stuck:

Can and Want To

> Once, when the Yehudi was walking cross-country, he happened on a hay wagon which had turned over. "Help me raise it up!" said the driver. The rabbi tried, but he could not budge it. "I can't," he finally said. The peasant looked at him sternly. "You can all right," said he, "but you don't want to."
>
> On the evening of that day, the Yehudi went to his disciples: "I was told today, we can raise up the Name of God, but we don't want to."
>
> (*Buber, Late Masters, p. 228*)

When I am stuck, blocked, baffled, slowed down, the first issue that I sort out is: Is it because of internal or external reasons? Is it psychological or something outside of me?

Is the overturned wagon physically beyond the Yehudi's strength or is it a psychological problem?

Of course, the physical and psychological elements are often intertwined, the but initial rough assessment is extraordinarily helpful in directing my attention where it is most needed.

Our minds play many tricks on us. We can use external reasons (i.e., reality) to cover up internal fears, and internal doubts to cover up reality problems. Ask first: Am I doing this or that because I can't or because I don't want to? I try to be very honest in answering this question. And I ask it a lot because I am often stuck!

THE MOST ETHICAL

I find the following story hard to believe. I feel that no one today would do what Rabbi Yehiel Meir did 200 years ago:

First Prize

> Rabbi Yehiel Meir, later the Rabbi of Gostynin, who was a poor man, went in to his teacher, the Rabbi of Kotzk, with a beaming face and told him he had won the first prize in a lottery. "That wasn't through any fault of mine," said the *tzaddik*. Rabbi Yehiel went home and distributed the money among needy friends.
>
> (*Buber, Late Masters, p. 285*)

Integrity is the practice of principle. The slightest deviation leads to a slightly larger one, and so on, and so forth. Let's assume that the message in the above story is that only what you earn is worth having, a principle found in many Hasidic stories. If that is so, and Rabbi Yehiel Meir is a man of principle, then his logical recourse was to give the money away.

To act otherwise, for example, holding onto the money, buying more lottery tickets, or the like, would have violated this principle. Note how subtly the Rabbi of Kotzk conveys the principle to Rabbi Meir: "That wasn't through any fault of mine." That means, "You, Rabbi Meir, did not earn this prize," and Rabbi Meir instantly grasped the message.

The confrontation is direct, compelling, inescapable. Why is this so, and why is it so important for understanding Hasidim and, even more important, for understanding ourselves?

Suppose, just for a moment, that you and I believed that only what we earn is worth having. We really believed in the principle and it was an important principle. Now if you and I won money in a lottery, would we in a million years give it away? Rabbi Meir did. What's the difference?

The difference is that today we are so removed from practicing our principles that we are *alienated from our alienation.* We are so alienated that we no longer are aware how unprincipled we are. We could and would create a thousand rationalizations (including that God has chosen us to be lucky) for holding onto the money. Rabbi Meir gave it away.

This story teaches me how corrupt I (you, too?) and our society have become. Even now, with all this exquisite and profound understanding of integrity, character and principle, even now, if I were to win a lot of money, would I give it away to needy friends? Would you? Rabbi Meir did.

Incidentally, man's ability to rationalize his actions was a phenomenon clearly understood by Hasidim and vigorously opposed:

Nothing but Abuse

Said the Dubner: "A charitable man who was gathering money to assist a needy person came to a certain citizen for a donation. The latter abruptly refused, without, however, offering any reason. The man of charity went to another citizen, and the latter began to abuse the man in need for whom the collection was being taken. 'He is a shiftless, lazy creature,' said the second citizen. 'Otherwise he would not be in such circumstances. I refuse to give a single penny to a worthless drunkard.' The man of charity replied: 'Your neighbor gave nothing but he kept silent; you, however, not only give nothing, but you also abuse and insult a needy man.'

"From this we learn that a wicked man invents false accusations against those to whom he gives nothing."

(*Newman, Maggidim and Hasidim, p. 224*)

THE MOST SIMPLE

I cherish this story:

How He Became a Hasid

Rabbi Mendel said:

"I became a Hasid because in the town where I lived there was an old man who told stories about *tzaddikim*. He told what he knew, and I heard what I needed."

(*Buber, Early Masters, p. 270*)

The sheer elegance of this story is so overwhelming I believe it is worth the effort to memorize the punch line: "He told me what he knew, and I heard what I needed."

Why am I so utterly enchanted with this uncomplicated, off-the-cuff comment? I think it is related to the idea of "entitlement." Neither the storyteller nor the listeners are claiming anything from each other. Storytellers are not responsible for enlightening, entertaining, solving problems, teaching, relaxing people, and saving the world. And you, listener, don't have to get anything out of this story now or later, or you may get something entirely different from what I got out of it now or later, or it may get you to think about an entirely different story from which you may or may not get something—or all of these. Whatever you get is o.k., and whatever I give is o.k., because you are you, and I am I!

THE MOST PUZZLING

This story will not leave me alone. I really enjoy being puzzled by it, because I feel some great insight or truth lies beneath its teasing seduction:

The Teaching of the Soul

> Rabbi Pinhas often cited the words: "A man's soul will teach him," and emphasized them by adding: "There is no man who is not incessantly taught by his soul."
>
> One of his disciples asked: "If this is so, why don't men obey their souls?"
>
> "The soul teaches incessantly," Rabbi Pinhas explained, "but it never repeats."
>
> (*Buber, Early Masters, p. 121*)

This is a super-curious and tantalizing statement about not listening to and obeying our soul:

- The soul teaches incessantly.

- The soul never repeats.
- Therefore, we don't learn to obey our souls.

And I would add:

- If I can figure this out, I will have a great illumination—an epiphany!

Now when I am stuck, I have two major alternatives: I can brainstorm, free-associate, just let go and make all kinds of random connections, the sillier the better. Or I can let it go, "forget" it, and let my subconscious marinate it. I don't give up hope (this is important) that something may pop up when I least expect it.

Before I let go of it consciously and let my subconscious take over, I will take a shot at brainstorming ("the soul teaches incessantly but never repeats") with the ten qualities I listed (and their stories) and see whether anything helpful emerges:

- **Provocative.** Every mortal I know who talks a lot, also repeats a lot. How is it my soul never repeats? The only thing I can come up with is that the soul constantly makes new connections, however ridiculous and far-fetched they may seem at first blush.
- **Funny.** Is this a joke, not to be taken seriously? If you believe this, you'll believe anything.
- **Liberating.** Tune in and concentrate when you do listen to your soul. Jump at what your instinct says to you is useful, and jump at it again and again.
- **Wise.** What is initially confusing is often, when understood, profound and wise. So hang in there. The better part of wisdom is in the ripening, which has its own pace.
- **Ridiculous.** You must have something better to do with your time. You are making a fool of yourself. To which another part of me says: "So what?"
- **Moving.** Obviously this story has touched me in a special way; otherwise I would not let it continue to bug me. So go with that movement, trust it, because I am a very feeling guy.

- **Challenging.** Anything you can't do, especially that which takes a lot of time, is probably worthwhile—as long as you don't despair. The bigger the challenge, the bigger the prize.
- **Helpful.** Very helpful . . . learning how to live with something you can't resolve is very helpful. It's a great builder of patience and humility.
- **Integrity.** Is "never repeating yourself," a distinguishing quality of a man of integrity? Can the soul go beyond the static surface to the underlying depths, where everything is in motion every second?
- **Simple.** I am holding out for a simple explanation that will strike like lightning with thunder, a magnificent flash of light and a palpable feeling of tremendous relief, and then I will know something I never knew before.
- **Puzzling.** What is the central *thrust* of all the puzzling connections made in the previous pages? Simply this: I don't know what it means when I'm told that my soul talks to me incessantly but it never repeats. So I will now give my subconscious a chance to encounter my soul. But something else has occurred. Following in the footsteps of Rabbi Pinhas and Martin Buber, I have released this puzzle into the world, and you may take up the challenge. I am convinced one of you will come up with a "solution" and will tell it to someone else and, as the solution makes the rounds in ever-widening circles, I will also hear it.

Light can enter only where darkness has been.

YAELLA WOZNER'S TEN BEST STORIES

This is not intended to be a selection of the best or most significant Hasidic stories, but of those that may help the reader to focus on subjects of personal interest and to consider options for solving personal problems.

My choices were based on the following assumptions:

- Each personality has a number of subsections that conduct a constant internal dialogue, which could be overheard if we were really listening. These are daily conversations which we hold with ourselves.

- Each of these inner parts has a positive intention to serve us, though sometimes they appear to be disturbing. A personal dilemma arises as a result of an unfinished internal debate among these inner parts.
- In order to solve a dilemma or to reach a solution compatible with all these inner parts, we have to pay respect to all the parts. If a part is not respected, it will continue to voice its demands and prevent us from reaching a satisfactory solution. Only if we assure this part that we have indeed understood its positive intentions and given it due consideration, will it cooperate and enable us to reach a satisfactory decision.
- The story serves as a means of expressing different parts within us and of conducting a dialogue between our different parts.
- Sometimes, one or more parts covers up the internal dialogue and keeps it a secret from ourselves and from others, because its revelations may upset our equilibrium by strengthening one part and weakening another. By means of the story, we can expose the unconscious self that is responsible for the existing equilibrium, and without a threat to the conscious self enable it to take steps to change the existing equilibrium and to create a new one that can serve us more harmoniously and efficiently.

For this process to take place, we must pinpoint for ourselves answers to the following questions:

- What in the present state needs to be changed?
- What is our desired state?
- What are the various options leading to the achievement of these aims?

We must also recognize, however, that the answers may not come so easily. Sometimes it is hard to identify the difficulties in the present state. Aims that are desirable in the present may change with time. There may be more available options than we first thought when examining the subject. The process of examining all of the options requires consideration of the pros and cons of each hypothetically available course.

After examining all available courses and clarifying which course of action will bring us nearer to our self-declared goal, we can attain satisfaction and peace of mind. Each civilization has developed the language, vocabulary, and imagery to describe this state of mind. This method of personal goal attainment consists of investigating five questions:

- What is the central problem within the story?
- What is the desired state?
- What are the options to get from the present state to the desired state in the story?
- What is the subjective message that the story conveys?
- What are the key words or key concepts that lead someone to select the stories he has chosen to retell or to cherish?

To demonstrate this method, I would like to describe the three stages I went through in selecting my ten best stories:

Stage 1. The first stage was choosing the stories. I thought about them for many days. I read many stories and put them aside. I was afraid to commit myself to a choice of stories that would be the best expression of myself. The deadline for handing over this chapter to my co-author arrived. Even at the last moment, a part of me kept on persuading the other parts not to cooperate, not to surrender to the pressure of time. The dialogues within me were sometimes so boisterous that they kept me awake at night. Since time had run out, the argumentative part in me resigned finally and I wrote feverishly.

Remember, the choice is right for the given moment. Tomorrow you and I might choose other stories. The stories themselves have little importance: Their importance lies in what they mean to you at a given moment. Seize this moment, look in the written mirror and love what you see, and with this loving and open eye, learn to accept what the stories have to tell you!

Stage 2. After choosing my ten "best" stories, I wrote them and noted the page references.

Copying the stories was a kinesthetic test of feeling myself going through the stories the way I would go through them in Stage 3, which became my tour guide.

Stage 3. Now I analyzed the stories according to the five questions previously posed.

First I tried to identify the problem and how it is described in the story. Sometimes the story is a solution to an implied problem only. Take into consideration that the problem implied by the story is mine, the one I see in it. You may find a completely different problem in the story.

That problem will be your own. It is not a matter of being right or wrong. We both look in the same mirror and behold different images.

When the message of the story "arrived," I discovered that a dialogue had developed between me and the story. When I refer the story to "you," it is because I heard the story giving me the message! It may give you a different message.

1. *"WHAT YOU GET OUT OF LIFE"*

The Rabbi of Zans accompanied the following story with gestures that conjured up a picture:

> "People come to me who ride to the market every day in the week. One such man approached me and cried: 'My dear rabbi! I haven't gotten anything out of life. All week I get out of one wagon and into another.' But when a man stops to think that he is permitted to pray to God Himself, he lacks nothing at all in the world."
>
> (*Buber, Late Masters, p. 210*)

The problem: What is the meaning of my activities in life? There is much trouble in them and little satisfaction. The "trouble," in the words of the storyteller, is that "All week I get out of one wagon and into another." The little satisfaction received from all this trouble is expressed by "I haven't gotten anything out of life."

The aim (implied): "To get something out of life."

The solution: Prayers to God.

The message: God is not supposed to get you "something out of life." The prayer itself provides satisfaction, and the person no longer feels he has nothing. The prayer is a means of ascending from daily matters to a more spiritual level.

There is an exciting stage between acknowledging the

need and attaining the goal. While concentrating on the need you often find that you have already received what you wanted. Revealing the need in this story makes you transcend your daily drudgery.

2. "ACCEPTANCE OF THE WORLD"

> One of the followers of the Rabbi of Kobryn was very poor. He complained to the rabbi about his straits, which, as he said, put him off his studies and made him unable to pray. The rabbi told him: "In these times the greatest piety, which supersedes study and prayer, is to accept the world as it is."
>
> (*Buber, Late Masters, p. 354*)

The problem is twofold—a problem within a problem: poverty which prevents me from praying.

The goal: Change the suffering caused by the inability to pray. In other words, to experience the good, even though the harsh reality remains unchanged.

The means: Accept the world as it is.

The message: Suffering is an expression of our personal interpretation of reality, how we experience it. If we change the interpretation, we change the suffering. Acceptance of the world is a change from the concept that poverty and inability to pray are evils that aggravate suffering. Accepting that poverty and nonprayer are just neutral phenomena, neither good nor evil, alleviates the suffering they cause. The forceful element in this story is the concept that nonprayer is also subject to interpretation. That is to say, accepting the world as it is, is no less important than prayer. It is clear that Rabbi Moshe of Kobryn recognized the paradox of change, which is: "In order to change a phenomenon you must first accept it." He knew that once the poor man accepted the world as it is, his mind would be set free for prayer. Though he could not solve the problem of poverty, he could solve the problem of the inability to pray.

The message to me: Accept yourself for what you are and stop tormenting yourself for what you are not.

3. "THE VERSE WITHIN"

> Once, when Rabbi Mordecai was in the great town of Minsk expounding the Torah to a number of men hostile to his way, they laughed at him. "What you say does not explain the verse in the least," they cried.
>
> "Do you really think," he replied, "that I was trying to explain the verse in the book? That doesn't need an explanation! I want to explain the verse that is within me."
>
> (*Buber, Late Masters, p. 156*)

The problem: Whether one should persuade others or himself.

The goal: Inner peace, an inner recognition that what is right for me is right.

The means (not stated explicitly but implicit in the story): The act of persuasion is not in the explanation to others, but in understanding the difficulty yourself, and satisfying yourself that it is right for you.

The message: Here it is very complex. There is an a priori acceptance of truth as outside the person, i.e., the verse does not need modification. It exists as a truth on its own. The aim of man is to understand "the truth" which exists independently of his explanation, outside him. Does this cognitive process involve the persuasion of others? The message is a loud and clear No. The other person serves merely as the means for persuading oneself. The conscious aim is the inner peace and perfection of the person with himself.

This applies to my own anxiety about this book. Now I am aware that my real anxiety is whether the book can persuade *me.* To be frank, I would like to be in harmony with the verse that is within me.

4. "WHAT HE PRAYED WITH"

> The rabbi once asked his son: "What do you pray with?" The son understood the meaning of the question, namely, on what he based his prayer. He answered: "With thc verse: 'Every

> statue shall prostrate itself before thee.'" Then he asked his father: "And with what do you pray?" He said: "With the floor and the bench."
>
> (*Buber, Early Masters, p. 269*)

The problem: How to perform a spiritual action suffused with a deep meaning toward God who is outside us? This is a central question of Hasidic thought. The rabbi instructs his followers how to do this.

The goal: is only suggested here. For me, it is knowledge of the way a spiritual action is performed. A spiritual action is performed by transforming sensual experiences.

The means: "With the floor and the bench." I think this response is wonderful. It signifies through the simplest means.

The message: Even while striving for "higher" worlds, keep in touch with the most simple sensual experiences. Perhaps there is a hint here about the importance of humility—a most important value in Hasidic thought. But for me, the message is to be close to primary experiences; do not belittle them in the name of the spirit.

5. *"THE REFUSAL"*

> Once on Rosh Hashana (New Year), about the time for afternoon prayers, Rabbi Mendel entered the synagogue and found about forty of his Hasidim there who had come from a long distance to spend the holy day with him.
>
> "This is a splendid congregation," he said, "but know all of you that I cannot carry all of you on my shoulders. Each one of you must work for himself."
>
> (*Buber, The Hidden Light, p. 324*)

The problem (implied and not stated explicitly): What is the responsibility of a rabbi towards his Hasidim? For me, the question is what is the responsibility of the therapist, the educator, or the group-leader toward his charges?

The answer: Each one of you must work for himself. This story reflects two major Hasidic beliefs: The goal of service

—every person is responsible for himself; the holy office, or spiritual work, cannot be performed by proxy. Each person is responsible for himself *and* must undertake the work himself.

The message: Since the responsibility for a person to get well is first of all his own, the role of the rabbi, the educator, or the therapist is to make this clear. When the Hasidim gather to learn how to connect to higher worlds, the rabbi should make it clear that he cannot do this for them.

6. "DRUGS"

> A learned but ungenerous man said to Rabbi Abraham of Strityn: "They say that you give people mysterious drugs and that your drugs are effective. Give me one that I may attain the fear of God."
>
> "I don't know any drug for the fear of God," said Rabbi Abraham. "But if you like, I can give you one for the love of God."
>
> "That's even better!" cried the other. "Just give it to me."
>
> "It is the love of one's fellow men," answered the *tzaddik*.
>
> (*Buber, The Hidden Light, p. 341*)

The problem: How to attain the fear of God, or as the rabbi amended it, "the love of God." The man wanted to reach a high spiritual level in which man is connected to God by emotional ties.

The goal: Attainment of emotional ties with God, the highest spiritual achievement—the love of God.

The means: Loving fellow men. Since man was created in the image of God, who is everywhere, even within man, the way to the love of God leads through the love of His creatures who are in His image—a lower manifestation of Divinity, as it were.

The message (for me): Love yourself, since you are a creature of God, too, and love your fellow creatures, not in order to stay at a high spiritual level, but because that is the way to a higher self-realization. There cannot be self-actualization without love for oneself and for one's fellows.

7. *"MEN MEET SOONER THAN MOUNTAINS"*

On one of his journeys, Rabbi Judah of Stratyn, the disciple of Rabbi Uri, was informed that Rabbi Simon of Yaroslav was traveling on the same road toward him. He stepped down from his coach and walked to meet him. But Rabbi Simon also heard that the former was coming, so he left his carriage, too, and set out on foot to meet him. They met and greeted each other warmly. Rabbi Judah said, "Only now do I understand the meaning of the saying, 'Men I do meet, mountains never.' If one regards himself as an ordinary man and the other one, too, they are able to meet each other. But if one thinks that he is a lofty mountain and the other one, too, they can never meet."

(*Buber, The Hidden Light, p. 340*)

The problem: How to establish contact, particularly if two spiritual giants are concerned?

In this story both the problem and the goal are only suggested. The story revolves on the means.

The goal: How to establish contact, how to meet?

The way: Each one should regard himself as an ordinary person, an ordinary pedestrian human being, not an immovable mountain, an important personage riding in a carriage. The accessories of comfort, the paraphernalia of status, are barriers.

The message (for me): The communication in this pleasant meeting in which the two rabbis greeted each other warmly is a central issue in my occupation as a therapist. The precondition for such a meeting between two people is that they lower the barriers between them, including status symbols. For me personally, it is a reminder to be unassuming and simple. Pride is an enemy of the human relationship.

8. *"THOSE WHO TRUST THEE"*

On the eve of Rosh Hashana, before the afternoon prayers, the Rabbi of Kobryn had bent over his little heap of petition-cards and said: "Lord of the Universe, You know that I am but a simpleton and a sinner, but what can I do with people? They think that I've got something! So I beg of You not to disappoint those who have trust in You."

(*Buber, The Hidden Light, p. 355*)

The problem: Though the Rabbi of Kobryn is only human, and aware of his limitations, he did not want to fail those who turned to him.

In other words, the Rabbi knows that there is a great disparity between what he is and what he is thought to be, but he wants God to close the gap.

The goal: The gap between reality and the expectations of the rabbi's followers should be bridged and thus the glory of God enhanced, because the rabbi is regarded as His messenger.

The way: The whole issue seems to be complicated by the appearance that the rabbi is negotiating with God unfairly. He tells Him to be a party in the fraud so that he can glorify His Name. But on second thought, the negotiation is not so fraudulent after all, because if the Hasidim believe that the rabbi is special, that God listens to him, their faith and piety would facilitate God's help.

This reminds me of a recent experience as a therapist with two different persons—one a relative, the other a student. Both had previous therapeutic experience with me, and they fully trusted my ability to help them. Because of this, they could skip the initial barriers of doubt, suspicion and argumentativeness, and could make use of me according to their needs. As a result, the treatment was short and efficient. My wish, like that of the Rabbi of Kobryn, is that those who turn to me should think "I have something"—not to increase my honor, but in order to have them make use of me and be helped by me efficiently.

9. "THE MORNING PRAYER"

> "There are *tzaddikim*," said Rabbi Naftali, "who pray that those in need of help may come to them and find help through their prayers. But the Rabbi of Roptchitz gets up early in the morning and prays that all those in need of help may find it in their own homes, will not have to go to Roptchitz, and will not be deluded into thinking that the Rabbi has helped them."
>
> (*Buber, Late Masters, p. 193*)

This story manifests a reversal of attitude from that of the previous story.

The problem: What is the role of the rabbi? Is he to pray that those who need help will come to him, so he can serve as a "mouthpiece" before God? Or should the rabbi pray that those who need help will not require his services as a go-between? To be sure, even then he serves as an intermediary, because he prays that God will directly help those in need, but his role as intermediary is then less obvious.

The *goal*: Affording help to those who need it. According to the Rabbi of Roptchitz, this can be accomplished without the direct agency of the rabbi in order to glorify God's Name.

The way: Ask God to help the needy directly, wherever they are; assume the role of a covert agent.

The message (for me): The approach is the opposite of that in the previous story. The rabbi wants his Hasidim to avoid the mistaken belief that it is the rabbi who helps them. The real helper is God.

There is a hint that the real helper of man is man himself, because he says, "All those in need of help may find it in their own homes."

The way of the Rabbi of Roptchitz, which is more modest, is based on faith that man's awareness that it is God Himself who has helped him will strengthen him more than the delusion that the help is from the rabbi.

10. "EVERYTHING AND EVERYONE"

> Rabbi Bunam said: "When my house is full of people on the holy Sabbath, I find it difficult to preach, because everyone needs a particular sermon for himself. Each one needs his particular *tikkun* ('resolution' or 'salvation') from my sermon, but what I give them is really taken from them."
>
> (*Buber, The Hidden Light, p. 410*)

The problem: How to say something from which every listener can find his own *tikkun*? What to say that will be meaningful to every listener?

The goal: To deliver a sermon that would be a *tikkun* for every person in the audience.

The way (implied): First, Rabbi Bunam notes the difficulty.

What he gives is really taken from the audience. He acts as a good group leader. He uncovers from the listeners what is significant to them, and then states it in such a way that each listener hears what is significant to him.

The message: Everyone has his own needs. The sensitive rabbi, therapist, or educator, should enable all his listeners to find in his words what is significant to them. The therapist's approach is characterized by sensitivity and by understanding of the individual needs of his patients, so the therapist gives the patient only what he has taken from him.

CONCLUSION

Ten stories significant for me have been examined in relation to four criteria: the problem, the goal, the resolution, and the message.

The following themes from the stories are significant for me:

1. Life: I have nothing. No, stop and think. But I lack nothing.
2. Acceptance of yourself and of the world may be your most powerful prayer.
3. Inner peace derives from awareness of what is right for you.
4. What do you pray with? With the floor and the bench!
5. The goal of service is to teach others to be responsible for themselves.
6. Love of God requires love of one's fellow men.
7. The best way for people to experience each other is to be on the same level.
8. If others think I am special, I am more effective.
9. The real helpers are God and the person in need of help.
10. What I give to others is essentially what is taken from them.

At this stage of my life I am struggling with "big chunk" problems, on personal and professional levels. The key words I have used in analyzing the stories describe and illuminate my personal issues. The main questions are:

- What is the meaning of life for me?
- What am I able and unable to do as a person and as a therapist?
- How do I meet, help, trust, accept, love others and myself?

The messages I have taken from these ten stories strengthen my beliefs and my ways, and remove my doubts.

SUMMARY OF THE PROCESS

The method of reading Hasidic stories to extend personal awareness consists of seven steps:

- Choose relevant stories.
- Identify the problem in the story.
- Identify the goal in the story.
- Identify the alternatives for reaching the goal.
- Connect personally to the story.
- Note the significant words (concepts) in the story.
- Draw your personal message from the analysis.

16

How to Tell a Story

It is time to get into the basics of telling a story, because it is by telling it that you get to the heart of it. You can react to a story upon hearing it, but when you see how the story can apply to others' situations and to different circumstances, your reaction takes on more vitality, depth and truth.

Whenever you receive an insight passively without applying it actively, it begins to wither from disuse. Application includes telling it to yourself under conditions that can delight and be useful to you. The advantage of retelling stories to yourself is that they become eternally vibrant by affecting your life and invigorating your beliefs, actions and feelings.

One story that I (Howard Polsky) refer to often, makes my life more worth living. It is the tale of the rabbi informing a melancholy and desperate Hasid that Satan uses sin to make us feel bad all the time about sinning. (See page 379.)

That was a real eye-opener for me. I don't think I sin more than your average cracker-barrel, bagel-and-lox American Jew, but I tell this story to myself a lot and it helps me! This story is a part of me—it is me!

The stories that you tell yourself make you more aware of the different circumstances under which you tell it to yourself. This helps tune you in to the manifold opportunities you will encounter in telling stories to other people.

Three essential elements make up storytelling:

1. *The context of storytelling.* The ecological, social, cultural, and psychological elements that contribute to a story's significance. Context includes the situation and the circumstances that stimulate you to tell the story.
2. *The structure of storytelling.* When you launch into telling a story, you will discover a process, a recurring beginning, middle, and end that ties you, your audience, and the story together. A story is often related to an expressed need which it helps illuminate and resolve.
3. *Enculturation—the after-effects of the story.* How the story affects the relationship between the storyteller and his listeners, and how it contributes to their culture: the intellectual, moral and aesthetic development of a common outlook and perspective on life and humanity.

THE CONTEXT OF THE STORY

We can think broadly of three different kinds of circumstances under which you will tell stories:

On the wing. While you are "in flight"; in other words, you don't have much time to tell, develop, or savor the story, but have to be incisive and precise, right on the mark, with the point of the story riveted to the topic.

Homespun. This is a story spun in a comfortable and sociable "homelike" setting where you can stretch it out and explore its subtle and hidden dimensions as well as venture into other complementary stories and situations which it evokes.

Propaedeutic. This is a story prepared beforehand for an occasion and designed to convey enlightenment as well as pleasure. In this category are stories for toasts, lectures, family events, introductions to speakers, prologues to debates.

You will find yourselves telling stories on the run, in friendly social groups, and in formal, prepared presentations. Each of these situations evokes a different mind-set in telling a story.

TELLING A STORY ON THE WING

One morning I got up at 5 A.M. to play tennis at 6. I showed up at the court promptly at 6, but there was no partner; at 6:15, no partner; at 6:30, still no partner.

I turned to Thelma, the receptionist, bookkeeper and general manager, beginning to steam up a bit, and I suddenly heard myself saying: "There is a story about a Hasidic rabbi who came home one evening to discover that his wife had not prepared the evening meal and he had to rush out to perform a good deed right after eating. He began to get angry, but suddenly he stopped and said to himself: 'Why should I double my loss? I will be late to perform the good deed, but why should I double my loss by getting upset and taking out my anger on my wife?'" (*Newman, The Hasidic Anthology, p.* 8)

"That's the way I feel, Thelma, why should I double my loss?"

"Exactly . . . how right you are, Howard!" Thelma enthusiastically responded, "I feel the same way." And she smiled: "It's part of maturity, being grown-up. What's happened is over. There are enough stressful situations without adding to them."

We congratulated each other on our mutual good sense and, whistling a sprightly tune, I went upstairs to take a leisurely shower, an even more leisurely breakfast, dawdling a little over *The New York Times.* I felt absolutely great!

A couple of days later a tennis player, inadvertently I'm sure, walked out without paying for a can of balls he had purchased, and Thelma's eyes and mine met for a moment, and her irritation suddenly vanished. She burst out laughing: "I know, I know, Howard. Why should I double my loss?"

* * *

An English friend telephoned me long-distance while he was visiting the United States, and we chatted a bit. He was not able to come to New York, so we could not arrange to meet. I asked him his impressions of California.

"California is fine," he responded, "but we spent an evening in Las Vegas and were appalled at the people gambling.

They seemed dazed and glazed, out of it and so sad, grim. So many of them—appalling."

We got into a discussion about gambling. I then told my friend the story about Rabbi Meir who, as a beaming disciple, once told his rabbi he had won a lottery, and his rabbi replied that he had nothing to do with that, whereupon Rabbi Meir promptly went away and distributed his winnings among the needy. (See page 385).

My friend paused for a long moment, then responded quietly:

"Yes, Howard, that's it. Gambling is so disconnected from what one is and has become, isn't it?" Then (long-distance, mind you) we got into a discussion on gambling, luck and the like, and agreed that most gamblers really don't think very much of themselves, and that gambling is an escape from their insubstantial lives and selves.

My friend told me he would never forget that story.

STORIES TOLD IN A FRIENDLY, SOCIABLE, SETTING

This is our favorite setting: a group of friends sitting around, drinking espresso, shooting the breeze. Good company is an end in itself.

When good company is reinforced by good talk, we get a glimpse of what Heaven is like. When the Messiah does finally arrive, we believe he will be found sitting among good friends, swapping stories.

One Sunday afternoon, in the midst of warm, special friends, I casually tossed out the Kotzker Rebbe's observation that everything in the world can be imitated except truth, and truth that is imitated is no longer truth. (See page 148).

The casual remark ignited a conflagration of feelings, observations, witticisms, and other stories that went on for several hours.

Someone immediately commented that truth is like a fingerprint—each one is unique! Then someone quoted the Bible that there is nothing new under the sun, which was countered by Heraclitus's famous assertion that you cannot step in the same river twice. Whereupon someone added, "Every woman is unique."

At one point we became very philosophical. Is originality always good? Is it true that you cannot be on the wrong road if it is your own road?

We then veered off into discussions of individuality and originality, and argued about the proposition that whatever you are is infinitely richer and more original than being like someone else. Of course, everybody remembered the story about the man who dreamed he could find a treasure in another city and went there only to discover the treasure was under his own hearth. (See page 312.) And the story about the man who could not find in the morning any of his things he had put away the evening before, including himself. (See page 275.)

All this was heady stuff and, to my amazement, I dredged up the story about our not being helped by the soul because even though it talks to us incessantly, it never repeats.

This stopped everyone in his tracks and I repeated the story.

Again, everyone was quiet. Then a quiet member of the group spoke up: "It suggests that the soul is original and has something new to say all the time, and we don't or can't understand our soul because each of us is not his own person. And when the time comes that each of us is comfortable being what he is, then the soul will be comprehensible." And someone else half-jestingly added, "and the Messiah will have arrived."

I was dumbfounded. Here was an answer to the puzzle that had been bedeviling me. And I said secretly to my heart, "I'll bet my shoelaces this man can listen to his soul."

THE PROPAEDEUTIC SETTING

Each of us will be called upon at times to make some "original" remarks on formal occasions. Some of these occasions occur frequently: classroom sessions, workshops, or committee meetings. Some occasions occur only once: making a speech at a conference or bidding farewell to someone at a going-away party.

For formal occasions, you have time to prepare your remarks and use a story to help make your point. The time to dwell on an appropriate story is before the occasion, although I have known colleagues who can, under pressure, produce an appropriate story on the spot.

I like to meditate on an appropriate story well in advance of the occasion; I play around with several themes and then let my subconscious come up with a pertinent story.

Sometimes, I stimulate my subconscious by thumbing through summaries of 200 of my favorite stories or by speed-reading the stories in Martin Buber's collection.

Last year, my secretary at Columbia University retired after thirty years of service. A big party was organized, and I was asked to speak.

I thought a lot about the retiring secretary—a very religious, consistent, reliable person who rarely distorted things but told it like it was, and was the soul of integrity.

I realized that this woman maintained very high personal standards. In a flash the story came to me about the student who left his village for five years and on his return told his family and the villagers that he had learned the true meaning of the Sixth Commandment, "Thou Shalt Not Steal." Certainly it is not right to steal from others, but it is much worse to steal from yourself.

During my highly charged peroration, I turned to the secretary and said that, because she was true to herself and never stole from herself, she was very straight and first-class with all of us.

Many months later, people told me that they still remembered the story I told and that it was beautiful.

THE STRUCTURE OF STORYTELLING

Do the stories have a common underlying foundation? Everything clothes itself in some form, and is thereby distinguished from every other form. The story, of course, is much more than its structure.

The structure of a story is a vital linkage between it and the audience. A subtle, pervasive and deep isomorphism emerges between what is transpiring in the story and in the listener. It turns out that the two processes are identical.

Both real life and the story have a protagonist: a person who takes a leading part, a fighter, an advocate, perhaps even a hero or heroine. In life and in the story there emerges a central figure of some significance (see Chapter 3, page 47).

The central figure in the story is matched by every listener's becoming a central figure, and the two undergo the same process insofar as the listener identifies with the central figure and experiences vicariously the following general sequence of activities:

Story's central figure — Listener as central figure

1. *Present State:* Someone has a question, problem, or difficulty in reaching a goal. The problem may not be fully understood and often attracts speculation and resists explanation. It may be some saying or behavior that is difficult to interpret; often the situation is paradoxical. The problem challenges one's ingenuity. Light can enter only where darkness has been.
2. *Desired Outcome:* The person with the problem seeks an outcome that will resolve the difficulty. In some cases he may feel hopeless about resolving it, but generally there is hope for its resolution.
3. *Strategy to Overcome Problem:* This requires a plan, a stratagem or scheme that will enable the individual to achieve his goal. Sometimes, the problem can be reframed, and the new perspective results in a satisfactory resolution.
4. *Resolution:* This is an action or process by which the problem is solved or the goal is attained. It is an answer to the problem. Sometimes, the resolution means making something clear or understandable. A story may clarify what is not immediately obvous; often the resolution of the story uncovers obscure motives; sometimes it involves using one's imagination.
5. *Lesson (or moral):* Many Hasidic stories carry an underlying message, a lesson or moral; frequently they define right behavior or the importance of conforming to a standard of behavior sanctioned by a religious judgment. Sometimes, more general truth relates to an ideal of conformity to a religious virtue. Very often, the transcendental, fundamental significance of spiritual reality is re-emphasized; but there also may be practical gener-

alizations that can help people lead productive, joyous, and divine lives.

The Hasidic story, like a person's problematic situation, is constructed on the basis of these five points. Awareness of this structure can help the storyteller recognize the issue, how to approach it, and how it is resolved, so that he can add or subtract, elaborate, and embroider it in his/her own way.

The structure helps a storyteller define a problem, issue, or theme related to the story. The core of the story revolves around the issue, problem or goal that needs resolution.

Once this basic structure is mastered, you can go to the underlying scaffolding of the story and recreate it in your own inimitable style:

The Reward of Frugality

The Karliner told the following parable: "A wealthy man took pity on two poor men and advanced them money to enable them to earn a living. The wiser man opened a small store, and, living very frugally, saved enough money to return the loan; at the same time he had money left over wherewith to maintain his business. The benefactor was delighted and made him a gift of the original sum.

"The other borrower began to live expensively, and could not meet his obligation. The lender was angered, and foreclosed on him. The point is obvious: He who plans his life to fit his circumstances oftentimes meets with pleasant surprises. The reverse is true in the case of the unthinking and improvident."

(*Newman, The Hasidic Anthology, p. 26*)

Knowing the structure frees the storyteller to play around with the story to maximize the response of his listeners:

The Sign of Pardon

"In this day and age, when there are no prophets," Rabbi Bunam once said to his disciples, "how can we tell when a sin we have committed has been pardoned?"

His disciples gave various answers, but none of them pleased the rabbi. "We can tell," he said, "by the fact that we no longer commit that sin."

(*Buber, Late Masters, p. 253*)

This story has all the structural components outlined above:

Present state: Rabbi Bunam asks his disciples how they can tell when a sin is pardoned.
Desired outcome: The pardoning of sin.
The strategy: The rabbi asks the disciples who give answers that deal with asking for forgiveness but not for the end of sinning. The rabbi reframes the asking for forgiveness to the cessation of sin. So the strategy is not in asking forgiveness for the past, but for sinless behavior in the present and future.
Resolution: One indication that the problem is solved is that the disciples do not continue to question the rabbi and the rabbi has nothing more to say.
The lesson: The resolution is part of the general Hasidic philosophy that action speaks louder than words. The Hasidim were wary about talk and confession that was not accompanied by a change in behavior. In one story after another, we are told that acting properly supersedes prayer and seeking redemption for past sins.

The following story attests to the compassion of Hasidic rabbis:

The Two Caps

Rabbi David Moshe, the son of the Rabbi of Rizhin, once said to a Hasid:

"You knew my father when he lived in Sadagora and was already wearing the black cap and going his way in dejection; but you did not see him when he lived in Rizhin and was still wearing his golden cap." The Hasid was astonished. "How is it possible that the holy man from Rizhin ever went his way in dejection! Did I not hear him say that dejection is the lowest condition!"

"And after he had reached the summit," Rabbi David replied, "he had to descend to that condition time and again in order to redeem the souls which had sunk down to it."

(*Buber, Late Masters, p. 68*)

The central problem in this story concerns a well-known rabbi who wears a black skullcap and seems to go around in a dejected way. This is contrary to the Hasidic way of life. The Hasidim celebrated life and rejoiced in God's creation, and felt it was a virtue to be joyful, and sinful to be downhearted. A famous rabbi who at one time wore a golden cap, a sign of ecstatic joy in life, now suddenly is gloomy and dejected. How can this be reconciled?

The strategy is to find a greater good that is performed through depression. To be maximally helpful to people who are down and out, the rabbi mirrors their situation and shows his compassion for them. He has to partake of their life situation in order to help them.

The message is that to help another, one must experience that person's problems and feel his sadness. The troubled person feels a great sense of support, and is more open to what the rabbi has to say.

Empathy, heartfelt support, is a concept central to all contemporary schools of psychology. All of them stress the importance of the counselor's pacing the client so that the latter can feel the counselor's support; it makes the counselor's efforts more credible. Pacing feelings enables the counselor to realize more fully the dimensions of the problem, not only intellectually, but also in an emotional sense, and he is then able to offer counsel in a way that can be most useful. The lesson is that one must constantly make choices, and that the sin of melancholy is not as grave as that of failing to help a burdened person.

The rabbis were constantly discoursing on and debating all kinds of problems stemming from daily life as well as those suggested by reading the Holy Scriptures and the Talmudic commentaries. Statements from the Bible were often chosen to enlighten people in their daily concerns. Here is a typical example:

Everyone Has His Place

Rabbi Abraham was asked:

Our Sages say: "'And there is not a thing that has not its place.' And so man too has his own place. Then why do people sometimes feel so crowded?"

He replied: "Because each wants to occupy the place of the other."

(*Buber, Late Masters, p.* 72)

The story begins with the general proposition that God ordered the world, yet it doesn't work out in practice. If there is a place for everything, why do people feel deprived? The answer is that they are envious of what others have, and they want to occupy their places. This is a wonderful play on the word "place."

The rabbis were well aware that envy is disastrous. Man is not content with what he has. Compared to others, he feels "crowded" because he does not have as much as other people do.

Generally, the rabbis were censorious of people not accepting their own situations and envying others. They saw jealousy as a self-defeating trait that can forever harass an individual. They also saw this striving after someone else's status as going against the moral order of God—in which everyone has his place:

The Humble Visitor

Rabbi Ber Alesker paid a call upon the Lubliner. To the surprise of the Hasidim, the visitor addressed the Master in these words: "By right, O Master, it was your duty to make the first call." Noting their surprise, Rabbi Ber explained: "The Zohar says that the *tzaddik* should seek out the sinner in order to save him."

(*Newman, Maggidim and Hasidim, p.* 78)

The Hasidic rabbis were not of one mold. They were very distinctive. Each one was unique. In that sense, the rabbi was a model for people to express themselves as they were and not try to be what they were not.

Still another angle to accepting oneself is seen in Hasidic tales. The rabbis were very playful and often would create problems in humorous ways. For example, suppose someone would ask you: "If God put the whole world into your hands to do with it just as you like, what would you do?" This is the "problem" that was put to Rabbi David Moshe:

The Faithful Servant

> Rabbi Nahum of Stepinesht once said of his brother, Rabbi David Moshe of Tchortkov:
>
> "When my brother David Moshe opens *The Book of Psalms* and begins to recite the praises, God calls down to him: 'David Moshe my son, I am putting the whole world into your hands. Now do with it just as you like.' Oh, if He only gave me the world, I should know very well what to do with it! But David Moshe is so faithful a servant that, when he gives the world back, it is exactly as it was when he received it."
>
> (*Buber, Late Masters, p. 75*)

This theme goes to the heart of the Hasidic outlook. This is, indeed, the best possible of all worlds, and every person is the best possible of all people. It is necessary to accept what is and work with it. There is something very powerful in accepting oneself and one's condition, because then one can create what a person can truly be. But if an individual tries to be someone else, there is no possibility of freeing the creative person that lies within him.

And so it is with the world that is. It is not the world that conspires against people; it is people's conspiring against themselves that keeps them from realizing their potential.

Through stories, the rabbis set up situations which demonstrated the inner power of faith, what Martin Buber called the "inner light," to overcome all kinds of material and physical obstacles.

In order to bring this mighty truth home in a practical way to their followers, the rabbis seized every simple activity and event to illustrate the great spiritual power that lies within an individual. Next is a typical story which demonstrates the power that lies within, once one commits himself to the holy life:

The Scroll of the Torah

> Once, a new Torah scroll was being dedicated in the House of Prayer. Rabbi David Moshe held it in his hands and rejoiced in it. But since it was large and obviously very heavy, one of his Hasidim went up to him and wanted to relieve him of it. "Once you hold it," said the rabbi, "it isn't heavy any more."
>
> (*Buber, Late Masters, p. 76*)

Let us break the story down according to the analytical framework that underlies stories:

Present state: The Torah is too heavy for the rabbi to carry.

Desired outcome: to relieve the rabbi of the heavy Torah.

Strategy: to ask him if someone could take the Torah.

Resolution: relieving the rabbi of his heavy burden.

Message: The followers are concerned about supporting their rabbi.

This is all turned around and reframed by the rabbi so that an expected outcome becomes a surprise ending.

Redesigning the issue from the point of view of the rabbi, we come out with the following framework:

Present state: The rabbi is very involved in holding the heavy Torah and enjoying it. The problem is that his followers believe the Torah is too heavy for him.

Desired outcome: The rabbi wants to continue to enjoy the Torah and be "lost" in it, and finds a way to convey this to his followers.

Strategy: The rabbi, in effect, tells his followers that once he held the Torah, it was not the heaviness he felt, but joy and lightness in being identified with it, and he no longer felt it was a burden.

Resolution: The followers accept the rabbi's resolution to hold the Torah because they realize it is not heavy but, in fact, gives him joy and "carries" him!

The lesson is the supreme importance of inner faith and devotion for overcoming all burdens. A mundane situation is turned on its head by the rabbi and is used to demonstrate the power of inner conviction and faith.

Ultimately, the Hasidic goal was to teach its followers to become self-reliant, but not to the point where they became immersed only in themselves; they were to be self-reliant as a way of dedicating themselves to God. This must be clearly understood as the ultimate triumph of the Hasidic faith: namely, that only the individual can save himself, but he can't do it alone. He requires God for salvation. And he can appeal to God only on the basis of a constantly self-substantiating ego. God is available to everyone who is someone; through God, everyone becomes someone:

God's Dwelling

> "Where is the dwelling of God?"
>
> This was the question with which the Rabbi of Kotzk surprised a number of learned men who happened to be visiting him. They laughed at him. "What a thing to ask! Is not the whole world full of His glory!"
>
> Then he answered his own question: "God dwells wherever man lets him in."
>
> (*Buber, Late Masters, p.* 277)

The relationship between a man with a strong ego and God, no matter how powerful that person may feel himself, ultimately involves submission to God.

The relationship between God and the Hasid is extraordinary. The Hasid reaches out to God not with words mechanically recited, but with all his heart and spirit in his everyday actions amidst the vicissitudes of daily life. Conquering the difficulties of everyday life had no meaning unless one was thereby partaking of God's spirit.

It was not enough to be successful the way we think about success in today's world. That is a trap. There is greater happiness in singing joyfully about the daily wonders of God's world. This outpouring of faith in God had much more meaning for those individuals who were strong and self-reliant and struggled heroically at the most mundane levels. Stories were helpful only when the audience was willing to deal with the "bitter truth."

The Sugar on the Pill

> Said the Dubner: "A physician prescribed for a boy patient some pills coated with sugar. The patient failed to show any improvement, and the physician resolved to investigate the cause. By carefully watching the boy, the doctor noticed that the foolish lad licked off the sweet coating with his tongue but spat out the pill itself. He then took the proper measures to remedy this unsatisfactory situation.
>
> "From this we learn: Many a member of an audience in a synagogue will swallow appreciatively the stories and anecdotes, but will refuse to heed the bitter truths which the preacher seeks to impress upon the congregation."
>
> (*Newman, The Hasidic Anthology, p. 65*)

It is important for an individual to succeed and thereby express himself more powerfully and joyfully to God; but it was alien to the Hasidic approach to believe that God could be a substitute for an individual's pain and suffering and misfortune. In other words, only you can be the initiator of a better life—or a worse one. In either case, prepare to treat both impostors, success and failure, just the same, for God is the ultimate reality and He works in ways that are beyond mortal comprehension.

HOW STORIES ENHANCE THE QUALITY OF LIFE

Individuals, couples, families, groups, institutions, professions, countries, and peoples—all have a cultural heritage; this integrated pattern of shared beliefs enables us to gear into each other and lies at the basis of our capacity for learning and transmitting experiences and knowledge to succeeding generations.

The culture of a group is not static, but an ever-changing tapestry of attitudes toward every aspect of life. Running through the culture of Hasidism are central themes that touch upon relationship with God: joy, independence, feeling from the heart and others that are discussed in Part III, "Hasidic Teaching." The stories reinforce a people's culture because they highlight key values in the listener's current life experience in a dramatic, narrative form.

Thus, stories that stick in people's minds and are frequently shared can contribute significantly to their culture. We have already amply demonstrated how often different stories with diverse contents are really stressing cumulatively a basic Hasidic value, such as independence (see Chapter 5).

The function of the stories in consolidating basic values in a tightly unified culture such as Hasidism is quite different in the context of fractured cultures to which the many Jewish and non-Jewish readers of this book belong. This has disadvantages, but also several important advantages.

The biggest disadvantage is unfamiliarity with the general Hasidic ethos, both in personal experience and in literature. This includes history, traditions, symbols, terms, organizational structure, daily, weekly and annual routines. The big advantage is the adventure of extracting from this strange culture what is pertinent to the listeners' present situation. Discovering that these vital people were coping with issues very similar to our own adds credibility to their importance and to their relevance to us. Some of the past is to us as our present will be in others' futures.

The question remains: How can we anchor meaningful stories into our culture and our way of life? Let us consider a strategy for rooting selected stories in your life and culture so that they become part of your thinking, feeling and behavior.

SUPPORTING POSITIVE VALUES THROUGH STORIES AND STORYTELLING

We believe stories come alive when they touch a belief close to your heart about the way you want to live; when you become eager to share those stories with others; when you begin to experiment with them in widening circles of acquaintances; and, finally, when you begin to tell stories in groups, meetings and conferences in which you may not know personally many of those present. The more the stories are shared at these different levels, the more they become an integral part of your personal heritage, as well as the culture of your friendships and groups (like your family) that you belong to.

HOW STORIES INFLUENCE YOUR CULTURAL ORIENTATION

When a story begins to intrude itself on you, it is time to begin paying attention to it. I cannot let go of the next story, or perhaps it will not let go of me:

For Himself in the World-to-Come

The Neshchizer Rabbi related the following: "Late at night, a man came to the home of Rabbi Liber of Berditchev and asked for lodging. Rabbi Liber extended to him a gracious welcome and began to arrange a bed for the guest. The man asked him: 'Why do you trouble yourself to arrange my bed?'

"Rabbi Liber replied: 'It is not for your sake, but for my own that I am doing this.'"

(*Newman, The Hasidic Anthology, p. 185*)

Now, how can the next story be also valid morally when its message seems to be diametrically opposed to the previous story?

The Most Earnest Prayer

The Yehudi became dangerously ill, and the inhabitants of his town proclaimed a fast and universal prayer for the rabbi's speedy convalescence. A villager chanced to come to town and went to the tavern for a drink of brandy. Several townsfolk overheard him and informed him that drinking was prohibited for the day.

The villager at once went to the synagogue and prayed: "O Lord, please cure the Holy Rabbi, so that I may have my drink."

Soon after, the rabbi began to recover his strength, and he said: "The prayer of the villager was more acceptable than any of yours. He expressed the greatest longing and the most earnest supplication for my prompt recovery."

(*Newman, The Hasidic Anthology, p. 64*)

Do these two stories contradict each other? At first blush, it may seem so. Rabbi Liber apparently is going out of his way to do a good deed for someone else, although he says he is doing it for his own sake.

In the second story, the villager seems to be praying for the Yehudi's recovery, but is really interested in getting his drink.

Actually, the second story helps clarify the first. Not only is there nothing wrong in doing something for someone else based on self-interest, but the giving to others that also serves your own interest makes the giving more valid.

In effect, Rabbi Liber's giving is primarily to himself as he gives to others. The villager's prayer is so he can get back to drink. For the Hasidim that is the preferred way to give to others. Wanting a drink does not take away the genuineness of the prayer for the Yehudi. Enjoying giving does not take away from the giving to someone else. In both cases it makes the giving more "earnest."

The deeper question of how we can learn to enjoy giving to others may very well have to await the coming of the Messiah. Realizing that there is no contradiction between giving to yourself and giving to others, and that in giving to others you do give to yourself may, God willing, hasten the Messiah's arrival.

In summary, stories will enter and become part and parcel of your cultural outlook through a process of meditation. Stories talk to your soul and it talks to you, especially when it is perplexed. Light can enter only where darkness has been.

Insofar as you are able to broaden your audience from yourself to ever-widening groups, the stories begin to contribute to the group culture and to your philosophy on new qualitative levels that not only summarize past experiences, but also significantly shape your future development. Let's take a look at a case where a story became a part of the cultural fabric of a large institution and influenced its future course.

HOW A STORY CONTRIBUTED SIGNIFICANT MEANING TO AN ORGANIZATION'S CULTURE

For many years I have served as a consultant to a multi-agency social service organization in New England. Since I helped train workers and staff for many years, I was well known throughout the agency, and my role placed me in a special position of influence—that of an inside-outsider.

I was asked to keynote an agency-wide fifteenth-year celebration to be attended by over 300 staff, clients, state and local officials.

At such events, speakers are expected to look backward and forward, to summarize past accomplishments, and predict future achievements.

The major speaker is expected to capture the "soul" of the organization; this includes not only its genius, invaluable contributions, and selfless service, but particularly its unique moving spirit!

I decided to use the "tightrope story" (see page 380) in my speech.

I realized that this agency, too, had walked a tightrope for fifteen years in maximizing services to the most vulnerable, poor, disadvantaged, mentally ill strata in the population, while adroitly dealing with the state, which subsidizes its programs. In fact the agency was always tilting from one side to the other, as a conscious, planned policy! It was willing to take sides without being foolhardy, and to develop a sound administrative base without becoming an over-bloated bureaucracy. They were willing to take chances, but always calculated the down-side costs.

Perhaps this is a way of life, a philosophy, for individuals as well as organizations, I told them. We want security and adventure.

Perhaps the secret of life is tilting from side to side: balancing "the rolling stone gathers no moss" with "nothing ventured, nothing gained." In many respects, life itself is a tightrope between security and adventure. We need both—either extreme robs us of our genius and talent. It is always possible to come back to the center by tilting to the other side, but if you always keep to the center, you lose the sparkle, growth and challenge of adventure which is so important in life.

17

Let Two Stories Tell the Story

Every good story concludes with inevitability. Our lives can be visualized as a series of stories with destinies that cannot be resisted. *Hamlet* and *Oedipus Rex* immediately come to mind.

An ending forces us to search through the story and to determine what compels us to believe that this, and only this, ending makes sense.

Once you are born, you are destined to die, and every breath, choice and act challenges your mind, heart and will to breach again and again the new, the strange, and the unknown. What you did is seeking you, as you seek to go beyond your past. What we seek is what we have and have not already sought. Inevitability is always crowding us: Smoke travels upward, and leaves fall to the ground.

Does an awareness of the pattern of your fate influence your capacity to modify your destiny? That seems to be the point of the following story about our ultimate destiny:

Ultimate Insight

Sometimes, the Yehudi said that every New Year's Day gave him fresh insight into the service of God, and then every-

> thing he had done in the past year seemed insignificant compared to the new, and thus he went from one crossing to the next, on an endless way. But once toward the end of a year when he was reading the Book of the Angel Raziel, it was revealed to him that he would die soon after New Year's Day. He went to his teacher, the Seer of Lublin, and told him this. "Stay with us over New Year's," said the Seer, "and you will be spared." But the Yehudi bade him farewell and returned to his own house.
>
> The day the Yehudi died, Rabbi Kalman was walking with Rabbi Shmuel in a distant part of the country. Rabbi Kalman said: "There is a certain unification which can be accomplished on this day, but only in the Land of Israel. Whoever accomplishes it in any other place must die on the selfsame day. That was what happened to Moses, our master, peace be with him."
>
> (*Buber, Late Masters, p.* 233)

The Yehudi chose his death by refusing to be spared by the Seer of Lublin. This choice resulted in a second "inevitability," the privilege of dying in exile on that one day. He could achieve a "unification" awarded only to others living in the land of Israel. Thus the Yehudi's death celebrates a special unity with God.

The story implies that a person's destiny lies inside and outside of himself, and that awareness of that interaction and interrelationship gives one some measure of determination of his "fate" throughout life, including its conclusion.

These musings about inevitability were prompted by the thought that this and any concluding chapter, act, movement, has an irrefutable logic that flows out of its previous parts, and yet it surprises us and points to a new future for everyone upon whom the creation has had an impact.

And so it is with this book. Somewhere in the previous chapter it dawned upon us what this book is really all about. You can imagine how delighted we were to discover the essence of this enterprise!

We now believe that every story is really two stories: the story that is told, and a more or less matching story carved out of the flow of the listener's experiences. This is a dynamic interchange, like the double helix of DNA (Deoxyribonucleic Acid) (see Figure 17-1).

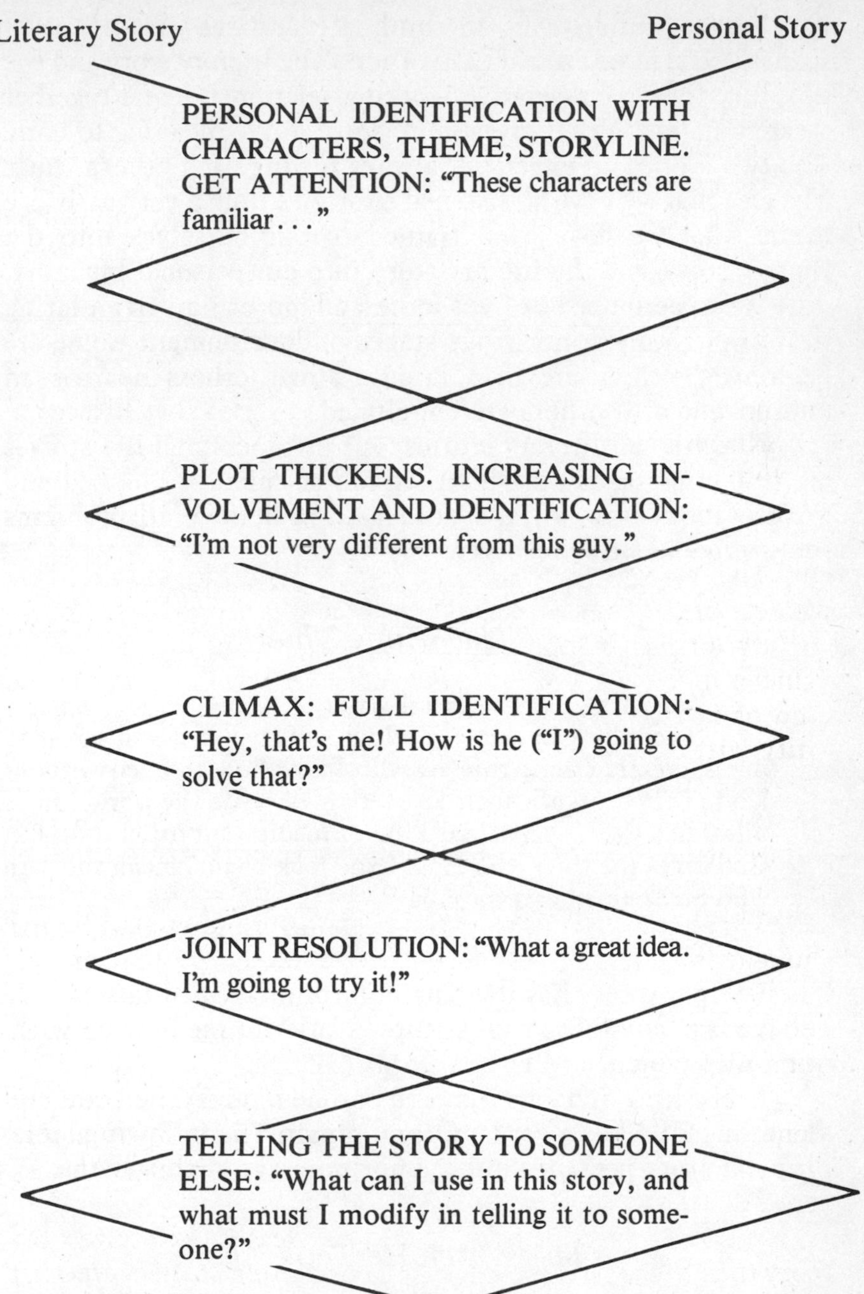

Figure 17-1. The Double-Helix Story Line

Stories stimulate us to think of our lives as a series of stories, some more crucial than others. The literary story and the life story form a cooperative working relationship and together create a narrative that gives more substantive meaning to both. The two stories, in effect, are always testing each other's truth. The fact that we have all listened to stories from a very early age means that we have been trained to put ourselves into the literary story, and the literary story into our personal life story.

We experience our lives more and more as an articulating network of stories in various stages of development. Some are beginning, others are in a middle stage, others nearing an ending, and still others are concluded.

And like all literary stories, our own personal life stories are full of plateaus on which we are stymied or blocked and unsure about how to proceed. Hasidim believe all problems ("mysteries") can be resolved:

The Strong Thief

The Maggid of Mezeritch said:

"Every lock has its key which is fitted to it and opens it. But there are strong thieves who know how to open without keys. They break the lock. So every mystery in the world can be unriddled by the particular kind of meditation fitted to it. But God loves the thief who breaks the lock open: I mean the man who breaks his heart for God."

(*Buber, Early Masters, p. 104*)

Every mystery has its "particular kind of meditation." We believe it is possible to substitute "story" for meditation without doing violence to either word.

Everything and every person can be straightened out, and sometimes it takes a very minimal repair. The following metaphorical story becomes quite emotional about this theme:

The Watch He Took Apart

Rabbi Yerahmiel, the Yehudi's eldest son, who was a watchmaker before he became a rabbi, once told this story to the congregation assembled in the House of Study:

"When I had learned the watchmaker's trade, I lived with my father-in-law, and he too knew quite a bit about watches. Once I wanted to go to a great *tzaddik* and had no money for the journey. Then I told my father-in-law if he gave me ten gulden, I would repair his watch which had been out of order for a long time, and which he had not been able to repair himself. He agreed. So I took the whole watch apart to see what was wrong with it. And then I saw that there was nothing wrong with it at all, except that one hairspring was the least bit bent. I straightened it out, and the watch was as good and true as when it left the hand of its maker."

When Rabbi Yerahmiel had ended his story, the entire congregation wept.

(*Buber, Late Masters, p. 233*)

That is really moving when you meditate upon the fact that small changes can have such huge consequences. This either takes your breath away, or makes you weep with joy, or both.

Straightening out one slightly bent hairspring is important because the watch is again "as good and true as when it left the hand of its maker." The Hasidim wept because being renewed to wholeness contains the promise of total ecstatic reunion with that other Maker!

His Watch

When Rabbi Elimelekh said the Prayer of Sanctification on the Sabbath, he occasionally took out his watch and looked at it. For in that hour, his soul threatened to dissolve in bliss, and so he looked at his watch in order to steady himself in time and the world.

(*Buber, Early Masters, p. 253*)

What a way to live—so blissfully that he needs a watch to locate himself temporally and spatially in our mundane world!

If our thesis is correct, that every story is actually a double helix of two intertwining stories, then Rabbi Bunam is fundamentally and profoundly correct in his belief that he alone cannot give each person his own Torah (message):

All and Each

> Rabbi Bunam once said:
>
> "On a Sabbath, when my room is full of people, it is difficult for me to 'say Torah.' For each person requires his own Torah, and each wishes to find his own perfection. And so what I give to all I withhold from each."
>
> (*Buber, Late Masters, p. 248*)

If, indeed, every story is really two stories, it is possible to start with either one and subsequently integrate it with the other story. I could read Martin Buber's book and contemplate how the Hasidic stories are related to my life stories. Or I could start with a personal life story and discover a relevant Hasidic story that sheds light on my situation. Between these two polar approaches, there are many serendipitous possibilities.

Let us demonstrate how a search starts with a personal life story.

Recently I (Howard Polsky) was looking for help as I undertook more risks in a couple of different situations. I began to search among Hasidic stories and made a connection between my own "story" thus far and the following literary one:

For the Light

> Rabbi Moshe, the son of the *Maggid* of Kiznitz, said:
>
> "It is written: 'Pure olive oil beaten for the light.' We are to be beaten and bruised, but in order to glow with light."
>
> (*Buber, Late Masters, p. 177*)

"Well, that makes sense," I said to myself. "Dues have to be paid. I can't be very good at any new venture. I will have to take my lumps for a while, and eventually I will 'glow' like pure olive oil."

Well, that was helpful but not very inspiring, so I looked further. I am sufficiently sophisticated to realize that without inner peace and sufficient self-esteem very few challenges will be chanced, but with inner peace everything is possible and risks can be taken. I discovered confirmation for this point of view in story and Scripture:

World-Peace and Soul-Peace

> Rabbi Bunam taught:
>
> "Our Sages say: 'Seek peace in your own place.' You cannot find peace anywhere save in your own self. In the psalm we read: 'There is no peacc in my bones because of sin.' When a man has made peace with himself, he will be able to make peace in the whole world."
>
> (*Buber, Late Masters, p. 264*)

Both these stories were of limited usefulness because they were too general for me; I could not take their general usefulness and make it relevant to my specific risk-taking.

So the search continued, and then the following story "attacked" me:

Adam's Sin

> Rabbi Yitzhak was asked: "What do you think was Adam's real sin?"
>
> "Adam's real sin," said he, "was that he worried about the morrow. The serpent set out to reason with him: 'There is no service you can perform, for you cannot distinguish between good and evil and are unable to make a choice. Eat of this fruit and you will be able to distinguish; you will choose the good and receive the reward.' That he gave ear to this—that is where Adam was at fault. He worried that he would not be able to serve, yet at that very hour he had his service: to obey God and to resist the serpent."
>
> (*Buber, Late Masters, p. 291*)

I didn't like the title, "Adam's Sin"; I would have preferred "Adam's Problem." Now that rang a bell, and the two stories merged in my mind and I felt a surge of belief that said to me: "That's it!"

In risk situations, I still dwell too much on the negative consequences, that anti-change (serpent-part-of-me) that looks too far ahead rather than focusing on the here-and-now.

When I reflect on this story, I meditate on how cleverly deceptive parts of us are to our whole selves. Forethought, planning, saving for a rainy day are admirable virtues which can turn into formidable enemies.

A good thing becomes bad when it prevents us from attaining a greater good, as Spinoza once observed. Satan utilizes all these virtues in a super-deceptive way. And that is reason why we have to get all the help we can from each other:

The Rooster and the Goose

> A preacher decided to settle in a small town. When he met the rav of the community, he explained his purpose. The rav was surprised and protested: "But the community pays its rav an exceedingly small amount; how will you make a living here as well?"
>
> The *maggid* narrated the following parable by way of answer: "A goose belonging to a thoughtless owner often suffered from hunger because her master forgot to feed her. One day, the man bought a rooster and placed him in the same coop with the goose. The goose was greatly concerned. 'Now I shall surely starve. There are two of us to eat from my small portion.'
>
> "'Do not worry,' retorted the rooster, 'I can crow when I feel hungry, and this will be a reminder to our owner. Then we shall both be fed.'"
>
> (*Newman, The Hasidic Anthology, p. 349*)

Another lesson to be derived from this example is the importance of trusting your intuition for what works for you. A story can be enjoyed because it is funny, enlightening, inspiring, or witty; but Hasidic stories are mostly practical (and moralistic). They can help you cope with your problems.

Our experience is that the stories are helpful to the degree that you can translate them into specific strategies that make a difference in your attitude, behavior, and understanding of your problematic situation.

The counsel to stick to the here-and-now and not to worry about consequences was liberating. Undue emphasis on the here-and-now could be harmful in other situations, as the story about the brooding watchman illustrated. (See page 26.)

The rabbis were aware of this issue: How specific or general should a story be so that it can be most useful to the audience? Their answer, of course, would be, "It all depends," which may be too general and needs more specification. Another strategy they would offer would be to involve the listener in the story and let him figure out the rest for himself.

That is their favorite methodology, and they relished being puzzling so as to hold the listener's interest:

The Fish in the Sea

> Rabbi Yitzhak of Neskhizh told:
>
> "Once my father said to one of his friends in the month of Elul: 'Do you know what day this is? It is one of the days when the fish tremble in the ocean.'"
>
> One of the men standing near Rabbi Yitzhak, observed: "People usually say, 'when the fish tremble in the waters.'"
>
> (*Buber, Early Masters, p. 164*)

Now that is a puzzler!

The only sense that we can make out of it is that it is more accurate to say fish tremble in the "waters" than in the "ocean." Both are "right," but "waters" is more precise. Perhaps this difference does not matter much to the fish, but the puzzle-lesson does make us aware of the values of accuracy and specificity.

* * *

The thesis of this chapter is that storytelling combines your own story and someone else's in a dynamic interchange that will change your life forever. You can begin with your own story and find in it gaps, uncertainties, dilemmas or even *weltschmerz*—a mental depression caused by comparing the real and ideal worlds, or a sentimental sadness brought on by the gap between what you feel you can do and what you ought to do. Or you can find the same theme in a Hasidic story and relate it to yourself and work yourself into and out of a weltschmerz:

Master and Disciple

> Rabbi Hanokh told this story:
>
> "For a whole year, I felt a longing to go to my master, Rabbi Bunam, and talk with him. But every time I entered the house, I felt I wasn't man enough. Once though, when I was walking across a field and weeping, I knew that I must run to the rabbi without delay. He asked: 'Why are you weeping?'
>
> "I answered: 'I am, after all, alive in this world, a being created with all the senses and all the limbs, but I do not know what it is I was created for and what I am good for in this world.'
>
> "'Little fool,' he replied, 'that's the same question I have carried around with me all my life. You will come and eat the evening meal with me today.'"
>
> *(Buber, Late Masters, p. 251)*

Rabbi Bunam said two important things to Rabbi Hanokh, and the second "message" could be easily missed. The first "obvious" answer and a very comforting one, is: "You think you are alone in struggling to find out who you are and what you should do. Listen, little fool, I have been struggling with this question all my life!"

The implication is that everyone is struggling with that question and will struggle with it all his life, and ultimately will find a way to deal with it.

So Rabbi Bunam starts where Rabbi Hanokh is and paces him and then very adroitly leads him to the next step: "You will come and eat the evening meal with me today."

In other words, all the weltschmerz in the world can never taste as delicious as bread in good company. What a simple, subtle, and insightful suggestion, with all the profundity and elegance of a witty philosophical work.

Rabbi Bunam was saying: "Speculate and ponder all you like, and that is important, but enjoy a meal with me today."

The Hasidic rabbis would be the first to say that an answer to one question leads to another question and another problem.

The question the answer provokes is this: Generally, isn't a point reached where all this preoccupation with oneself becomes not only counterproductive but even fatuous?

A Piece of Advice

Rabbi Hayyim had married his son to the daughter of Rabbi Eliezer of Dzikov, who was a son of Rabbi Naftali of Roptchitz. The day after the wedding, he visited the father of the bride and said: "Now that we are related, I feel close to you and can tell you what is eating at my heart. Look! My hair and beard have turned white, and I have not yet atoned!"

"O my friend," replied Rabbi Eliezer, "you are thinking only of yourself. How about forgetting yourself and thinking of the world?"

(*Buber, Late Masters, p. 214*)

Eliezer's answer is not the whole answer either. One can be very busy caring for others and "the world" and still be personally very much lost amidst all of the activity:

The Busy Rabbi

Said the Besht: "When the Berditschever was about to be born, the Satan complained that henceforth he would have no work to do, inasmuch as the Berditschever would be able to induce every Jew to become a *tzaddik*.

"'Do not worry,' replied the Lord. 'He is destined to become a rabbi, and hence he will be busily occupied with congregational affairs.'"

(*Newman, The Hasidic Anthology, p. 470*)

Self-abandonment is as fruitless as self-preoccupation. So how can we be useful to others and be situated solidly in the real world, and still be legitimately concerned about who we are, what we value most and what we want to do? Can all of this come about by throwing ourselves into the real world?

Jews all over the world are famous for answering a question with another question. This very practical manifestation of experiencing and promoting the mysterious and the unknown must ultimately have its source in the final mystery of mortality and immortality.

It will not be very productive to pursue that last question at this time in our human development. A more practical mystery is how to live a life that is fully self-conscious without being narcissistic, and how to be fully engaged in the real world with awareness of our own integrity and uniqueness:

In Their Own Estimation

> The Strelisker recalled to his Hasidim the saying of Rabbi Simeon ben Yohai to the effect that he had looked about him and had observed that superior persons are small in number. Said the rabbi: "How could he identify the superior persons? He did so by discovering those who were small in their own estimation."
>
> (*Newman, Maggidim and Hasidim, p. 122*)

That's the issue in these concluding pages: how to know and be concerned with ourselves individually and yet be caringly connected to others.

In order to probe this question (and come up with some better questions) we will bring together some mystery stories that have plagued us and see if they can form a coda, distinct in itself, and also serve as a reasonably rounded-out summary of this book.

The stories in this book are our story; even the puzzling stories are related to what is puzzling in our lives. Perhaps most puzzling is why we try to resolve some puzzles and abandon others. A puzzle is a tease: It cannot be too bewildering or too easy. A puzzle that disturbs and baffles and is even momentarily dumbfounding leads to invigorating guesswork and brainstorming. Above all, a puzzle is a promise that you will learn something new—if not about the outside world, certainly about your inner world.

Our intention is to juxtapose the following three mystery riddle-puzzles with a life centered in oneself and the world, and examine the hypothetical combinations that emerge:

Today as Yesterday

> The Rabbi of Rozniatov, Rabbi Eliezer Lippmann, persistently inquired from Rabbi Mendel of Kossov why the Messiah has not come, and why the Redemption promised by the Prophets and Sages has not been fulfilled.
>
> Rabbi Mendel answered: "It is written: 'Why has the son of Jesse not come, either today or yesterday?' The answer lies in the question itself: 'Why has He not come? Because we are today just as we were yesterday.'"
>
> (*Newman, The Hasidic Anthology*, p. *247*)

The soul is constantly telling baffling mysteries, which we continue to repeat to ourselves. This is the distinctive mark of human beings: curiosity—an insatiable desire to learn and to know about everything. Curiosity is letting go of what we know and have for what we don't know and what the soul has told us only "once." This curiosity dates from Adam and Eve in the Garden of Eden and has cost us dearly.

Mystery is one (or at least one) of the ways that we can be drawn to what we don't know. Once the challenge to learn something we don't know is made, we are hooked into finding a solution in order not to remain perpetually in doubt. Questions lead to wisdom. Questions are fueled by curiosity. Perhaps this is the *raison d'être* of our life on earth, as a Yiddish proverb (Ayalti 1949) suggests: "A man should live if only to satisfy his curiosity."

Of all the trillions of puzzles in the world, about which our restless soul is forever telling us, our favorites are about things that have inherent contradictions, such as dilemmas, paradoxes, antinomies and anomalies. Contradictions abound to constantly rework into tantalizing resolutions. Selecting the best resolution raises many new questions, and intuition plays a very big role here, perhaps nine-tenths.

We started with a question: How can one concentrate on

self-development, and yet be of constructive use in the world? If we could learn this—make way for the Messiah. Why not listen to our soul? Well, there is another problem—it talks non-repetitively and in riddles.

We decided to welcome puzzles and mysteries, especially paradoxes.

What more challenging paradox could we find than the one we started with—how to go north and south at the same time? How can that be related to living maximally in the real world and in our inner, egotistical, imaginary world? Can we answer that question in such a way that the next question does not leave us even more perplexed?

Let us turn to an archetypical paradox:

How to Become Spiritual

In the days of the Great *Maggid*, a well-to-do merchant, who refused to have anything to do with Hasidic teachings, lived in Mezeritch. His wife took care of the shop. He himself spent only two hours a day in it. The rest of the time he sat over his books in the House of Study. One Friday morning, he saw two young men there whom he did not know. He asked them where they were from and why they had come, and was told they had journeyed a great distance to see and hear the Great *Maggid*. Then he decided that for once he, too, would go to his house. He did not want to sacrifice any of his study time for this, so he did not go to his shop that day.

The *maggid*'s radiant face affected him so strongly that, from then on, he went to his home more and more frequently and ended up attaching himself to him altogether. From this time on, he had one business failure after another until he was quite poor. He complained to the *maggid* that this had happened to him since he had become his disciple. The *maggid* answered: "You know what our Sages say: 'He who wants to grow wise, let him go south; he who wants to grow rich, let him go north.' Now what shall one do who wants to grow both rich and wise?" The man did not know what to reply. The *maggid* continued: "He who thinks nothing at all of himself, and makes himself nothing, grows spiritual, and spirit does not occupy space. He can be north and south at the same time." These words moved the merchant's heart, and he cried out: "Then my fate is sealed!" "No, no," said the *maggid.* "You have already begun."

(*Buber, Early Masters, p. 108*)

This is a powerful story, mostly because of the reverberations it gives off: Rich and wise? North and south? Innerworldly and other-worldly? Secure and adventurous? Self-concerned and concerned for others? Saintly and humble? Bold and prudent? One could go on and on. Are we fated to seize one horn of the dilemma and let the other go, or to be torn apart by trying to assume both contradictory qualities at the same time?

The *maggid* in the story has an "answer": "He who thinks nothing at all of himself, and makes himself nothing, grows spiritual, and spirit does not occupy space. He can be north and south at the same time." We think the merchant's instinct was correct about the sealing of his fate, despite the *maggid*'s last rejoinder: "No, no, you have already begun."

We believe the *maggid* was on the right metaphysical track, but he did not quite get the answer on how to go north and south at the same time.

The spatial-spiritual metaphor is a sound direction. We suggest two additional reinforcing metaphors. When you travel north, you are also traveling south, because you will reach a point at which you will return to where you started: *home base.* Going north turns into going south.

This suggests an even more compelling metaphor. Every time you take a step to the north, you are also taking a step south into yourself (and vice versa). So the *maggid* was right: The merchant had already begun, to which we would add: "to go north and south." Once the merchant decided to go to the *maggid*'s house to study, he grew wiser and richer in a whole new way. Once he made a decision and followed through on it, he would grow wiser and less wealthy (in money), but in adding to his store of knowledge, going north, he went south into himself and became far richer. He changed himself radically (thus going south), while pursuing single-mindedly his goal of study (and thereby going north also).

When a person wholeheartedly decides to do something in the real world, he is also transforming himself in an immeasurably enriched way.

Make a decision and act on it, and choirs of angels will sing "Amen." One decisive act leads to another, and you become accustomed to listen to your non-repeating soul.

And what about the Messiah?

Every time you make a decision and act on it, you will discover an overwhelming truth about yourself. You will be different today from yesterday, and tomorrow from today. You will become your own savior, and we may have to find another reason for the coming of the Messiah.

Part V

EPILOGUE

18

The Legacy: The Impact of Hasidic Stories on Jewish People Today

Dissatisfaction

The Lizensker said: "When a person becomes dissatisfied with his business or profession, it is a sure sign that he is not conducting it honestly."

(*Newman, The Hasidic Anthology, p. 194*)

Good Sense

An author showed his work, "Good Grace," to Rabbi Geshon of Shkliv, and asked his opinion. "It is a good book," replied the rabbi, "but it has one defect; namely, it lacks the 'sense' mentioned in Proverbs 3:4: 'So shalt thou find grace and good sense.'"

(*Newman, The Hasidic Anthology, p. 122*)

After a year of immersion in Hasidic stories, we felt the need to explore their impact on us and our contemporaries. Though not religious, we identify closely with our Jewish cultural heritage. We define ourselves as Jews—lovingly, proudly, assertively.

We were surprised by the degree to which the key values of Hasidism continue to influence our lives. We hypothesize a similar influence on other Jews; hence, this chapter offers tentative assumptions about the influence of Hasidism in order to assess the logical and intuitive consequences.

Our criteria for selecting core Hasidic beliefs that continue to influence us are quite straightforward. We selected stories originally for their current relevance, and heard recurrent themes.

We dug into the subtext for hidden themes and integrated them into a *gestalt*. We are confident the diagnostic scheme that emerged will only partly surprise you, as it did us.

Hasidism was, from the start, a mass religious movement. A Talmudic religion was retooled to become suitable for a poor, simple, nonscholarly, depressed people who were excluded from God's chosen among "the chosen." Religion was simplified and made understandable to the general public. Hasidism became general currency among the masses because it allowed a direct communication to God. If you passionately want to touch God, you *will* touch God. And they did!

Within this populist-religious frame, the Hasidic rabbis created a distinctive amalgam of the mystical-esoteric literature of the Kabbala and the *halakha*—the vast body of Jewish law supplementing the scriptural law, especially the legal part of the Talmud. The result was a folksy culture that combined the mystical, the legal, and the practical, and consequently was preserved for us through stories and legends. The stories are of vital importance to us today, for they tell us about the active living norms—the common people's shared expectations of how to behave and what to believe. These Hasidic values preserved in the tales are the precipitates of Hasidim's daily conduct.

Hasidism has directly touched millions of Jews over the last 200 years. It is no longer a vast popular movement. We are examining the *residues*—residual norms and values—now considerably modified, that remain with us and in us, often subconsciously, and which are not easily forgotten even after generations. One reason they are not easily obliterated is that they continue to be useful.

To avoid misinterpretation we must warn that the source of the value system that makes up contemporary Jewish character is in no way exclusively Hasidic. Hasidism contributed importantly to the Jewish character, because of its popular mass base for 200 years, but many other sources and forces in Jewish history were of equal importance. It takes *chutzpah* to presume to say in one book what Hasidism is all about. Be that as it may, here is one definition: Hasidism is a different qualitative level of *self-consciousness*, with its forebears and contemporaries in Montaigne, Cervantes, Shakespeare, Voltaire, Goethe, and Dostoevsky. They all celebrated a revolutionary self-awareness that culminated in different ways in Marx or Freud.

By taking "self-consciousness" as the central thread, it is possible to illuminate the impact of Hasidism upon Jewish people today. Again, this exploratory-hypothetical interpretation is based on the study and analysis of several thousand Hasidic stories that stem from the eighteenth century and the first half of the nineteenth century (see Figure 18-1).

THE REVOLUTION OF SELF-CONSCIOUSNESS

1. *Faith in God.* By this phrase, the "revolution of self-consciousness," we mean the evolving awareness of ordinary people that everyone is unique, like God, and each has to find his own way to God. Each person is responsible for creating a unique spiritual partnership with God, which has two major outcomes. One group of believers, the mystics (comparable to our contemporary *gurus*), through altered states of consciousness, experienced an ecstatic communion with God. Total identification with God transported them daily to an extraterrestrial spiritual sphere.

This daily mystical communion was true of only a small percentage of Hasidim. The great mass of people were gradually educated by the rabbis and *tzaddikim* to a paradoxical faith in God: The way to show faith in God is to continue to maintain this faith even when receiving nothing in return from God. God owes you nothing; you owe everything to God. If that does not build character, nothing will!

The human representative of the godly way of life was the *tzaddik*. He was also very human. He modeled all the human

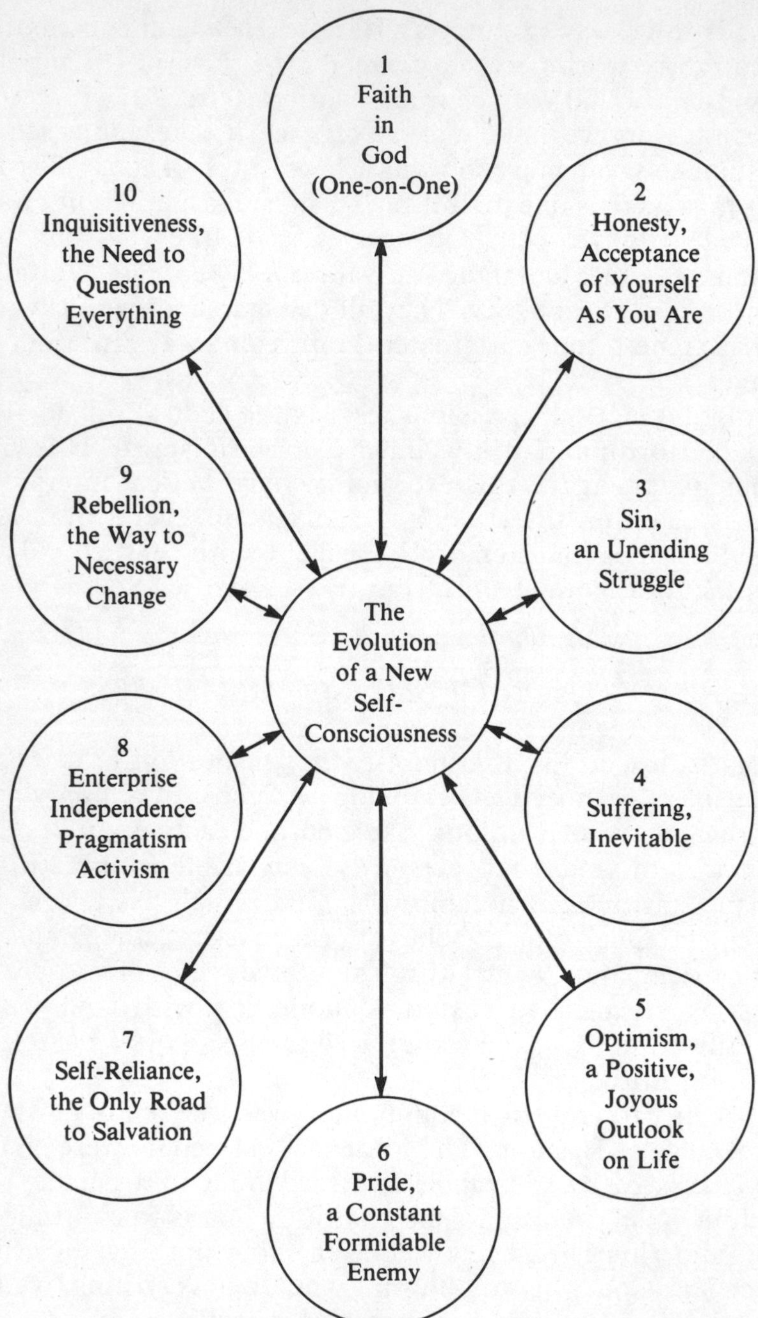

Figure 18-1. Main Elements in Early Hasidism's New Self-Consciousness

virtues in his constant struggle to overcome his human deficiencies. The new self-consciousness stressed not only virtuous behavior, but inner feelings and thoughts. This was a whole new concept.

It was not enough to act right; not enough at all, if it was not done wholeheartedly. Inner conviction now must match conduct. The Baal Shem made it quite clear—he could help anyone but a liar!

2. *Honesty.* Facing and accepting yourself becomes the key to serenity and wisdom. Accepting yourself certainly does not mean resigning yourself to who you are, but constantly improving yourself. But improvement cannot occur without ridding yourself of delusions, deceptions, and distortions about the real you.

In many stories, the rabbis alternately threaten and cajole their followers into accepting themselves wholeheartedly. Everything could be tolerated that was frankly admitted—a kind of mass purgation of sins, evil, unholy (sexual) thoughts, and dishonesty. Everything was grist for the honesty mill.

When you reflect deeply about these honesty "trips" and how they can affect you, you can become terrified. Despite all the defense mechanisms of which Freud has made us aware, it is difficult to hide yourself from yourself. Massive guilt was inevitable. And guilt became intolerable, because it included imagined culpability as well as real offenses. You were guilty if you committed or didn't commit an offense, as long as you harbored thoughts about committing sins. In the face of this onslaught, could anyone survive?

> The wicked flee when no man pursueth;
> but the righteous are bold as a lion.
>
> *Proverbs 28:1*

Is there enough courage in the world to deal with all this honesty and guilt? Is that why we need God? He not only is the one who can peer into our hearts to see all our unimaginable sins, but is the sole agent who can forgive us. And what happens to all the joy that abounds on earth in the face of all this abundant guilt? Clearly, something had to be done about sin.

3. *The Democratization of Sin.* One of the most useful social policies Hasidic leaders stressed was the democratization of sin. By "democratization" we mean sin favored equally everyone—all classes, all statuses, the learned and unlearned, rabbi and *tzaddik*, *tzaddik* and Hasid, male and female. Sin is an equal-opportunity employer! There were no hereditary distinctions. Sin appealed to the masses and favored equally the common people and the snobs. No one was exempt. Sin was universal, inescapable, and undeniable.

> Be sure your sin will find you out.
>
> *Numbers 32:23*

Sin, in part because of the revolution in self-consciousness, had really gotten out of control and had to be defused. The rabbis devised a variety of strategies to help their followers cope:

- Know that sin will always be plentiful and available, and the battle is endless.
- Remember, we, the rabbis and *tzaddikim*, suffer from sin just as you do.
- More sinful than sinning is dwelling on sins and becoming obsessed with sin.
- Concentrate on the future, not on the past: Stop sinning, and get on with your life.
- God in his wisdom assigns to sin an important role in ultimately doing good.
- Sin is punishment enough; undue repentance is unnecessary.
- A sin is undone by not repeating it.

A sin punishes itself:

> Whoso diggeth a pit shall fall therein.
>
> *Proverbs 26:27*

> There is no peace, saith the Lord, unto the wicked.
>
> *Isaiah 48:22*

The upshot of sin, as dealt with in the Hasidic stories, was to remove its sting and bite. It is pervasive but manageable. It is human—God realizes that. Don't make too much of it. Stop it, and forgive yourself. Be wary: Satan is tricky and treacherous. What is important is how you deal with sin. Don't permit it to overwhelm and immobilize you. And above all, there is nothing wrong with you for having sinful thoughts—we all do.

4. *Suffering.* The word "suffer" suggests acceptance or passivity rather than courage or patience in response to pain. Zealous rabbis were active, even aggressive, in attacking pain and suffering. Two main approaches, which are not mutually exclusive, for overcoming suffering are revealed in the stories.

One approach is to enter what we call today an altered state of consciousness. Through intense prayer, meditation, self-hypnosis and concentrated use of the imagination, assume a trance. This profound absorption or abstraction often includes varying degrees of suspended animation. This state of semiconsciousness mutes or eliminates physical pain.

Psychic suffering, the kind stemming from the loss of a family member, was approached by cognitively reframing suffering as either good because it will lead to goodness, or good in itself because it tests faith in God. Good and evil, like suffering, are both really good because they are God-given. Our limited mortal understanding puts labels of good and evil on actions and events, and those distinctions are not valid from a Divine perspective.

We have a surprising hypothesis about suffering. We feel that neither ecstatic, altered states of consciousness nor reframing the meaning of suffering has worked or taken hold among the masses of Jews during the eighteenth and nineteenth centuries, nor, as a matter of fact, in this century.

In today's view, suffering is to be avoided at all costs. The notion that suffering can lead to a higher good, or is good in itself, is not a Jewish norm. The various forms of brainwashing, from hypnosis to laughter therapy, to combat pain and suffering have limited success today, but they may expand in the future. What is emerging forcefully is the idea that ideas and feelings can affect the body's physical functioning, giving new impetus to believers in the power of positive thinking and positive feeling. This was the centerpiece of *kavvana*, the new Hasidic self-consciousness.

5. *Optimism.* A persistent outlook of joy and wonder in everything God has created is the distinctive emblem of Hasidism. Joy ideally permeates every moment in prayer, work, home, friendship, song, dance, and even death. Joy is the most powerful characterological residue that the Hasidim bequeathed to the Jewish people today, the Holocaust notwithstanding.

Joy is active and forward-looking. Joy is buoyant—it floats. Joy overflows. Joy conquers. Joy always raises you when you are down. Joy warms the heart, brightens the face and invigorates the body. Joy begets joy.

Joy makes everything good and beautiful. Joy knows everything will be better. Joy cheerfully tolerates unbelievers in joy.

The Jewish people's unquenchable joy in life despite suffering, misery, persecution, and the wanton mass destruction of millions of innocent Jews is the single most distinctive bequest from Hasidism. In fact, some believe the Jews' faith in joy today after the Holocaust is obscene.

Joy abounds among Jews today not only because it is taught and reinforced from childhood, but because joy itself stimulates a continuous joyous life:

> He that is of a merry heart hath a continuous feast.
>
> *Proverbs 15:15*

6. *Pride.* According to one definition, pride as reasonable or justifiable self-respect or as the joy and delight in a notable action, is eminently proper and desirable. However, the new self-consciousness was inordinately vulnerable to exaggerated self-esteem.

Arrogance, haughtiness, an overbearing manner were attacked with sharp caustic wit and every barbed tool at the Hasidim's command. In fact, a *mensch* can be defined as someone who is not haughty.

In story after story, the Hasidim waged a relentless war against the vain and the prideful, particularly inveighing against haughty rabbis. This vehement opposition to arrogance among Jews is a potent residue of Hasidism.

We are all familiar with the biblical injunction against pride:

Pride goeth before destruction, and a haughty spirit before a fall.
Proverbs 16:18

This injunction was strongly embraced by the Hasidim and undoubtedly exerted a major role in the waning influence and downfall of the "high and mighty" rabbis.

7. *Self-reliance* and *Enterprise.* These two qualities, for Jewish people, are interrelated and interactive. The dependence upon oneself as the road to personal salvation also embraces an activistic and initiating outlook on life. The world exists to be acted upon. There are no guarantees in life; independent activity is essential to make something happen. God does not really provide, and therefore it is up to you to do so. These two traits, self-reliance and entrepreneurship are powerfully interlinked in the Hasidic tradition and in their legacy to us today.

Hasidism emerged in opposition to the *mitnagdim* who stressed the spiritual value of scholarly study of the Bible and its commentaries. The wealthy were highly regarded because they supported the scholarly studies of the rabbis. It was a closed, self-perpetuating system that excluded the poor Jews—ninety-percent of the Jewish population—from the charmed circles of the rich and scholarly famous.

When the Baal Shem Tov initiated the Hasidic revolution to break up this arrogant cabal, he removed a plug from the repression that downgraded and degraded mundane work and activities. Daily life was sanctified. Each Hasid could connect to God, not only through prayer and study, but through wholehearted dedication in any mundane activity. The repressive dam burst. The entrepreneurial spirit was sanctified, and only later was it categorically profaned as the secular and sacred worlds were split into separate spheres. This dichotomy today for Jews and Gentiles alike makes a mockery of a spiritual life guided by God.

The two characterological qualities, self-reliance and entrepreneurship, have proved of inestimable value in the rapid expansion of the capitalistic system.

8. *Rebelliousness.* Without doubt a strong streak of rebelliousness runs through the Jewish character. Hasidism was founded by a rebel, the Baal Shem Tov, who always remained the father of the movement.

Hasidim were not stupid. Life changes, people change, perhaps God Himself changes. Change is necessary, though sometimes painful. What was extraordinary about the Hasidim was their flat-out welcome to the deviant, the innovator, the challenger of the *status quo.* Bored by the tired old cliches of the super-virtuous. Hasidim yearned for creativity. Imitation was reviled, and innovation was admired.

Rebelliousness encouraged Jews to think for themselves, and for individuals and groups to split off and form their own independent programs. There remains to this day a potent critical counter-dependent stripe in the Jewish character. Every Jewish leader was eventually opposed by the people or by individuals who sought change. Even God was never exempt from challenge: Some religious leaders after the Holocaust, declared Him to be dead.

Underlying rebelliousness is potent to this day.

9. *Inquisitiveness.*

A man should live if only to satisfy his curiosity (Ayalti 1949).

A Jew cannot be too inquisitive in both the positive and negative meanings of the term. Jews examine, investigate and ponder everything. Jews are also a prying people—impertinently, officiously and presumptuously interrogative about every visible and invisible phenomenon in the universe. The desire to know why a thing ticks, how it ticks, what ticks, and when and where it ticks, and how tick is related to tock can go on forever. This desire to get to the bottom of things often suggests to bystanders an objectionable intrusiveness or officiousness. Curiosity can be seen as impertinent and meddling.

Jews are meddlesome, aggressively so, hence the introduction of *chutzpah* into the English language. They may exceed the bounds of propriety in showing interest, doggedly pursuing, and then offering hypotheses about everything. This often can be tactless, interfering, and unwelcome. Although some would decry these negative consequences of an overactive curiosity, it is in reality the basis of a vigorous intellect. Jews will probe and probe, and even break a thing to find out what it is. They question everything, because this stimulates them to find answers. A question is never embarrassing.

Hasidism played a unique role in directing Jews' inquisitiveness in new directions. Hasidism inherited two main lines of inquiry that evolved over hundreds of years. One line of inquiry consisted of piling up commentaries and interpretations primarily of the Torah, the five books of Moses, which were built cumulatively upon each other and resulted in the magnificently systematic, scholarly, and rationalistic Babylonian and Palestinian Talmuds. This solid authoritative body of Jewish tradition is a monument to the Jewish people's delight and love of probing in fascinating and exhaustive detail. Every question an answer raises, and every answer a question raises, in an endless circuit. The miles of Talmudic inquiry were exact, methodical, and logical.

At the other end of the pendulum was the Kabbala, a medieval system of Jewish mysticism characterized by the manipulation of letters and numbers in interpreting the Bible. This modality of mystical insight was profoundly irrational and subjective, as befits hidden mysteries and esoteric secrets.

Hasidism synthesized both these modalities and created a unique brand of inquiry. We will try to be precise although the subject matter does not quite lend itself to methodical inquiry. Hence, the following propositions are exploratory and hypothetical:

We believe that the Hasidim transmuted their interest in hidden mysteries from the occult to matters of the heart. The whole new world of inner feelings and fantasies, the human psyche and such psychological issues as despondency, anxieties, obsessions, motivation, sin, pride, integrity—the new self-consciousness—began to preoccupy their inquiring minds.

The other transformation was the refocusing of the Hasidic rabbis' attention from Talmudic study in the *yeshiva* to the study of human relationships and practical problems of daily life.

These two revolutions were momentous for the Jewish people. The Jews' prodigious powers of inquiry were now let loose to investigate thoroughly what motivates people individually, how people love and fight and negotiate, and how to attain a life of joy, wisdom, and serenity.

It is no accident that the Hasidim used the story as their

vehicle for transmitting the fruits of their new inquiries and new self-consciousness.

Why the story? The Bible is mostly story, the Talmud has stories, parents always have told children stories; the nonscholarly masses could learn best through stories. The story is a marvelous mixture of fact and fantasy for teaching new truths about Hasidic life and practice as well as human nature in general.

The Hasidim literally had a new story to tell. They invented a new culture. They told that "story" by telling tales about their way of serving God and living together. The story of the Hasidic movement lies in the tales the rabbis told each other and their Hasidim. The Hasidic movement achieved its distinctive role in Jewish history by consolidating its values and culture through storytelling and using the story to tell the world about Hasidism. This book continues that process. The Hasidic stories became Hasidism's Talmud.

DID HASIDISM BROKER MARX, FREUD, AND EINSTEIN?

We think the early founders of Hasidism, particularly the Baal Shem Tov, would appreciate the awesome irony of this outrageous question.

All the residues discussed in the previous section clustered around *kavvana,* the new self-consciousness that permutes in many different combinations. Hasidism was the midwife in the evolution of Jewish life from scholasticism and mysticism to enlightenment and secularism.

The Hasidic approach essentially was to facilitate the wholehearted connection of each Hasid's soul to God's spirit. And in the short-term this approach was spectacularly successful. What went wrong?

The liberation of Jews from scholasticism coincided with the rise of capitalism, modernity, and democracy. The new consciousness begot an independent, nationalistic, pragmatic, robustly optimistic, smart entrepreneur, who left God further and further behind, the more successful he became in the aggressive bourgeois society.

Secular Jews rebelled against the Hasidim as the latter had against the *mitnagdim.* The rebellious utopian-scientists became Marxists. The self-searchers dug deeper and became Freudians. The inquisitive turned to the scientific study of the physical world and became Einsteins. And the entrepreneurs became Rothschilds. Secular spiritualists became *gurus.* And the other permutations produced a magnificent array of professionals who rapidly rose to top positions in their fields.

WHAT IT ALL MEANS—FINALLY

This is a ridiculous assertion. It reminds us of the hoary joke about "What is life?" Answer: "A cup of tea." *Pause.* After listener's surprise, "You mean it is not a cup of tea?"

Yes, we do have to be more specific about "what it all means" in the context of this chapter, which is about Hasidism's brokerage role in the prodigious transformation of the Jewish people from a traditional-ritualistic religious community to a secular-humanistic society. Hasidism brought individuals closer to God while promoting individualistic, entrepreneurial self-help egos. The unintentional outcome was not entirely unpredictable to the Hasidim—they knew Promethean forces were being unleashed and fought valiantly against their successful followers' overweening pride. Hasidism, or something like it, would have had to be invented to serve as a midwife into secularism from traditional-orthodox scholasticism.

Is there a story that could shed light on such a momentous metamorphosis of Jewish life? We must do some tinkering, in fact, turn the following story "on its head":

The Two Strangers

In Psalm 119, the psalmist says to God: "I am a sojourner on the earth, hide not Thy commandments from me."

Concerning this verse, Rabbi Barukh said: "He whom life drives into exile and who comes to a land alien to him, has nothing in common with the people there, and not a soul he can

> talk to. But if a second stranger appears, even though he may come from quite a different place, the two can confide in each other, and live together henceforth, and cherish each other. And had they not both been strangers, they would never have known such close companionship. That is what the psalmist means: 'You, even as I, are a sojourner on earth and have no abiding place for your glory. So do not withdraw from me, but reveal your commandments, that I may become your friend."
>
> (*Buber, Early Masters, p. 89*)

The above story speaks to man's sojourn on earth and his need for a continuous supportive relationship with God. "Look here," says man to God, "my sojourn is all too brief. I will therefore be able to pay limited homage. Be a good sport and let me know what I have to do. I really want to be your friend."

The metaphor the storyteller uses is the stranger in an alien land who links up with another stranger, and through their bond builds up a close supportive friendship.

This is a super story for any religious person who may be experiencing some estrangement from God. Rabbi Barukh's metaphor is apt in helping a Hasid, or any believer in God, realize that it takes time to develop a friendship with God, and that as it evolves He will certainly inform you of His "needs" (i.e., commandments) as occurs in every friendship.

And now for some heresy as we turn the above story on its head. Most Jews today are not very religious. God is no longer in the center of our lives as He was with the Hasidim; but He is still around and mostly with us if we lead fairly decent lives. As Charlie Chaplin says in *Monsieur Verdoux*, in response to a priest who asks him to repent, "My quarrel is with man ('society'), not God."

Here is how we would rework the above story in heretical modern garb:

The Two Strangers

> In Psalm 119, the psalmist says to God: "I am a sojourner on the earth, hide not Thy commandments from me."
>
> Concerning this verse, Rabbi Polsky-Wozner said: "Wherever you go and however far you distance yourself from our

established traditions, and because of your independent spirit, have not another soul to talk to, do not dismay because God will continue to confide in you and you will cherish each other. God, too, is a sojourner, and had not both of you been 'strangers,' you would never have known such close friendship.

"So do your thing. This may drive you into 'exile', and your native society may become alien, and you may have very little in common with the people there, and not a soul to talk to.

"But just as you will always have God (as long as you remain a basically decent fellow), a second stranger will certainly appear, even though he may come from quite a different place, and you two will be able to confide in each other and cherish each other.

"And had you not been strangers, you would never have known such close companionship. That is what the psalmist means: 'You, even as I, are sojourners on earth and have no abiding place for our glory. Do not withdraw. Let us understand our heritage and whence we came, that we may remain fast friends.'"

AMEN

POSTSCRIPT

The Story of Stories in This World and the World to Come

A young competent disciple told his rabbi that he did not want to leave him. The rabbi insisted that the young disciple was ready to go forth on his own. Every day, the disciple found excuses to stay with the rabbi. However, the rabbi firmly repeated to the disciple it was time for him to leave.

One day, the disciple asked his rabbi: "Is there any sign that could let me know that indeed I was ready to leave?"

The rabbi then told his disciple a story: "A rich, unhappy man once sought penance from his rabbi. After the rabbi was convinced that the rich man truly desired penance, he told him the following: 'Go to Reborovitz where there are many poor Jews and give away all your money in such a way that no one will know that you are the benefactor.'

"The rich man was shocked at such a severe penance, but he nevertheless proceeded to make plans to leave for Reborovitz. Before he left, he asked the rabbi: 'And how will I know that my penance is performed properly?'

"The rabbi replied: 'When someone comes to you to tell you his story.'"

APPENDIX

The Linguistic Foundation of Hasidic Stories (or: Why Truth Should Never Get in the Way of Telling a Good Story)

For better and worse, language is a communal enterprise and herein lies its soaring majesty and its severest restrictions. Rabbi Bunam thoughtfully considered the limitations of language:

All and Each

Rabbi Bunam once said:

"On a Sabbath, when my room is full of people, it is difficult for me to 'say Torah.' For each person requires his own Torah, and each wishes to find his own perfection. And so what I give to all I withhold from each."

(*Buber, Late Masters, p. 248*)

In this story, "Torah" stands for "instruction" in the broadest sense, and we are using it as a metaphor for a "story." So how can a story instruct everyone when each individual is unique and requires his own story?

The irony, of course, is that we all can understand the difficulty of a story appealing to many people when each person is unique! Rabbi Bunam would reply that in telling a story from which everyone can learn something, he also withheld from each individual a uniquely personal message.

Our tale about communication through stories becomes even more complicated in the following story, which contradicts it:

How to Become a Hasid

> Rabbi Mendel said:
>
> "I became a Hasid because in the town where I lived there was an old man who told stories about *tzaddikim.* He told what he knew, and I heard what I needed."
>
> (*Buber, Late Masters, p. 270*)

This story introduces a new kettle of fish. First of all, it flatly contradicts the previous story. Rabbi Bunam tells us he cannot craft a special story for every individual, and therefore he robs every individual.

Rabbi Mendel is "telling" Rabbi Bunam that he is too hard on himself: "Just tell what you know, and trust each listener to take what he needs." Rabbi Bunam's response would be that in telling a story for all, he dilutes its potency.

If both stories are true, then they are also both false unless we can find a more general proposition that can encompass the "truth" about both stories. One solution is that a story can be both general enough to appeal to many different people and yet specific enough to serve different people, depending on how it is crafted linguistically. Underlying the stories is a linguistic foundation that creates a general form which can mean different things to different listeners.

This is why both stories are true, although each one contradicts the other. Every story is purposely incompletely told so that the listener can fill in his or her necessary details.

The best linguistic tool designed to help people accurately connect language to experience is called the "meta-model," developed by Richard Bandler and John Grinder (1975).

The fundamental idea behind the meta-model is that language is *not* experience but *represents* experience, the way a map represents a physical territory. The map is not the territory, and language is not the experience; the meta-model guides us in making sense out of our experience by using the most accurate language to represent it.

When we grossly dilute or falsify an actual experience by using very general terms, deleting and omitting vital information or distorting by exaggeration, we are violating one or another meta-model principle. This violation of specificity and accuracy in storytelling is purposely done to force the listener to fill in the missing parts with his own experience, and thereby to make it his own.

Let us briefly review ten important meta-model violations which enable the storyteller to weave a story in which the listener is impelled to supply information, ideas and feelings from his own personal experience. Examples are the two stories just discussed.

DELETION

Deletion is omitting information that tells us specifics of the story. In the following sentence, the reader will observe, in somewhat more detail, the deleted information and begin to get a fuller picture of the experience the story is omitting.

"I became a Hasid because in the *town* where I lived there was an *old man* who told *stories* about *tzaddikim."* Here are some of the deletions in that sentence:

"I became"	— when did you become?
"town"	— which town?
"old man"	— who?
"stories"	— which stories?
tzaddikim	— which *tzaddikim*?

There are many deletions in each of these two brief stories.

LACK OF REFERENTIAL INDEX

The lack of specific and accurate language leaves out details important for an understanding of the issue in the story. It generalizes without indicating any background references, and therefore the communication lacks perspective, proportion and clarity. This is intended to activate the listener to provide the requisite detail and richness of context. To challenge the lack of referential index, you ask: Who specifically? Or, what specifically?

For example: "Each [person] wishes to find his own perfection."

Lack of referential index: Who, specifically wishes? What, specifically, is "perfection"?

Another example of lack of referential index: "He told what he knew." Who, specifically, is he ("the old man")? What, specifically, did he know (about *tzaddikim*)?

UNSPECIFIED VERBS

If someone says merely that he is tired, it could be from running several miles, constant pressure on the job or anxiety about a sick child. Verb specifications connect a person more clearly and substantially to the experience that is described. The challenge to unspecified verbs is: how specifically?

Examples of unspecified verbs:

"And so what I give to all I withhold from each."

How, specifically, Rabbi Bunam, do you manage that neat trick? How do you give to all and withhold from each?

"And I heard what I needed."

How did you, Rabbi Mendel, separate what you needed from what you didn't need? How did you manage to hear what you needed?

NOMINALIZATIONS

Nominalization is the process of transforming verbs, ongoing processes, into nouns so that they become a fixed thing or event. Thus, instead of seeing the continuing process which is "in the verb," nominalization makes the process finished and into an event that is concluded. The illustration Bandler (1978) uses is visualizing a wheelbarrow in which you can put a pencil, yourself, your hat, etc.; but how about success, struggle, learning, happiness? To change a nominalization into an ongoing action, use a verb in place of the noun.

For example:

"Each person requires his own Torah" becomes "Each person constantly develops his own way of studying Torah. . . ."

"Each wishes to find his own perfection" can become "Each finds ways of becoming what he wishes to become."

"He told what he knew" becomes "He told what he was most excited about, which is . . ." or "what he himself was thinking about recently, which is . . ."

The central point is that finishing off a process by turning it into an event or thing means that people are deprived of choices to keep changing and to be connected to an ongoing dynamic process. Storytellers tend to work in modes of sharp distinctions—black-and-white, either/or, this or that, was or is, there or not there, doing or not doing, know or don't know—rather than the multihued, ambiguous, ongoing dynamic processes of which our lives really consist. It is a rare storyteller who will let truth get in the way of telling a story.

UNIVERSAL QUANTIFIERS

"All," "every," "never," "always," "everywhere," "nobody" are "universal quantifiers." By challenging a person's universal quantifiers, one finds exceptions and, therefore, more choices for dealing with the situation.

A storyteller likes to keep his story neat, clean, clear-cut, definite and universal, and abhors the niceties, exceptions, and ambiguities. Universal quantifiers abound in all stories.

For example:

"Each person requires his own Torah."

"Each wishes to find his own perfection."

"I give to all."

"I withhold from each."

MODAL OPERATORS OF NECESSITY

"Have to," "it's necessary," "must," "no alternative," "can't," "forced to" are modal operators of necessity. They place severe limits on further action, and they limit choices. Again the storyteller heightens the drama of the story by employing this violation of the meta-model.

The challenge to a "must," "have to," or "can't" is to ask: "What stops you?" Or, "What would happen if you did?" "What forces him to . . ."

For example:

"For each person requires his own Torah."

"Each wishes to find his own perfection."

CAUSE AND EFFECT

"Cause and effect" is a shorthand way to say that someone believes that one person's action, feeling, thought or belief can cause another person to feel in a certain way and create an inner emotional state. Here again, the further implication is that *because* someone is making me feel angry, resentful, anxious or happy, I have little choice to respond otherwise and am controlled emotionally by outsiders. If X causes Y, the challenge is, "How does X cause Y?"

For example: "When my room is full of people, it is difficult for me to 'say Torah.' For each person requires his own Torah, and each wishes to find his own perfection."

Assuming that Rabbi Bunam is right, how do those attitudes make it difficult for him? Can they also be an advantage, for example?

Storytellers heighten the drama by using "cause and effect" to intensify the conflict and complicate the resolution.

MIND READING

"Mind reading" is the reputed ability to know what another person is thinking or feeling without being told. The subject can respond to the mind reading by asking the mind reader how he knows this to be true.

Stories abound with mind reading. It enables the storyteller to establish the characters, plot, complications, and resolution quickly and get directly to the punch line.

For example: "He told us what he knew."

How do you know that he did not tell about some things he knew, or perhaps about things that he did not know? He could not tell everything that he knew.

"For each person requires his own Torah."

"Each wishes to find his own perfection."

Rabbi Bunam, as far as I know, never took a poll of his followers or even asked them informally. So how does Rabbi Bunam know this? He doesn't; he is mind reading.

LOST PERFORMATIVE

In setting the stage for a story, or introducing a complication, heightening the conflict, a storyteller often will introduce a statement or a judgment in the form of a generalization about "life," "people," "the world" that everyone naturally accepts. Thus, the "lost performative" is a situation in which the speaker's assumption about a generalized truth really belongs to him, not to everyone. In other words, the speaker is "laying a trip" on others. The challenge to the lost performative is: for whom? Or according to whom?

Examples:

"For each person requires his own Torah."

"Each wishes to find his own perfection."

* * *

We want to add a generalization of our own that we feel is smuggled into storytelling, one which can add or detract from the impact of a story. Each story contains "hidden assumptions" about the nature of man, the world, human relationships, the conduct of life. Hidden assumptions can include ideas, feelings and beliefs about how to influence people, how to learn, how to raise children and so on.

Let us go back to our two familiar stories (with Rabbis Bunam and Mendel) to point out significant assumptions about how people learn and are influenced:

All and Each

Rabbi Bunam once said:

"On a Sabbath, when my room is full of people, it is difficult for me to say 'Torah.' For each person requires his own Torah, and each wishes to find his own perfection. And so what I give to all I withhold from each."

(*Buber, Late Masters, p. 248*)

How He Became a Hasid

Rabbi Mendel said:

"I became a Hasid because in the town where I lived there was an old man who told stories about *tzaddikim*. He told what he knew, and I heard what I needed."

(*Buber, Late Masters, p. 270*)

Rabbi Bunam is assuming that each individual requires a specially created "Torah" or instruction. And since he is addressing many people, he assumes he will have to enlighten many and will therefore be less particularly effective with each individual. He seems to emphasize that different followers require different instruction.

Rabbi Mendel assumes just the opposite: The storyteller says what he knows, from which each listener will select what is useful for him.

Neither Rabbi Bunam nor Rabbi Mendel was aware of how storytelling violates the meta-model, thereby enabling each listener to participate actively and to get out of the story what both listener and storyteller put into it.

Today we know (here comes a "lost performative") that storytelling by its very nature, structure, and linguistic foundation heavily involves the listeners in co-participant and cocreator roles.

That is the point about stories—they interweave the lives of listeners into the storyteller's tale.

In the controversy we have created between Rabbi Bunam and Rabbi Mendel, we would have to ("modal operator of necessity") stand with Rabbi Mendel. But we also believe that Rabbi Bunam secretly (and openly) would be pleased ("mind reading" and "cause and effect") that his story helped ("unspecified verb") us understand better the profound teaching ("nominalization") of Rabbi Mendel.

And, needless to say, Rabbi Mendel would be pleased at Rabbi Bunam's gratification ("mind reading").

SUMMARY

We have detailed the linguistic mechanisms through which the storyteller stimulates the reader to fill in his own subjective reality. Of course, the largest part of that subjective reality is shared by other members of his group, family, religion and society. That is what we mean by a common cultural heritage, a set of shared beliefs and values about ourselves and the world. The stories reflect, modify and add to a culture in a never-ending process.

The story's situation is unspecified and is shaped in a way that leads the reader to fill in spontaneously the missing pieces in the general outlines. The storyteller knows the cues that signal the reader to go inside himself rather than to seek the what, who, when and where, which are found in a good newspaper article. The storyteller's job is to make something real that has a lot missing and makes an impact only by the listener's filling in the pieces from his subjective life situation, thereby making that story part of him and his subjective reality.

GLOSSARY

Ari: Rabbi Isaac Luria, a major Jewish mystic who lived in Safed. His teachings are recorded in the books of his disciple Hayyim Vital (1543–1620). His name, *Ari*, is an acronym of *A*shkenazi *R*abbi *I*saac. In Hebrew, the acronym also means "a lion," hence his disciples most often referred to him as *Haari Hakddosh*, "the holy lion."

Ashkenazi (pl. Ashkenazim): a term applied to German Jews since the ninth century. At later periods it was extended to include all Yiddish-speaking Jews and their descendants.

Baal Shem: literally "a master of names": a person who heals the sick, exorcises demons, writes amulets, and performs miracles by using the magical power of divine names.

Beit Midrash: (House of Study): usually, the small downstairs synagogue used for daily prayers and Talmudic study. The main, upstairs synagogue was used on Sabbaths and holidays. The *beit midrash* was more than a place of learning and worship. Travelers without lodging were often put up in the House of Study.

Book of Splendor: the *Zohar*, the foremost work of Jewish mysticism, composed in Aramaic during the thirteenth century as a commentary on the Pentateuch. The Zohar maintains that all things contain a divine element. God is everything, and everything is united in him.

Day of Atonement (Yom Kippur): the last of the "Ten Days of Turning" (repentance) which commence with the New Year (Rosh Hashana). It is a day of fasting and uninterrupted prayer for forgiveness.

Days of Awe: the days between Rosh Hashana and the Day of Atonement.

Deveikut: act of devotional cleaving to God in meditative or ecstatic communion with God (*unio mystica*); a key concept in Hasidism, representing the ultimate goal of the religious life and spiritual endeavor.

Divine Nothingness: See Habad. The *Habad* movement, organized by Shneur Zalman of Liadi and based upon the teachings of the Great *Maggid*, held that the Divine is without limitation and opposed to all "something," which is limited. The Divine is the "nothing" that subsumes all limitation and finiteness.

Elijah: According to legend, after his ascent to heaven the prophet Elijah continued to help and instruct the world of man in his function as a messenger of God. He appears at every *brit mila* (circumcision) and at every Passover Seder. There are many legends about righteous men and scholars who have seen Elijah in their dreams and received instruction from him in the mysteries of the Torah.

Elisha: the disciple and successor of Elijah the prophet.

Evil Urge: the inclination to evil, which is opposed to "the inclination to good." It is not considered as evil *per se*, but as a power abused by men. It is rather the "passion" in which all human action originates. Man is called upon to serve God "with both inclinations," directing his passion toward the good and the holy.

Frankists: followers of Jacob Frank (1726–1791), a pseudo-Messiah who taught and practiced a perverse mystical faith marked by violent antinomianism. Frank and most of his followers converted to Christianity, and the movement ended with his death.

Gabbai (pl. Gabbaim): usually the sexton or secretary of the synagogue of the Hasidic rebbe and his court.

Galut: exile, the dispersion of Israel among the nations outside their own land.

Gaon: 'Eminence,' originally a title for the heads of the leading rabbinic academies of Babylon between the sixth and twelfth centuries, and since then a term applied to outstanding rabbinic scholars. In a personal and unqualified context 'the *Gaon*' generally refers to Rabbi Elijah of Vilna (the Vilna Gaon), renowned for his extraordinary scholarship and the leader of the early movement against Hasidism (died 1797). In modern Hebrew, *gaon* means genius.

Gemara: literally completion (of the teaching); that which is fully learned. It consists of commentaries upon and discussions of the Mishna, the first written codification of the oral Torah and the basic section of the Talmud. The Gemara of the Talmud of Jerusalem and that of the far more extensive Babylonian Talmud (*Talmud Bavli*) were composed between the third and the sixth centuries C.E., one in Western Aramaic, and the other in an Eastern Aramaic idiom.

Goyim: literally nations, peoples; Gentiles, non-Jews.

Habad: an acronym of the Hebrew words *Hokhma* (wisdom), *Bina* (understanding), and *Daat* (knowledge); the Hasidic sect established by Rabbi Shneur Zalman of Liadi in Russia.

Halakha: the religious, ethical, civil, and criminal Jewish laws and ordinances as they have been formulated in the Mishna and the Babylonian and Jerusalemian Talmuds and the literature related to these main bodies of oral law.

Hasid (pl. Hasidim): In current usage, it applies to a member of the religious mystical movement which emerged in the Ukraine and southern Poland in the middle of the eighteenth century and later spread to other parts of eastern and central Europe. At the present time, Israel and the United States are the main centers of this movement.

Hasidism: the pietistic movement founded by Rabbi Israel Baal Shem Tov.

Hasidut: Hasidism.

Haskala: the movement of "enlightenment," an attempt to bring secular knowledge and discipline into Jewish education. The *maskilim* were the founders and participants in this movement.

Heder: a private elementary Hebrew school.

Hitbodedut: Hebrew for "aloneness." The act of seeking solitude, of steeping oneself in solitude, in order to attain perfect communion with God.

Hitahavut: enthusiasm, fervor, ecstasy.

Isaac Luria: See Ari.

Kabbala: Jewish mystical doctrines and their systems, which developed in southern France and Spain from the twelfth century on, and subsequently spread into Palestine, North Africa, Yemen, and eastern Europe.

Kavanna (pl. Kavvanot): "intention, devotion"; the intention directed toward God while performing a (religious) deed. In the *Kabbala*, *kavvanot* denote the permutations of the divine name that aim at overcoming the separation of forces in the Upper World.

Lamdan: one who is well versed in rabbinical lore.

Learning (study): to learn in the Jewish sense of the word is to occupy oneself with the study of the Bible, the Talmud, and the later rabbinical literature, for its own sake. The duty of "learning" is considered binding on all males throughout their lives and forms a more or less large and very often important part of the lives of all classes of Jews.

Lilith: A female demon that seduces men.

Maggid (pl. maggidim): a Jewish and often itinerant preacher. Customarily, the preacher's discourse would draw upon a biblical text, which would be embellished by parables drawn from the rabbinical commentaries and folklore. The most popular *maggidim* created original parables of distinction which were later assembled and published.

Messenger of the Messiah (i.e., the Prophet Elijah): According to Jewish legend, the Prophet Elijah has been God's constant messenger to mankind. He gives help in need, guidance in uncertainty, and, as a forerunner of the Messiah, as arouser and summoner, he is destined, to prepare a sluggish mankind for the coming of the Messiah.

Messiah (Greek form of the Hebrew "Mashiah"): "the Anointed." The man anointed by God to bring salvation to the world at the end of time. He will end the exile of Israel and restore the Kingdom of God, which will then be established over the entire world.

Midrash: literally, study; more especially, the interpretation of scripture that goes beyond the literal meaning of the text. The *midrashim* (pl. of *midrash*) are the many collections of these interpretations of the various biblical books. They contain a wonderful mass of legends, parables, stories, similes, and sayings.

Mishna: the first written codification of the Oral Law (*Torah She-be'alpeh*), which supplemented the written Torah. Compiled in Hebrew in the second and third centuries C.E., it is the basic portion of the Talmud.

Mitnagdim: opponents (of Hasidism) were so called. Today, the term is applied loosely to non-Hasidic Jews.

Mitzva (pl. Mitzvot): literally, a "commandment"; by extension, the performance of a good deed.

Niggun (pl. Niggunim): a melody or popular song introduced by a Hasidic rebbe or his court.

Nistarim (sing. *Nistar*): 'anonymous'; a group of mostly itinerant mystics who concealed their identities and undertook the dual task of encouraging and assisting their co-religionists and spreading the teachings of Jewish mysticism. Active mostly in the seventeenth and early eighteenth centuries, the *Nistarim* were the forerunners of the Hasidic movement.

Rabbanim: plural of rav (master), as well as of rabbi (literally, "my master"). But rav and rabbi are titles for religious teachers, rav designating the religious judge, and rabbi the religious leader of the congregation. However, the functions of the rav and those of the rabbi may at times be performed by the same person.

Rabbi Akiva: one of the most influential figures, celebrated in legend, among the early masters of the Oral Law and among the earliest to record his teachings in writing. He helped Simon bar Kochba, the "Son of the Star," in his great revolt against Roman Emperor Hadrian (132–135 C.E.) and died a martyr.

Ransom Money: the Hasid, visiting the *tzaddik* hands him together with a Note of Request, a sum of money. This sum is taken to be a "ransom" for the soul of the applicant.

Return of the Souls (Gilgul, i.e., cycle): doctrine of the transmigration of souls, developed in the Kabbala under Oriental influences, systematized chiefly by Isaac Luria, and from this source taken over by Hasidim.

Sanctification of the Name (of God): designates every sacrificial act of man; by it man participates in the establishment of the Kingdom of God on earth. The death of a martyr is the highest instance of Sanctification of the Name.

Sephardi (pl. Sephardim): a term applied to Spanish and Portuguese Jews and their descendants who, after the expulsion of the Jews from Spain in 1492, settled in Mediterranean countries and, in smaller numbers, in western Europe.

Seven Shepherds: mentioned in the Bible (Micah. 5:4), and identified by the Talmud (*Sukka 52 b*) as Adam, Seth, Methuselah, Abraham, Jacob, Moses, and David.

Shabbetai Tzvi: born in Smyrna, Turkey, in 1626. He proclaimed himself Messiah; central figure of the greatest messianic movement in the history of the Diaspora. The movement broke down and its founder embraced Islam.

Shekhina: "indwelling," the "glory" of God, the presence of God in the world. The Divine Spirit, which does not dwell in the world but rests entirely in itself, is called *Elohut* ("Divinity"), that is, the divine side of God, in no way comprehensible by man.

Shulhan Arukh: *The Set Table.* Title of the most popular compilation of the rabbinical laws regulating the practices of Judaism. It was written in 1555 by Joseph Caro (1488–1575).

Sparks: according to the Kabbala, in the primeval creation of the world, the divine light-substance burst and the "sparks" fell into the lower depths, filling the "shells" of the things and creatures of our world.

Talmud (learning, teaching): canonical collection of the Oral Law. Judaism holds that, along with the "written teaching" contained in the Bible, an "oral teaching" had also been revealed, which, from Moses' time on, was transmitted by word of mouth from generation to generation. The Oral Law was finally edited and compiled in the Mishna. The rest of the Talmud consists of interpretations and discussions of the Mishna.

Thirty-six Hidden Tzaddikim: the Talmud (*Sukka 45b*) speaks of thirty-six pious men who welcome the presence of God every day; in later legends, they are described as humble, unrecognized saints. Disguised as peasants, artisans, or porters, they perform good deeds and constitute the true "foundation of the world."

Turning (Teshuva, usually "repentance"): man's turning from his aberrations to the "way of God." It is interpreted as the fundamental act by which man contributes to his redemption.

Torah: "instruction," teaching, law: (preserved "in writing" and handed down "by word of mouth"). As a book, Torah means the Pentateuch. It is divided into weekly portions to be read before the congregation.

Tzaddik (the proven one, the perfected one): In the Bible this word denotes the man perfected in righteousness. In the Kabbala, the *tzaddik* was elevated into the mediator between God and man. In Hasidism, exemplified by the Baal Shem Tov and his successors, the *tzaddik* is the man in whose life and being the Torah is embodied.

Wayward Thoughts: thoughts about immoral or profane matters which disturb a man during prayer and prevent him from obtaining the desired *deveikut.* Such thoughts may turn a prayer over to the evil forces. The Hasidim considered wayward thoughts as the means by which Satan tried to obstruct their prayer.

World of Confusion (Olam Hatchu): the realm in which souls exist after death before they achieve their redemption.

World-to-Come (Olam Habba): The true world; the other world, where the righteous dwell forever.

Zohar: See Book of Splendor.

TRANSLITERATION GUIDE

In transliterating Hebrew and Yiddish words we have used the following:

h for the letter Hey as in hat Hatikva, *hayom*
h for the letter Het (a hard "h" against the upper palate) *haver*, Hanukka
kh for the letter Khaf (deeper in the throat, as in Bach) *melekh, derekh*
tz for the letter tzadi *tzaddik, tzores*
a equals ă as in father *rav, haver*
e equals ĕ as in let, get *shtetl* (sometimes ei as in weight—*seder, heder*)
i equals ĭ as in mitt, hit *mitzva, minhă*
o equals ō as in go, row Torah, *tov*
u equals u as in put, pull *tikkun*, Purim, *mezuza*
ei equals ĕĭ as in freight, weight *sheigetz*
ai equals ăĭ as in Taiwan *gabbai*
ay equals ăĭ as in Thailand *dayan*, Hayyim
tch equals ch as in chip Berditchev
zh equals zh as in pleasure Medzibozh

If a vowel is repeated, it is pronounced twice; for example, Yaakov is pronounced Ya-ah-kov; *maase, ma-ah-se; maariv, ma-ah-riv*. Such words tend to change in the Yiddish and are transliterated differently: *maise* (mai-se), and *maariv* (mai-riv).

When Hebrew and Yiddish words end in e or a, the final letters are pronounced as follows: final e is pronounced as in set, met; final a is pronounced like the a in father. If the final vowels are not accented, they may be weakened somewhat, but this happens mostly with Yiddish words. Final e and a are never silent.

We have used the Sephardic pronounciation for Hebrew words.

Although Hasidim usually refer to their leaders as rebbes, we have, with only one or two exceptions, referred to all of them as rabbis. The word *rav* is used to indicate a non-Hasidic rabbi.

All place names in this book have many spellings and pronunciations, some as many as three or four—Polish, Russian, Ukrainian, and Yiddish. In all cases, we have tried to use the form and spelling most common among Jews, the Yiddish version.

REFERENCES

Ayalti, H. J., ed. (1949). *Yiddish Proverbs.* New York: Schocken Books.

Bandler, L. C. (1978). *They Lived Happily Ever After.* Cupertino, California: Meta Publications.

Bandler, R., and Grinder, J. (1975). *The Structure of Magic.* Vol. I. Palo Alto, California: Science and Behavior Books.

——— (1976). *Patterns of the Hypnotic Techniques of Milton H. Erickson, M.D.* Vol. I. Cupertino, California: Meta Publications.

——— (1976). *The Structure of Magic.* Vol. II. Palo Alto, California: Science and Behavior Books.

Buber, M. (1947). *Tales of the Hasidim: The Early Masters.* Vol. I. New York: Schocken Books.

——— (1948). *Tales of the Hasidim: The Later Masters.* Vol. II. New York: Schocken Books.

——— (1957). *The Hidden Light.* New York: Schocken Books.

Goffman, E. (1959). *The Presentation of Self in Everyday Life.* New York: Doubleday Anchor Books.

Haley, J. (1973). *Uncommon Therapy: The Psychiatric Teachings of Milton H. Erickson, M.D.* New York: Norton.

Homans, George C. (1974). *Social Behavior: Its Elementary Forms.* New York: Harcourt Brace Jovanovich.

Newman, L. I., and Spitz, S. (1944). *The Hasidic Anthology.* New York: Bloch.

——— (1962). *Maggidim and Hasidim: Their Wisdom.* New York: Bloch.

Rosen, S., ed. (1982). *My Voice Will Go With You: The Teaching Tales of Milton H. Erickson.* New York: Norton & Co., p. 56.

Scholem, Gershom (1941). *Major Trends in Jewish Mysticism.* New York: Schocken.

Zevin, S. Y. (1979). *A Treasury of Hasidic Tales on the Festivals.* Vol. I. New York: Mesorah Publications, Ltd.

——— (1980). *A Treasury of Hasidic Tales on the Torah.* Vol. I. New York: Mesorah Publications, Ltd.

——— (1980). *A Treasury of Hasidic Tales on the Torah.* Vol. II. New York: Mesorah Publications, Ltd.

——— (1982). *A Treasury of Hasidic Tales on the Festivals.* Vol. II. New York: Mesorah Publications, Ltd.

LIST OF STORIES

10 *Merging with God*

11 *Joy*

14 A Story for [Almost] All Occasions

15 Ten Best Stories Times Two

INDEX